THE MALAYAN PARLIAMENTARY
ELECTION OF 1964

D1482031

THE MALAYAN PARLIAMENTARY ELECTION OF 1964

by
K. J. RATNAM
and
R. S. MILNE

University of Malaya Press
Singapore
1967

Sole Distributors

Oxford University Press, Ely House, London W.1.
GLASGOW NEW YORK TORONTO MELBOURNE WELLINGTON
CAPE TOWN SALISBURY IBADAN NAIROBI LUSAKA ADDIS ABABA
BOMBAY CALCUTTA MADRAS KARACHI LAHORE DACCA
KUALA LUMPUR HONG KONG TOKYO
Bangunan Loke Yew, Kuala Lumpur
● University of Malaya Press 1967
First published 1967

The University of Malaya Press is a joint enterprise of the
University of Malaya and the University of Singapore.

PRINTED IN SINGAPORE BY MALAYSIA PRINTERS LIMITED

PREFACE

SINCE the 1964 election there have been some important political changes. Singapore separated from Malaysia in August 1965; a few days later Dato Donald Stephens, who had earlier been Chief Minister of Sabah, resigned from his post as Minister for Sabah Affairs in the Federal Cabinet. In June 1966 the composition of the Sarawak Cabinet was changed, following the removal of the Chief Minister, Dato Stephen Kalong Ningkan. In the last chapter reference is made to the most striking of these events, Singapore's separation from Malaysia, but it was obviously not possible to cover in any depth what happened after the election. The scope of the book is limited, substantially, to the election itself and the situation and prospects immediately afterwards.

This book would not have been possible except for funds provided by the Rockefeller Foundation. Our thanks are therefore due to the Foundation and, particularly, to its Vice-President, Dr. Kenneth W. Thompson. We also wish to express our gratitude to the University of Singapore for providing funds for a visit to Sarawak and Sabah. Thanks are also due to the Institute of Commonwealth Studies (University of London) and to Professor K. E. Robinson, who was then its Director, for secretarial assistance and other facilities which they made available to Professor Ratnam when he was on leave. But for their kindness, the book might have taken longer to complete.

Necessarily, the book is largely based on interviews, conducted over a period of three years, in every state in Malaysia. It is not possible to thank, by name, all the persons interviewed. But we were courteously received and helped by members of all the party organizations. Mention should be made of the co-operation given by the

Election Commission, in particular by its Chairman, Dato Dr. Haji Mustapha Albakri.

Three of the contributions are by outside scholars: Mr. T. E. Smith, Secretary of the Institute of Commonwealth Studies, University of London; Dr. Frances Starner, formerly Visiting Lecturer in Political Science at the University of Singapore; Dr. R. K. Vasil, formerly a research student at the University of Malaya.

For research assistance we are grateful to Miss Chan Heng Chee, Miss Perin Jumabhoy and Mr. Tan Joo San. For translations of newspapers and documents our thanks are due to Mr. Lim Hong Too, Inche Mansor Sukaimi, Inche Othman bin Haron Eusoff, Dr. T. V. Sathyamurthy and Mr. S. Kanagaratnam.

We were given excellent service by the Library of the University of Singapore, particularly by Mrs. Wang Chen Hsiu Chin and Mrs. Patricia Lim Pui Huen. Mrs. Wang, in her capacity as Secretary of the Publications Committee, University of Singapore, also assisted the book through the press.

Our thanks are due to Mrs. Lilian Wong for typing the manuscript efficiently.

Finally, our indebtedness to our respective wives was increased by the secretarial services which they performed for us under trying conditions.

K. J. Ratnam
R. S. Milne

TABLE OF CONTENTS

LIST OF TABLES

PAGE

I

Introduction

THE study of elections in developed countries may be defended along easily recognizable lines.[1] The most modest claim is that electoral studies provide material for future historians. A stronger claim is that the study of a political system at election time is more rewarding than at other times. Political activity is then at its most intense, and reaches a climax with the poll. Consequently political issues are sharply focussed and are thrown into bold relief by the assertions and counter-assertions of the parties. During the election period new interpretations or developments of party policy may be stimulated by the confrontation of claims and ideas. There is also the attraction that, unlike many other fields of political study, election results lend themselves easily to quantitative treatment. Lastly, the election period is limited in time, and the activities of the parties are regulated and confined by electoral law. This creates the impression that an election is a conveniently marked-out unit for study. Unlike many political case-studies it has an easily-recognizable end, although the political process, in the wider sense, continues. Election periods are, of course, atypical; it is neither possible, nor desirable, for politics to proceed day-in day-out at such a frenetic pace. Nevertheless, making allowance for this, it is undeniable that we are likely to learn more about politics by studying elections than by studying periods *in-between* elections.

The Nuffield type of study has been extended to developing countries[2] during the last few years, and this book

1 D.E. Butler, 'Introduction', *The British General Election of 1951*. London, 1952.

2 Notably, to list only the most prominent publications in book form: W.J.M. Mackenzie and Kenneth E. Robinson, eds. *Five Elections in Africa*.

follows the same general scheme. Like the series of Nuffield studies of British elections,[3] it will seldom explicitly assume the form of hypothesis and verification.[4] The concluding chapter will offer some hypotheses and speculations on some of the questions raised above, but only tentatively. The main body of the book will be devoted to an account of what the parties said and did during the campaign,[5] the role of press and radio and an analysis of the results. The chapters immediately following will give an outline of recent political history in Malaya, the party system and the arrangements for holding elections. Malaya is a small country, but it is far from being homogeneous: the accounts of the election in two particular constituencies, one in the Federal capital, the other in the underdeveloped north-east coast, are intended to give some notion of its political variety. A chapter has been added on elections in Sarawak and Sabah (North Borneo); one has also been included on the Singapore elections of 1963. These territories did not directly elect members to the Federal Parliament in 1964. Nevertheless, accounts of the elections in these territories, which were the basis of *indirectly* electing members to the Federal Parliament, have been included for two reasons. After the formation of Malaysia in 1963

London, 1960; M. Venkatarangaiya, *The General Election in the City of Bombay, 1952*. Bombay, 1953; Jorge R. Coquia, *The Philippine Presidential Election of 1953*. Manila, 1955; R.L. Park and S.V. Kogekar, eds. *Reports on the Indian General Elections 1951-1952*. Bombay, 1956; H. Feith, *The Indonesian Elections of 1955*. Ithaca, N.Y., 1957; I.D.S. Weerawardana, *Ceylon General Election, 1956*. Colombo, 1960; G. Bennet and C.G. Roseberg, *The Kenyatta Election: Kenya 1960-1961*. London, 1961; K.W.J. Post, *The Nigerian Federal Election of 1959*. London, 1963.

[3] *The British General Election, 1945*, by R.B. McCallum and A. Readman, was published by Oxford University Press. The volume on the 1950 election by H.G. Nicholas, those on the 1951 and 1955 elections by D.E. Butler, that on the 1959 election by D.E. Butler and Richard Rose, and that on the 1964 election by D.E. Butler and Anthony King, were all published by Macmillan.

[4] W.J.M. Mackenzie, 'The Export of Electoral Systems', *Political Studies*, Vol. V, No. 3 (1957), p. 250.

[5] As learned from party literature, newspaper reports, direct observation and a series of open-ended interviews with party officials, especially at state level, over a period of more than two years.

politics became Malaysia-wide in scope. There was a tendency for parties which originally operated in only one area to try to reach out into others. The chief example of this was the entry of the People's Action Party (PAP), hitherto only a Singapore party, into the elections in Malaya in April 1964. In spite of Singapore's separation from Malaysia in August 1965 the chapter on the Singapore elections has been retained. It helps to illustrate the style of politics which the PAP introduced to Malaya in its 1964 campaign there. More generally, the chapters on Singapore and on Sarawak and Sabah make comparisons of campaigning methods possible between areas which are at different levels of political development and sophistication.

In some developing countries public opinion polls have thrown some light on voting behaviour.[6] But it was not possible to arrange for any polls to be taken at the time of the 1964 general election in Malaya. Selection and training of interviewers and translation of questionnaires and replies (in at least four languages) would have been particularly formidable obstacles. Also, any questions on opinions might not have been answered or might not have been answered 'honestly'. If an interviewer were identified with the Government, the answers might have been deliberately deferential to the Government; if he were not so identified, no answer might have been forthcoming.[7]

[6] Although the polls have not been as comprehensive or as frequent as, say, those of the British Institute of Public Opinion. Among them, varying greatly in comprehensiveness, are those mentioned in: Park and Kogekar, *op. cit.* pp. 26, 36-7, 185-7; Bennet and Roseberg, *op. cit.* pp. 128 and 159ff; Post, *op. cit.* Ch. X; R.A. Scalapino and J. Masumi, *Parties and Politics in Contemporary Japan.* Berkeley, 1962, Ch. IV; Carl H. Landé, 'Political Attitudes and Behaviour in the Philippines,' *Philippine Journal of Public Administration,* Vol. 3, No. 3 (1959).

[7] One opinion poll on politics was attempted by a reputable polling organization in the Kuala Lumpur area in March and April 1964. Questions were asked on which political leader in the Far East was admired most: the respondents overwhelmingly chose Tengku Abdul Rahman, the Prime Minister of Malaysia (54 per cent. compared with 11 per cent. for both Mr. Nehru and Mr. Lee Kuan Yew). Respondents were asked what they liked best, and least, about the government. They liked best 'economic development' and 'national unity and peace'. Only 1 per cent.

Even if there had been no problem of finance, the polling
operation would have required so much supervision and
control that the authors would have been unduly distrac-
ted from the main course of the election study. A more
promising line of research, at present being undertaken in
Singapore,[8] is to survey political attitudes between elections without asking any questions directly relating to political parties.

Another limit to research was the absence of voting figures for individual polling stations in Malaya.   In countries where such figures are available, such as France and
the United States, there is a great deal of scope for statistical investigations which follow the lead of André Siegfried, by looking for correlations between voting data and
the social characteristics of quite small groups of electors.
The only relevant voting figures for areas below parliamentary constituencies in Malaya were the figures for the
state elections, held in portions of each parliamentary constituency.   These elections took place on the same day, so
the voting figures approximate to a partial breakdown of
the parliamentary voting figures.   The limited relevance
of local elections is discussed in Chapter XII.

Without explicitly formulating hypotheses, it is still possible to indicate how election studies like this may throw
light on certain aspects of the political process.   One important question is the extent to which politics has been

referred to the formation of Malaysia. Less than half the respondents
answered the question on what they liked least. Those who did answer
mentioned privileges given to the Malays, taxation, education policy. The
limitations of public opinion polls at elections, already indicated by the
reluctance to criticize Alliance policy, were confirmed by the answers to
the question: 'If a general election was held tomorrow, for which party
would you vote?' 44 per cent. refused to answer, 46 per cent. said 'Alliance', only about 10 per cent. named a party other than the Alliance.
Yet in the Kuala Lumpur area the opposition parties won about 60 per
cent. of the vote. In the absence of any evidence that there was a late
swing of support away from the Alliance, it must be concluded that only
about one in six of the opposition party voters was willing to state his
preferences openly.

8 By Dr. Robert E. Gamer, Department of Political Science, University
of Singapore.

'nationalized' in Malaysia. To test this, one would need to know the importance, or otherwise, of local issues and personalities, the extent to which parties varied their propaganda when appealing to various groups, and the degree of uniformity of changes in the pattern of voting, 1959-64, over wide areas. It would, presumably, be encouraging in a multi-racial country like Malaysia, to find that sectional appeals by parties were few or were diminishing.[9] What, if anything, was the effect of Indonesian confrontation in increasing or decreasing sectional appeals by the parties? A number of other questions suggest themselves. Who are the political élite and how are they recruited? What are the parties' methods of selecting candidates? Are the parties acquiring a mass base?[10] Do the parties have a permanent 'life' of their own, or are they merely a 'front' for traditional institutions which is hurriedly erected at election time?[11] Have any parties developed coherent ideologies or philosophies, as opposed to slogans?[12] How are parties related to pressure groups, and how are they financed? How strong is the political appeal of personalities?[13] What is the role of opposition parties at an election held in a country exposed to invasion and internal subversion?

9 Cf. on tribalism in African parties, Mackenzie and Robinson *op. cit.* p. 484; Post *op. cit.* p. 395 ff.

10 Cf. Scalapino and Masumi, *op. cit.* p. 5ff; S.E. Finer, *The Man on Horseback.* London, 1962, p. 114.

11 R.S. Milne, 'Elections in Developing Countries', *Parliamentary Affairs,* Vol. XVIII, No. 1 (1964-5), p. 53.

12 Cf. Mackenzie and Robinson, *op. cit.* p. 479. Of the parties discussed in the book perhaps only the Bloc Populaire Sénégalais 'aspires to have a philosophy'. On the ideologies of Asian parties see Guy J. Pauker, 'Political Doctrines and Practical Politics in Southeast Asia', *Pacific Affairs,* Vol. XXXV, No. 1, 1962. F.G. Carnell lays stress on the eclectic nature of 'Nehruism', 'Sukarnoism' and other ideologies. ('Political Ideas and Ideologies in South and Southeast Asia' in Saul Rose, ed. *Politics in Southern Asia.* London, 1963, pp. 279-91.) Judged by the strict standards of Asoka Mehta, *The Political Mind of India.* Bombay, 1952, pp. 69-70, there are few Asian parties with a 'coherent policy' and fewer still which are searching for a 'philosophy'.

13 Cf. the hypothesis that where 'party tradition or doctrine and party organization are both weak, it is natural for a party to make its appeal through the personality of an individual'. Mackenzie and Robinson, *op. cit.* p. 480.

How can they function responsibly if the Government regards them as subversive?[14]   On the other hand, how can a
Government do its duty in combating subversion, including subversion in opposition parties, and still maintain
the essential features of 'free'[15] elections?

It is hoped that this election study will provide information on these questions as well as on other aspects of the
political process.   In the early days of a country's independence there is a good deal to be said for looking at its politics by considering the 'crowded hour', or cross-section, of
its political life represented by an election.[16]   Studies in
depth, for instance, by the methods of social anthropology,
or of the political process through time, may come later.
But an election offers a rich vein which can be tapped in
a short time.   Unless some of the material is quickly captured and recorded, by the collection of party propaganda,
through interviews and so on, it will disappear.   Moreover, the first few elections after independence do offer an
interesting spectacle of the extent to which elections may
become 'domesticated' when exposed to indigenous influences, if indeed they *are* domesticated and not shown the
door instead.

The repetition of descriptive studies of elections in any
country would in time become tedious and unprofitable.
In Malaysia, partly because direct elections have yet to be
held in the Borneo territories, descriptive studies of elections may be of interest for some years to come.   However,
the authors are aware of the limitations of the purely descriptive approach.   Within the framework they have chosen they have tried to make some comparisons, and, especially in the concluding chapter, to advance tentatively
towards the formation of a few general hypotheses.

14 Where there is a dominant party or group of parties and opposition
parties have not experienced power, and are even almost without the *hope*
of power, how can they become 'responsible'?   Scalapino, on Japan, *op.
cit.* p. 151.

15 Free elections being defined as 'elections in which voters believe that
they have a real though limited choice in some matter of importance to
the state and to themselves'.   Mackenzie, *Political Studies*, p. 255.

16 Cf. Mackenzie and Robinson, *op. cit.* pp. 486-8.

II

Politics in Malaya, 1959-64

THE Federation of Malaysia, a union of Malaya, Singapore, Sabah and Sarawak, was formed on 16 September 1963. However, the general elections held in April 1964 were confined to Malaya; the representatives from the other territories to the Federal Parliament in Kuala Lumpur were elected indirectly. So the elections with which this book is primarily concerned were *Malayan* elections to fill only 104 of the 159 seats in the Federal Parliament. Simultaneously, elections were held for the eleven *state* legislatures in Malaya, a total of 282 seats. However, the next elections for the Federal Parliament will probably not be held before 1969, when they will be direct in all areas of Malaysia. Since Malaysia was first proposed, politics in each area has become more and more linked with politics in the others. For this reason appendices have been included on the elections in Sarawak, Sabah and Singapore, which indirectly decided who should represent these states in the Federal Parliament.

As a background to the election it is necessary to know a little about the social and economic setting and the main features of constitutional and political development in Malaya.[1]

Before, and after, the first permanent European settlement in Malaya (the Portuguese in Malacca from 1511) a number of separate states existed; in each of these the

[1] A general introduction will be found in J. M. Gullick, *Malaya*. London, 1963. On economic aspects, see T.H. Silcock and E.K. Fisk, eds. *The Political Economy of Independent Malaya*. Singapore, 1963. On the working of the political system see R.S. Milne, *The Government and Politics of Malaysia*. Boston, 1967. On communal problems and their relation to politics and elections up to and including the 1959 election, see K.J. Ratnam, *Communalism and the Political Process in Malaya*. Kuala Lumpur, 1965.

ruler exercised intermittent control over several territorial chiefs. The states in the north were subject to invasion from Siam and were sometimes under Siamese suzerainty. Those on the west coast traded and fought with parts of what is now Indonesia, particularly Sumatra and the Celebes. Towards the end of the eighteenth century the British replaced the Dutch in Malacca, who had previously replaced the Portuguese. During the nineteenth and early twentieth century the whole peninsula came under various forms of British rule, direct rule in the three Straits Settlements of Singapore, Penang and Malacca and two types of indirect rule in nine states[2] which retained their rulers. There were no elections of any kind, except during some periods for local government bodies, such as George Town (Penang). However, 'unofficial' members, to voice the claims of various interests, were appointed to the advisory legislative bodies of the Straits Settlements and the state councils.

After the Second World War the political situation was very different. Previously 'politics' had consisted mainly of the efforts of the Malay rulers to preserve their traditional status and privileges, in spite of the presence of the British, and of British and Chinese businessmen to further their economic interests. But from 1945 onwards racial problems were revealed as even more complex than in the rest of South-East Asia, because the 'indigenous' Malays were actually in a minority, compared with the other races taken together.[3] While colonial rule continued, the British could, to some extent, control the effects of their admission of Chinese to work in the tin mines and in trade, and of Indians to the Government service and to jobs on rubber estates. They could, as it were, 'hold a balance' between the races, or, in the language of opponents of colonialism, practice a policy of 'divide and rule'. But after

[2] Less direct in Johore, Kelantan, Trengganu, Kedah, Perlis (Unfederated Malay States) and more direct in Pahang, Perak, Selangor and Negri Sembilan (Federated Malay States).

[3] By 1947 'Malaysians' (including aborigines) were 49.5 per cent. of the population, Chinese 38.4, Indians (including Pakistanis) 10.8, others 1.3. *Federation of Malaya Official Yearbook 1962*. Kuala Lumpur, 1962, p. 40.

the war 'nationalism', in the sense of loudly-asserted claims
by groups of persons with similar ethnic origins, became
prominent.   Disharmony between the races was encouraged by the Japanese during their occupation of Malaya,
because they were committed to an anti-Chinese policy.
Nationalism among the Malays was stimulated by a British
post-war proposal in 1946 for a 'Malayan Union',[4] which
would have degraded the position of the rulers and would
have made it possible for Chinese, Indians and others to ac-
quire citizenship relatively easily.   Malay reaction against
these proposals, which were abandoned as a result, took
the form of creating an organization to fight for the rights
of the Malays, which eventually became known as UMNO
(the United Malays National Organization).

The ill-fated Malayan Union scheme was replaced by a
Federation of Malaya Agreement, which operated from
1948 onwards.   From 1951 there was the familiar pre-independence device of a 'Member System' by which nominated members of the Legislative Council were made responsible for various functions and departments of government,
such as Education and Health.   Full independence was
retarded at first by the 'Emergency', during which a small
number of communist guerillas terrorized large areas of
the country.   But eventually local politicians argued successfully that the existence of the Emergency was a reason
for granting, not withholding, independence; after independence the communists could no longer claim convinc-
ingly that they were engaged in an anti-colonialist struggle.
In 1957 Malaya became independent, with a constitution
patterned on those of Britain and India.   Government was
'parliamentary' in the sense that the cabinet was responsible to a directly-elected lower house.   The upper house,
or Senate, was to consist of appointed members, some of
whom were to represent the states.   The system was to be
federal, but with the more important functions concentrated in the central government.   The Malay rulers were
embodied in the new constitution.   The states in the new

[4] Not including Singapore, which after the war became a separate British colony.

federation corresponded to the nine states still under Malay rulers plus two new states consisting of the former Straits Settlements of Penang and Malacca. Each of the nine rulers (and also the two new non-hereditary governors of Penang and Malacca) was to be head of one of the states in the federation. In addition a Conference of Rulers, in some respects a 'third house' of parliament, was set up, which has competence, among other things, over legislation altering the boundaries of a state, affecting the position of the rulers themselves or concerning certain aspects of the Muslim religion. The Conference of Rulers is also responsible for electing the Head of State (the Yang di-Pertuan Agong) chosen from among the rulers themselves for a five-year term, and his deputy. At the same time that the constitution was being drafted and put into operation the civil service was also being 'Malayanized', compensation being paid to British officers whose services were no longer needed.

However, these constitutional operations would have been pointless, unless during this period it had become clear that there was a promising local alternative to government by the British. By 1953 a possible alternative had appeared in the form of the Alliance Party, which consisted of the UMNO, the Malayan Chinese Association (MCA) and, later, the Malayan Indian Congress (MIC). The political scene had been radically changed by the Emergency. The Malayan Union proposals had resulted in the birth of UMNO, and also stimulated a number of other parties and heterogeneous alphabetical 'fronts', many of which were left-wing. When communist terrorist attacks began in 1948 and the Emergency was proclaimed, many of these organizations were outlawed. However, the Emergency was also indirectly responsible for the *creation* of another party, the MCA. Its formation was encouraged by the British in the hope that it would provide a focus of Chinese loyalties, which would compete with the attractions of communism. One of its immediate functions was to help with the resettlement of Chinese who were moved into 'new villages' by the Government in order to remove them from areas where the communists could intimidate them into providing food.   In the longer run, the MCA, whose first President was the respected Straits Chinese Tan Cheng-lock, was a body sufficiently representative of influential Chinese opinion to ensure that any future constitutional changes did not neglect Chinese interests.   The MCA joined with UMNO to fight the first municipal elections held in Malaya in Kuala Lumpur in 1952.   This alliance was a purely *ad hoc* and temporary expedient, but it worked sufficiently well to be continued at other local elections and to take the form of a permanent Alliance Party.

The Alliance was an answer to an apparently insoluble problem.   In so complex a multi-racial society as Malaya, what effective form could a political party take?   If it assumed an explicitly communal form, it could not hope to be trusted to aggregate the interests of all communities. Certainly the British, before 1957, would have been most unlikely to give up power into the hands of an obviously communal party.   On the other hand, in a country with so small a degree of consensus between the races, how could there be mutual co-operation between politicians of different ethnic origins *inside* a single party?   The failure of the latter possibility was shown by the fate of Dato Onn bin Ja'afar, who had been President of UMNO, but had wished to work, inside UMNO, also for the interests of other races.   Only the Alliance had solved the dilemma how to construct an effective party in Malaya through the device of communal parties, which were linked at the top in a non-communal union.   Even this 'solution' was not necessarily permanent, and was subject to perpetual strain, as the history of the Alliance has shown.   The Alliance policy as embodied in the single agreed memorandum which it submitted to the Constitutional Commission of 1957, and as substantially enacted in the Constitution of Malaya, was essentially a compromise, a 'bargain' between the élites of the two major races.   An increasing number of Chinese were to become citizens, and so to become qualified to vote. This was partly the reason for the dramatic rise in the proportion of Chinese in the electorate between 1955 and 1959. Also, tacitly, the predominant position of the Chinese in business (apart from the important role played by foreign firms) was accepted, although long-term measures were envisaged to encourage and train more Malay entrepreneurs. On the other hand, the framework of government, the Head of State, the rulers and, predominantly, the administrative civil service were to be Malay. Islam was to be established as the religion of the Federation, but this was mainly a symbolic provision. Unless otherwise provided by Parliament, Malay was to be the sole official language after 1967, as compared with Malay and English up to that time. The educational system was to be oriented towards Malay and English at secondary school level. In government, or financially-aided, secondary schools, other languages could be taught, but the medium of instruction had to be either English or Malay. Malay land privileges were to be safeguarded, and, by Article 153 of the Constitution, their 'special position' recognized, *inter alia,* for entry into some branches of the civil service and for certain types of trade and business licences. This agreement between the major partners of the Alliance was based on a certain rough 'balance' between racial interests. But particular items can easily, and sometimes plausibly and profitably, be attacked by parties which are in essence communal. For instance, pro-Chinese communal parties have persistently attacked Alliance policy on Chinese education and on the official language. These attacks, in turn, have set up stresses and strains inside the MCA, particularly in 1959, and consequently, at one remove, inside the Alliance.[5]

The electoral system adopted in 1955 and 1959 was the same as the British 'first past the post' system, by which, in each constituency, the candidate with a plurality of the votes is elected. There were no provisions for 'communal rolls' by which there would have been internal competition in each ethnic group, but the groups would have been sheltered from competition with each other. It was pre-

5 See **Chapter III.**

cisely because of the *lack* of such provisions that the Alliance problem of allocating seats among its different racial components arose.

The outstanding feature of the 1955 election had been the overwhelming victory of the Alliance, based principally on the large number of votes cast for UMNO. The Alliance won 79.6 per cent. of the votes, compared with 7.6 per cent. for Party Negara and 3.9 per cent. for the religiously-oriented Pan-Malayan Islamic Party (PMIP). No other party won more than 2 per cent. of the vote. The Alliance success in terms of seats was even more striking: it won fifty-one, the PMIP one. The other main point to note is that Chinese and Indian Alliance candidates were returned even in constituencies where the Malays were in a majority. For this election at least, the independence issue, with which the Alliance was identified, dwarfed any communal considerations.

By 1959 the situation had changed. The Alliance proportion of votes had fallen from 79.6 to 51.8 per cent. However, because of the scattering of the opposition among different parties and different areas, it won seventy-four seats. The parliamentary elections were preceded by elections for the state legislatures, which were held at intervals in the months preceding the federal elections. The general regional picture and strength of the opposition parties is suggested in Table 1.

The Table brings out the regional character of the opposition vote. The four northern states of Kedah, Perlis, Trengganu and Kelantan are predominantly Malay, traditional and underdeveloped. However in the former two, where communications with the rest of Malaya are adequate, the PMIP, although showing strength, was unable to win any federal seats from the Alliance. On the less accessible East coast, in Trengganu and Kelantan, they defeated the Alliance, and, as a result of the state elections, won control of the state legislatures. Party Negara won its only success in Trengganu. Even this was achieved only by the personality of the candidate, Dato Onn, and the fact that the PMIP did not fight the seat. In Johore and Pahang[6] the main opposition was provided by the the Socialist Front (SF), which had been formed in 1957,

TABLE I

TRENDS IN SUPPORT FOR THE ALLIANCE

STATE	PERCENTAGE OF VOTES				NO. OF SEATS	
	ALL. 1955 FEDERAL ELECTION	ALL. 1959 STATE ELECTIONS	ALL. 1959 FEDERAL ELECTION	LARGEST OPPN. PARTY VOTE 1959 FEDERAL ELECTION	ALL. 1959 FEDERAL ELECTION	OPPN. PARTIES 1959 FEDERAL ELECTION
Kedah	92.8	70.5	65.1	26.8 PMIP	12	—
Perlis	66.8	64.0	59.6	40.4 PMIP	2	—
Penang	79.9	51.1.	44.0	38.2 SF	5	3 SF
Perak	70.5	55.0	49.6	26.9 PPP	15	4 PPP 1 IND.
Selangor	71.2	57.8	44.3	30.4 SF	9	5 SF
Malacca	87.9	67.0	58.9	16.1 PMIP	3	1 MP
N. Sembilan	83.9	55.8	51.9	16.7 PMIP	4	2 IND.
Johore	86.1	67.1	65.7	14.2 SF	16	—
Trengganu	84.9	35.4	37.4	47.6 PMIP	1	4 PMIP 1 PN
Kelantan	78.1	26.9	31.4	68.3 PMIP	1	9 PMIP
Pahang	90.0	63.6	66.9	21.4 SF	6	—

ALL. = Alliance; PMIP = Pan-Malayan Islamic Party; SF = Socialist Front; PPP = People's Progressive Party; Ind. = Independent; MP = Malayan Party; PN = Party Negara.
T. E. Smith, *Report on the First Election of Members to the Legislative Council*, Kuala Lumpur, 1955; 'The Malayan Elections of 1959', *Pacific Affairs*, XXXIII, No. 1, 1960, 38-47; and *Report on the Parliamentary and State Elections, 1959*, Kuala Lumpur, 1960.

6 There are large tracts of unsettled land in Pahang. But the parts which are settled are less poor and less 'traditional' than Kelantan and Trengganu.

out of the alliance of the Labour Party (mainly Chinese) and the Party Rakyat (People's Party, mainly Malay). However the Alliance retained all the seats. In the other four states the situation was more complicated, although a common factor was that the opposition parties drew their support mainly from non-Malays. In Penang, the SF, which had previously gained control of the municipal council of George Town, won three seats to the Alliance's five. In Perak the main opponent was the People's Progressive Party (PPP), which had contested the 1955 election as the 'Perak Progressive Party'. In spite of its change of name it was still a Perak party. It stood for equal rights and privileges for non-Malays. The main opposition to the Alliance in Selangor was provided by the SF, which returned five members. Independents who were formerly MCA also polled well. In both Malacca and Negri Sembilan the Table conveys an inaccurate impression of the PMIP as the largest opposition party. In each of these states the non-Malay opposition was split. In Malacca it was shared between the SF and the Malayan Party, another 'equal rights' party, led by Mr. Tan Kee Gak. In Negri Sembilan it was split between the SF and the Independents, two of whom, both formerly in the MCA, were returned. The opposition was therefore regionalized. The PMIP was strong in the four northern states. The SF was potentially strong in the more industrialized parts of the country with the largest non-Malay population, but (apart from the MCA) it had to face stiff competition from regional parties in particular areas, the PPP in Perak, the Malayan Party in Malacca and also from Independents in Negri Sembilan and Selangor.

It would be tedious to recount in detail the political history of Malaya between the 1959 and 1964 elections. But there was one outstanding event which dominated the 1964 election, the formation of Malaysia and the Indonesian objections to Malaysia which, early in 1963, resulted in the 'confrontation' of Malaysia by Indonesia.[7] These re-

7 See *Malaysia Act*, 1963; *Report of the Commission of Enquiry, North Borneo and Sarawak*. Kuala Lumpur, 1962; T. E. Smith, *The Back-*

lated issues made themselves felt in four main ways. First, the Alliance used them as election issues, while some of the opposition parties, notably the SF and the PMIP, were placed at a disadvantage, because, especially after the start of confrontation, their opposition to Malaysia was difficult to distinguish from lack of patriotism. Second, the activities of the SF were physically weakened by the arrest of some of their workers for reasons of internal security. Apart from actually reducing the number of party workers, this must have affected the morale of some who were not arrested. The most important political figure arrested was Inche Ahmad Boestamam, one of the SF leaders, who was detained in February 1963 on the ground that he had been concerned in the planning of the Azahari revolt in Brunei the previous December. There is no official figure of the total number of SF members who were arrested. Shortly before the campaign period began, on 11 March, a former secretary-general of the Party Rakyat was detained. Two days later the Johore Bahru branch treasurer of the same party and one other person were also detained after a police ambush which uncovered hidden arms and ammunition.[8]

These arrests were made on different grounds from the arrests of some PMIP members. Although the latter arrests were made under the Internal Security Act, there was no allegation of collaboration with an external enemy. The grounds were incitement to violence through religious and communal appeals. For instance, when three PMIP Kelantan State Assemblymen were arrested on 24 February 1964, a police statement said: 'Their mischievous and distorted utterances, if allowed to continue, are likely to lead to a breach of the peace and threaten the

---

ground to Malaysia. London, 1963; G. P. Means, 'Malaysia — a New Federation in Southeast Asia,' Pacific Affairs, Vol. XXXVI, No. 2, 1963; R.O. Tilman, 'Malaysia: The Problems of Federation', Western Political Quarterly, Vol. XVI, No. 4, 1963.

8 Straits Times, 12 and 14 March, 1964. Seven rather less prominent Party Rakyat members had been detained a few days previously. (Ibid. 8 March 1964.)

security of the country'.[9]   The President of the PMIP, Dr.
Burhanuddin, was also a casualty of the law in that he was
legally disqualified from standing at the election, although
not from campaigning.   The Chairman of the Election
Commission confirmed that he was disqualified by reason
of having been found guilty of a (somewhat technical)
offence under the Companies Ordinance and having been
fined $25,360.[10]   It is unlikely that this encounter with
the law cost the PMIP many votes, because the company
with which Dr. Burhanuddin had been associated had been
formed for the estimable purpose of providing sea transport for Muslim pilgrims.

A third consequence of confrontation was that it was at
least partly the reason why a few well-known politicians
left an opposition party and joined the Alliance.   Prominent among them was Mr. D. S. Ramanathan, a former
President of the Labour Party and a former mayor of
Penang, who left the SF,[11] and the paid executive secretary
of the Malacca SF, Inche Hamzah bin Kimin.[12]

The final consequence of Malaysia and confrontation
combined was the effect on the prospects of electoral
alliances among the opposition parties.   After the 1959
elections, there were effectively five opposition parties, the
PMIP, SF, PPP, Party Negara and Malayan Party.   The
last one was largely a one-man party, and that man, Mr.
Tan Kee Gak, was temporarily in poor health.   However,
two new parties soon appeared.   The previous president
of the MCA, Dr. Lim Chong Eu, who had left active politics in 1959, founded a new United Democratic Party
(UDP) in April 1962.   The other new party arose from
the forced resignation of the Minister of Agriculture in
the Alliance Government, Inche Abdul Aziz bin Ishak.
The immediate cause of his leaving the Government in
October 1962 was his objection to a switch of ministerial

---

9 *Ibid.* 25 February 1964.

10 *Ibid.* 4 March 1964.   Any fine of more than $2,000 would have dis-
qualified him from standing as a candidate.

11 *Ibid.* 2 November 1963.

12 *Ibid.* 6 March 1964.

portfolios.   But for several years he had disagreed with
the rural development policy of the Government on the
ground that it was not doing enough to protect Malay
farmers and fishermen from middlemen.   He also thought
that Malaya had not achieved 'real' independence and was
still under the domination of foreign (mainly British)
capital and advisers.   On leaving the Government Inche
Aziz did not immediately form a new party, although it
was widely believed that he would do so.   Eventually, in
July 1963, he founded the National Convention Party,[13]
which was joined by one other UMNO member of Parliament.

Before then, however, there was a move to form a common front against the way in which the Alliance Government proposed to bring about Malaysia.   In March 1963
representatives of the SF, the PPP, the PMIP, the UDP
and some Independents met with Inche Aziz and agreed
on a number of points.   Among them was opposition to
Alliance methods in bringing about Malaysia; desire that
Malaysia should be postponed until the people of North
Borneo, Brunei and Sarawak were represented by fully-
elected governments or until a free referendum on Malaysia was held in these territories; and disapproval of the
Government's use of the powers of arbitrary arrest.[14] Inche
Aziz was chairman of the meeting, and, as far as the Malaysia issue was concerned, became for a short time a sort of
unofficial 'Leader of the Opposition'.

The precise stands of the various parties on Malaysia
will be discussed later.[15]   Perhaps it is enough to say at
this stage that the opposition parties might conceivably
have had more success in forming a front which would
have lasted until after the election (in spite of possible
disputes about which parties should fight which seats) but
for one thing — confrontation.   Indonesian opposition to
Malaysia, which led to confrontation and to actual armed
attacks on the Borneo territories, had a double effect on

13 *Ibid.* 16 July 1963.
14 *Ibid.* 12 March 1963.
15 See Chapter VI.

the PPP and UDP. Some party members obviously reacted patriotically to the attacks as Malaysians. But some
also reacted as Chinese. Many who deplored the manner
in which Malaysia had been formed, deplored still more
the treatment which had been given to the Chinese in
Indonesia. On this score they were decidedly more anti-
Indonesia than anti-Malaysia.

This was seen in the resignation of Mr. Chin See Yin
from the UDP.[16] He was a founder member of the UDP,
but now left it because it was proposing to form a united
front with pro-Indonesian parties.[17] The PPP also withdrew from negotiations on a united opposition front before any agreement had been reached. Its leaders had
always distrusted the SF for being too left-wing and in-
sufficiently pro-non-Malay. Perhaps a decisive reason for
their breaking away was the proposals for 'Maphilindo'
which were made in the middle of 1963. Maphilindo
would have taken the form of a confederation of Malaysia, Indonesia and the Philippines. To the PPP, Maphilindo, which might bring with it the prospect of the persecution of Chinese in Malaya, was even more detestable
than confrontation.[18]

By February 1964 there was an apparent decline in
PMIP interest in the negotiations.[19] The remaining parties were four in number: SF, UDP, National Convention
Party and Party Negara. The SF was decidedly the strongest and the UDP probably the next strongest. The most
important point was therefore whether or not these two

16 See Chapter V.

17 *Straits Times*, 19 April 1963.

18 The PPP was still sometimes mentioned as a possible partner in a
united front as late as February 1964. But the possibility was denied
by Mr. Chew Choo Soot, President of the PPP Kuala Lumpur branch.
(*Straits Times*, 13 February 1964.)

19 In that month it had twice omitted to send a representative to meetings of opposition parties. (*Ibid.* 12 and 22 February). Dr. Burhanuddin,
the PMIP leader, later compared the 1963 negotiations with those which
resulted in the heterogeneous coalition of the AMCJA and PUTERA in
1947. In Dr. Burhanuddin's view some of the other parties' leaders in
1963 were not 'mature enough' to reach agreement. (Interview, 16 August
1964.)

parties could reach agreement, particularly with regard to Penang, where both were strong but where failure to form an electoral pact would probably result in a split opposition vote and an Alliance victory. Early in March agreement in principle was announced,[20] but a second announcement revealed that the agreement had broken down when policies and the distribution of seats had been considered.[21] Apart from the question of seats, the UDP and Party Negara claimed *inter alia* that, while they accepted Malaysia in principle although deploring the manner in which it had been brought about, the SF still totally rejected it. Furthermore, the UDP and Party Negara said that, while they and the NCP had wanted to emphasize that the new front was non-communist and non-aligned, the SF wanted to delete the word 'non-Communist'.[22] The SF on the other hand, was apparently intransigent on the Malaysia question, and thought that the UDP had never been really serious in conducting the negotiations.

The prospect of a grand united opposition therefore faded away. The National Convention Party joined the other two parties in the SF, not just for the election but permanently.[23] Among the other parties there were some local agreements not to contest against each other, for instance between the PPP and the UDP and between the PPP and the PAP (People's Action Party). But these arrangements did not necessarily cover the whole of Malaya. In the Bungsar constituency a PAP candidate won in spite of the existence of a PPP candidate. In 1964, as in 1959, the opposition parties failed to find a sufficient area of agreement for a firm election coalition. As Asoka Mehta perceived at the Indian general election of 1957, there was a limited value in coalitions of parties which were not

20 *Straits Echo,* 4 March 1964.

21 *Straits Times,* 5 March 1964. There had been temporary alliances between the SF and the UDP in some local authorities, for example, Seremban, Taiping and Bentong, but these had not always worked smoothly.

22 *Straits Echo,* 9 March 1964 (Dr. Lim Chong Eu for UDP and Inche Garieb Raouf for Party Negara).

23 *Straits Times,* 17 March 1964.

like-minded. This could strengthen the opposition only if 'voters do not respond to policies and ideologies but only to antipathy to the ruling party'.[24]   In Malaya in 1964 most of the opposition parties depended largely for their appeal on 'policies and ideologies', in the widest sense, but on *divergent* policies and ideologies.   Some opposition leaders saw quite clearly that the mere fact of 'adding' one party to another did not of itself create strength. 'Nothing plus nothing equals nothing.'[25] Tengku Abdul Rahman put the problem in homely and unflattering terms: attempts of the opposition parties to co-operate with each other would end like an alliance between frogs and rats.[26]

Between the 1959 and 1964 elections the Alliance gained on balance from changes of party by prominent politicians.   UMNO lost Inche Abdul Aziz bin Ishak, but in December 1963 it gained Dato Nik Ahmad Kamil, who had been a Party Negara candidate in 1955 and later Ambassador to Washington.[27] It was believed that he would strengthen the Alliance election campaign in Kelantan. The MCA, in contrast to 1959, when its education policy had proved to be unpopular, actually gained supporters instead of losing them.   Mr. Tan Kee Gak of the Malayan Party rejoined the MCA, because of the threat of confrontation.[28] So did several prominent UDP members from Negri Sembilan, some of whom had previously been MCA officials, notably Mr. Quek Kai Dong, M.P.[29] But later moves for perhaps the 'most independent' Independent of all, Mr. Chin See Yin, to rejoin the MCA came to nothing.[30] Probably because of confrontation and the threat

24 S.L. Poplai, ed. *National Politics and 1957 Elections in India.* Delhi, 1957, p. 41. This volume also contains the counter-arguments of Jayaprakash Narayan (p. 41) and documents on an electoral alliance (pp. 145-54).

25 Inche Zulkiflee (PMIP), interview, 16 August 1963.

26 *Tamil Malar,* 2 April 1964.

27 *Straits Times,* 3 December 1963.

28 *Ibid.* 5 March 1964.

29 *Ibid.* 5 May 1963.

30 See p. 89 below.

of PAP intervention,[31] there was no great agitation on the part of the MCA for a larger share of Alliance candidates.[32] The MCA also gained the support of Mr. Yeo Tat Beng (Independent, Bruas) when he crossed the floor in the Federal Parliament and joined the Alliance.[33] The only really disturbing internal incident in the MCA was that a prominent returned 'rebel' gave up his intention of standing for Parliament.[34]

Ordinarily, any election losses by the MCA would have benefited parties already operating in Malaya, mainly the SF, the PPP and the UDP. But there was a distinct possibility that the MCA, after Malaysia came into force in September 1963, might also have to face the competition of the PAP. It had been clearly placed on record in 1954, in the original manifesto setting out the aims and objectives of the PAP, that the party's political horizons extended beyond the Johore Causeway. 'Though, because of the division of Malaya into two territories, we are technically a political party operating in Singapore we shall in all our approach to the problems of this country disregard the constitutional division. We are as actively interested in the problems of our fellow Malayans in the Federation as we are in those of Singapore. When Malayans in the Federation who agree with our aims join us we shall work throughout Malaya.'[35]

Perhaps the first hints that the day of the PAP's entry into the politics of Malaya might not be so far distant appeared during the negotiations between Malaya and Singapore on the terms on which Singapore would enter Malaysia.[36] The bargaining, particularly between the Singa-

31 Which in fact materialized, as shown below.
32 But see Chapter V, footnote 11.
33 *Straits Times*, 21 August 1963.
34 See pp. 102-3 below.
35 Lee Kuan Yew, *The Battle For Merger*. Singapore, 1962, p. 148, in a reference to the PAP 1954 Manifesto.
36 The outcome, financially, was embodied in an *Agreement between the Governments of the Federation of Malaya and Singapore on Common*

pore Prime Minister and Mr. Tan Siew Sin, who was at
the same time the Finance Minister of the Federation of
Malaya and the President of the MCA, developed with
more acerbity than might have been expected. The PAP
attitude was at this time at least partly defensive. The formation of Malaysia led the MCA to believe that, in the
coming Singapore elections, as a partner in the federal
government they could expect increased support, especially from businessmen, in Singapore. Mr. Lee denounced
the visits of two MCA senators, Mr. T. H. Tan and Mr.
Khaw Kai Boh, to Singapore in order to obtain such support.[37]   Later Mr. Lee re-opened the theme of a future
PAP entry into Malayan politics.[38]   Mr. Tan Siew Sin
quickly counter-attacked; Mr. Lee, he said, 'has unleash-
ed against us a ceaseless and violent propaganda barrage,
using all the paraphernalia of the State Government at his
disposal for the time being, such as radio and TV'. Whereas Mr. Lee had spoken of the MCA losing support in the
towns in Malaya, the PAP in Singapore had lost every by-
election held since it had come into power. Mr. Tan went
on to accuse Mr. Lee of trying to pose as a champion of
the people of Singapore against the Federation and of not
understanding what federalism really meant.[39]   Although
in the Singapore elections, which were held on 21 September 1963, the PAP was fighting, among other parties,
both the Singapore UMNO and the Singapore MCA, its
attitude to these two parties was quite different in the context of Malaysia. Only twelve days before the poll Mr.
Lee stated the position thus: 'It is my belief that the
Tengku and Tun Abdul Razak will work with us — not
today or next month, but in years to come. We calculate
in terms of decades, not in terms of elections.' The MCA

Market and Financial Arrangements. Federation of Malaya, Cmd. 27 of
1963. At one point in the negotiations Mr. Lee accused the MCA of
blocking an agreement on finance between Malaya and Singapore. But
the Tengku warmly defended the MCA. *Straits Times,* 21 May 1963.

37 *Straits Times,* 18 May 1963.

38 *Ibid.* 27 July 1963.

39 *Ibid.* 4 August 1963.

had suffered defeat after defeat in the large towns of the Federation of Malaya. In the long run UMNO and the PAP would have to work together in Malaysia. But the PAP would not contest the elections in Malaya in 1964. 'We want to show the MCA that even if the PAP keeps out of the elections on the mainland, the MCA will still lose.'[40]

After the PAP won the Singapore elections, and the Singapore MCA and UMNO had been totally defeated, a period followed in which the PAP seemed to be assiduously wooing the Tengku and the UMNO. Under the new Constitution of Malaysia, the PAP, which was in control of the Singapore Legislative Assembly, was in a position to nominate two senators to the upper house of the Federation. However, Mr. Lee Kuan Yew requested the Tengku to nominate one of the two and the Tengku agreed. The PAP also showed in the Federation House of Representatives that it intended to behave, not like other opposition parties, but rather as a 'loyal' opposition. At the same time there was a running battle carried on in speeches and in newspapers between the MCA and the PAP. Another reference to PAP expansion into Malaya was made in January by Mr. S. Rajaratnam, Singapore's Minister of Culture, when he said that the PAP must start operating as a Pan-Malaysian party to help build a prosperous, independent and peaceful Malaysia.[41]

Yet in all this guerilla warfare there was little to prepare the public for the bombshell dropped by the Singapore Deputy Prime Minister, Dr. Toh Chin Chye, on 1 March 1964. Dr. Toh announced that the PAP would after all contest the Malayan elections, which, it turned out, were then only eight weeks distant. The long-term reasoning behind the statement, and his amplification of it the following day, was not new. Within five years (that is, by the 1969 election) the PAP hoped to develop itself into a force to be reckoned with in Malaysia. By that time the party could muster enough support to convince the

---

40 *Ibid.* 10 September 1963.
41 *Ibid.* 18 January 1964.

UMNO that it was strong enough to be worth co-operating with. If the PAP did *not* extend its activities to Malaya, then electors who inclined to the left would support the Socialist Front, which was under the influence of the Malayan Communist Party. But the intervention was to be on a limited scale only. At the forthcoming election the PAP would 'play a token part' by fielding 'a very small number of candidates'. It was not the intention of the PAP 'to fight the Central Government of Malaysia or the UMNO'.[42] The PAP would therefore concentrate on fighting urban areas[43] (that is, the areas where the MCA were contesting, not UMNO). The PAP did not intend to try to supplant the MCA or align itself with UMNO.[44] From these conciliatory statements it could be gathered that the PAP's 'bombshell' was intended to be conventional, not nuclear.

The PAP intervention will be described elsewhere in this book. But in order to provide the necessary background, it may be said here that the MCA recognized the challenge as a mortal attack on itself,[45] while the PAP went ahead with its plans by registering itself as a political party in Malaya and by setting up a headquarters in Kuala Lumpur.[46] The question remains: why did the PAP suddenly decide to contest the Malayan elections in the light of their previously-announced decision not to contest? This is quite a different question from the one: what were the forces impelling the PAP to enter politics in Malaya in

42 *Ibid.* 2 and 3 March 1964.

43 *Ibid.* 3 March 1964 (Mr. S. Rajaratnam).

44 *Ibid.* 16 March 1964 (Mr. S. Rajaratnam).

45 Mr. Tan Siew Sin, *ibid.* 3 March 1964. The MCA received immediate support from eminent UMNO members, including the Chief Minister of Malacca and the Minister of Health (*ibid.* 4 and 7 March 1964). The Tengku also took up the issue on 14 March. 'Tengku Abdul Rahman today reaffirmed his faith in the MCA. He said the PAP was trying to supplant the MCA by trying to align itself with UMNO. "But we don't want them", he said amidst loud cheers as he launched the Alliance election campaign with a rally in Serdang Bharu...' (*Sunday Times*, 15 March 1964).

46 *Straits Times*, 11 March 1964.

the long run? Most of the PAP leaders' statements[47] answer the latter question, not the former. If the PAP entry
was the result of calculation, and not of impulse, the calculations have not yet been revealed.[48]

A pointer to the 1964 general election results might be
found in the results of by-elections between 1959 and 1964.
In most countries these results are notoriously difficult to
interpret, mainly because some voters will express their
dissatisfaction with a government party by voting against
it at a by-election, although drawing the line at voting
against it at a general election and so possibly contributing to an actual change of government. Nevertheless, the
trend of by-election results in a country is sometimes suggestive. In May 1960 the Government lost the seat of
Kampar to the PPP with a swing of 7.5 per cent. and in
May 1961 it lost Telok Anson to an ex-MCA Independent,
Mr. Too Joon Hing, with a swing of 17.5 per cent. Both
these reverses could be attributed largely to discontent
with the Alliance's Chinese education policy on the part
of Chinese voters. The other three by-elections for parliamentary seats were all in largely Malay areas, but they gave
the Government increasing ground for confidence. It was
only to be expected that when Dato Onn died, Party
Negara would suffer, because of the loss of the personal
vote for the original champion of Malay rights. The Alliance did in fact win the seat, Kuala Trengganu Selatan, in
March 1962 by a comfortable margin of over 2000 votes.
The by-election at Kuala Lipis in October 1962 was complicated by the entry of the Socialist Front, which turned
the previous Alliance-PMIP fight into a three-cornered
contest. The Alliance and the PMIP lost approximately
the same proportion of their vote to the Socialist Front.
The Alliance had an 8,500 majority over the Socialist
Front, which came second. Perhaps the most suggestive
result was that of the last parliamentary by-election, for
Muar Selatan, held in December 1963. The Alliance,

---

[47] E.g. Dr. Toh, *ibid.* 10 March 1964; Mr. Lee, *ibid.* 16 March 1964.
[48] Cf. Milton E. Osborne, *Singapore and Malaysia.* Ithaca, 1964, p. 83;
Chapter XIII, below.

PMIP and Party Negara had contested in 1959. In 1963 Party Negara dropped out, and the Alliance vote went up by almost the full amount of the previous Party Negara vote, leaving the PMIP vote almost unchanged. It is significant that by this time Malaysia was in existence and confrontation was in full swing. The by-election results for State Assembly seats in 1959 and 1960 showed a tendency for the Alliance to lose votes to the Socialist Front and the PPP. Later this tendency was checked, although as late as December 1963 the Socialist Front made a spectacular gain in votes at the Balik Pulau election (1,331 compared with an Alliance gain of 509) and nearly won the seat. During the entire inter-election period the Alliance consistently improved its 1959 position relative to the PMIP whenever the latter party contested a state by-election.

Local government elections gave similar indications that the Alliance would not lose much ground, if any, in the 1964 general elections. Once again, local elections, apart from any changes in voting behaviour over time, cannot be a completely accurate guide to general elections. For one thing, the number of voters concerned is much smaller, because local government bodies do not cover the entire territory of Malaya. Nevertheless, a careful analysis of the 1961 Local Authority elections[49] showed hardly any change in the strengths of the various parties from the position as at the 1959 general election. The 1963 local authority elections gave a rather similar indication. In these elections the Alliance won 48·9 per cent. of the votes and 70·9 per cent. of the seats, compared with the same proportion of the vote but 73·7 per cent. of the seats in 1961.[50]

Finally, the prospects of the parties might be influenced by the *timing* of the election. In one possibly important

[49] T. E. Smith, 'The Local Authority Elections 1961 in the Federation of Malaya', *Journal of Commonwealth Political Studies*, Vol. 1, No. 2, 1962.

[50] These 'local authority' elections should be distinguished from the 'local council' elections held in 1962 in what were originally the new villages set up for resettlement during the Emergency.

respect there was to be a difference from 1959; in 1964 the parliamentary and state elections were to be held on the same day. When Dato Haji Mustapha Albakri, chairman of the Election Commission, announced this in May 1963 he stated that the proposal had come from the Tengku and that the purpose was primarily to save the parties money. He estimated the saving at about 25 per cent. of the campaign expenses.[51] The two possible drawbacks of the new scheme were that the voters might be confused about the mechanics of voting and that the simultaneous elections would tend to obscure the dividing lines between federal and state issues. There was a marked increase in the percentage of spoilt ballots.[52] However, it is doubtful whether, even if the elections had been held separately, the voters would have made fine distinctions between which issues were a federal responsibility and which were within the province of the states. They do not seem to have had federal and state issues presented to them separately at the 1959 elections, although these were *not* held simultaneously.[53] As regards expense, the Government would certainly spend more on running the elections under the new scheme. With 'staggered elections' some equipment, such as ballot boxes, could be used, then moved and used again. Now this would no longer be possible. Among the parties, most Alliance officials supported the change, although their reasons for doing so sometimes seemed to consist merely in approving it because the Tengku had proposed it. One objection was that the Alliance could not use the state elections to 'test the ground', and, if necessary, adjust its propaganda for the parliamentary elections. Some opposition party officials were opposed to

51 *Straits Times*, 10 May 1963.

52 The percentage of spoilt votes was almost four times as great at the combined parliamentary and state elections of 1964 as it had been for the parliamentary elections of 1959. In 1964 spoilt parliamentary votes were 4.2 per cent. of those cast.

53 '... during the State election campaigns there was as much a tendency by candidates to concentrate on national as on local issues....' Federation of Malaya, *Report on the Parliamentary and State Elections 1959.* Kuala Lumpur, 1960, para. 31.

simultaneous elections simply on the ground that they would lead to confusion. But one other argument appeared to run along the following lines. The Alliance had more nationally-known politicians and more money than the other parties. They also had the advantage of more publicity via the mass media.[54] Even with simultaneous elections they could make an impact on every constituency, parliamentary and state. The main strength of opposition parties, such as the PMIP and the SF, however, lay in their large numbers of devoted party workers in particular areas. If the state elections were held on different days, as in 1959, these workers could be switched from one area to another. In 1964, with all state elections (as well as the federal election) held on the same day, they could not.

The parliamentary and state elections were in fact held on the same day in 1964. But there was an important change from the previously expected[55] target date of July 1964. Early in March 1964 a statement was made that the date would be April 25.[56] The reasons for the switch from July to April are not hard to understand. It could be argued that the Government was anxious to 'seek a mandate' on the issues of Malaysia and confrontation. 'The election in actual fact should be held sometime in August or September this year, but because of the seriousness of the situation and the charge made by the other political parties to the effect that the Alliance Government has no mandate from the people to pursue the course we are now pursuing, it has been decided to hold it earlier. The decision to hold an early election is to seek a mandate from the people and for them to decide as to whether we are doing the right thing in boldly facing Indonesia's confrontation.'[57]

From an opposition point of view, the Government could be described as wanting to 'cash in' on the patriotic feelings of the population aroused by Malaysia and con-

[54] See Chapter VIII.
[55] *Straits Times*, 10 May 1963.
[56] *Ibid.* 3 March 1964.
[57] The Tengku, Radio Malaysia broadcast, 14 April 1964.

frontation. The longer the election was delayed, the greater the possibility that these feelings might diminish and be obscured by the adverse effects of confrontation on the Malaysian economy. There is reason to believe that the Government wished to hold the elections even earlier than April. But an important consideration stood in the way. A new register of electors was being compiled, which was not expected to be ready until about March 1964. To use the old register would be to deprive about a quarter of a million persons (whose names were on the new register but not the old) of their right to vote.[58] The actual date of the election was consequently about the earliest possible, given that the election was to be held on the new register.

[58] Interview, Chairman of the Election Commission, January 1964.

III

Political Parties

EVER since the introduction of municipal elections in 1952, the Alliance Party has enjoyed an unchallenged pre-eminence in Malayan politics. Although the party represents inter-communal ideals and contests elections as a single unit, its main strength lies in the support directly given to its constituent organizations. These organizations are the United Malays National Organization (UMNO), the Malayan Chinese Association (MCA) and the Malayan Indian Congress (MIC). They function purely on communal lines, and cater to the interests of their respective communities. Individual membership is confined to these organizations, and there is no provision for direct membership of the Alliance. The 'Alliance Party' exists only at different co-ordinating levels, and comprises delegates from its member bodies. This arrangement has had its advantages and disadvantages, but before these are discussed some attention will have to be given to the way in which the constituent bodies are organized and function.

The UMNO was formed in 1946, to lead the Malay agitation for the withdrawal of the Malayan Union scheme. This scheme, introduced soon after the war, sought to create a streamlined and highly centralized administration in place of the pre-war arrangement under which there were three distinct groups of states (the Straits Settlements, the Federated Malay States and the Unfederated Malay States) and ten different sovereigns (the British Crown in the Straits Settlements and the rulers in the nine Malay States). It implied, among other things, the termination of the privileged status previously enjoyed by the Malay community and a drastic reduction in the powers of the rulers. It also threw the citizenship doors wide open, thereby enabling the vast majority of non-Malays in the country to become citizens. Under the dynamic leadership of Dato Onn the UMNO succeeded in rallying the mass of the Malay population behind it, and was able to impress the Colonial Government sufficiently to bring about the abandonment of the Malayan Union scheme. The Federation of Malaya Agreement, which followed, recognized the special position of the Malays and the rights and prerogatives of the rulers, and imposed stringent regulations to cover the eligibility of non-Malays for citizenship.[1]

The origins and initial functioning of the UMNO thus reflected a very strong communal tone. Malay solidarity was the sole concern of the party, and little attraction was found in the idea of an inter-communal approach to politics. Indeed, so strong was the preoccupation with the exclusive welfare of the Malay community that even Dato Onn was unable to get the rank and file of the party to support his proposal, made after the immediate constitutional objective had been achieved, to broaden the UMNO's base by providing for non-Malay participation. After two unsuccessful attempts Dato Onn resigned from the party and formed the non-communal Independence of Malaya Party (IMP). He was replaced in the UMNO by Tengku Abdul Rahman, who has led the party since then and is now the Prime Minister.

The introduction of elections brought a new variable into party politics in the country. Before then political parties had acted mainly as pressure groups, which sought to influence official policy without having the opportunity actually to participate in government. After 1952 their activities were influenced by the fact that they had to compete with each other with a view to gaining popular support. This led the UMNO and the MCA to reappraise their positions, and they decided that it would be to their mutual advantage to present a common electoral front. Initially their partnership amounted to nothing more than

[1] The citizenship laws were subsequently liberalized in 1952 and again in 1957. As a result of these changes, there are now few barriers which effectively prevent non-Malays from becoming citizens.

a purely electoral arrangement, whereby UMNO candidates were put up in predominantly Malay wards and Chinese candidates in Chinese wards.[2] The success of this experiment led the two parties to consider their partnership more seriously, and resulted in the formation of a permanent Alliance Party in 1953.

Today the UMNO is undoubtedly the 'senior' partner in the Alliance, and is helped in this respect not only by the wide support it receives from the Malays (who form the majority in about 60 per cent. of the constituencies) but by the willingness of the other two partners to recognize the political pre-eminence of the Malay community. It has a very extensive organization which penetrates to every part of the country, although the main emphasis is in the rural areas. 'Branches' constitute the party's basic units. They are expected to correspond to polling districts, but in practice it is not uncommon for some polling districts to have more than one branch.[3] The next level in the organizational hierarchy is made up of 'divisions'. As provided in the party's constitution, the usual practice is for each division to encompass the territory covered by a parliamentary constituency. There are, however, a few divisions which cover two or more constituencies,[4] the usual explanation for this being that it promotes efficiency where the leadership is united and would prefer to work as a single unit. At the next level there are State Liaison Committees, comprising the leaders of the various divisions in each state, which supervise the activities of the branches and divisions. The status of these Committees has been a source of some disagreement within the UMNO, for it has been felt by the lower levels that entrenched cliques have tended to use them to promote their own personal interests. The Liaison Committees have consequently been given very few powers in recent years.

[2] This was for the municipal elections held during 1952 and 1953.

[3] On the other hand, there are also polling districts where the party has no branch at all.

[4] The most extreme deviation from established practice is in Malacca, where a single division covers all four constituencies in the state.

The party's main policy-making authority is its General Assembly, which meets annually. It consists of delegates from the various divisions,[5] three delegates each from the Women's Section and the Youth Section, and the members of the Supreme Executive Council elected by the Assembly at its previous meeting. The Supreme Executive Council is the party's highest administrative authority, and is responsible to the General Assembly. The Women's Section and the Youth Section[6] have their own organizational hierarchy, but their activities are merged with those of the main organization especially at the lower levels. Although both are effective in mobilizing workers during elections, their strength varies from one part of the country to another.

The UMNO has had to face two kinds of internal problems. First, there have been rivalries for nomination as candidates and for positions within the party. These have not always been restricted to individuals, and have on occasion led to the emergence of antagonistic factions. But there have been few outward manifestations of this at the national level, mainly because the chief positions have been held by men who enjoy wide support within the party and whom few would aspire to replace. The best examples are undoubtedly the Tengku and Tun Razak who, in addition to being the President and Deputy President respectively of the UMNO, are also the Prime Minister and Deputy Prime Minister of the country. In some of the states, on the other hand, the situation has been quite different. Rivalries involving individuals and factions have been quite noticeable, and have led to serious problems of discipline. The best example of this was seen in Kelantan, following the Alliance's defeat in 1959. Different groups within the UMNO began blaming each other for

[5] Calculated on the basis of one delegate for the first 500 members and an additional member for every other 250.

[6] There are no age restrictions which govern membership of the Youth Section. Its present leader is the Minister for Information and Broadcasting, who is 45 years old. His predecessor (the present Minister for Transport) was 47 when he was replaced, and had been the President of the Youth Section for thirteen consecutive years.

their party's virtual annihilation by the PMIP, and the situation deteriorated to a point where it was impossible either to get the existing leaders to co-operate with each other in rebuilding the party or to find an alternative group of leaders who were prepared to do so. The Tengku had to summon those involved for talks in Kuala Lumpur, and a solution was eventually found by sending an outsider, chosen by the national leadership, to reorganize the party in Kelantan.

Secondly, there have also been disagreements over some of the policies followed by the Government. In this connexion, the main conflict has been between those who feel that the Government's first duty is to promote the material and cultural interests of the Malay community and those who maintain that due regard must also be given to the welfare of the other communities. As in the case of the rivalries just discussed, this conflict has also been kept from assuming any serious proportions by the deference shown to the national leaders (especially the Tengku, who is a strong advocate of inter-communal partnership) by the party's rank and file. There has consequently been a reluctance on the part of the critics outwardly to challenge the wisdom of the policies that have been followed. Needless to say, the desire for the continuing success of the party (and hence the common fear of rocking the boat) is another factor which has helped to keep the UMNO's internal problems within fairly manageable limits.

Although there was a great deal of political activity during the immediate post-war years, most of it was dominated by the Malay response (through the UMNO) to the Malayan Union and the attempt by the left-wing parties to gather mass support.[7] As a community the Chinese did not show a great deal of enthusiasm for furthering their interests and this was reflected, among other things, by their failure to make any forceful or sustained effort to defend the Malayan Union scheme and to prevent its re-

[7] For a discussion of party politics during the immediate post-war period, see K.J. Ratnam, *Communalism and the Political Process in Malaya*. Kuala Lumpur, 1965.

placement by the Federation of Malaya Agreement. Part of the reason for this undoubtedly lay in the fact that there was no specifically Chinese organization which set out to mobilize support in an attempt to protect the interests of its own community. Such an organization emerged in 1949, with the formation of the MCA.

The founding of the MCA served two immediate purposes: it gave the Colonial Government a medium through which it could obtain the support of the Chinese community with a view to combating the communist insurrection;[8] and it gave the Chinese themselves the organizational backing which they needed to improve their constitutional status in the country. The MCA also provided the wealthy and middle-class Chinese with better facilities for competing with the communists for the allegiance of the poorer classes within their community, especially the 'squatters'.[9]

Although a great deal of attention was given to the constitutional objectives of the Chinese community as a whole, an important feature of the early life of the MCA was its performance as a social organization which dedicated itself to helping the less privileged Chinese. Most outstanding in this respect was the initiative and financial assistance which it provided in helping the 'squatters' to be resettled into 'new villages'. This resettlement has subsequently acquired a wider political significance, by making a large number of Chinese who were previously scattered in remote areas easily accessible to political parties. The MCA is now well supported in most of these new villages.

The MCA's organization is broadly similar to that of the UMNO. 'Ward branches' form the basic units, and are normally expected to correspond to 'a city, town, or Local-Council Electoral Ward where more than 50 members re-

[8] The vast majority of communist guerrillas were Chinese.

[9] Since they lived mainly on the periphery of the jungle, these 'squatters' (who numbered about half a million) had been exposed to intimidation and extortion by the communist guerillas. They were resettled into 'new villages' which were fenced and guarded, so as to make them inaccessible to the communists.

side'.[10]   The next level, the division, is administered by a
Divisional Assembly made up of delegates from the ward
branches.   As in the case of the UMNO, the divisions are
ideally expected to correspond to parliamentary constituencies, but there are some which cover more than one
constituency.[11]   The reasons given for this deviation were
the same as those given by the UMNO, but MCA leaders
also explained that leadership of a high calibre was not
available in every constituency and that it was therefore
better in some cases to bring adjacent constituencies under
the same leaders.   The main organizational difference between the two parties is that the MCA's State Assemblies
have more effective powers than their counterparts in the
UMNO (the State Liaison Committees).   This may be explained in terms of the fact that ward branches and
divisions were not even provided for in the MCA's constitution until it was amended in 1959.   The relevant amendments were apparently introduced, not only because it was
thought that a broadening of the party's base was desirable in itself, but because powerful and self-perpetuating
cliques had come to dominate certain states and damaged
the popularity and internal unity of the party.   Another
difference between the MCA and the UMNO is that the
former has a special 'President's Committee' in addition to
its Central Working Committee (the equivalent of the
UMNO's Supreme Executive Council), which is personally appointed by the President from the members of the
Central Working Committee and acts as a kind of super
policy-making authority.   This Committee was created in
1961, as part of a more general reform.   The MCA's
Youth Section is at least as active as its UMNO counterpart, and is acknowledged by the party's leaders to be valuable during elections.   Unlike its partner, the MCA has
no separate Women's Section.

The MCA has for some time been beset by serious internal problems.   Most of these have been related to the

[10] *Constitution of the MCA,* Article 7.

[11] In Johore, for example, where there are sixteen parliamentary constituencies, there are only nine divisions.

attempts made by the younger groups within the party to oust some of the established leaders. Those aspiring to office have often blamed the leaders of the party for projecting an unfortunate image, not only by being aloof and unenergetic, but also by giving the impression that the MCA is run by the rich for their own benefit. The first major crisis over leadership occurred in 1958 when Dato Sir Cheng-lock Tan, the 'father' of the party and its President since its inception, was defeated by Dr. Lim Chong Eu, the leader of a faction which sought to inject young blood and a new dynamism into the party. A more severe crisis occurred in 1959, as a result of which Dr. Lim and other important leaders resigned from the party following their failure to persuade the majority to take a 'tougher' attitude in negotiating with the UMNO over the allocation of seats.[12] After Dr. Lim's resignation from the Presidency, and following an interim appointment, Mr. Tan Siew Sin, the son of Dato Sir Cheng-lock Tan, was elected President of the Party.

Recently, there have been fresh and more vigorous attempts by the younger groups to get rid of some of the leaders in an attempt to foster a new image. Matters came to a head at the meeting of the General Assembly in November 1963, when a 'new image group' launched a major campaign for reform. In the event they succeeded in infusing some new blood into the party's leadership. Presumably in an attempt to prevent a major rift, the President gave his support to the cry for a new image. Saying that the party was 'probably facing the most serious threat to its very survival in its nearly fifteen years of existence', he told the General Assembly:

> Our opponents and our detractors have always stated that the MCA is an association which exists for the rich and the well-to-do, or for those who want to become rich through politics. It may not be true, it may not be fair, but if this belief becomes increasingly accepted

12 This is discussed in Chapter V.

by wide sections of the Chinese public, then the MCA is doomed.[13]

Obviously mindful of the various pressures, Mr. Tan then went on to outline certain proposed changes in the party's organization. The most important of these was the formation of a Youths' 'Brains Trust' which initially would comprise 'back-room members' who would give thought to the various problems faced by the party and suggest ways of solving them. 'Their thinking', said Mr. Tan, 'could range far and wide. They would advise the President and the various top-level committees on what they feel should be the signposts for the future.'[14] As a counter-measure, he also proposed the setting up of a 'Council of Elders' whose relation to the Central Working Committee would be like that of the Senate to the House of Representatives in the Malaysian Parliament. These arrangements, he felt, would ensure 'a correct blending of youth with age, of boldness and enthusiasm with maturity and experience'.[15] In the course of interviews, however, many leaders of the party were forthright in admitting that, while the first proposal was an attempt to placate the younger elements, the second was essentially a face-saving device. The view was unanimously held that the changes would be beneficial to the party's long-term interests. It was also felt that the reforms were necessary in order to forestall the PAP, since that party might otherwise have taken advantage of the MCA's internal disunity.[16]

The MIC was founded in 1946, for the purpose of representing Indian interests in the country. For a short while it was a member of the All-Malaya Council of Joint Action (AMCJA), a left-wing front comprising several organizations. When, with the declaration of the Emergency in 1948, the other organizations in this front either dissolved themselves or were driven underground, the

13 *Sunday Mail,* 17 November 1963.

14 *Loc. cit.*

15 *Loc. cit.*

16 At the time of these reforms, it was not known whether or not the PAP would participate in the forthcoming elections.

MIC returned to its original function of representing Indian interests alone. Just before the 1955 Federal Election, the party was incorporated into the Alliance. Its present importance derives almost entirely from its membership of the Alliance, especially since the Indians do not constitute as much as one-quarter of the electorate in any constituency. If the Alliance has gained by bringing the MIC within its fold, it is only because that move has enabled it to embrace all three of the major communities within its organization. In terms of electoral strength alone, the MIC is no asset. For this reason, it is perhaps unnecessary to go into any details about its organization. It may however be worth pointing out that, like the MCA, it has had to cope with serious internal tensions. But these tensions have almost exclusively been the result of personal rivalries. The intensity of these rivalries could perhaps be attributed to the fact that since the party receives only a very small share of the Alliance's nominations (for parliamentary as well as state elections), the choice of candidates depends a great deal on a person's importance within the party. Further, there is not the same need for the MIC to be concerned with its policies and public image, since these are not the main factors which influence the success of its candidates. What matters is not the following which the party has within the Indian community but the support which Chinese and Malay voters give its candidates because they stand on an Alliance ticket. The mere fact of gaining nomination is therefore far more important within the MIC than within the UMNO or the MCA.

As pointed out earlier, the 'Alliance Party' exists only at certain co-ordinating levels. Its organization does not involve any general meeting of the members of the constituent bodies, and is restricted to committees which comprise delegates from these bodies. The 'division' is the lowest level at which these committees function, branch activities being conducted entirely by the member organizations. Each state has it own (Alliance) Liaison Committee and Executive Committee, which co-ordinate the activities of the member parties. The supreme authorities are the National Council and the National Executive Committee, which comprise the leaders of each party and decide on all matters of policy.   At each level the UMNO and the MCA have the same number of delegates, while the MIC has fewer.   In the National Council, for example, the first two have sixteen representatives each while the third has only six.   The corresponding figures in the National Executive Committee are six, six and three.[17]

The fact that it has no direct membership and exists only as a co-ordinating body is in some ways the Alliance's main source of strength.   It gives the member organizations the opportunity to project themselves as the champions of their respective communities while at the same time enabling them to promote inter-communal ideals.   It also helps the candidates of each party to have more than a purely communal base for their support, thereby giving them an advantage over most of their opponents.[18]   But this arrangement also has its weaknesses.   The preservation of three separate identities means that the leaders are responsible to different sets of members and in some ways represent different (and at times conflicting) interests. There is thus a constant need for bargaining and compromise, and there are obvious difficulties in reaching agreement, especially over policies which have communal implications.   The most serious conflicts, however, have not been over policies but over the allocation of seats during elections.   This is discussed in Chapter V.

The way in which the Alliance functions also makes it impossible for its member organizations to do as much as they would like for their respective communities. The UMNO, for example, must always bear in mind its relationship with the MCA and the MIC in promoting the interests of the Malay community, since that relationship could be destroyed if it strives to achieve too much.   Thus each organization has to confine itself within

[17] The National Executive Committee is elected by the National Council from among its own members.   From all evidence its exact composition is of no practical significance since decisions have to be unanimous.
[18] See p. 164.

the limits which are necessary for the preservation of its partnership with others, and must always be prepared to make concessions. This has exposed each member organization to accusations of having failed to look after the interests of its community properly, and of having given in too easily to its partners. Thus the MCA is accused of having sold out the interests of the Chinese to the Malays by being too subservient in its relations with the UMNO. Similarly, the UMNO is accused of having failed to dedicate itself properly to the task of serving the interests of the Malay community, by allowing itself to be manipulated by the MCA. Nor are these accusations confined purely to the member organizations. It is not uncommon for the Alliance as a whole to be characterized as a Malay-dominated party by some Chinese and as a party of Chinese interests by some Malays.

Despite these shortcomings, the Alliance continues to be by far the most successful party in the country. The potential gravity of many of its internal problems is offset by the concern among all the partners not to endanger the success which they have enjoyed so far. Each organization realizes that its strength depends on the continuation of its partnership with the others, and is therefore anxious not to precipitate any major crisis. The Alliance also has the advantage of a more widespread organization and considerably larger funds than any of its opponents. It still benefits from being the party which achieved independence, and is fortunate in having a leader (Tengku Abdul Rahman) who enjoys wide support from all sections of the population and whose stature within the party is a valuable aid in resolving internal conflicts. Although the party lacks any conventional ideology which can promote enthusiasm and help to keep it united, it has made itself attractive by showing the electorate that it is the only party which can provide an inter-communal basis for politics and at the same time represent specifically communal interests. Despite all the criticisms made against it, it was significant that most of those interviewed from rival parties were agreed that the Alliance was the 'next best party' in the country, either because it was 'reasonable' or because it was felt that the other parties were antagonistic towards some community or communities.

The Socialist Front (SF), like the Alliance, is made up of three separate organizations: the Labour Party, Party Rakyat and the National Convention Party (NCP). It was formed in 1957, and originally comprised only the Labour Party and Party Rakyat. The NCP, which was founded in 1963 by Inche Abdul Aziz bin Ishak, an ex-Minister in the Alliance Government,[19] was incorporated into the SF just before nomination day and is by far the smallest of the three partners. Unlike the Alliance, the constituent organizations of the SF are not exclusively communal, although the Labour Party is essentially non-Malay, while Party Rakyat and the NCP cater to the Malay community. Thus the SF is also primarily an inter-communal alliance, and, for this reason, has many problems in common with the Alliance Party. But the main factor which brought its member organizations together and keeps them under the same roof is less related to the communal implications of partnership than to their allegiance to a common ideology, socialism. However, communal considerations are not altogether irrelevant in the sense that they have at least prevented the constituent bodies from merging to form a single organization with direct membership. Ideology may be crucial to the SF's support and internal unity, but is not a sufficient counterweight for the electorate's preoccupation with communal issues and for the different communal viewpoints of the party's own leaders. This was conceded by all those who were interviewed, and it was felt that the interests of the party would be best served by retaining some communal basis for support even if the main emphasis was to be on ideology. It was feared that if the member organizations were to sacrifice their separate identities the Malays would view the SF as a Chinese party since the Labour Party was the most active component and had more members than the other two partners put toge-

19 See Chapter II, above, for the circumstances which forced Inche Aziz to resign as Minister.

ther. The view was also expressed that in such an event party activity in different localities would tend to be dominated *either* by Malays or non-Malays since communal fraternity was an important ingredient of sustained enthusiasm.[20] As will be shown shortly, the present arrangement enables the Malays and the non-Malays to have their own separate organizations where this is thought desirable.

Branches form the basic units of the Labour Party. They do not correspond to any electoral unit, and the decision to set them up is made by the 'divisions', which, in the Labour Party, represent the state level. The party's constitution provides that a branch may be formed whenever forty adult members are available. In practice, however, the divisions also take into consideration such factors as the total population of the proposed area to be covered by a branch,[21] the type of people who live in the area,[22] and the number of 'activists' who will be available for party work. It was claimed that the divisions do not take into account the proximity of a proposed branch to one that already exists, and use as their main criterion the extent to which a new branch will help the party to be 'in close touch with the people'. Those interviewed also maintained that the electoral convenience of having a branch was not too important since the party's main aim was to encourage its 'activists' and provide them with scope for party work.

Unlike the UMNO and the MCA, the Labour Party has no organization at the constituency level. The unit immediately above the branch is the 'division', which covers an entire state. The supreme body in each division is the Divisional Committee, which is elected annually at the Divisional Conference and is expected to meet at least once every month. This Committee is advised in its work by a Divisional Advisory Committee, which includes among its members delegates from all the branches

20 These fears are felt even more strongly in the Alliance.

21 To see how far the party can benefit by having a new branch.

22 For example, their occupational composition. A working class population was naturally considered desirable.

in the division.[23] At the national level, the Labour Party's activities are managed by a National Executive Council, which is elected at the party's annual Conference and comprises 'a Chairman, two Vice-Chairmen, General Secretary, Treasurer, one representative from each Division and an equal number of members as those nominated from Divisions to be elected by the National Conference from Conference delegates.'[24] The main administrative burden is delegated to a National Working Committee, which is made up of the five principal office-bearers of the National Executive Council and four others elected by that Council from among its own members.

Party Rakyat's organization is similar to the Labour Party's and therefore need not be described. The third partner, the NCP, was only a small organization at the time of the election, and there was very little scope for observing the way in which it functioned. The formally approved structure provides for 'divisions' (which correspond to parliamentary constituencies), State Councils and a National Council. According to the party's leader, eleven divisions had initially been established but four of them had soon collapsed. From all available evidence, Inche Aziz's own personality was the main driving force behind the NCP.

Like the Alliance, the SF exists only as a co-ordinating body. It comes into existence at the state ('divisional') level, and here comprises five representatives each from the Labour Party and Party Rakyat, who together form an SF State Liaison Committee.[25] At the national level

[23] The rest of the Divisional Advisory Committee is made up of the members of the Divisional Committee. This Committee is expected to meet at least once every quarter.

[24] *Constitution of the Labour Party of Malaya,* Section VI, Article 1.

[25] Since the NCP was incorporated into the SF only a few weeks before the election it was difficult to ascertain its position in relation to the other partners. It was, however, often stated that it would enjoy the same status as the others, but then it has also to be borne in mind that the NCP did not have any organization in most of the states and hence could not have been represented in the majority of SF State Liaison Committees.

the party is made up of a National Council in which each of the partners has six representatives.[26]

The SF has no clear policy on how the branches of its constituent organizations should be distributed. Although there was a great deal of conflicting evidence given in the course of interviews, the general policy seems to be that one or the other of the organizations should be allowed, wherever possible, to operate in any given area. There are, however, several areas where both the main partners have their own branches, but this duplication is partly explained by the fact that these branches existed before the SF was formed. Some of those interviewed stated that in forming new branches preference was usually given to the party which represented the dominant community in the area concerned. This would mean that, wherever possible, Party Rakyat branches are set up in Malay areas and Labour Party branches in Chinese areas. Others, however, were insistent that communal considerations were not taken into account and that new branches were approved purely on the basis of which party had requested their establishment. The evidence on the whole would suggest that the SF machinery is in some way involved in decisions which concern the setting up of new branches. But this involvement can only be informal, since the constitutions of the member organizations state quite clearly that they are solely responsible for the setting up of their own branches.

By retaining their separate identities the SF partners, like those of the Alliance, find it necessary to continue representing different interests and, for this reason, often come into conflict with each other. Because each of them is primarily communal, at least in composition, issues related to communal interests have often formed the basis for disagreement. But these issues have not assumed the same prominence within the SF as they have in the Alliance, not only because the party appeals mainly on ideological grounds but because, not being in power, it

26 Once again, there was some uncertainty about the NCP's position in this arrangement.

has been able to avoid taking a clear-cut stand on many communal issues. The main rivalry between the partners is consequently over the allocation of seats. The chief difficulty in this respect arises from the fact that the SF's popularity is concentrated in the urban areas. Theoretically, the partnership of the Labour Party and Party Rakyat in the SF is supposed to be one between an urban-based non-Malay party and a rural-based Malay party. This means that, in apportioning seats, urban constituencies should ideally be assigned to the Labour Party and rural constituencies to Party Rakyat. But in one respect such a distribution would make nonsense of the assumed equality of the two partners, since one party would get all the 'good' seats while the other would have to be satisfied merely with going through the motions of putting up candidates in areas where it had little chance of success. For this reason, Party Rakyat has tended to insist that it should be given at least some of the seats in the urban or semi-urban areas. This has naturally been resented by the Labour Party although, in the interests of unity, it has shown itself willing to make some concessions.

Because they attempt to have at least some communal basis for their support, and because they have to make concessions to each other, the component units of the SF, like those of the Alliance, are exposed to the accusation that they are not sufficiently dedicated in promoting the interests of their respective communities. Unlike the Alliance, however, this accusation does not flow equally strongly in both directions: the main criticism of the SF on communal grounds comes from the Malays, who accuse it of being dominated by the Chinese. The failure of Party Rakyat to gain any appreciable support among the Malays in the rural areas has been one of the SF's main disappointments. If this failure has largely been the result of the SF's image as a Chinese-dominated party, Party Rakyat seems to have done very little to improve the situation. Almost all its leaders are from urban areas, and appear reluctant to extend their party's activities into rural areas. But this reluctance is not altogether unjustified since experience has shown them that it is difficult for their party to make any impression on the UMNO and the PMIP which are both extensively organized and enjoy an entrenched popularity among the Malays. Given the Malay community's great concern for its communal interests, it will be difficult for Party Rakyat to compete with these two parties as a champion of Malay rights. It apparently also suffers because many Malays believe that socialism implies a rejection of God.

The most serious handicap faced by the SF, however, has been its failure to become accepted as a 'respectable' party. Many still associate left-wing politics with communism and subversion. If this view has been deliberately encouraged by the other parties, it is also true that various members of the SF have been shown to have been involved in clandestine activities. In any event the SF is the party which has suffered most as a result of official concern over its activities, and there have been sporadic arrests of its members under the Preventive Detention Ordinance. There are some grounds for believing that there is a certain amount of conflict between the 'extremists' and 'moderates' within the party, and that this has served to weaken some of its internal unity.

The Pan-Malayan Islamic Party (PMIP) is the most extreme communal party in the country. Its main appeal is religious, but the party also places a great deal of emphasis on its claim that the Malays are the only 'true sons of the soil' and that the policies of the Government should therefore be more exclusively geared to promoting their welfare. It advocates a more equitable distribution of wealth, in a manner which is claimed to be prescribed in the Koran. Most of the PMIP's support is found in the predominantly Malay states in the north and north-east of Malaya, where it has successfully exploited the religious sentiments and anti-Chinese feelings of the tradition-bound and economically backward local population.

Compared to the Alliance and the SF, the PMIP has a less elaborate formal structure. According to its constitution, its 'branches' can be established 'in any place as ap-

proved by the PMIP Central Executive Committee'. It is
also stipulated that 'a branch can be established to cover
one state or a district, or a group of districts or an area in
which there are at least 50 members'.[27] In the course of
interviews, however, it was pointed out that branches are
in fact ideally expected to correspond to state constituencies. But in some states (e.g. Selangor) there are fewer
branches than state constituencies, while in others (e.g.
Kelantan) there are more. The constitution also provides
for 'sub-branches'. It is stated that they can be established
'in any place as approved by the Branch Executive Committee', and that only fifteen members are required for
the formation of a sub-branch.[28] Again, a different account
was given during interviews, when it was maintained that
sub-branches were normally expected to correspond to
polling districts. In practice, however, their distribution
is haphazard. In each state there is a 'Liaison Officer' (or
'Commissioner') who co-ordinates the activities of all the
branches and sub-branches under his control, and through
whom the national leaders communicate with the lower
levels of the party.[29] This official is appointed by the
President of the party on the advice of the Central Executive Committee, and is assisted in his work by a Liaison
Executive Committee made up of branch representatives.

The PMIP's supreme policy-making authority lies in its
Annual General Meeting. This is attended by the members of the Central Executive Committee (the chief administrative body), the various Liaison Officers, branch presi-
dents, delegates from the branches,[30] and representatives
from the party's Religious Council (*Dewan Ulama*), Youth

27 *Constitution of the PMIP*, Article 15, Clauses 1 and 2.

28 *Ibid.* Article 16, Clauses 1 and 2.

29 The constitution is not specific about the territory which falls under
the control of each Liaison Officer. It states: 'A state or a district or a
place which has more than one PMIP Branch shall [have] a Liaison
Officer who shall be the District Commissioner' (Article 26, Clause 1).
It was, however, explained during interviews that the normal practice was
for each Liaison Officer to have control over a state.

30 The number of delegates from each branch is determined by the
strength of its membership.

Council (*Dewan Pemuda*) and Women's Council (*Dewan Muslimat*).[31] Interestingly, it is also provided that certain religious scholars who are ordinary members of the PMIP will be invited to attend the Annual General Meeting, without having voting rights conferred on them. Those specified in this category are administrative heads of religious departments in Malaya, members of the Religious and Customary Councils in the Malay States, and members of the Islamic Advisory Council in Penang, Malacca and Singapore.[32] Another indication of the emphasis placed on religion and religious principles by the PMIP is found in the article in its constitution which states: 'The highest rule in the PMIP belief is God's book (the Koran) and the sayings of the Apostle (Al-Rasul) as well as the clear and obvious consensus of opinion of the Muslim scholars. The PMIP's power which resides in the General Meeting is subject to this highest rule.'[33] It is also stipulated in the constitution that only persons professing the Islamic faith are eligible for membership of the party.[34]

Many of the PMIP leaders who were interviewed admitted that their party's organization was weak. But they also felt that this was not a serious shortcoming since their party was less dependent than the others on the effectiveness of its formal organization. Where it was successful, it was because of grass-roots enthusiasm rather than the strength of its organization. But this enthusiasm was not, as was often claimed, purely the result of a spontaneous reaction to the party's policies. Although the PMIP's main policies have a great emotional appeal among some sections of the Malay community, an important counterbalance for the lack of a strong organization usually consisted in the dedicated support which the party received from religious leaders in the rural areas. This is discussed

[31] The PMIP's women and youth sections are on the whole much less active than their UMNO counterparts.

[32] *Constitution of the PMIP*, Article 5, Clause 10.

[33] *Ibid.* Article 4, Clause IA.

[34] *Ibid.* Article 8.

in other parts of the book, and need not be elaborated here.[35]

The PMIP benefits from the fact that it has an immediate appeal among Malays who resent the economic superiority of the Chinese and who live in areas where traditional values are dominant. It is also favourably placed by being the only effective alternative to the UMNO among the Malays, as a result of which it is bound to gain from any dissatisfaction with the latter's performance. Its outlook is especially attractive to those who are preoccupied with religion and whose nationalism is based on communally exclusive ideals. But if this outlook serves to guarantee a basic core of support, it is ultimately also the party's main weakness. As long as the PMIP attempts to consolidate its support through uncompromising religious propaganda and by evoking hostile feelings towards the non-Malays, it will forfeit all chances of ever gaining control of the central Government. Its tactics may have been ideally suited to help it to come to power in Kelantan and Trengganu in 1959, but they can have little appeal in the more advanced states in western and southern Malaya. Further, these tactics will certainly serve to deny the party any support from the non-Malays, who in 1964 constituted about 45 per cent. of the total electorate.

The strong ideological unity provided by religion is one of the important factors which has helped to preserve the internal unity of the PMIP. Those interviewed were often keen to point out that the party's leaders did not have much personal control, and that disputes which arose were solved either in the most democratic manner or by common agreement over what was best in the interests of Islam. But this was not always borne out by observation, although it is true that the PMIP has no leaders who have a status comparable to that of the Tengku and Tun Razak in the Alliance.[36] On important matters like the selection

[35] See especially Chapters VII and IX (a).

[36] In this connexion it should also be pointed out that the support enjoyed by the PMIP is not in any important way dependent on the personal popularity of its national leaders.

of candidates, for example, the national leaders of the party wielded a great deal of influence and did not have many effective restraints on their personal authority. Further, internal squabbles have not altogether been avoided. Discipline broke down most seriously in Trengganu in 1961, when some of the party's state assemblymen crossed the floor to give the Alliance a majority.

None of the other parties was sufficiently large or well-organized at the time of the election to merit detailed consideration here. The one that came closest to being a 'big' party was the United Democratic Party (UDP), which fielded twenty-seven parliamentary candidates and contested in five states.

The UDP was formed in 1961, by the key figures who had resigned from the MCA after the crisis in 1959. It is led by Dr. Lim Chong Eu (its Secretary-General), who was the President of the MCA before he left that party. Due mainly to the political background of those who founded it, the UDP is commonly regarded as a 'Chinese' party. But its leaders have tried in many ways to alter this image, being aware that their party will have to prove itself acceptable to the Malays if it is to make much headway. It is only by recognizing this motive that one can reconcile the party's predominant Chinese image with the fact that its president is a Malay and that eight of its twenty-seven parliamentary candidates in 1964 were also Malays. This attempt to broaden its appeal has so far met with little success. The tendency has been for the few Malay members of the party not to be taken seriously by their own community, who regard them as mere 'front men' who have little or no influence. Further, the effective leaders of the party have been reluctant to allow their desire for an inter-communal appeal to damage their popularity among the Chinese, whom they know to be their main supporters. Thus the main issues which have been raised by the UDP since its inception have been aimed primarily at gaining Chinese support. Of special significance has been its criticism of the Government's policy towards Chinese education. It must however be emphasized that the UDP does not by any means cater to Chinese interests alone. It supports the reservation of special privileges for the Malay community, while maintaining that these privileges should only be temporary. It also approves of Malay as the sole official language. Up to the present, the party's efforts have been concentrated in the predominantly Chinese areas in Penang, Perak, Negri Sembilan, Johore and Malacca.

Although the People's Action Party (PAP) fielded only a small number of candidates and had practically no formal organization in Malaya at the time of the election,[37] it occupies a very important place in Malaysian politics. One would certainly be mistaken in thinking that its future significance was in any way reflected by the number of seats it contested in 1964, or by the fact that only one of its candidates was successful. The decision to contest was made only at the last moment, and the party therefore had very little time to organize an effective campaign at the grass-roots level. Even if it fails to get much support in the Malayan states in future, the PAP is bound to exert a great deal of influence on national politics. The fact that it is firmly entrenched in Singapore gives it considerable importance, but what is significant for the future is the possibility that it will benefit from non-Malay fears of Malay domination, and also be able to exploit dissatisfaction in the Borneo territories, if the central Government fails to give due regard to state autonomy. Should the question of preserving states' rights ever become a dominant issue, it could provide a convenient platform for concerted action by Singapore, Sarawak and Sabah. These states have a wider area of autonomy than the others and, having only recently become federated, are likely to place greater emphasis on their own separate identities.[38] Understandably, the two Borneo states, which are both controlled by the Alliance, are bound to be less keen in coming into open conflict with the central Government

[37] An account of the PAP's activities in Singapore is given in Chapter XI.

[38] The Malayan states, on the other hand, have been accustomed longer to a highly centralized form of federal government.

since they will also consider the advantages provided by the common Alliance bond.[39]   But there will be a limit beyond which this party bond will not be able to offset the tensions brought about by federal-state conflict.   Thus if the Federal Government comes to be identified with too much central control, it is possible that the Alliance will lose its present popularity in Sarawak and Sabah, and some of its leaders there may find it advantageous to emphasize their state identity rather than their ties with the Federal Government.   This might be followed by a new political alignment embracing Singapore and these two states, nourished by a concern for state autonomy.   It is, of course, quite possible that dissatisfaction with the Alliance in the Borneo states will never become so severe as to encourage them to seek new alignments.   It is also possible that the political leaders in these states, even if they are prepared to sever their Alliance connexions, will not be prepared to subordinate themselves to the PAP.   What is important, however, is that the PAP is commonly regarded as the party most capable of undermining the popularity of the Alliance, particularly in the urban areas.   Its reputation has been enhanced by its success as a moderate left-wing Government in Singapore, and the amount of attention which it received during the election was proof of the extent to which the other parties in the country regard it as a major political force.

The People's Progressive Party (PPP) is the sole advocate of complete equality between Malays and non-Malays. It is opposed to the 'special position' accorded to the Malay community in the Constitution, and is also the only party which campaigns for multi-lingualism.   It is therefore not surprising that its appeal is almost totally confined to the non-Malay communities.   Its strength is limited to the area around Ipoh, the main city in the state of Perak.   This is where its leaders (the two Seenivasagam brothers) live,

---

39 It should, however, also be pointed out that the component units of the Alliance in Sarawak and Sabah are not the same as in Malaya (see Chapter X).

and the support enjoyed by the party is mainly the outcome of their personal popularity.[40] No serious attempt
appears to have been made to extend the party's organization to the other states, or to co-ordinate its activities in
the different parts of the country. Some party officials have
explained that this was the result of the difficulty in finding good local leaders in the other states. Others, however,
felt that it was due simply to a lack of enthusiasm among
the party's leaders, who were satisfied with the one base
they had, and were also reluctant to decentralize the party
for fear of losing their own influence.

Party Negara, like the PPP, is essentially a one-state
party. Its activities are confined almost wholly to Trengganu, where its four parliamentary and seventeen state
candidates contested in 1964. It stands next to the PMIP
as a champion of Malay rights but, unlike that party, has
neither a strong religious bias nor any intense hostility towards the non-Malays. Party Negara was formed under
the leadership of Dato Onn in 1954, following the IMP's
demise.[41] It was the Alliance's chief rival at the 1955 election, but was completely routed by its opponent.[42] Since
then its fortunes have not improved, but for Dato Onn's
own success (in a Trengganu constituency) at the 1959 parliamentary elections. With Dato Onn's death in 1962, the
party lost even its limited appeal, which depended on his
personal popularity. Even in Trengganu its organization
at present is only rudimentary.

None of the parties was able to give a proper estimate
of its current membership. It was often pointed out that

40 The two seats in Ipoh (Ipoh and Menglembu, contested by the
Seenivasagams) were the only ones won by the PPP in 1964. Originally
the party was in fact called the *Perak* Progressive Party, but changed its
name after the 1955 elections.

41 Once it became clear the IMP (which was non-communal) had no
popular following, Dato Onn reverted to his original role as a champion
of Malay rights.

42 None of the party's thirty candidates was successful. Of the fifty-
two seats that were contested the Alliance won fifty-one and the PMIP
one.

full membership figures were kept only at the branch or divisional level, and that in any event many of those whose names appeared on party lists had long ceased to be paying members. The MCA, for example, estimated that only about a fifth of its 'members' (roughly placed at 200,000) had actually paid up their subscriptions. It was maintained by one party official that the difficulty of contacting every member in order to collect his subscription was usually not worth the return. The SF, which claimed a 'membership' of 90,000, probably had only 15,000 paying members.

Although important, the financial incentive was not always the most important one which encouraged the parties to recruit members. It was frequently believed that the mere fact of 'membership' (regardless of the payment of dues) usually encouraged a person to have a greater commitment to a party, and that by having a large number of members a party was able to increase the number of its propagandists. Those who were less optimistic were at least satisfied that by being formally enrolled as a member a person was made less receptive to the propaganda of rival parties. These considerations must have been foremost in the mind of the UMNO when it decided in 1961 to launch a special membership drive in Kelantan under which people could become members of the party without having to pay any dues.

Notwithstanding their desire to increase their members, all parties were emphatic that they were not prepared to make membership available on demand, since there was a risk of infiltration by agents belonging to rival parties. Some of the opposition parties also claimed that many of their supporters were reluctant to become members because this might antagonize the ruling party. They therefore argued that membership figures did not in any way reflect the actual following which a party had. A top PMIP official stated that, for this reason, his party preferred to make a list of its supporters rather than launch a membership drive in order to estimate its popularity. Especially in the rural areas, the view was also frequently expressed that even an annual fee of M$1[43] was considered by many to be prohibitive. For this reason, it was not uncommon for some members to be exempted by their party from paying their entrance fee (usually $1) and for some others to be allowed to pay a reduced annual subscription or to have their subscription waived altogether.

Subscriptions are always collected at the branch or divisional level, whichever happens to be the basic unit. The usual procedure is for this level to keep a certain percentage and to forward the remainder to be shared by the various levels above it. In theory all branches and divisions are expected to be self-supporting. In practice, however, they often need special grants from their state headquarters in order to remain active throughout the year.[44] The state and national levels usually get some part of their income in the form of donations from well-wishers. It is also a common practice for successful candidates to make compulsory contributions to their parties.[45]

Of the main parties, the Alliance is the one which depends most on donations from sources outside the party. Being in power, and because its policies are favourable to free enterprise and to business interests, it has not had much difficulty (especially during elections) in getting substantial contributions to help defray the cost of running a vast and relatively expensive organization. This gives it a considerable advantage over its opponents, but some of it is offset by the fact that it usually has to pay more than its rivals for obtaining the same services during elections. Its main opponents, the SF and the PMIP, are able to compensate for their relatively poor finances by receiv-

43 Party subscriptions range from $1 for three years (PPP) to an annual fee of $2 (MCA and the Labour Party).

44 This is most pronounced in the case of the Alliance.

45 In almost all cases, this is a fixed percentage of the allowance they receive as members of parliament, as state assemblymen, or as local councillors.

ing a great deal of voluntary help from their more enthusiastic and dedicated supporters.[46]

[46] This is discussed in Chapter VII. For a more detailed study of
party finance in Malaya, see R. S. Milne and K. J. Ratnam, 'Politics and
Finance in Malaya', *Journal of Commonwealth Political Studies*, Vol III,
No. 3 (1965).

IV

The Administration of the Election

T. E. Smith

The Election Commission

THE parliamentary and state elections held in April 1964 in the states of Malaya were the second in the series of general elections held under the supervision of the Election Commission which was established shortly after the Federation of Malaya gained independence in 1957. If the first and only election of members in 1955 to the part-elected and part-nominated Federal Legislative Council is taken into account, the 1964 election can be regarded as the third in this series.

The Election Commission was appointed under the provisions of Article 114 of the 1957 Constitution. In accordance with the clauses of this Article, the Commission so constituted consisted of a Chairman and two other members, each of whom was appointed by the Yang di-Pertuan Agong after consultation with the Conference of Rulers 'having regard to the importance of securing an Election Commission which enjoys public confidence'.[1] The original trio still held office in April 1964. They were an administratively very experienced and capable Malay (Dato Dr. Haji Mustapha Albakri) as Chairman, and an Indian (Mr. Ditt Singh) and a Chinese (Mr. Lee Ewe Boon), both of whom had held key posts in state election offices prior to their appointment, as the two other members. The Constitution did not require representation of all the three major ethnic groups of Malaya, but there seems little doubt that justice and expediency demand a continuation of this arrangement. The Chinese member in fact

[1] Clause 2 of Article 114.

reached the age limit of sixty-five[2] in 1964 and the Indian member reached it in 1965. They were replaced by a new Chinese member and a new Indian member, respectively. The Malaysia Constitution of 1963 read in conjunction with the Report of the Inter-Government Committee on Malaysia (the Lansdowne Committee) provides for an additional member of the Election Commission to be appointed from one or other of the Borneo States, but such an appointment had not been made at the time of the 1964 election in the States of Malaya.

The duties and the degree of independence of an election commission in any country are matters of more than academic importance. The 1957 Constitution required the Election Commission to 'conduct elections to the House of Representatives and the Legislative Assemblies of the States and delimit constituencies and prepare and revise electoral rolls for such elections'.[3] The high reputation which the Election Commission won for itself in 1959 in conducting elections efficiently and impartially was reflected in the decision taken in 1961 that the Commission should take responsibility not only for parliamentary and state elections but also for local authority and local council elections.

Power to delimit constituencies was however withdrawn as the result of the Constitution (Amendment) Act of 1962,[4] and the Commission's powers in respect of constituencies are now limited to the making of *recommendations* for changes in boundaries in accordance with fairly closely defined principles and procedures. There can be no doubt but that the reason for this amendment to the Constitution lay in the Alliance Government's dismay on reading the Election Commission's 1960 report[5] on the delimitation of parliamentary and state constituencies. It is however unusual for an election commission or for boundary

2 Clause 3 of Article 114.
3 Article 113 (1).
4 Section 20.
5 *Report of the Election Commission on the Delimitation of Parliamentary and State Constituencies under the Provisions of the Constitution of the Persekutuan Tanah Melayu, 1960.*

commissioners to have the final word in the delimitation
of constituencies, and, in limiting the Malayan Election
Commission's authority by amendment of the Constitution, the Parliament of the Federation of Malaya has done
no more than provide itself with the powers possessed by,
for instance, the British Parliament.

Inevitably there have been pressures on the Election
Commission from time to time both by the Alliance
Government and by the opposition parties. It is relatively
easy for the Commission to ignore any seemingly unreasonable demands or attacks from the opposition parties,
but the Commission is in a far more difficult position in
its relationship with the Government. Amendments proposed by the Commission to any of the Acts dealing with
electoral affairs must of course be approved by Parliament,
whilst proposed changes in the Regulations made under
such Acts must pass the Cabinet before being submitted
to the Yang di-Pertuan Agong for his approval; thus no
changes in electoral legislation are possible without the
approval of the party in power. It is, however, rather in
the field of personal relationships between the Election
Commission and the Ministers of the Government that
the real difficulties are likely to arise. For instance, the
electoral regulations state with admirable clarity which
persons are allowed and which are not allowed to enter
polling stations on polling day: at least one Alliance Minister expressed resentment in the 1959 election at being
instructed to leave a polling station which he had no right
to enter.

The Alliance Government for their part made one dramatic but unsuccessful attempt to oust the Chairman of
the Election Commission by amendment of the Constitution in 1960. The original 1957 Constitution made the
following provisions:

114 (3). A member of the Election Commission shall
cease to hold office on attaining the age of sixty-five
years or on becoming disqualified under Clause (4) and
may at any time resign his office by writing under his

hand addressed to the Yang di-Pertuan Agong, but shall not be removed from office except on the like grounds and in the like manner as a judge of the Supreme Court.

(4). A person is disqualified for appointment as a member of the Election Commission if he holds any other office of profit or is a member of either House of Parliament or of the Legislative Assembly of any State.

The Chairman of the Election Commission had not at any time since his appointment held 'any other office of profit' as defined in the Constitution but he did have business interests which brought him certain remuneration over and above his salary as Chairman of the Commission. In 1960, Clause 4 was repealed and the following new Clause was substituted:

(4) Notwithstanding anything in Clause (3), the Yang di-Pertuan Agong may by order remove from office any member of the Election Commission if such member —

(a) is an undischarged bankrupt; or

(b) engages in any paid office or employment outside the duties of his office; or

(c) is a member of either House of Parliament or of the Legislative Assembly of a State.

This manoeuvre aimed at removing him was foiled by the Chairman who was able to point to Article 114 (6) which provides that 'the remuneration and other terms of office of a member of the Election Commission shall not be altered to his disadvantage after his appointment'.

It would be wrong to make too much of any friction which there may have been in the past between the Election Commission and the Government. The very fact that the Chairman was successful in resisting attempts to remove him is a fair illustration of the degree of independence of the Commission so far. Probably the next test of its independence will be in the extent to which the new members, appointed to the Commission recently to take the place of those who had reached the maximum age, succeed in commanding public confidence generally and not merely the confidence of supporters of the Alliance.

The House of Representatives and State Legislative Assemblies

The description of the electoral system which follows relates to the election of members to the House of Representatives and the state Legislative Assemblies. Both parliamentary and state elections are conducted under the same electoral laws. Members of the Senate are not at present elected and the dissolution of Parliament at the end of February 1964 did not affect the Senate.

The direct election of members of the House of Representatives and of state Legislative Assemblies on 25 April 1964 was held in the States of Malaya only, and not in Singapore, Sabah and Sarawak. For these three states, the Malaysia Constitution, as a temporary measure, provides for the indirect election of members of the House of Representatives by their own state Assemblies and, on the dissolution of Parliament in 1964, the only elective action necessary was for the three state Assemblies to take a fresh vote on their representation in Parliament. The Constitution of Malaysia requires that there must be directly elected members of Parliament for these three states at the first dissolution of Parliament after the end of August 1968 or at such earlier date as the Yang di-Pertuan Agong may direct.

The Constituencies

In the Legislative Council of the Federation of Malaya which sat from 1955 to 1959 there were fifty-two elected members.[6] The terms of reference of the Commission which delimited these constituencies required that there should as far as possible be an approximate equality in the number of inhabitants within each constituency except that a measure of 'weightage' for area should be given to the rural constituencies. 'In view of the very great distances involved in some of the more sparsely settled portions of the country', the terms of reference said, 'it would not be

[6] For details of the electoral boundaries of the fifty-two constituencies and a detailed commentary on the methods used in deciding upon them, see the *Report of the Constituency Delineation Commission* (Chairman — Lord Merthyr). Kuala Lumpur, 1954.

regarded as unreasonable if in some instances a rural constituency contained as little as one half of the inhabitants
in the more populous urban constituencies returning single members.' In the event, each constituency defined by
the Commission was contained entirely within the boundaries of a single state, and the range of population within
the various constituencies was such that the most populous
contained just over two and a half times the number of
people living in the least populous, based on the 1947
census figures which were the latest reliable data available
in 1954 when the Commission performed its task.

In 1958 the Election Commission divided each of the
fifty-two constituencies used in the 1955 election into two
parts to create 104 new single-member parliamentary constituencies in accordance with the provisions of Article 171
of the Constitution of 1957.[7] Each of these 104 parliamentary constituencies was further subdivided to form
state constituencies for the purpose of elections to the state
Legislative Assemblies. These constituencies delimited in
1958 were used in the 1959 general election and again, as
things turned out, in 1964. The constitutional intention
at the time of the 1958 delimitation was that the 104 parliamentary and 282 state constituencies should be used for
the purpose of the 1959 general elections and subsequent
by-elections only and that a completely fresh division of
the country into parliamentary and state single-member
constituencies should be made for the next general election following that of 1959, in accordance with the provisions of Articles 116 and 117 of the 1957 Constitution.
These Articles provided for the allocation of parliamentary constituencies to the states in such a way that the
average number of electors per constituency in each state
should be approximately equal to the country-wide average, unless a large difference in the state and country-wide
average population per constituency would thus be caused,
in which case both factors should be taken into considera-

---

[7] For details, see the *Report of the Election Commission on the Delimitation of Constituencies for the first Elections to the House of Representatives and the State Legislative Assemblies.* Kuala Lumpur, 1958.

tion. After allocating parliamentary constituencies to each state, Articles 116(4) and 117 made provisions for the further division of each state into parliamentary and state constituencies, making some allowance for differences in density of population and means of communication. The proviso was that this allowance should not increase or reduce the number of electors in any one parliamentary or state constituency to a number differing from the average number of electors per parliamentary or state constituency respectively in that state by more than 15 per cent. As has been stated above, the decisions of the Election Commission using this formula, as published in the 1960 *Delimitation of Parliamentary and State Constituencies Report*, proved unacceptable to the Alliance Government, which feared, probably unnecessarily, that the adoption of the new boundaries would be detrimental to their chances of returning to office at the next general election. With their large majority in the House of Representatives, the Alliance was able to amend the Constitution, cancel the 1960 delimitation, and provide new procedures[8] for the determination of constituency boundaries which will be used for the delimitation due to take place sometime between 1966 and 1968. These new procedures will allow a substantially greater weightage for rural areas than was provided in the 1960 delimitation.

The 1964 parliamentary election was thus held in constituencies formed by the division into two parts of each of the fifty-two constituencies delimited by the Merthyr Commission of 1954. This Commission had to base its estimates of the distribution of the population on 1947 census figures. Since 1947 there has been a considerable redistribution of population, due mainly to migration from rural to urban areas, and, to a much smaller degree, to the resettlement during the Emergency in the 1950's. This was largely responsible for the wide variations in the population and registered electorates of the constituencies, urban areas in general being under-represented and rural areas over-represented. The variations in population may

8 See Section 31, Constitution (Amendment) Act, 1962 [No. 14 of 1962].

be somewhat greater than the variations in the electorates because of the tendency for a larger proportion of the population to be registered electors in predominantly Malay rural areas than in the more urbanized and industrialized areas of mixed population. Within the state of Selangor alone, the 1964 electorates of parliamentary constituencies ranged from over 58,000 (Bungsar) to 17,750 (Ulu Selangor). In Perak the range was from 46,000 (Menglembu) to 15,800 (Hilir Perak). The smallest electorate in a parliamentary constituency in the States of Malaya was in Johore Tenggara (12,854) and the largest in Bungsar.

The Electoral Rolls

There is a single electoral roll for parliamentary, state and local government elections. Registration is voluntary, though potential electors are given every encouragement to submit applications to the Registering Officer of the registration area in which they are resident. The Registering Officers are usually Assistant District Officers or other Government officers of equivalent status. Each parliamentary constituency constitutes a separate registration area,[9] and each polling district within a parliamentary constituency is a separate registration unit and has its own separate portion of the electoral roll. In 1964 there were 3,229 polling districts in the States of Malaya as a whole giving an average of thirty-one for each federal constituency. This is over double the corresponding figure in 1959, when there were only 1,513 polling districts. The explanation for the increase is that the roll for each polling district must now be usable in local authority and local council elections without further sub-division and no polling district boundary must therefore cross a ward boundary. It will be remembered that the Election Commission were not given responsibility for local government elections until after the 1959 series of elections.

Any citizen, male or female, who has attained the age of twenty-one years on the qualifying date (31 August) is entitled to submit an application for registration as an

[9] Reg. 3 (1) of the Elections (Registration of Electors) Regulations.

elector. Such applications are receivable between 1 September and 12 October in each year by the Registering Officer of the parliamentary constituency in which the applicant is resident. For some years after the Federation of Malaya became independent, there was a constitutional qualification[10] requiring six months' residence in the particular constituency in which the applicant wished to have his name entered on the electoral roll. This absurd and all too common method of temporarily disfranchising electors who move their residence from one constituency to another is now fortunately a thing of the past, following a constitutional amendment in 1960.[11]

During the period of six weeks each year when applications from new would-be electors may be submitted, those who have moved house may apply to have their names transferred from the electoral roll of one constituency to another or from the roll of one polling district to another in the same constituency. All too frequently the elector who has changed his address completes the form for new electors instead of the form for change of address of an already registered elector; this would lead to his or her name being included in the electoral rolls of two separate constituencies or in the rolls of two parts of the same constituency, unless the Registering Officer's assistants spotted a change of occupancy in the elector's old residence and made a corresponding deletion. Errors of this kind, almost always unintentional, are undoubtedly the most common reason for duplications in the electoral rolls.

It also happens occasionally that an elector is registered twice at the same address. Political parties take part in canvassing of new electors during the registration period and an illiterate man or woman might well sign or put a thumbprint on two application forms at the behest of two different sets of canvassers. Alternatively his name may already be in the electoral rolls and he may not realize that it is unnecessary to register again when an election is in the offing.

10 See Article 119 of the 1957 Constitution of the Federation of Malaya.
11 Section 14 of the Constitution (Amendment) Act, 1960.

The electoral roll for each polling district is compiled in three parts. List A is the register in force at the beginning of the period for revision; List B contains the names of applicants for entry in the electoral roll; List C contains the names of persons who have died or have ceased to be qualified for inclusion in the polling district electoral roll. After the claims and objections have been dealt with in the normal way, the electoral roll is certified in these three parts. Consolidation by the deletion from List A of the names of persons appearing in List C and the addition to List A of the names of persons appearing in List B does not have to be completed until just before the beginning of the next subsequent revision of the register. At an election the electoral roll in use is the most recent one certified by the Registering Officer. The duplication of the name of an elector in List A and List B (as might happen if an already registered elector had applied for fresh registration in the same polling district) could pass unnoticed on polling day. Again, although instructions were given by the Election Commission that all names appearing in List C should be deleted from List A before polling commenced, such instructions may not always have been effectively carried out.

This necessarily lengthy description of the forms used by applicants for registration and of the lists in which the electoral rolls are arranged has been given in order to explain in detail the possibilities of duplication of names. It is not possible to determine the extent of duplication with any certainty, but, in view of the high percentage of electors who were given ballot papers and the absence of allegation of actual double voting, it seems unlikely that duplication is on a very large scale. In this connexion it should be noted that no offence has been committed if an elector's name is included twice in the electoral rolls; an elector does however commit an offence if he votes twice in the same election.

Complaints were made by the People's Progressive

Party,[12] and by some would-be voters who went to polling stations and were refused a ballot paper, that the names of some electors had been incorrectly included in List C for deletion by the Registering Officers.   Such voters presumably failed to inspect the draft electoral rolls at the time for making claims and objections.   Mistakes of this kind did occur and were probably for the most part occasioned by reports from Assistant Registering Officers that such electors could not be contacted and were assumed to have moved, when in fact they were but temporarily away from home.   It is of course possible that political motives may have been behind some of the names put forward for inclusion in List C by Assistant Registering Officers, but it seems far more likely that any such errors were inadvertent.

The first register of electors compiled in 1954-5 prior to the 1955 election of members to the Federal Legislative Council contained just over 1,280,000 names.   In 1958, prior to the 1959 parliamentary and state elections, there was a considerable addition to the number of electors and the 1959 election took place with a total electorate of 2,170,000 persons.   In 1960 there was a complete re-registration of electors and since that year, revisions of the register have taken place annually.   The electorate at the time of the 1964 general election numbered about 2,775,000.   Probably some 85 to 90 per cent. of the potential electorate are now registered as voters.

The registers compiled in 1955 and 1958 were duplicated.   More recently the electoral rolls have been produced by the Department of Statistics which, in 1963, took over all responsibility for the punching of cards (one for each elector), the maintenance of the card file and the printing of the rolls.   This interesting and desirable development is still in the teething stage and there is as yet a lack of adequate co-ordination between Elections Officers and the Department of Statistics, the former not always

12 See the remarks made by the Member for Ipoh (Mr. D.R. Seenivasagam) in the House of Representatives on 20 May 1964.

realizing either the capabilities or the limitations of statistical machinery.

The rolls are arranged by localities within each polling district in identity card number order for each locality. The fact that electors are so ordered in the electoral rolls rather than in alphabetical order in rural areas or by house numbers in streets in urban areas apparently caused some difficulties for canvassers trying to contact electors during the election campaign. There was a fresh identity card registration which started in 1960, and some of the entries in the electoral rolls give pre-1960 identity card numbers whilst others give the new number. Until all electors are registered under their new numbers, it will be technically impossible even for an electronic computer to trace all duplications in the rolls. The accuracy of the electoral rolls would certainly be improved with a complete re-registration, new regulations dispensing with the necessity for separate B and C Lists, and the provision of the necessary statistical machinery to produce consolidated electoral rolls by the statutory target dates. It must be stressed, however, that electoral registers are never completely accurate and that those of the States of Malaya are probably better than those of many other countries with a voluntary system of registration.

The Conduct of the Election

The system of conducting an election in the States of Malaya has not changed greatly since the election of members to the Federal Legislative Council in 1955. The general election of 1964 was however the first occasion on which members of Parliament and members of the State Assemblies were elected simultaneously.

In broad outline the Malayan electoral system involves a two-hour period for nomination of candidates; a further period of one and a half hours on the day of the nomination for making objections to nomination papers; a rather lengthy period of not less than three weeks and not more than eight weeks between nomination day and polling day; and voting in secret by means of numbered ballot papers on which are printed the names and symbols of each candidate. Each voter in a parliamentary election (as in a state election) may vote for one candidate only, and the winning candidate in each constituency is determined on a simple majority basis. There is postal voting for certain categories of electors. There is an Election Offences Ordinance which deals with corrupt and illegal practices and other electoral offences, provides for the return of election expenses and explains the procedure for the submission and hearing of election petitions.

Before nomination day, recognized political parties are permitted to apply to the Election Commission for registration of a party symbol for the use of its candidates. Such symbols must meet with the approval of the Commission. For independent candidates the Commission has a variety of symbols which are allocated by the returning officer in each constituency by lot.

Candidates for election to the House of Representatives must be citizens of Malaysia not less than twenty-one years of age and must be resident in Malaysia on nomination day. A Singapore citizen, although also a citizen of Malaysia, is not qualified to be an elected member of the House of Representatives except as a member for Singapore itself; conversely a citizen who is not a Singapore citizen is not qualified to be a member of the House of Representatives representing Singapore or any part of it. There is no language qualification for candidates in parliamentary and state elections in the States of Malaya. Disqualifications include unsoundness of mind, undischarged bankruptcy, the holding of an office of profit and the acquisition of rights of citizenship in a foreign country. Persons who, as candidates or election agents, have failed to lodge returns of election expenses and persons who have been convicted of an offence and sentenced to at least one year's imprisonment or a fine of at least two thousand dollars are also temporarily disqualified. Finally the Election Offences Ordinance imposes disqualifications for certain offences, and this last type of disqualification was the subject of a successful appeal against a candidate nominated by the People's Progressive Party in both a parliamentary and a state constituency in the state of Perak. On an election petition heard in 1959, this candidate had had his election voided on the grounds of having committed a corrupt practice and, as the law requires, his statutory five-year period of disqualification had not expired by nomination day in 1964.

Members of the federal and state public services, of the armed forces and the police force, of the judicial and legal service and of the railway service are among those debarred from being elected to Parliament or to a state Legislative Assembly on the grounds of holding an office of profit. On the other hand, this type of disqualification has been ruled not to apply to teachers in the unified teaching service, to employees of local authorities and statutory boards, and to civilian employees of Commonwealth Military Authorities.

The procedure for nomination is simple. The candidate is required to submit nomination papers in triplicate together with a statutory declaration of qualification to the Returning Officer of the constituency between 10.00 a.m. and 12 noon on nomination day. Each nomination paper must be signed by a proposer and seconder and at least four other persons, all of whom must be registered electors of the constituency in which the candidate seeks election. A deposit of five hundred dollars in the case of a candidate to the House of Representatives and two hundred and fifty dollars in the case of a candidate to a state Legislative Assembly must be paid not later than noon on nomination day. This deposit is forfeited if the candidate fails to obtain at least one eighth of the valid votes cast in the election in his constituency. In the election of 25 April 1964, deposits were forfeited by forty-seven of the 279 candidates who stood for Parliament.

Withdrawal of candidature is not permissible after noon on nomination day. Thus, although the People's Action Party stated after the close of nominations that they intended to withdraw two of their candidates in certain Johore parliamentary constituencies, the withdrawal could not be made legally effective, and the names of these candidates were printed on the ballot papers, each polling a few hundred votes.

The length of time between nomination day and polling day is determined in Malaya not by political considerations but by the length of time required by the Government Printer in Kuala Lumpur to print and distribute ballot papers. Elections, however, must be held within sixty days of the dissolution of Parliament and, as already stated, the period between nomination of candidates and polling must not exceed eight weeks. In 1964 the gap was five weeks. This proved in fact to be slightly too short a period to enable Returning Officers to distribute ballot papers to postal voters with sufficient time for the more distant of such voters to return their ballots for the count.

Postal voters include members of the regular armed forces and their wives, members of the Police Force (but not their wives), members of the public service posted outside the Federation of Malaya and their wives, students at universities and similar institutions outside the Federation of Malaya and their wives, and a few other categories. All such persons must of course be registered electors as a condition of obtaining a postal vote. A last minute application by the Army authorities for Territorial Army personnel called up for active service to be given postal votes had to be refused, on the grounds that it would be impossible to trace such persons in the electoral rolls without the full home addresses and electoral numbers of those concerned. Difficulties also arose over the distribution of postal votes to the wives of many members of the regular armed forces, because the electoral rolls did not contain details of the army rank and number of their husbands and the army authorities responsible for the distribution could not trace the wives through names and home addresses only. In Malaya, the procedure for the issue of postal ballot papers and for their return to and receipt by the Returning Officers is similar to that of the United Kingdom, and the details need not concern us here save to say that 5 p.m. on polling day is the closing time for their receipt by the Returning Officer if they are to be counted. Some postal voters, for instance, a number of soldiers serving in the jungles of Borneo and students attending overseas universities, did not receive their ballot papers in time to return them before zero hour. The writer understands, however, that this factor could in no case have affected the results of the election in any constituency.

On polling day, 25 April 1964, some 3,400 polling stations were provided and about 34,000 persons, mostly Government clerks, teachers and Government pensioners, were on duty in polling stations or at the counting of votes. The number of persons employed on polling day was greater than in 1959, because this time parliamentary and state elections were being held simultaneously. The majority of polling districts contained one polling station to which all registered electors on the relevant electoral roll had to go if they wished to cast their vote. If the electorate of the polling district numbered more than about 800, the voters were divided into two or more streams at the polling station with a presiding officer and poll clerks and, usually, a separate room for polling for each stream. In a few polling districts with a scattered population, two separate polling stations were provided, and in this event the presiding officers and the electorate had to be carefully briefed regarding which section of electors were to vote at one polling station and which at the other.

Outside the boundaries of each polling station, there was a 'no canvassing' zone extending outwards for fifty yards in all directions from the polling station limits. This 'no canvassing' zone was under police control, whereas the polling station itself was under the control of the presiding officer. Outside the 'no canvassing' zone, the agents of each candidate were permitted to set up not more than four booths, but in practice the sites chosen for polling stations were such that it was unusual for a candidate to consider it necessary to have more than one such booth at each polling station. Although a candidate was permitted to identify his booth by posters, such posters were allowed to bear only the party symbol of the candidate and were limited by law to four in number per booth and to fifty square inches per poster.   Candidates were reminded before the election that booths were permitted by law for the purpose of assisting electors to ascertain their numbers in the electoral roll.   There seems to be no reason to suppose that serious attempts were made to exercise undue influence on voters at these booths immediately before they entered the polling stations.   Both the Election Commission and the Police would, however, have been much happier had the Alliance Government accepted the Commission's proposal that the law should be amended to forbid canvassing of any kind anywhere on polling day.   We deal later with the question of the exercise of undue influence and of bribery during the election campaign.

Passing through the 'no canvassing' zone, the voter first takes his place in the waiting queue, and then enters the polling station and establishes his identity.   Polling station staff in the 1964 election were instructed that:

> The easiest method of establishing identity is the use of identity cards and all voters will be warned to bring their identity cards with them to the polling station.   In practice the work of identification of voters will be done by the first polling clerk who will check the photograph in the identity card with the face of the voter and check that the identity card number coincides with that shown in the electoral roll.   Only where doubt exists will the Presiding Officer be called upon to use his discretion in the matter.

> The law now gives to the Presiding Officer power to demand the production of an identity card and if he (the voter) refused the Presiding Officer is legally entitled to refuse to give a ballot paper to that person. This does not mean that any person who cannot produce his identity card or whose name or identity card number does not exactly correspond with the particulars shown in the electoral roll should be refused the right to vote.   Evidence other than identity cards may be taken. . . .

After the voter had been identified, his or her electoral number, identity card number and name were called out by the polling clerk and he was given his parliamentary and state ballot papers, the former coloured white and the latter buff. The original intention had been that state ballot papers should be coloured green, but objection was taken to this colour by the Alliance Government very shortly before nomination day on the ground that green, the colour of the Pan-Malayan Islamic Party, might suggest to unsophisticated voters the desirability of voting for that party. The necessary large supplies of white and green paper had been obtained from overseas by the Government Printer months before the election; buff was the only practical quick alternative to green, as many government forms are printed on paper of this colour and large stocks are therefore carried as a matter of course!

As has been stated, the names and symbols of each candidate were printed on the ballot papers and the voter's task was merely to mark a cross in the space provided for the purpose on the right-hand side of the ballot paper opposite the name and symbol of the candidate for whom he wished to vote. This was the first occasion on which parliamentary and state elections were held simultaneously, and it may well have happened that a number of electors marked one ballot paper but not the other. At any rate the proportion of rejected votes to the total number of voters polled was higher in 1964 than in previous general elections: in the 1955 election, for instance, the percentage of rejected ballot papers was only about 2.5 per cent. but in the Parliamentary election of 1964, a typical constituency percentage was 4 to 5 per cent. and in a few constituencies considerably higher.

Having marked his ballot papers in the secrecy of a polling booth, the voter was required to put his white parliamentary ballot paper in a ballot box which had a white-painted band around the sides of the box and a white-painted square on the top of the box, whilst his buff state ballot paper had to be put in another ballot box with similar painted pattern but of a buff colour. If the voter in error placed his ballot papers in the wrong ballot box, this did not lead to the rejection of his votes at the count, as the Attorney-General had ruled that a state ballot paper found in the ballot box from the same polling station for the parliamentary election could be handed over for inclusion in the count of votes for the state constituency and vice versa.

The Presiding Officer is permitted by law to assist blind or otherwise incapacitated voters. Any such voter may be accompanied into the polling booth by the Presiding Officer and asked by him there how he wishes to have the ballot paper marked. No polling agent or polling official other than the Presiding Officer is permitted to interfere or be within low-voiced earshot. The Presiding Officer is not however permitted to help illiterate voters merely on the grounds of their illiteracy; he could ask voters at his discretion when the latter received their ballot papers whether they know the method of voting and, in the event of a negative response, he could describe how to cast a vote without suggesting which candidate should be favoured. Experience has shown that illiterate voters can easily be taught to identify the symbols and to mark a cross against the symbol of the candidate supported.

The law provides for the admittance of one polling agent per candidate at any one time in each polling station, with the provisos that the President Officer must be notified of the name and address of any such polling agent before the commencement of polling, that any such polling agent should bring a signed and attested oath of secrecy to the polling station for presentation to the Presiding Officer and that where there are two or more separate streams of voters at a polling station with separate teams of polling officials, there may be one polling agent for each such stream. Polling agents are not permitted to talk to voters in the polling station but may submit criticisms or comments on the identification of voters and the general process of voting to the Presiding Officer for his consideration. The officially recommended lay-out of a polling station for simultaneous parliamentary and state elections places the polling clerks on one side of the room, the polling agents on the other side, and the presiding officer in between with the ballot boxes immediately in front of him. The polling booths are sited with entrance on the wall side so that neither the polling clerks nor the polling agents can see the voter mark his ballot papers.

There are, as in many other Commonwealth countries, provisions for the use of tendered ballot paper, coloured differently from ordinary ballot papers. These tendered ballot papers are utilized when 'a person representing to be a particular elector named in the electoral roll applies for a ballot paper after another person has been recorded as having voted as such elector'.[13] We need not be concerned with the detailed procedure relating to tendered ballot papers here except to say that in 1964, as in 1955, tendered ballot papers were issued in error instead of ordinary ballot papers at the beginning of polling in one polling station. In 1964 this error (at a Malacca polling station) affected only thirteen electors; the corresponding error in 1955 (at a Perak polling station) led to the rejecttion of some hundreds of votes.

Another error of some consequence occurred in the 1964 election when the Returning Officer of one of the Perak State constituencies sent ballot papers for the wrong constituency to one polling station. That such an error could occur is explained by the fact that the Returning Officer of a parliamentary constituency is also the Returning Officer of the state constituencies contained within its boundaries. The polling station in question had a small electorate of 269 living in a compact Local Council area, and the fact that the error was not discovered until shortly after noon, when 161 electors had voted, is a clear indication of the reliance placed by voters, in this area at least, on the symbols rather than the names of the candidates on the ballot papers! When the mistake was discovered, gallant efforts were made to recall the electors who had already been to the polling station to enable them to cast their votes properly.

13 Reg. 22 (1) of the Elections (Conduct of Election) Regulations.

The counting of votes in each parliamentary constituency and in the state constituencies contained within its boundaries took place centrally under the control of the Returning Officer.   In most constituencies the count was completed during the night after the close of polling, but in a few constituencies with a very scattered electorate it was not possible to begin the counting until the day after polling. The count is conducted in four stages, very much as in the United Kingdom.   The first stage involves the verification of the total number of votes found in each ballot box and the separation of tendered ballot papers from ordinary ballot papers.   The tendered ballot papers are sealed and kept with the records of the election for the six-month statutory period prior to destruction; none of these records or documents may be opened or inspected except at the direction of a Judge of the Supreme Court. The second stage of the count involves the mixing of all the ballot papers, other than tendered ballot papers, from all polling stations in the constituency.   The third stage involves sorting of ballot papers for each candidate and the making of decisions by the Returning Office on doubtful ballot papers.   The fourth and last stage is the counting of the ballot papers for each candidate and the announcement of the result, if necessary, after a recount. This last stage, though purely arithmetical, was too much for one or two tired Returning Officers in the small hours of the morning, and one defeated candidate was credited with some 5,000 more votes than he actually received!

Conclusion
How fair were the 1964 parliamentary and state elections in Malaya? The most bitter critic was Mr. D. R. Seenivasagam who, in a speech in the House of Representatives on 20 May 1964, was reported[14] as having commented on 'the disgraceful and shameful manner' in which the elections were conducted, referring specifically to the thousands of names which were removed from the register 'for no reason whatsoever' and also suggesting that, on polling day,

14 See *Straits Times* and *Malay Mail*, 21 May 1964.

non-voters were allowed to vote. Even Mr. Seenivasagam, however, was reported as having admitted that the Alliance would have emerged victorious in any event. Another critic in the House of Representatives on the same day was Enche Mohammad Asri bin Haji Muda, the Pan-Malayan Islamic Party member for the Pasir Puteh constituency in Kelantan; he was reported as having stated that a few government officers and police officers had 'taken sides' in the election.

Mr. Seenivasagam was certainly justified in complaining that the names of some electors had been incorrectly deleted from the electoral rolls, and the number over the country as a whole probably did run into a few thousands. Few electors bother to inspect the electoral rolls at the time for making claims and objections, and it can be argued with some justice that those electors whose names had been deleted were at least as negligent as the Registering Officers concerned. He was perhaps on more doubtful ground in claiming that non-voters were allowed to vote. He may have been thinking of those with red-coloured identity cards, the colour indicating that the holders had been deprived of citizenship. Such persons, if they have not re-acquired citizenship since the date of issue of the red identity card, commit an offence in voting because they are not qualified, as non-citizens, to vote. The presiding officer however can warn but cannot refuse a ballot paper to any person whose name appears as a currently registered elector in his portion of the electoral rolls. It is more difficult for this writer to comment on Enche Mohammad Asri's complaints which undoubtedly related mainly to the state of Kelantan.

The truth is, of course, that when many thousands of persons are engaged in a task such as the running of an election, there will certainly be a few whose efficiency and effectiveness in performing their duty leaves a good deal to be desired. There may also be a few who prove incapable of exhibiting that impartiality which is needed on such an occasion. It would nevertheless be wrong to leave the impression that the writer agreed with Mr.

Seenivasagam that the elections were conducted in a 'disgraceful and shameful manner' (if such words were in fact used); the known instances of inefficiency were few and far between and, in general, in the writer's opinion, there can be little doubt that the Alliance were just as liable to suffer as the opposition parties from the mistakes which were made.

As far as the candidates and their supporters are concerned, the campaign was full of personal invective, and some election offences were probably committed. A case was brought in Penang for alleged bribery of a few voters. The Alliance claimed that it was only the alertness of their polling agents which prevented a number of cases of double voting in one constituency in the island. Certainly there were rumours that one opposition political party had deliberately registered some of its supporters twice in different polling districts, but no evidence had been produced to support this allegation at the time of writing. Again the Election Offences Ordinance restricts the expenditure of parliamentary candidates to ten thousand dollars during the election campaign and that of state candidates to seven thousand five hundred dollars.[15]   It is all too easy for actual expenditure as opposed to expenditure included in the return of election expenses, to exceed these amounts.

Despite such possible blemishes it is difficult to resist the conclusion that the result of the election would have been the same in almost every constituency had every election official performed his duty perfectly and every candidate and his supporters observed every section of the Election Offences Ordinance.   Only in some of the closely contested Kelantan and North Trengganu constituencies, it would seem, could the use of undue influence by party canvassers or the words and actions of government and police officers conceivably have swayed the balance.

15 Election Offences (Amendment) Act, 1961.

V

The Candidates

THERE were altogether 279 candidates who contested the
104 parliamentary seats. This was twenty-one more than
the total in 1959, the increase being accounted for mainly
by the entry of the UDP and the PAP, and by the larger
number of candidates fielded by the Socialist Front.[1] The
Alliance, once again, was the only party to contest all the
seats. Each of the three remaining larger parties contested fewer seats in 1964 than it had in 1959 — four fewer
in the case of the PMIP, ten in the case of the PPP and
six in the case of Party Negara. There was also a significant decrease in the number of Independents, from
twenty-six to eight. Three small parties which had contested in the 1959 Parliamentary Election were now absent
from the political scene. They were the Malayan Party,
Province Wellesley Labour and Semangat Permuda Melayu.[2]

Only the Alliance put up enough candidates to secure
a majority in the new Parliament. The largest opposition
party, the Socialist Front, would have had to perform an
impossible task in order to form a Government. Not only
would it have had to win every seat that it contested; it
would also have had to win the support of seventeen out
of the twenty-one non-Alliance members from Singapore,
Sarawak and Sabah.[3] This absence of any effective challenge to the Alliance led one newspaper to comment:

[1] Having fielded only thirty-eight candidates in 1959, the SF now put
up sixty-three.

[2] The Malayan Party had contested two seats in 1959, while the other
two had contested one each.

[3] These twenty-one were made up of fifteen from Singapore (twelve PAP
and three Barisan) and six from Sarawak (three SUPP and three PANAS).
At least in the case of the PAP and PANAS members, there could have
been no possibility of any co-operation with the SF.

The certainty of an Alliance victory deprives the election of fundamental excitement. But there are many secondary issues to sustain interest. The margin by which the Alliance will win, and the fate of the Opposition parties will be an important weather vane for Malaysia's political future.[4]

Although none had ever seriously doubted that the Alliance would once again come to power, it had commonly been assumed until nomination day that the opposition parties would field a larger number of candidates than they in fact did. Some estimates (apparently based on statements by party spokesmen) had given figures as high as 95 for the SF and 80 for the PMIP.[5]

Of the candidates 168 were Malays, 94 Chinese and 17 Indians. The equivalent figures for 1959 were 157, 79 and 23. The SF was mainly responsible for the increase in the number of Malay candidates, its (Malay) nominations having gone up from eleven to thirty. There were also eight Malays in the UDP's line-up. The increase in the number of Chinese candidates was largely the result of the entry of the UDP and the PAP which, between them, put up twenty-six Chinese. The SF, which fielded eight more Chinese in 1964 than in 1959, also contributed to this increase. A significant feature, however, was the substantial *decrease* in the number of Chinese who stood as Independents (from seventeen to three). There had been a special reason for the large number of Chinese who stood as Independents in 1959, namely the pre-election crisis within the MCA which had led to the resignation of certain key figures, some of whom stood as Independent candidates.[6] By the time the candidates were chosen in 1964, most of these rebels had either returned to the MCA or had joined the UDP. The decrease in the number of Indian candidates was largely accounted for by fewer Indians being put up by the PPP and the SF.

4 *Straits Times,* 22 March 1964.
5 *Ibid.*
6 The circumstances which led to the crisis were discussed in Chapter III.

TABLE II

COMMUNAL BREAKDOWN OF PARLIAMENTARY CANDIDATES
BY PARTIES, 1964

(1959 figures in parenthesis)

	MALAYS	CHINESE	INDIANS	TOTAL
Alliance	68 (69)	33 (31)	3 (4)	104 (104)
SF	30 (11)	28 (20)	5 (7)	63 (38)
PMIP	53 (58)	– (–)	– (–)	53 (58)
UDP	8 (–)	18 (–)	1 (–)	27 (–)
PAP	1 (–)	8 (–)	2 (–)	11 (–)
PPP	1 (1)	4 (9)	4 (9)	9 (19)
Party Negara	4 (9)	– (–)	– (–)	4 (9)
Malayan Party	– (–)	– (1)	– (1)	– (2)
Independents	3 (8)	3 (18)	2 (3)	8 (29)
Total	168 (156)	94 (79)	17 (24)	279 (259)

Although it did not reflect any major change of policy, the communal breakdown of candidates within the Alliance deserves some comment. The allocation of seats between the different partners had always been one of the thorniest problems faced by the party, a problem which in 1959 had very nearly brought about a dissolution of the partnership. On that occasion the UMNO had demanded 78 nominations, while the MCA had insisted on 40. A period of bitter negotiations followed and it was finally decided that they would be given 69 and 31 nominations respectively, 4 going to the MIC. This compromise, and the manner in which their candidates were alleged to have been chosen,[7] angered a significant section of the MCA leadership who felt that the only honourable thing for their party to do was to withdraw from the Alliance. When, after much heated debate, this faction failed to get the majority within the party to support its stand, several prominent figures (including the party's Secretary-General) resigned forthwith.

Although a General Election had previously been held in 1955, it was only in 1959 that the full force of the rivalry

[7] It was alleged that the MCA leaders had not been given a say in the final selection of their own candidates, and that the line-up had not been revealed to them (by the Tengku and some of his advisers, who made the final choice) until it was too late to propose any changes.

for nominations was first faced within the Alliance. In 1955, due mainly to the citizenship laws which then prevailed, the Malays had constituted 84·2 per cent. of the electorate and the Chinese a mere 11·2 per cent; further, of the fifty-two constituencies into which the country was then divided,[8] Malay voters had formed the majority in fifty and Chinese voters in only two. This clearly meant that the MCA was not in a position to strike a hard bargain as regards the allocation of seats within the Alliance. However, so as not to make a complete mockery of the inter-communal structure of the Alliance (and possibly also in an attempt to make the election more representative than the citizenship laws and the delimitations of constituencies had made it appear), the MCA was given 15 nominations against the UMNO's 35, 2 seats being allocated to the MIC. In the event, all the MCA and MIC candidates were returned. Helped by the fact that 'independence' (of which the Alliance was the chief advocate) was the main issue at the election, a large number of Malays had obviously chosen to vote along party lines at the expense of purely communal considerations.

In 1959, however, the Chinese formed almost as large a proportion of the electorate as they did of the general population.[9] In addition, they now constituted the most numerous section of the electorate in forty-one out of the 104 constituencies. To the UMNO, this meant that there was no longer any need to make concessions to the MCA: indeed, it had to be kept in check if its own position as the 'senior partner' in the Alliance were to be effectively maintained. To the MCA, on the other hand, the vast increase in the number of Chinese voters meant that it did not any longer have to regard itself as an ineffective participant in the electoral process, depending almost entirely on Malay votes for seats in Parliament. These were essentially the

8 Although the total strength of the Legislative Council was ninety-eight, only fifty-two seats were filled by elected members.

9 They formed about 36 per cent. of the electorate and 38 per cent. of the total population.

considerations which led to the dispute over the allocation of seats in 1959.

The crisis of 1959, together with the subsequent increase in the proportion of Chinese voters,[10] prompted a better deal for the MCA in 1964. Its share of the nominations was therefore raised from thirty-one to thirty-three, the increase being made at the expense of both the other partners who sacrificed one seat each. Although this compromise was achieved without any open conflict, it nevertheless appeared that agreement was not easily forthcoming. Evidence of this became public when the Tengku, speaking at an election seminar organized by the MCA a little over a week before nomination day, warned that party not to create any difficulties over the allocation of seats.[11] The following day he issued the same warning to UMNO members, emphasizing the importance of avoiding friction with the MCA through quibbling over seats.[12]

This question of apportioning seats between the different communities did not affect the other parties to quite the same extent. In the case of the PMIP and Party Negara there were no comparable internal pressures, because both of them were explicitly communal organizations which sought to represent the interests of the Malay community alone. A different explanation would apply in the

10 In 1964 the Chinese constituted 38 per cent. of the electorate, and were the most numerous group in forty-two constituencies.

11 'There is talk now that the MCA will demand all the seats where Chinese voters are in the majority, but should you take this line then I am afraid you are not going to succeed. So you have to think twice before you work on this basis for allocation of seats.' Earlier in the speech he had said, 'The MCA cannot go on any chauvinistic line because they must depend on the Malay votes to get the MCA candidates in and once the Malays feel that MCA is not toeing the Alliance line then they can only hope to get a few Chinese votes but will lose the Malay votes.' At the same election seminar Mr. Tan Siew Sin said, 'The main problem of our Government is Sino-Malay relations. We have to accept that the Chinese are economically stronger than the Malays. The Malays, therefore, feel that in order to counter-balance their weak economic position they have got to have political power. They feel that with this political power or special position they could cope with the other races politically and economically.' (*Straits Times,* 6 March 1964).

12 *Ibid.* 7 March 1964.

case of the other parties. Having contested only a limited number of constituencies (or none at all) in 1959, they invariably had more room than the Alliance in which to manoeuvre: new pressures could always be accommodated simply by deciding to contest new seats. For the Alliance, on the other hand, every change had to imply a *reallocation*,[13] with all its attendant tensions and disappointments.

Turning now to the way in which the parties chose their candidates, all those Alliance officials who were interviewed maintained that a strict procedure was followed within their party. Each ward branch in the country was entitled to submit a name to the divisional level, which then passed on the names it had received to the state headquarters. The divisions acted merely as conveyors, and did not have the right to add or delete any names. The various state headquarters then made consolidated lists of all the names they had received from the divisions and submitted them (again without any amendments) to the national headquarters. The final choice was made at the national level, by a committee set up for this specific purpose — the Candidates Selection Committee, headed in 1964 by Inche Mohamed Khir bin Johari, the Minister for Agriculture and Co-operatives. In submitting names for consideration the various levels of the party were not to indicate where particular candidates should be put up: this was to be left to the Candidates Selection Committee, which, in addition to making the final choice of candidates, was also given the task of deciding where each person would stand.[14]

The procedure just outlined was followed by each partner of the Alliance, and the Candidates Selection Committee thus received three separate lists of names. It is, however, worth pointing out that, although every branch of each member organization had the right to submit a name, not all of them in fact did. In areas where one of the communities formed a large majority of the electorate, the parties representing the other two often did not bother to

---

13 Since it had contested all the seats previously.

14 Naturally, the area from which a person was nominated (and hence his popularity there) was usually a decisive factor.

submit names of their own. This was generally the case in Kelantan, Trengganu and Perlis, where there was practically no likelihood of a non-Malay candidate being adopted. Indeed in many parts of these states the MCA and the MIC did not even have separate branches.

To appreciate the full complexity of the selection procedure within the Alliance, one needs to look beyond the formal procedure which has been just outlined. To begin with, although this procedure appeared to give the rank and file of the party an important say in who their candidates would be, it remained possible for the national leaders to exercise a great deal of control. They were able to do this in two ways. First, it was they[15] who decided how the seats were to be apportioned between the different partners of the Alliance for the country as a whole. This meant that the Candidates Selection Committee could not, in making its final choice, rely purely on the relative merits of the individual candidates and their popularity in their own areas: it had to work within the limits set by the way in which the seats had been apportioned.

Second, it was also possible for the national leaders of the Alliance and the Candidates Selection Committee to render virtually valueless the right of the branches to submit names. As indicated, the procedure that had been adopted did not establish any connexion between the amount of support a person received from the branches and his eventual selection as a candidate: all that was needed was for his name to be on the consolidated list, even if he had been nominated by only one branch. On this basis it obviously could not have been too difficult for the party's leaders, when they wanted to see a particular person nominated for reasons of their own, to use their influence on some branch to make sure that his name was submitted.[16] This was certainly implicit in the last-minute efforts by MCA leaders to induce some of their 1959 rebels to return to the party by offering them seats. These efforts

15 Apparently just the Tengku, after he had consulted the other leaders.

16 This would have been particularly easy where the branch concerned had no definite choice of its own.

often took the form of personal negotiations between the two, evidently without much suggestion that the latter's chances of being adopted would have to depend on their being nominated by the party's branches. There was, however, one known instance where the party's national leaders failed to have things their own way. In this case their attempt to lure back Mr. Chin See Yin, one of the leaders of the 1959 rebels, was strongly objected to by the entire MCA organization in the state concerned, Negri Sembilan. Since his resignation Mr. Chin had carried on an active campaign against the MCA in his state, and was commonly thought to have been instrumental in undermining its prestige and influence. He had been returned as an Independent at the 1959 Parliamentary Election,[17] and had thereafter played an important role in the formation of the UDP from which he later resigned as a result of certain disagreements with its other leaders.[18] Although it was prepared to accept some of the others who had left the party with him, the Negri Sembilan MCA firmly drew the line at Mr. Chin's nomination as a candidate and threatened to walk out *en bloc* if he was forced on them. The national leaders eventually decided not to insist on his candidature and thus averted a showdown with the state organization.

But generally there was very little conflict between the preferences of the national leaders and those of the rank and file within the Alliance. The nomination procedure had one important merit in that, while it did not stifle democracy within the party, it nevertheless gave the leaders adequate opportunities to implement their own wishes. In terms of the need to preserve unity and discipline, what mattered most was that the rank and file of the party felt satisfied that the system in operation was a democratic one

17 Several MCA rebels had contested the 1959 state and parliamentary elections in Negri Sembilan as Independents. The press collectively referred to them as 'Chindependents', a term imaginatively derived from the name of their leader, Mr. Chin See Yin.

18 Following the Alliance's defeat at the Seremban Town Council election, Mr. Chin had also for a time been the President of that Town Council.

and that they had an important, although limited, say in who their candidates would be.

Broadly, the SF's candidates were also chosen from those whose names were submitted by the branches. Compared to the Alliance, however, the formal nomination procedure gave wider powers to the state and national levels of the party in that they were entitled to nominate candidates of their own choice.[19] Although it was earlier observed that the SF did not have as serious a problem as the Alliance in apportioning seats between its different components, rivalry was by no means avoided in every part of the country. The most glaring example of this was in Johore, where a major crisis developed within the SF following disagreement over the nomination of candidates. It was reported that certain Malays from Party Rakyat who had not been chosen as candidates were planning to leave the SF, and that there was even a possibility of Party Rakyat's being dissolved immediately after the election.[20] But this was an extreme case, and conflicts were usually resolved in a much more conciliatory manner.

Where there were disputes between the different partners, the agreed procedure was to give preference to the party which was seen to be the most active in the constituencies concerned. This was usually ascertained by comparing the number of branches which each party had in these constituencies.[21] Even in deciding whether or not a constituency should be contested, a great deal of weight was given to the strength of active membership in that constituency and to the amount of popular support that could be expected. It was argued that this was necessary

[19] Since the final selection was made by the national headquarters, there could not have been much doubt about the eventual adoption of those whose names were suggested by the national (and possibly state) level of the party. But it was also pointed out by those interviewed from the SF that it was extremely rare for a person's name to be suggested only at the state or national level.

[20] *Utusan Melayu,* 26 March 1964.

[21] As in the case of the Alliance (but to a much lesser extent) there were some constituencies where only one of the partners had any serious intentions of putting up a candidate.

if the party was to make the most effective use of its limited resources. In identifying the areas of strength, the evidence of local officials was not always automatically accepted. It was felt that these officials might in certain cases be tempted to give an exaggerated account of the amount of active support in their constituencies with a view to enhancing the claims of their own nominees. Whenever this was suspected the state or national headquarters sent its own men to the constituences concerned so as to verify the evidence that had been received.

As pointed out earlier, there was a substantial increase in the number of candidates put up by the SF in 1964. This had been forecast some months earlier by the party's officials, who attributed the intended increase to better finances, improved party organization and a greater confidence in the support that could be received in areas which had earlier been ignored. As things turned out, the increase was accounted for not by the party's venturing into states which it had previously neglected, but by its putting up more candidates in those states where its organization was already strong in 1959.[22] The increase was greatest among the Malay candidates and this could have signified an attempt to placate Party Rakyat and to avoid giving the Malays the impression that the SF was dominated by the Labour Party.[23]

22 The number of SF candidates put up for parliamentary seats in the various states was as follows in 1964 (1959 figures in brackets): Johore 11 (7); Kedah 4 (4); Kelantan 1 (0); Malacca 4 (2); Negri Sembilan 6 (2); Pahang 4 (3); Penang 8 (6); Perlis 0 (0); Perak 9 (4); Selangor 13 (9); Trengganu 3 (1).

23 Three of the SF's Malay candidates were in fact from the NCP, but it is quite possible that even if that party had not been incorporated into the SF the seats concerned would have been given to Party Rakyat. It became evident during interviews that the last-minute incorporation of the NCP resulted in new frictions within the SF over the choice of candidates. The two original partners (who were both much larger than the NCP) were naturally reluctant to give up seats which they had initially expected to contest. The NCP, on the other hand, was keen that it should be given a 'respectable' number of seats in order to make its membership in the SF worthwhile, but could not point to many constituencies where its own strength would warrant the adoption of its

In the case of the PMIP, those interviewed did not always give the same account of the procedure that was followed within their party in the selection of candidates. Nevertheless, it was evident that the main features of this procedure were similar to those followed by the Alliance and the S.F. Names were suggested by the various branches to their respective state organizations, which then submitted a short-list to the national headquarters for final selection. Compared to their equivalents in the Alliance and the SF, the state and national headquarters of the PMIP openly exercised wider powers in the selection of candidates. They appeared to give greater weight to their own evaluation of persons who were known to them, and were also less influenced by the views of the branches in deciding where each candidate would stand. The use of such initiative was justified on the grounds that while the party's popularity was restricted to a few states (or to particular parts of states), it had many men of good calibre outside them. Thus if these men were to be put up as serious candidates, they had to be given constituencies in areas where the party was strong and this often meant that local nominees had to be by-passed.

Technically the Alliance Candidates Selection Committee was also empowered to act in the above manner and to adopt 'outside' candidates whenever necessary. But there were two factors which usually discouraged this. First, although the Alliance had 'strong' and 'weak' states, such as Pahang and Kelantan, respectively, there were not many areas of the country where it could have been said that it was pointless to put up a candidate. This meant that there was usually no pressing need to move good candidates from one state to another, since it was not too difficult to find them reasonably safe constituencies in their own states. Secondly, the party's rank and file (as represented by the branches) were not sufficiently committed to any ideology or sense of mission in order to be encouraged to sacrifice their own preferences. Consequently, a bla-

---

nominees. The main friction, it would appear, was between Party Rakyat and the NCP, since both were competing for the SF's Malay nominations.

tant disregard for their wishes could have led to serious problems of discipline for which solutions could not have been found simply by appealing to 'higher interests'. The PMIP, on the other hand, was aided by the binding quality of its mission and ideology and this made the lower levels of the party more amenable to persuasion.[24]

The 'outside' candidates were usually from the urban areas and contested in constituencies which were predominantly rural. This is understandable, since 'good quality' was measured mainly in terms of educational and professional attainments and urban dwellers are much more likely to have superior qualifications in this respect. Since the vast majority of the seats contested by the PMIP were in the rural areas, it was inevitable that a higher proportion of its candidates should come from outside their constituencies and in some cases from outside the states in which they contested.[25] Even in the case of the Alliance many of the candidates who contested rural constituencies came from urban areas; but at the same time there was also a great deal of scope for well-qualified urban candidates to be put up in urban or semi-urban constituencies. Candidates were 'moved' even less in the SF, since that party concentrated its efforts mainly in the urban or semi-urban areas. Compared to the PMIP, there were very few instances in the Alliance and the SF where candidates were moved from one state to another.

As far as the other parties were concerned, the most significant feature of their selection procedure was that it was highly centralized. The most extreme example of this was naturally the PAP. Having no organization in Malaya at the time its candidates were chosen, its leaders in Singapore had a free hand in deciding which constituencies they would contest and who their candidates would

24 There was, however, one instance where the choice of 'outsiders' was reported to have caused a considerable amount of disaffection in local circles. This was in Kelantan, where the PMIP's effort was mainly concentrated. *Utusan Melayu*, 19 March 1964.

25 This was intensified by the fact that Kelantan and Trengganu, the PMIP's two 'strongest' states, are also among the most backward and rural states in the country.

be. The party's range was naturally limited by the fact that Singapore citizens were not eligible for nomination as candidates.

In comparing the nomination procedures of the different parties, the most significant point is that there appeared to be a noticeable difference between the methods adopted by the larger parties and those of the smaller ones.[26] The former followed a broadly democratic procedure, while at the same time ensuring that the final choice was made by their leaders and that they also had a long list of names to choose from. In the case of the latter, party leaders more openly had the right to nominate their own candidates. Part of the explanation for this could lie in the fact that it is easier (and, in the absence of a widespread organization, often necessary) for the leaders of smaller parties to exercise a greater amount of direct control. Extensive bureaucratization, on the other hand, is likely to be accompanied by certain (even if only formal) limitations on the leaders' freedom of action.

But this difference should not be over-emphasized, and it is worth remarking that the 'democratic' procedure adopted by the bigger parties was neither intended to, nor did it have the effect of, denying their leaders scope for initiative in the selection process. The 'democratic' element was in some ways more apparent than real, and was relied on not so much to ensure that the best or the most popular candidates would be chosen, as to reduce the risk of alienating support within the parties concerned. Although the evidence would suggest that this goal was successfully achieved, informed observers outside these parties did not always take the procedure seriously. The *Straits Times*, for example, observed:

> ...the constituencies have very little to say about [the selection of candidates] They get the candidates which party headquarters send them. Of course there are obvious local preferences which the parties can hardly

26 The Alliance, the SF and the PMIP are here regarded as the 'larger' parties.

disregard, and the natural rule holds good that it is easier to keep a seat than to win one.[27]

The *Utusan Melayu,* on the other hand, felt that local preferences as such should not be the deciding factor in the choice of candidates. In discussing the criteria for selection within the UMNO it commented:

> In the interests of the party and its victory, the candidates to be chosen must be good and have clean records. Those who were chosen previously and who have clean records and are popular among the voters and in the party should be chosen again. Those who have been elected before but who do not possess good records must be dropped, even if they are nominated by the divisions.[28]

Some attention may now be given to the candidates themselves, to find out what type of person was generally preferred and to see if there were any significant differences between the different parties in this respect.

The first general rule that was followed by all the parties was to put up Malay candidates in Malay-dominated constituencies and non-Malay candidates in the others.[29] It was obviously assumed that this was the safest thing to do, and the situation in this respect was no different from that in 1959. Of the 150 candidates who then stood in Malay-dominated constituencies, 136 were Malays and only 14 either Chinese or Indian. In constituencies where the Chinese were the most numerous group, 69 out of 108 candidates were Chinese, 17 were Indians and 22 Malays. In 1964, 135 of the 147 candidates who contested in Malay-dominated constituencies were Malays and only 12 were either Chinese or Indians. In Chinese-dominated constituencies only 32 candidates were Malays while 84 were Chinese and 15 Indians. This meant that, as in 1959,

27 *Straits Times,* 22 March 1964.

28 *Utusan Melayu,* 11 March 1964.

29 As has already been shown, the vast majority of non-Malay candidates were Chinese. There was no constituency in the country where the Indians and 'Others' accounted for more than 23 per cent. of the electorate.

most of the Malay candidates fought against other Malay candidates and non-Malays against other non-Malays.

With the exception of the Alliance, which contested all the seats, the parties generally showed a preference for either Malay or non-Malay dominated constituencies, thus showing that they expected their support to come from one or the other of these groups.[30]   This consideration was most frankly admitted by the PMIP, one of whose spokesmen was reported to have said: 'We know that non-Muslims will not support us, so it would be politically unwise for us to contest in non-Muslim areas'.[31]   This admission was not surprising, since the PMIP was the only party which did not stand to lose by advertising the fact that it was communally exclusive and which really hoped to gain support by so doing.   Table III following shows the extent to which communal considerations appear to have been relevant in the choice of constituencies contested by the various parties.

TABLE III

CONSTITUENCIES CONTESTED BY PARTIES
AND THEIR RACIAL COMPOSITION

PARTY	TOTAL NUMBER OF CANDIDATES	NUMBER CONTESTING IN CONSTITU-ENCIES WITH A MALAY MAJORITY	NUMBER CONTESTING IN CONSTITU-ENCIES WITH A NON-MALAY MAJORITY
SF	63	22	41
PMIP	53	47	6
UDP	27	10	17
PAP	11	0	11
PPP	9	0	9
Party Negara	4	4	0

The distribution within the Alliance is equally interesting.   Of the 62 candidates who contested in Malay-

[30] This was also evident in the allocation of seats *within* the Alliance. Thus UMNO candidates were generally put up in Malay constituencies and MCA candidates in Chinese constituencies.   See Chapter XII below.
[31] *Sunday Times*, 15 March 1964.

dominated constituencies 58 were from the UMNO, 4 from the MCA.   In the case of the non-Malay dominated constituencies, on the other hand, only 9 were from the UMNO while 30 were from the MCA and 3 from the MIC.

Malay candidates were on the average older than non-Malay candidates.[32]   Their average age was 42.5, while that of the Chinese was 38.1 and that of the Indians 44.1.[33] The average age for all candidates was 40.8.   Table IV gives the breakdown, by parties, in five-year groups.

Information on educational background was available for only 133 candidates, roughly 48 per cent. of the total.[34] Of this number 65 were either university graduates or had some professional qualification (mainly as lawyers and accountants), while 66 had completed secondary education. Only 2 were stated as not having gone beyond the primary level.

It is very possible that the majority of those for whom no information was given either had very little formal education or had not proceeded beyond the primary level.

[32] Assuming that this did not happen purely by chance, two possible explanations may be given for the higher average age of the Malays. First, a larger proportion of the sitting members were Malays, and those who were contesting for the second (and in some cases the third) time would have tended to be older than those who became candidates for the first time in 1964. Secondly (bearing in mind that most of the Malay candidates contested in rural areas) it is possible that respect for age is more peculiarly a rural phenomenon.

The average ages given here are based on the ages of 246 (out of the 279) candidates, of whom 145 were Malays, 86 Chinese and 15 Indians. Most of this information, along with the other personal details which follow, was obtained from the *Utusan Melayu* and the *Nanyang Siang Pau* which gave biographical data on a good majority of the candidates before the election. Some of the details were obtained verbally in the course of interviews and have been incorporated where necessary.

[33] Since there were only a few of them, the Indian candidates did not seriously affect the average age of the non-Malays as a whole. The small number would also make it misleading to offer possible explanations for their relatively high average age.

[34] In some cases the information was quite vague — for example, that a person had 'attended' a certain school, that he was 'educated in Malay and English', that he was 'fluent in English and Chinese', and so on. These cases have not been included in the present classification.

TABLE IV

AGE COMPOSITION OF THE PARTIES' CANDIDATES

	21-5	26-30	31-5	36-40	41-5	46-50	51-5	56-60	61-5	TOTAL	AVERAGE AGE
Alliance	–	4	16	22	20	13	8	3	6	92	41.3
SF	5	13	4	14	13	4	2	–	1	56	36.7
PMIP	–	5	5	16	10	6	2	3	–	47	41.1
UDP	1	2	3	5	6	4	2	1	–	24	41.3
PAP	–	1	6	1	1	–	–	1	1	11	38.5
PPP	–	–	1	1	4	1	–	–	–	7	41.6
Party Negara	–	–	–	1	1	–	1	–	–	3	45.3
Independents	–	–	3	1	–	1	–	1	–	6	40.7
Total	6	25	38	61	55	29	15	9	8	246	40.8

TABLE V

EDUCATIONAL BACKGROUND OF THE PARTIES' CANDIDATES

	PRIMARY	SECONDARY	UNIVERSITY DEGREE OR PROFESSIONAL QUALIFICATIONS
Alliance	–	26	32
SF	2	19	7
PMIP	–	9	5
UDP	–	7	8
PAP	–	4	6
PPP	–	–	5
Party Negara	–	–	–
Independents	–	1	2
Total	2	66	65

It might have been thought pointless (and possibly even harmful) to publicize the lack of an adequate education. In the case of many of these candidates the occupations were also not stated, presumably for a similar reason. Where they were stated, they were usually not indicative of much formal education. From the information available, the non-Malay candidates appeared on the whole to be better educated: two-thirds of those with higher education, for example, were non-Malays. Since almost all of them were from urban areas, this could have been expected.

Basic details of occupations were available in the case of 218 candidates. Of these, businessmen of one kind or another numbered 50, and constituted the largest single group. As could have been anticipated, a majority of them (32 out of the 50) were non-Malays, mostly Chinese, who contested in urban constituencies.[35] Teachers constituted the next largest group, numbering 42, 31 of whom were from the Alliance and the PMIP, and were mostly employed in Malay or Muslim religious schools.[36] Law-

[35] The proportion of non-Malays was even higher among lawyers, doctors and accountants.

[36] Naturally, there was a higher proportion of religious teachers in the PMIP's line-up.

TABLE VI

OCCUPATIONS OF EACH PARTY'S CANDIDATES

	TEACHERS	EX-GOVT. SERVANTS	BUSINESS-MEN	LAWYERS	DOCTORS	ACCOUNT-ANTS	TRADE UNIONISTS	JOURNA-LISTS	CLERKS	FULL-TIME PARTY WORKERS	OTHER OCCUPA-TIONS	TOTAL
Alliance	14	17	19	14	6	2	—	2	1	—	5	80
SF	4	3	9	1	2	1	6	3	6	4	7	46
PMIP	17	5	6	1	—	—	—	3	1	—	7	40
UDP	3	2	10	1	4	1	—	—	—	—	3	24
PAP	4*	—	—	2	2	—	3	—	—	—	—	11
PPP	—	—	3	4	—	1	—	—	—	—	—	8
Party Negara	—	1	—	—	—	—	—	—	—	—	—	1
Independents	—	—	3	1	1	—	—	1	—	—	2	8
Total	42	28	50	24	15	5	9	9	8	4	24	218

*One of these was a lecturer at the University of Singapore.

yers, doctors and accountants together totalled 44, exactly
half of them belonging to the Alliance.   There were 9
trade unionists all of whom, understandably, were from
the two left-wing parties, the SF and the PAP.   The
majority of those classified under the heading 'other occupations' in Table VI were either self-employed or earned
their living as land-owners and rubber smallholders.   It
could perhaps also be assumed that many of those from the
rural areas for whom no occupational details were given
in fact earned their living in one of these ways, since these
three are the predominant occupations among rural dwellers.

There was an impressive correlation between people's
participation in party activities and their selection as candidates.   In choosing candidates the parties did not normally cast around for men of good social standing, and
confined themselves to their own established (party) circles.[37]   Of the 271 party candidates,[38] 176 were known to
hold some office within their parties.[39]   Seventy-five were
from the Alliance, 48 from the SF, 32 from the PMIP,
12 from the UDP, 6 from the PPP, 2 from Party Negara
and 1 from the PAP.   This apparent regard for party
work in the selection of candidates reflected a situation
that was quite different from that which obtained in Ceylon in 1956, where it was a common practice for parties
either to invite prominent members of the community to
stand on their tickets or to choose their candidates from
voluntary applicants.[40]   The latter practice has also been

[37] There were some minor exceptions.   The PAP, for example, was not
an organized party in Malaya at the time its candidates were chosen and
hence relied on recruiting prominent individuals to stand on its platform.
Some of its candidates, however, were members of good standing in
Singapore. Being a fairly new party which did not have a well-
established organization, the UDP also did not entirely fit into the
generalization.   The MCA's attempt to lure back some of its 1959 rebels
by offering them seats constituted yet another exception.

[38] That is, excluding the eight Independents.

[39] Considering that information was not available on all candidates,
the actual number must certainly have been higher.

[40] I.D.S. Weerawardana, *Ceylon General Election, 1956.*   Colombo, 1960,
pp. 35-7.

reported as having been widely followed in India during 1951-2,[41] being accompanied, as in Ceylon, by the use of such devices as written undertakings from intending candidates that they would not contest on some other ticket if they failed to get a party's nomination. There was no need for these devices in Malaya, since none of the parties entertained voluntary applications. But this does not mean that there were no problems of discipline or that no steps were taken to diminish their likelihood. It was, for example, fairly common for nomination lists to be kept secret from everyone except a small group of national leaders until the very last moment.[42] It was felt that this would reduce the opportunity for unsuccessful nominees either to stir up local dissatisfaction and thereby force a reconsideration, or to seek nomination outside the party. This was particularly true of the Alliance where the nominations from the branches were several times as many as the number of seats available and where the number of disappointments was therefore bound to be very considerable.

Despite this precaution, there were a few instances where party discipline was threatened by disputes over nominations. The UMNO, for example, had to expel a few unsuccessful nominees because of their decision to contest outside the party.[43] The most serious crisis, however, occurred within the MCA where six candidates (three parliamentary and three state) declined nomination at the very last moment because they strongly disagreed with the party's line-up in Selangor.[44] Disagreement had apparently centred on one of the MCA seats in the state, and the dissidents, some of whom had been active in the 'new image'

[41] R.L. Park and S.V. Kogekar, *Reports on the Indian General Elections, 1951-2.* Bombay, 1956. Information given in many of the *Reports*.

[42] In some cases until a day or so before nomination day.

[43] Twelve such expulsions were reported in Negri Sembilan and six in Perak. *Berita Harian*, 4 April 1964. Most of those involved were candidates for the state elections.

[44] The line up was known to these men before it was officially released because some of them were important members of the party.

group, which had forced an alteration in the balance of power in the MCA Central Working Committee at the expense of some older leaders a few months earlier, decided that they had no option but to withdraw as candidates. One of them was an Assistant Minister and another a 'rebel' who had been ceremoniously welcomed back into the party only a few weeks earlier. In a joint statement the group declared:

> In our efforts to create a new MCA image in Selangor to win the confidence of the people, we have not been successful. Under the circumstances we feel that we are unable to accept nomination. Being unable to agree to a line-up that can command the support and the respect of the electorate as a political party, it will be futile for us as individuals to participate in the elections.[45]

Since the party's leaders resolutely refused to give in to their demands, these dissidents had to be hurriedly replaced by other candidates.

A special problem was posed by a UDP man who contested a state seat as his party's candidate, but stood as an Independent in a parliamentary constituency. He claimed that he had been offered the parliamentary seat in question (Port Dickson, in Negri Sembilan) at a meeting of party leaders and that it was only on nomination day (after he had filed his nomination papers for the state election) that he had suddenly been told that a different UDP candidate had been adopted for the parliamentary seat. He refused to let this interfere with his intention to stand, and explained: 'To prove my sincerity to my supporters in Port Dickson, where I have worked for a year, I decided to stand as an Independent.'[46] Despite the apparent injustice he claimed that he would continue to support his party's policies and fight the state election under its banner.

The tactic of delaying the publication of nomination lists was also defended on other grounds. Each party felt

45 *Straits Times*, 18 March 1964.
46 *Ibid.* 25 March 1964.

that its opponents would be at an advantage if they knew
in advance where its 'strong' and 'weak' candidates would
be contesting, since they could then utilize this information in arranging their own line-up.[47]   There was a special consideration in the case of certain constituencies
where no community formed a clear majority of the electorate and where it was thought that the outcome could
depend on which parties contested and to what community their candidates belonged. The main question facing
the parties in these situations was whether they should
concentrate on wooing the Malay or the non-Malay votes
and, in some cases, whether it was worth contesting at all.
The PMIP, for example, might have felt encouraged to
put up a candidate even in a constituency where the Malays formed only 45 per cent. of the electorate, if it knew
that the only other parties contesting were the MCA (Alliance), UDP and PPP, since there would then be a good
chance of a split in the non-Malay vote. It would probably have felt differently if it knew that the other parties
were the Alliance and Party Negara, since the non-Malay
votes would then have been solidly behind the Alliance.

To return to the apparent preference for party workers
in the selection of candidates, this could indicate that the
party organization is well-established and is taken seriously
by the leadership. It could also reflect a consolidation of
the role of parties in the country's political life. But other
interpretations should not be overlooked. It is fairly common for party officials to be in close contact with the society around them. Especially in the rural areas, the party
office is often the place to which people turn when they
have certain problems (for example, when they are applying for land) or when they seek explanations of government policy. Since their duties require them to give advice
and help where possible, party officials in the various local-

---

[47] They could, for example, attempt to defeat a 'strong' candidate by
putting up a good candidate of their own, especially where a seat was
known to be marginal. On the other hand they could also decide not
to contest if the opposition was known to be fielding a 'strong' candidate
in a safe seat.

ities usually have a great deal of opportunity to establish a good local reputation for themselves. Their role in this respect is very similar to the 'interpretative function' which Post has ascribed to the 'new men' in Nigeria.[48] Consequently, in addition to the internal party pressures which may have favoured them, those holding office must also have had the advantage, as potential candidates, of having an established local reputation.

Although a consolidation of the role of parties may be implicit in the high proportion of candidates who held party office, there was also something to remind the observer that the situation was in some ways still fluid and that party politics had not had a long history in the country. No less than thirty-five candidates were known to have switched parties some time during their political careers, most of them during the preceding five or six years.

It would have been interesting to find out if those who were nominated as candidates, in addition to being active within their parties, were also involved in more general social activities — for example, as officials of non-political organizations. In other words, was there any correlation between an active political life and prominence in non-political organizations? More specifically, did one of them contribute to the other or were they mutually reinforcing? Unfortunately, the information available was not sufficient to enable meaningful generalizations. It was, however, fairly clear that the vast majority of candidates who held office in non-political organizations were Chinese.[49] This is not surprising, since non-political voluntary organizations are mainly found in the urban areas where non-Malay candidates were predominant. Also important is the fact that the Chinese have a large number of guilds, chambers of commerce and clan associations for which the Malays have few equivalents. Thus the average Chinese has much greater scope (and, in the case of those with some

48 K.W.J. Post, *The Nigerian Federal Election of 1959*. London, 1963, pp. 46-8.

49 Of the 33 candidates who were stated to be officials of non-political organizations, 26 were Chinese, 5 Malays and 2 Indians.

standing, even a social obligation) to participate in communal, professional and other non-political associations.

Slightly more than 25 per cent. of the candidates had previous parliamentary experience. Sitting members did not generally have much difficulty in getting renominated, but there were a few who declined nomination for personal reasons. There were also some cases where dissatisfaction within the party was instrumental in preventing renomination. This usually occurred when there was strong feeling that a person had neglected his party after getting elected or when it was felt that he had, for some reason, lost the confidence of the voters.[50]   Previous defeat was usually a major disqualification, and there were only thirteen known cases of defeated candidates being put up again in 1964. The most dramatic change in the list of candidates was seen in Kelantan, where the Alliance followed a conscious policy of putting up 'new faces' in the conviction that its defeat there in 1959 had been caused by the poor image projected by its candidates. Consequently, none of its 1959 candidates was renominated in 1964.[51]

In discussing previous experience, reference might also be made to membership of state assemblies and local councils.   There were altogether twenty-nine candidates who had state assembly experience and forty-eight who had local council experience.[52]   In the case of the former, the figure would certainly have been much higher but for the fact that the Alliance, which controlled all but one of the state assemblies,[53] followed a deliberate policy of not putting up the same candidates for the state and parlia-

[50] It was, for example, alleged during interviews that certain sitting members had simply not bothered to maintain any contact with the electorate or with their constituency organizations, and that their renomination would therefore be damaging to the party's reputation.

[51] Only one out of its ten candidates had been successful in 1959. The successful candidate declined nomination in 1964 on the grounds that he wanted to devote more time to his business commitments.

[52] There is some duplication in these figures since some of the candidates belonged to both groups.

[53] Kelantan. Altogether the Alliance held 207 of the 282 state seats in the country.

mentary elections. Since there had been a tremendous pressure for nomination, it was decided that the interests of party unity would be best served by giving nominations to as many persons as possible. Consequently, of the sixty-four candidates who contested both parliamentary and state seats, only one was from the Alliance.[54]

Finally, a brief attempt may be made to interpret some of the attributes of the candidates chosen by the different parties. In particular, did these attributes contribute to, or confirm, a particular 'image' in the case of each party? Attention will be given first to the communal breakdown.

The Alliance line-up clearly reflected the party's inter-communal structure. There were 68 Malays, 33 Chinese and 3 Indians. These figures also show the relative dominance of the UMNO within the Alliance.[55] The PMIP's line-up, in contrast, was consistent with its communal composition and outlook: all 53 of its candidates were Malays. The SF, like the Alliance, revealed its inter-communal composition by putting up 30 Malays, 28 Chinese and 5 Indians. But these figures are misleading in so far as they may suggest that the Malay section of the party (comprising Party Rakyat and the NCP) is almost as strong as the non-Malay section (the Labour Party). The SF's strength lies mainly in the support it receives from non-Malay voters, and the decision to adopt thirty Malay candidates must in all likelihood have been prompted by the need to satisfy the different sections of the party. What was important was the fact that the majority of the 'winnable' seats were seats with a minority of Malays which the Socialist Front contested with non-Malay candidates. All the

54 The rest were made up of 23 from the SF, 13 from the UDP, 10 from the PMIP, 8 from the PAP, 6 from the PPP, 1 from Party Negara and 2 Independents.

55 It must however be remembered that since the Alliance contested every seat in the country, it was inevitable that a majority of its candidates should have been Malays. But the line-up was nevertheless favourable to the UMNO since Malay voters formed the most numerous group in only sixty-two constituencies.

other parties showed themselves to be either Malay or non-Malay oriented.[56]

SF candidates were on the average younger than those of the other parties. This is consistent with the fact that left-wing politics in Malaya is to a significant extent sustained by the enthusiasm and active support of the urban youth, particularly the Chinese-educated. Like the Barisan Sosialis in Singapore, the SF gets many of its active workers from this group and this has partly been responsible for the 'youthful' image of the two parties.

Of the three major parties, the Alliance had the highest proportion of businessmen and professional people among its candidates.[57] This was not surprising since, in addition to being the party in power, it also stood for conservative economic policies. But it should also be remarked that the proportion of businessmen was by no means sufficiently high to fit its description, especially by the left-wing, as a 'rich man's party'.[58] The PMIP, true to its preoccupation with religion and the Malay language, fielded the largest number of religious and Malay school teachers. The SF had the largest number of trade unionists, a fact obviously related to its left-wing character.

As indicated earlier, all parties except the Alliance showed through their choice of constituencies that they expected their support to be restricted to certain parts of the country. Even the SF, which spread its candidates fairly widely, chose its seats in a manner which indicated that it did not expect to receive much support in the predominantly Malay states of Kelantan, Trengganu, Kedah and

[56] See Table II.

[57] Two of the minor parties, the UDP and the PPP, in fact had a higher proportion. But in their case the main explanation probably lies in the fact that they only put up a small number of candidates who, in the absence of a large and decentralized party organization, were often hand-picked by their leaders.

[58] It is not, of course, being assumed that a party's description as catering to rich men or business interests cannot be justified unless its candidates are themselves businessmen or rich people. What we are concerned with at the moment is the extent to which the attributes of the candidates confirmed certain commonly-held stereotypes or views about their parties.

Perlis.   The constituencies chosen by the UDP and the PAP revealed that they expected their support to come mainly from Chinese voters.[59]   By putting up all but one of its candidates in Perak, the PPP reinforced the popular view that it was a party which was primarily confined to that state.   The PMIP, as expected, limited itself almost entirely to Malay-dominated constituencies, concentrating its efforts in the states in the north and north-east.

[59] Because of its aspiration to replace the SF as the main left-wing party in the country and to provide a more 'responsible' alternative to it, the PAP also tended to choose constituencies where the SF was known to be strong.

VI

Issues

THE main feature of the election was perhaps the pre-eminence of a single issue. This was the Indonesian 'confrontation' of Malaysia and the threat which it posed to the country's security. From the very outset of the campaign the Alliance showed its determination to make this the central issue and, helped by the PAP, succeeded in compelling the other parties (notably the SF) to concentrate their energies on refuting the various charges of disloyalty that were made against them.

Although the Alliance went through the motions of preparing and distributing a manifesto (and a great deal of other literature) which covered a fairly comprehensive list of subjects, its leaders made it quite clear that the only 'real' issue facing the electorate was whether they wanted to continue as an independent and prosperous nation or be an impoverished Indonesian colony. Other issues were said to be of only minor importance.[1] It was, therefore, not surprising that the election should have been described as 'something like a referendum' on this particular issue, to decide whether or not the Government had a mandate to continue with its policies in dealing with 'confrontation'.[2] It was even explained, by the Prime Minister, that this was the reason why the election was being held 'earlier than usual'.[3]

The Alliance argued that it was the only party which could safeguard national integrity and that the difference between voting for it and voting for other parties was in essence the difference between being loyal and being sym-

[1] *Straits Times,* 16 April 1964. However, as will be shown later, certain other issues did feature prominently during the campaign.

[2] *Ibid.* 23 April 1964.

[3] *Malay Mail,* 2 April 1964.

pathetic to Indonesian aggression. 'Every vote for the
Alliance', declared one of its officials, 'is the vote of a loyal
citizen .... Do not be a traitor by voting for the Opposition parties'.[4] An overwhelming victory for the Alliance,
it was argued, would convince Indonesia of the futility of
its aggression against Malaysia and therefore lead to the
termination of 'confrontation'.[5] It was thus necessary for
the voters to sink their other differences, because this was
the only way in which they could show the rest of the
world that they favoured the creation of Malaysia. To
stress the importance of this plea, attempts were made to
show how each of the other parties was or had been involved in some way with 'anti-national' or 'anti-Malaysia'
activities and how a vote for any of them could therefore
be construed to be a vote for Soekarno.[6] There were, however, only two main targets for this attack, the SF and the
PMIP. These parties were singled out as having direct
connexions with Indonesia and were bluntly accused of
carrying on fifth-column activities. Frequent reference
was made to the fact that some of their leaders — particularly Dr. Burhanuddin (PMIP) and Ishak Mohammad and
Ahmad Boestamam (SF) — had, after the war, been the
leaders of a movement which advocated union between
Indonesia and Malaya. The SF, in particular, was repeatedly challenged to denounce Indonesian aggression instead
of just blaming it on the way in which Malaysia was
formed. The party was also accused of complicity in the
Brunei revolt of December 1962 and of having made
moves to precipitate an uprising in Malaysia.[7] To indi-

4 *Straits Times,* 26 March 1964.
5 *Ibid.* 15 April 1964.
6 *Ibid.* 23 April 1964.
Even the PAP and the PPP, which were firmly behind the Government
in its stand against Indonesia, came in for criticism. The former was
blamed for attempting to disrupt unity at a time of crisis, and thereby
of playing into Soekarno's hands. The latter was accused of having
originally been anti-Malaysia and of having changed its stand 'for the
purpose of the elections' because it realized that the majority of people
supported Malaysia. *Loc. cit.*
7 These charges were originally made at the time of Boestamam's arrest
but were repeated during the campaign.

cate the extent to which the SF and the PMIP were actively involved in subversion and sabotage, the Alliance made
full use of the fact that arms and ammunition had been
discovered in a Party Rakyat branch in Johore and on a
beach near Bachok, a PMIP stronghold in Kelantan. In
commenting on the latter the Deputy Prime Minister,
Tun Abdul Razak, declared:

> The ammunition and the ship came from our enemy,
> Indonesia. It is now clear that the PMIP leaders have
> connections in this matter. The PMIP leaders have
> often been the champions of President Soekarno and his
> colleagues in our country. Now we have found deadly
> weapons in Kelantan — probably for their plans to re-
> sort to violence.[8]

The Alliance also accused the SF and the PMIP of receiving money from Indonesia for use in their election
campaign.[9] It was further alleged that armed Indonesian
gunboats were attempting to intimidate Malaysian fishermen in the Straits of Malacca into voting for the SF.[10]
To the obvious embarrassment of these two parties, it was
also pointed out that in broadcasts beamed at Malaysia,
Radio Indonesia was asking the Malayan voters to support
the SF and the PMIP.[11] Earlier in the campaign the
Alliance had given full publicity to an editorial in the
Indonesian Herald (which was described as the unofficial
voice of the Indonesian Foreign Office) in which it had
been alleged that the bomb explosions in Singapore during the preceding weeks had been brought about by the
Government's suppression of opposition parties, and that
'political violence' would increase. This, it was argued,
was further proof that the SF and the PMIP were involved
in sabotage. Leaders of these parties were quick to react
in their own defence. Saying that the Indonesian statement was 'regrettable', Mr. Lim Kean Siew, one of the

[8] *Straits Times,* 17 March 1964.

[9] Concrete details of this, however, were not made known until February
1965 when the Government published a White Paper entitled *A Plot
Exposed.* (Cmd 12 of 1965.)

[10] *Sunday Times,* 19 April 1964.

[11] *Straits Times,* 23 April 1964.

national leaders of the SF, explained that the Indonesians were probably referring to violence by aggrieved individuals. He added that the SF abhorred violence and took the opportunity to condemn the Government for failing to maintain security. Claiming that no one really knew who was responsible for the explosions, he suggested that it could have been the work of 'a few mad-caps or a mad bomber, or it may even have been organized to confuse and throw suspicion on political opponents'.[12] For its part, the PMIP denied that it had any connexions with Indonesia. Its Deputy National President, Zulkiflee Muhammad, asserted that there was no need for his party to resort to violence since it was quite happy to settle things 'by means of the elections' and to overthrow the Alliance 'politically and constitutionally'.[13]

Yet another piece of evidence produced against the SF was that its symbol contained the eagle found in the Indonesian emblem, and that the bull's head which was incorporated in it belonged to a type of bull found in Indonesia and not in Malaysia.[14] Dismissing this as 'a lot of bull', a spokesman for the SF replied that the head was that of a Malayan bull, the *seladang*, which was well known for its strength and endurance.[15] Another spokesman found this attempt to link his party with Indonesia 'rather pathetic', and went on to point out that in any case the Alliance was not in a position to make such accusations since the UMNO's flag had the same red and white design as the Indonesian flag, while that of the MCA resembled the Kuomintang emblem.[16] But this failed to put an end to the bull. A game warden was brought into the fray by the Alliance and solemnly pronounced that he had not seen a single *seladang* with horns similar to those of the bull found in the SF's emblem. His verdict was that the bull was definitely Indonesian. The PAP delivered the

12 *Ibid.* 3 April 1964.
13 *Ibid.*
14 *Ibid.* 6 April 1964.
15 *Ibid.* 9 April 1964.
16 *Loc. cit.*

coup de grâce in a statement issued by its Central Political Bureau. Here it was pointed out that the SF's claim (that the head was that of a *seladang*) had 'only evoked laughter from experts who know about the Malayan *seladang*'. The statement then went on to analyse the 'five faces' of the bull and showed that the head in question, in addition to being the symbol of Party Rakyat, was also that of Aza-hari's Party Rakyat in Brunei (which led the revolt there), the insignia of the Revolutionary Army of Kalimantan Utara (North Borneo), the official Indonesian crest and the crest of the so-called Revolutionary Government of Indo-nesia. 'The choice of the bull's head for these five groups, all of whom are anti-Malaysia and pro-Indonesian', the statement concluded, 'cannot be coincidence'.[17]

The most serious attack on the SF and the PMIP on the question of Malaysia and 'confrontation' was delivered a mere two days before polling day, with the timely publica-tion of a Government White Paper on *Indonesian Inten-tions Towards Malaysia*. In addition to tracing the his-tory of 'Indonesian imperialist intervention in Malaya and her neo-colonial attempts to deny Malaya the fruits of her freedom',[18] this publication also gave some detailed ac-counts of how certain leaders of the SF and the PMIP had over a period of years actively participated in clandestine activities in co-operation with known Indonesian agents. Needless to say, the White Paper in question featured very prominently in the last two days of the Alliance campaign.

Throughout the campaign, the PAP was at one with the Alliance in accusing the SF and the PMIP of complicity with Indonesia. But it was not always sympathetic to the methods that were used. It argued, for example, that the White Paper should have been released some two or three weeks earlier since it was 'naively optimistic' to expect people to read and comprehend a sixty-four page docu-ment in forty-eight hours. Said Lee Kuan Yew in this connexion: 'Now the Opposition is sure to claim that this

17 *Malay Mail*, 15 April 1964.

18 Malaysia, Ministry of Internal Security, *Indonesian Intentions towards Malaysia*. Kuala Lumpur, 1964, p. v.

is a dressed up piece of evidence published two days before polling day in order to embarrass them'.[19]   He felt that the information contained in the White Paper was far too important to be made to stand the risk of being interpreted as an instrument of party rivalry: the nation's survival was at stake, and it was therefore vital that the people should be constantly informed of what was happening. The PAP also deplored the way in which news of the discovery of ammunition near Bachok was released.   Said Lee Kuan Yew:

> To release information of a discovery of ammunition on the beaches of Kelantan with footmarks of a frogman through a Minister whilst he is campaigning during the general election is not the best way to bring home the gravity of the facts.   The use of data damaging to Opposition parties is legitimate and usual in all democratic countries.   But an effective and intelligently run democratic government should first disclose the facts coldly and without comment.   Later let the debate begin on the conclusion to be drawn from the facts.[20]

The main argument advanced by the SF and the PMIP was that those who asked them to condemn Indonesia were merely trying to divert people's attention from the fact that it was the way in which Malaysia had been created (without adequate consultation of opinion in the Borneo territories and without sufficient regard for Indonesian views) which had led to the strained relations between Indonesia and Malaysia.   To them it was therefore Malaysia which had been responsible for the provocation, and no amount of condemnation of Indonesian aggression was going to change this.   Each of them repeatedly claimed that the only way of ensuring peace would be for the voters to support its candidates and that an inevitable consequence of an Alliance victory would be war with Indonesia.   But there was one important difference in the attitudes of these two parties.   The SF based its objections to Malaysia on the grounds that it was the result of connivance between the

19 *Straits Times*, 23 April 1964.
20 *Loc. cit.*

colonialists and local reactionary elements aimed at the preservation of their own interests. The PMIP's reservations,
on the other hand, rested mainly on its contention that the
creation of Malaysia represented a dilution of Malay influence in the country since the proportion of non-Malays
was substantially increased as a result of the incorporation
of Singapore, Sarawak and Sabah.[21]   The fact that Indonesia was a 'Malay' country was an added consideration,
since this meant that Malaysia's conflict with it represented
a division within the Malay race.   According to some of
the Alliance officials who were interviewed, these communal considerations were so important to the PMIP that it
had gone to the extent of telling voters (in the course of
its house-to-house campaign) that domination by Indonesia
was preferable to domination by the Chinese in Malaysia.

However, it was the SF which was mainly responsible
for the denunciation of Malaysia.   It claimed that the new
federation was a 'neo-colonial plan' which was designed to
'suppress the independent and democratic movement of
the people in North Borneo'.[22]   This plan, according to
the SF, had been implemented by the British working
through the PAP and the Alliance in order to 'preserve
their large and fat interests'.[23]   The party also alleged that
Malaysia was merely a tool that was being used by the
'American and British power *bloc*' to strengthen the defence of SEATO and to isolate Indonesia.[24]   In apparent
justification of Indonesia's reactions, a statement issued by
the Central Publicity Section of the SF declared: 'The
establishment of Malaysia has brought about Indonesian
confrontation because it is a British colonialist plot aimed
at harming Indonesian interests and safety'.[25]   This statement also justified the earlier revolt in Brunei on the
grounds that the people in that state, having failed to gain

[21] In fact, the Chinese now formed the most numerous group in the
country.

[22] *Sin Chew Jit Poh*, 30 March 1964.

[23] *Loc. cit.*

[24] *Loc. cit.*

[25] *Ibid.* 6 April 1964.

independence through constitutional means, had been 'forced to take up arms against the British colonialists'.

Although the SF did not for a moment waver in its strong stand against Malaysia, there were some indications that complete unity was not achieved within the party concerning certain aspects of its policy on this issue. Statements released by the party's Central Publicity Section were always virulent and abusive in attacking the architects of Malaysia, and contained a full complement of clichés and jargon which one usually associates with 'revolutionary' propaganda. These statements viewed issues solely in black-and-white terms. At the same time there were also certain individuals within the party (some of whom were prominent leaders) who, while not conceding anything as far as their main arguments were concerned, were nevertheless prepared to make certain distinctions. A good example of this apparent lack of agreement was provided by the different reactions to the Government's decision to introduce conscription for males between 21 and 29 years of age. Mr. Lim Kean Siew, the Vice-President of the Labour Party and one of the SF's most outspoken leaders, said that his party was prepared to accept the call-up as 'inevitable', adding: 'If it is meant to prepare ourselves for national defence, then we accept it'.[26] Another leader maintained that his party would be prepared to fight only if the Indonesians attacked Malaya and that they would not fight in the Borneo territories. By fighting in Sabah and Sarawak, he claimed, they would only be 'assisting the lifespan of the colonialists'.[27] The SF Election Committee in Tanjong (Penang) expressed a similar view when it observed that Malayan youths were not obliged to become 'cannon fodder for the British in Sabah and Sarawak'.[28] The party's Central Publicity Section was not even prepared to make any such qualifications. In an outright condemnation of the conscription proposals, it viewed the call-up solely as a determined

26 *Malay Mail*, 11 March 1964.
27 *Straits Times*, 28 March 1964.
28 *Sin Chew Jit Poh*, 24 March 1964.

effort by the Alliance Government 'to push the Malayan people to war so that Asians will fight Asians — in conformity with the imperialist plot'.[29]

Two weeks before the close of the campaign, the SF put forward a five-point proposal to bring about a peaceful solution to the Malaysian crisis. The proposals were:

i.   'Immediate cease-fire in the Borneo territories.'
ii. 'Appeal to non-aligned Afro-Asian countries under the United Nations.'
iii. 'Withdrawal of all troops — British, Gurkha and Indonesian — from Sabah and Sarawak under UN supervision.'
iv. 'Release of all political detainees held without trial and the normalization of democratic life.'
v.   'The UN should conduct a referendum to ascertain the true spirit of self-determination of the Borneo people, as to whether they want (a) independence or (b) join Malaysia or (c) other wishes.'[30]

In announcing these proposals the Secretary-General of the Labour Party, Dr. Wee Lee Fong, declared that if the Borneo territories were freely to express their wish to join Malaysia and if Indonesian aggression continued despite this, the SF would then 'call on the whole nation to fight against Indonesia'.[31] Earlier, another spokesman had stated that the only peace which the Alliance was capable of achieving was 'the peace of an opium den or the mortuary'.[32]

The strongest attack on these proposals came from the PAP. Each of the five points, argued Lee Kuan Yew, either echoed an Indonesia demand or was designed to assist the Indonesians. The demand for the withdrawal of British and Gurkha troops, in particular, was criticized as directly representing Indonesian interests since the only

29 *Ibid.* 6 April 1964.
All the other parties gave their whole-hearted support to conscription.
30 *Straits Times,* 11 April 1964.
31 *Loc. cit.*
32 *Ibid.* 3 April 1964.

outcome of such a move would be that Malaysia would then be left defenceless in the face of any Indonesian attack.[33]

The SF also accused the Alliance of using the Malaysian crisis to create mass hysteria and to frighten the people into voting for it at the election. The publication of the White Paper shortly before polling day was seen as an attempt to intimidate the electorate and was therefore called 'a dirty trick, a dastardly and cowardly act by a group of power-hungry men who in their anxiety to retain authority over our destiny and to cling to their autocratic privileges, resort to the most vile and vicious methods of propaganda'.[34] A similar interpretation was given to the reports which had been released in the early stages of the campaign that parachutes had been dropped by unidentified planes.[35]

The UDP and the PPP, while having certain reservations about the haste shown by the Alliance Government in the formation of Malaysia, were both unreservedly opposed to Indonesian aggression. Of the two, the PPP was the one which most frequently and unreservedly condemned Indonesia and which also repeated many of the allegations made by the Alliance and the PAP against the SF. Party Negara, receiving very little publicity during the campaign, made one extravagant bid for attention when its leader, Inche Garieb Raouf, boldly announced that he was prepared to go to Indonesia to negotiate peace provided he was given a mandate by the Alliance. 'I am prepared', he announced, 'to do anything to prevent war. I am even prepared to lay down my life even if it means getting shot in Indonesia. I hate Asians killing Asians. That is why I am offering my services to find a way to ensure that our boys do not get killed unnecessarily.'[36] Alas, far from getting a mandate, the only reply he got from the Alliance was the Tengku's comment at a rally:

33 *Straits Times,* 16 April 1964.
34 *Malay Mail,* 25 April 1964.
35 *Straits Times,* 24 April 1964.
36 *Ibid.* 20 April 1964.

'It is better to send a goat than Inche Garieb'.[37] And there the matter rested.

Next to Malaysia and confrontation, communal issues were the most prominent during the campaign. Of these the most important were religion, Malay privileges and language.

On religion, the bitterest conflicts were between the PMIP and the UMNO,[38] both Malay parties. This was so, not because the non-Malay parties were any less opposed to the PMIP's policies than the UMNO, but because the main rivalry in the rural areas (where the PMIP fielded almost all its candidates) was between these two Malay parties. In fact, religion was in many ways the main issue in Kelantan, Trengganu, Kedah and Perlis. In all these states the UMNO and the PMIP were the chief contenders for office.

The PMIP's main argument was that the establishment of Islam as the state religion in the Constitution was nothing but a mere sham since it had not led to the adoption of specifically 'Islamic principles of administration'. It promised to follow these principles if returned to power, but very little explanation was given as to what this really implied.[39] The UMNO was continuously accused of 'betraying Islam', not only because it was sacrificing spiritual values for material advancement, but because its partnership with the MCA and the MIC in the Alliance amounted to co-operation with 'infidels'. From many accounts, the PMIP used its house-to-house campaign to warn Malay voters that they would be going against the dictates of Islam if they voted for a non-Islamic party or even for a party (like the UMNO) which was working in close co-operation with non-Muslims. To show the extent of the

37 *Loc. cit.*

38 More strictly the Alliance, but almost all its candidates who stood against the PMIP were from the UMNO.

39 Even in the course of interviews party leaders were always hazy about the specific policies which they had in mind. Often they merely insisted that these 'principles' were contained in the Koran and that all that was required was for more 'research' to be done in order to ascertain their full meaning.

UMNO's disregard for Islam, it was alleged that the Alliance Government had been responsible for allowing Chinese to rear pigs near Malay homes.[40] In a similar vein, the accusation was also made that the Tengku had danced the twist with female competitors after a Koran reading competition during the fasting month.[41]

Although the PMIP concentrated on gaining support through emphasizing its concern for the welfare of Islam, it is possible that the efficacy of its religious appeal depended at least as much on the active support it received from rural religious leaders as on the religious issues which were raised. In other words, many voters may have been influenced by the mere fact that their religious leaders had advised them to support the PMIP rather than by their own evaluation of the religious arguments used by the PMIP and the UMNO. These two are admittedly difficult to separate, but the point is that voters may have been influenced purely by their trust in their religious leaders. This is gone into in greater detail in other parts of the book, and need not be further discussed here.[42]

In its attempt to offset the PMIP's religious appeal, the UMNO argued that it was no less concerned with the welfare of Islam than its rival. It was pointed out, for example, that the Alliance Government had spent vast sums of money in building mosques and prayer houses throughout the country whereas the PMIP, which posed as the custodian of Islam, had done no such thing in Kelantan where it was in power. At the same time, voters were also warned that the PMIP's interpretation of the Koran was perverse and that its leaders were doing a great disservice to Islam (and indeed to the country) by misinterpreting its tenets. In this connexion, special attention was given to that party's alleged insistence that it was forbidden (*haram*) for Muslims to co-operate politically with non-Muslims. It was revealed that its workers had distributed talismans

<hr/>

40 The speaker who made this allegation at a rally was also careful to point out that such a practice had hardly been heard of during the colonial days. *Warta Mingguan,* 12 April 1964.

41 *Utusan Melayu,* 9 April 1964.

42 See Chapters VII and IX (a).

which incited Muslims to wage a holy war (*sabil*) against the non-Muslims in the country. In commenting on this the Prime Minister, Tengku Abdul Rahman, observed while addressing a rally:

> I have warned the PMIP before to cease inciting the people [to fight] each other. This time I will take stronger action. If they dare defy me, go ahead. I'll fight back. I will arrest those who want to destroy the unity of our people. Democracy should be pursued through persuasion. That is the essence of democracy. We cannot force people into accepting our point of view, leave alone incite them to wage a holy war against those who are not members of the PMIP.[43]

At another rally he observed:

> There are few democracies left in Asia. But our democratic way of life is being threatened by a political group which seeks power through incitement to violence which would lead to bloodshed. If these people preach violence it means that they reject democracy. Election is the essence of democracy so that the people can elect their own form of government freely. I, too, can change the law and maintain power like some dictators in Asia. But the Alliance is dedicated to maintain the principles of democracy.[44]

Another allegation made against the PMIP was that it was forcing people to swear on the Koran that they would vote for it at the election. Support was apparently urged on the grounds that its candidates were strictly not party representatives but 'messengers of the prophet' who were opposing 'infidels' and not merely candidates from the UMNO.[45] Observed an Alliance candidate in Kelantan: 'It is not the party...or the candidate that is projected to the voters, but God and the Prophet. It is not Dr. Burhanuddin or Zulkiflee [the President and Deputy President of the PMIP] who are leaders of the party now, but the Prophet, the messenger of God'.[46]

43 *Malay Mail*, 16 April 1964.
44 *Straits Times*, 18 April 1964.
45 *Ibid*. 15 April 1964.
46 *Loc. cit.*

In trying to discredit the PMIP, the Alliance also made full use of the misdemeanours of some of that party's leaders in an attempt to show that their pious fronts should not be seriously taken. Just before nomination day, a PMIP Member of Parliament had been found guilty of *khalwat;*[47] earlier, another prominent member had been convicted on a charge of outraging a woman's modesty. These convictions were obviously embarrassing to the PMIP, and provided the Alliance with good propaganda material. As on most other issues, ample support was given by the Malay newspapers. *Utusan Melayu*, for example, commented in an editorial:

> ...the PMIP is cheap and low. The party is ready to sell and use the verses handed down by God without heed to his warning: 'Do not sell my verses cheaply....' What truth is there in the PMIP's claim that it is God's party and that its leaders are God's messengers and apostles...when the leaders themselves do not follow the Prophet's traditions? The question should be thought over by all faithful and intelligent Muslims.... We heard about the honourable PMIP leader... who tried to outrage the modesty of a young midwife. Immediately after this we heard about the President of the PMIP, Dr. Burhanuddin, who was on trial...[48] and after this we heard about Harun Pilus, an honourable PMIP member in Ulu Trengganu who...was sentenced because of 'khalwat' (close proximity) with a waitress. All these are punishments handed by God to the PMIP leaders who broke their promises to God ...we hear that among the PMIP leaders there are those who indulge in vices — some drink alcohol and entertain 'wild women'.... To promote a nation of God is not within the capacity of the present personalities and leaders of the PMIP, who themselves are ignorant of Islamic philosophy and who cannot control their desires.[49]

47 *Khalwat* is 'retirement in close proximity' by members of the opposite sex who are not married to each other. It only concerns Muslims, and is a punishable offence in certain states.

48 See p. 17 above.

49 *Utusan Melayu*, 16 April 1964.

In condemning religious fanaticism, the Alliance repeat-edly emphasized the obvious dangers of communal dis-cord. Neither the country nor the Malay community could gain from the type of communal solidarity advocated by the PMIP since that solidarity would antagonize the other communities and isolate the Malays. Describing the PMIP's policies as 'narrow-minded' and 'virulent', the Tengku told a rally:

> Its policy is particularly dangerous because there are almost the same number of Malays and Chinese living in Malaysia. No party should ever play the game of religious and communal politics. If ever the people ac-cept the policy and propaganda put out by the PMIP and other opposition parties, then there will be trouble and chaos in the country. Malaysia might even end up worse than Cyprus.[50]

On the question of Malay privileges,[51] the PMIP held the view that the special rights given to the Malay com-munity by the Constitution were grossly inadequate and that they should be both extended and made more per-manent. At the root of its argument was the claim that Malaya was a Malay country and that steps should there-fore be taken to guarantee that community's dominance in the country's political (and, ultimately, economic) life. 'There is nothing in the Constitution', lamented one of its leaders in this connexion, 'to guarantee the Malays per-petual political power in the country.'[52] It was felt that the existing privileges, far from being adequate as instru-ments which could facilitate the attainment of this goal, were doing very little to check the creeping tide of non-Malay economic control. For this reason, the achieve-ment of independence in 1957 was dubbed as an empty victory for the Malays since it had done nothing to im-prove their lot. It was thus PMIP's contention that the

[50] *Straits Times,* 31 March 1964.

[51] The Constitution guarantees a 'special position' for the Malay com-munity. This involves land reservations (Article 89) and the reservation of quotas in respect of civil service appointments, educational benefits, and certain business licences (Article 153).

[52] *Straits Times,* 18 April 1964.

aims of Malay nationalism were yet to be realized and that
it was the only party which could spearhead the continuing struggle.

The Alliance, in explaining its own views on this subject, gave due emphasis to the need for giving certain special privileges to the Malay community. But it was also
insistent that a balance should be struck between these
privileges and the legitimate rights of the non-Malay communities. Despite this emphasis on compromise, the approach to the problem was noticeably different in the case
of each partner. The UMNO appealed to Malay voters
by reminding them of the great efforts that were being
made to promote their welfare. It projected itself as the
party best able to look after their interests, but, unlike the
PMIP, avoided giving the impression that there was any
inherent conflict between the Malays and the non-Malays.
The MCA, on the other hand, concentrated on reassuring
the Chinese that their own interests were being properly
looked after by the Alliance and that the concessions which
had been made to the Malay community did not in any
important way curtail non-Malay opportunities. This approach helped the Alliance partners to preserve their essentially communal appeal while at the same time encouraging their respective communities to have a proper regard
for the welfare of the others. While this had its advantages, it also meant that each partner was exposed to accusations of betrayal by the other parties which sought to
represent its community. The UMNO was accused by the
PMIP and Party Negara of having sacrificed Malay interests because of its conciliatory attitude towards the non-
Malays. Equally, the PPP and the UDP were emphatic
that the MCA had for all intents and purposes totally suc-
cumbed to the UMNO and that it had long ceased to be
an effective spokesman of the Chinese community. They
claimed that too many of the major policies adopted by
the Alliance Government had been aimed solely at benefiting the Malays and establishing their superiority, and that
the MCA had done nothing to prevent this. This view,
obviously aimed at a non-Malay audience, occasioned vehe-

ment attacks against non-Malay communalism in the Malay press.[53] Interestingly, although the Malay newspapers firmly supported the policies of the Alliance Government, many of their comments in this connexion echoed views which were more specifically held by the PMIP. The main target of these attacks, however, was neither the PPP nor UDP but the PAP which, although it was critical of certain pro-Malay policies, was in fact a strong supporter of the special position of the Malays. The *Utusan Melayu*, in particular, conducted a virulent campaign against the PAP which began well before nomination day and which continued, with increased vigour, during the election period. Indeed, nothing received more attention in its editorials than that party's alleged duplicity, its enslavement of the Malay community in Singapore and the inevitable oppression of that community if the PAP were ever to gain control, and the ruthlessness, arrogance and personal ambition of Lee Kuan Yew.[54] While this attention is difficult to explain, it is possible that the PAP was seen as the party most likely to pose a threat to Alliance power in the future, and also a party which might challenge the preeminence of Malay political leaders.

There were two main aspects to the language issue. First, there was the controversy over the achievements of the Alliance Government in promoting Malay as the national language of the country and the progress which had been made towards the abandonment of English as a second official language.[55] In this connexion, the main critic of the Alliance was the PMIP which argued that not enough had been done to expand Malay educational facilities and to do away with English at the earliest possible opportunity. This accusation was denied by the Alliance which was emphatic that vast progress had been made in giving the national language its due status in the country's

[53] See for example *Warta Negara*, 4 April 1964, and *Berita Harian*, 18 April 1964.

[54] See p. 206 below.

[55] The Constitution provides that English will continue as a second official language until 1967, when Parliament will decide whether or not its use should be extended for a further period.

educational system and administration. Secondly, there was a great deal of argument over the treatment given to Chinese education, especially the preservation of Chinese as the main medium of instruction in Chinese schools. It was this which commanded the greatest attention during the election and which gave the language issue its prominence during the campaign. Understandably, the main debate was confined to the urban areas. Before discussing the stand taken by the different parties, a brief historical background may be helpful.

The first major attempt to formulate a national education policy was made in 1956. This policy, contained in the *Report of the Education Committee, 1956* (usually referred to as the *Razak Report*, after the Chairman of the Committee) enabled the Chinese schools in the country to receive a full Government subsidy while continuing to use Mandarin as their main medium of instruction. It was, however, stated that all students (that is, students from all the language 'streams') would follow the same syllabus and sit for a common final examination. Although this provision caused no controversy at the time of the *Report*'s publication, there was an outcry from Chinese educational authorities when, in 1959, it was decided that a 'common final examination' meant an examination conducted in the same language, Malay.[56] Sections of the MCA joined the general protest, and dissatisfaction with this alleged misinterpretation of the 1956 policy contributed to the resignation of many important members from the MCA in 1959.[57] In 1960, the provision in question was officially defined to mean that all students would sit for their final examination in either Malay or English. This interpretation failed to receive the full support of the Chinese community and a certain amount of dissatisfaction has since continued. It was feared by the MCA that this dissatisfaction could lead

[56] The Chinese had assumed that their students would sit for the same examination as all the others, but in their own language.

[57] The immediate cause of these resignations, however, was the conflict between the UMNO and the MCA over the allocation of seats for the 1959 general election.

to a loss of votes at the 1964 election, especially since it was evident that the issue would be exploited by some of its opponents.

Shortly before the commencement of the campaign, the Finance Minister, who was also the National President of the MCA, toured the country distributing money to Chinese schools.[58] The money was from a supplementary budget, and was to enable these schools to renovate or add to their premises and to buy new furniture. In the course of his speeches during the tour, the Minister was careful to point out that this gesture by the Government was clear proof of its deep concern for the welfare of Chinese education and that it disproved the various attacks by opposition parties on the Government's policy towards Chinese education.[59] Malaysia, he pointed out, was the only country in South-East Asia (and the only country in the world, except for China and Taiwan) which provided Chinese education from primary to university level. Unlike the opposition parties, the Alliance did not merely issue 'blank cheques', but emphasized 'sincere work'. The voters were asked to bear this in mind in judging the MCA and the Alliance.[60]

At least on one occasion, the distribution of funds took place in an MCA Assembly Hall. This special subsidy for Chinese schools featured prominently in the MCA's propaganda during the campaign.

It was the MCA's view that while every step should be taken to preserve Chinese culture by enabling Chinese schools to have their own medium of instruction and by making the Government responsible for financing Chinese education, it would be unreasonable to demand that Chinese should be made an official language. The party was therefore critical of those who insisted on multilingualism and accused them of playing up to communal sentiments.

[58] The total sum distributed was $5 million. *Sin Chew Jit Poh*, 29 February 1964.

[59] *Ibid.* 25 February 1964. This claim was also made by other MCA spokesmen during the campaign.

[60] *Loc. cit.*

There was, however, one instance where one of its candidates (Tan Kee Gak) was reported to have told a rally that by supporting the Alliance one could ensure that Chinese would be adopted as an official language.[61] This view was a direct contradiction of Alliance policy, but there was no evidence that the party (or even any of its opponents) did anything to pursue the matter. The candidate in question, a man of some wealth and a wide personal following in his constituency, had earlier been the leader of the Malayan Party and had successfully contested the 1959 election on its ticket.[62] Early in 1964 he had been persuaded by the MCA to wind up his party (which had really ceased to function some time earlier) and to stand on an Alliance ticket.

Throughout the campaign, the UDP was the sternest critic of the Government's policy on Chinese education. While not discounting the need for physical improvements in Chinese schools, it pointed out that this was merely one of the minor problems which confronted Chinese education. 'The basic problem', it argued, was 'that of protecting and preserving a truly good Chinese education, and it lies in the medium of teaching and examination.'[63] The Alliance was accused of 'deceit and insincerity' for trying to give the impression that it was promoting Chinese education merely by giving away money for the building and renovation of Chinese schools, when it was clear that the existing policies discriminated against Chinese education. In this connexion, the UDP also deplored the Alliance's use of public funds for party propaganda immediately before the election.

The controversy over Chinese education was by no means confined to these two parties. The SF, the PAP and the PPP were also involved, and there was in effect a general free-for-all among these five parties. Each was accused of either betraying the Chinese community (an accu-

---

61 *Nanyang Siang Pau*, 4 April 1964.

62 The Malayan Party was an advocate of multi-lingualism and equal rights for non-Malays.

63 *Sin Chew Jit Poh*, 2 February 1964.

sation made most frequently by the UDP and the PPP against the MCA) or of playing up to Chinese chauvinism (an accusation chiefly made by the MCA against the UDP and the PPP).[64] The PAP, although it did not openly advocate any change in the education policy in Malaya, was in the position of being able to point to its own achievements in Singapore where, it claimed, equal treatment had been given to the various language streams. This claim was vigorously contested by the SF which, in a very detailed statement issued by its Publicity Section, attacked the PAP for its 'ugly effort to develop English education' at the expense of the other language streams. Using a vast amount of statistics, this statement set out to prove how the PAP was 'stealthily' killing all but English education and how devious means had been employed to discourage parents from enrolling their children in Chinese schools. It showed that there had been a decrease in admissions to Chinese schools, but insisted that this had nothing to do with public concern over 'student disturbances' in these schools as had been argued by the PAP. Such an argument was 'heartless and irresponsible', and was 'the utterance of a madman, talking in his dreams'.[65] Concerning the earlier boycott of Government examinations by a section of the Chinese school student community in Singapore, the statement was emphatic that this was a genuine and inevitable protest against the Government's unfair education policy, and that there was not the slightest truth in the PAP's allegation that it had been communist-inspired. The PAP replied with an even lengthier statement, in which it gave a detailed account of how the communists and certain communist-front organizations had made use of the Chinese education issue, and Chinese school students, to foment political unrest in Singapore.[66] This statement also contained a detailed explanation of the Singapore Government's education policy, to show how

---

[64] The PPP was the chief advocate of multi-lingualism.
[65] *Sin Chew Jit Poh*, 16 April 1964.
[66] *Ibid*. 20 April 1964.

Chinese education had in no way been discriminated against.

The communal appeal of the different parties was by no means confined to the positions they took on the communal issues which have just been discussed. Each party also made an attempt to project a more general image of itself as being essentially a Malay or a non-Malay party. The PMIP and the PPP were the ones which appeared most obviously to depend on the projection of such an image for their support, and were followed in this respect by Party Negara and the UDP.[67] As pointed out, each of the Alliance partners approached the electorate as the chief protector of the rights of its own community, but without evoking any hostile communal feelings. The tactics adopted by the constituent units of the SF were not very dissimilar, although their separate communal identities were perhaps not as overtly displayed. It was nevertheless also evident that the main communal issues raised by the SF at the national level were designed primarily to appeal to Chinese voters. The PAP, while professing to be totally non-communal in its politics, confined itself to the urban (and hence Chinese) areas. This did not fail to influence its campaign, and it was evident that it presented itself as the party which could best serve the interests of the non-Malay communities.

Each party was vigorous in accusing the others of being communal. The PMIP was convinced that every other party in the country (with the possible exception of Party Negara) was in one way or another the tool of Chinese interests. Each of the other parties accused its opponents either of Malay or non-Malay communalism. The PMIP was commonly condemned for its Malay racist propaganda, while the PPP and the UDP were the parties most frequently accused of encouraging communal attitudes

[67] The UDP, however, was different from the other three in one important respect. As shown in Chapter V, its candidates (unlike those of the other three) were relatively well distributed between the different communities: there were eighteen Chinese, eight Malays and one Indian. But this was misleading in terms of the support which the party hoped to receive, which was mainly from the Chinese.

among the non-Malays. The MCA was attacked by the UDP and the PPP for failing to safeguard the interests of the Chinese community while the UMNO was accused by the PMIP of having failed the Malays. The PAP was condemned for Chinese chauvinism by the Alliance and the PMIP. The parties which least attacked each other were the PMIP and Party Negara; the UDP and the PPP; and the PAP and the PPP.

Most of the parties also laid stress on the need for communal harmony. With the exception of the PMIP (which did not subscribe to this goal) each claimed that its own policies were the ones best suited to achieve this, and accused the others (with the exceptions mentioned above) of inciting hatred. The Alliance never failed to claim credit for what it had already achieved in this respect, and always pointed out that it was the only party which had made inter-communal partnership its main philosophy. The PMIP, however, was of the opinion that the 'partnership' which the Alliance represented amounted to nothing more than the dominance of non-Malay over Malay interests. The PPP and the UDP, on the other hand, were equally convinced that the reverse was the case. The SF condemned the brand of partnership practised and preached by the Alliance, claiming that its only consequence would be the perpetuation of communalism in the country's political life. The Alliance, it argued, was a collection of specifically communal parties, each of which claimed a solely communal justification for its existence.

An argument frequently used by the Alliance in the urban areas was that by supporting anti-Malaysia parties people would in the long run only be inviting an Indonesian régime which would suppress the Chinese community. This argument was directed mainly at the SF, since the PMIP (the other main anti-Malaysia party) was not a contender for Chinese votes. Said Mr. Tan Siew Sin, the President of the MCA, at a rally:

> It is incredible that in spite of its pro-Indonesian attitude, the Socialist Front should get so much Chinese support. A take-over of Malaysia by Indonesia, how-

ever, would subject the Chinese population of this country to the most unspeakable horrors and agony, and yet
many Chinese in this country support a party which
practically invites the Indonesians to take over this
country.[68]

The PAP and the PPP, the latter in particular, also went
to some length in describing the vicious oppression of the
Chinese community in Indonesia. Soekarno was portrayed
by the PPP as the 'slaughterer of the Chinese'.[69]

Economic development featured prominently in the
Alliance campaign, particularly in the rural areas. A great
deal of emphasis was placed on the Government's achievements in this field and voters were always reminded that
this had been made possible only as a result of the sober
and far-sighted policies that had been adopted. The importance of sustaining the progress that had already been
made was thus a recurrent Alliance theme, and was accompanied by the warning that a change of Government
would lead to chaos and confusion: it was essential that the
ruling party be given a chance to complete its development programme. The Alliance also argued that its economic policies had produced a great deal of confidence
among investors, and that the flow of foreign capital into
the country was a testimony to this fact. Whatever one's
feelings, the country could not do without foreign capital;[70] and there would not be any further inflow of such
capital if there was a change of Government.[71]

The main emphasis, however, was always on rural development. This occupied a very important place in the
party's manifesto, and, next to 'confrontation', received the
greatest amount of publicity during the campaign.[72] The
rural areas were naturally the ones where this subject received the greatest attention, and the vast expenditure on
Federal Land Development Authority (FLDA) schemes was

[68] *Straits Times*, 11 April 1964.

[69] *Ibid.* 9 April 1964.

[70] *Straits Times*, 24 April 1964.

[71] *Ibid.* 15 April 1964.

[72] However, as has been pointed out, there was a greater amount of
controversy over communal issues as a whole.

usually given pride of place.[73] In emphasizing the Central Government's achievements through the FLDA, the Alliance leaders were convinced that the shortage of arable land was the problem which commanded the greatest attention in the rural areas and that the most obvious way of impressing the rural population would therefore be to tell them how much the Government had spent and intended spending in solving this problem. The opening up of new land, it was felt, was the main index of 'development' in the eyes of the rural population.

For some time after the 1959 election, it had been a sore point with the Chinese community that the Government's rural development plan had hitherto been confined to the Malay areas and that the 'new villages'[74] had not been included. The MCA had been subjected to some criticism as a result of this and it was felt that the dissatisfaction might be harmful to its future electoral prospects. One was therefore not surprised when, in 1962, the 'new villages' were formally incorporated into the rural development scheme. One was even less surprised to see the MCA make full use of this in the 'new villages' during its 1964 campaign.

Although its development programme was in many ways its trump card in the rural areas, the Alliance was heavily criticized by the PMIP and the SF for its alleged lack of achievements in this field. The PMIP, being its main rival in the rural areas, was naturally the chief critic. In its attempt to belittle the Alliance's achievements it argued that an accelerated programme of rural development would have been the first duty of any government that had been returned to power. There was thus no reason for the Alliance to claim any special credit since other parties, if

[73] Under the FLDA new areas of land have been opened up, at the Federal Government's expense, for settlement. Each settler is given ten acres of land, eight for rubber cultivation and two for mixed farming. In addition to clearing the land the Government also plants the rubber and provides homes for the settlers. The settlers also receive a monthly subsidy until the rubber is ready for tapping. Then they begin repayment on a fixed scale.

[74] See footnote 9 of Chapter III.

they had been returned to power, would have achieved at least as much. Having said this, the PMIP also went on to maintain that the Alliance's achievements had in fact been most inadequate and that its policies were misguided.

The main argument advanced by the PMIP was that a large proportion of the money spent on rural development had failed to bring any direct benefits to the rural population. The vast sums that had been spent on building roads in the rural areas were usually singled out for special criticism, the point being made that this bore little relation to living standards in the rural areas and that it only made driving more comfortable for those touring the country by road. The chief beneficiaries were not the Malays but the Chinese capitalists who controlled the country's distributive trade.[75] While not denying that there had been an increase in wealth in Malaya as a whole, the PMIP constantly repeated its claim that the real advances had taken place only in commerce and industry, both dominated by the Chinese. There had been no increase in rural productivity and hence in the living standard of the Malay community.

The PMIP also attacked the FLDA schemes for placing too great a burden on those who 'benefited' from them. It was alleged that the settlers were indebted to the Government for too long a period (about fifteen years) and that, by being compelled to commence repayment the moment they started tapping their rubber, they could not really feel that they owned their land and that they enjoyed the fruits of their own labour. The party claimed that its own land schemes in Kelantan which were based on self-help and which did not lead to any serious indebtedness, were therefore superior, although there were not many such schemes. The Central Government's failure to promote co-operative schemes in the rural areas was also criticized, both by the PMIP and the SF.

[75] The Alliance, however, maintained that the new roads had a direct bearing on the economic uplift of those living in hitherto inaccessible areas. For one thing these roads had made it easier for them to market their produce.

Unlike the PMIP, the SF did not concentrate its attack on any particular aspect of the Government's economic policies. The way in which the economy in general was being managed was severely brought to question, although special attention was always given to the continuing dominance of foreign capital. The Alliance was constantly accused of being an 'agent of colonialism', and of selling out the interests of the people. The achievement of independence in 1957 had brought no real benefits to the people of the country since Alliance rule was merely a continuation of colonial rule. In elaborating on this, a statement issued by the Central Publicity Section of the SF observed:

> The cunning British colonialists then devised a form of administration for saving their monopolistic economic interests and political rule. On 31 August 1957 they handed the administration over to the local feudalistic comprador ruling clique — the Alliance Government — which had been nurtured and brought up by them. In name Malaya became independent but there was no change in the power of the British colonialists who still can enslave and exploit our people through the Alliance Government . . . the Alliance has gone all out to suppress anti-colonial patriotic struggles and sell out the interests of the people.[76]

The statement then went on to give details of the extent to which the country's important industries (notably rubber and tin) were controlled by British and American capitalists, the profits they made, and the way in which the Alliance was continuing to operate as their agent.

Attention was drawn by the Alliance to the 'special importance' of the election. Most of this, as already shown, was related to the fact that external aggression had made it necessary that the outcome should reflect a high degree of unity behind the Government. Such a unity would be the most effective way of encouraging Indonesians to change their attitude, but also important was the fact that the rest of the world was anxious to see how far the Mala-

[76] *Sin Chew Jit Poh*, 6 April 1964.

yan electorate supported the creation of Malaysia. It was further pointed out that the outcome of the election would determine the future of democracy in the country. The Alliance, it was argued, was firmly dedicated to democratic values, and had decided to go back to the people although the 'situation facing the country would have justified its not doing so'.[77] Malaysia was one of the outstanding democratic nations in Asia, but this would no longer be so if the Government did not take a firm stand against those parties which abused their democratic privileges to undermine the nation's stability.[78] The dangers of communist subversion were given a great deal of prominence, the SF always being considered the main threat in this respect.[79] The SF replied to this by saying that the alleged 'communist threat' was entirely a figment of Alliance and PAP imagination and that the former, while claiming to be the saviour of democracy, was in fact leading the country towards dictatorship. The SF bitterly attacked the Government's use of preventive detention (from which it had suffered the most casualties) and frequently demanded that those who had been detained should either be released or be tried in the normal manner.

Another argument used by the Alliance was that it was the only party which could possibly form a Government since none of the others had fielded enough candidates to gain a majority in the House of Representatives. This, it was claimed, made it futile to support opposition parties since no amount of help could enable any of them to come to power. A special word of advice was given to those who intended supporting the smaller opposition parties: not only would they be wasting their votes but, by not sup-

77 *Straits Times*, 30 March 1964.

78 *Utusan Melayu*, 18 April 1964.

79 On a few occasions the PMIP was also accused of communist leanings. In replying to this 'baseless lie', one of its leaders pointed out that such an accusation could make no sense since the PMIP and the Communist Party had conflicting ideologies. 'The PMIP', he claimed, 'believes in the existence of an Almighty God and preaches good, while the Communists don't believe in God or religion.' (*Straits Times*, 8 April 1964.)

porting the Alliance, they would be helping the SF and the PMIP and hence, indirectly, Soekarno.[80]

In urging the voters to support it regardless of minor grievances, the Alliance also pointed out that it was the only party which had any experience of running the country and that no risks could be taken at such a critical time. It reminded the people of its achievements since coming to power in 1955, special attention being given to the attainment of independence, the maintenance of communal harmony, the high rate of economic growth and the preservation of peace and order. The opposition parties, understandably, were determined that these general claims should not be allowed to impress the electorate, and made every attempt to discredit the Alliance by drawing attention to more specific issues. The bitterest and the most comprehensive attack came from the SF in documents issued by its Publicity Section. Its views on economic development and the fruits of independence have been mentioned, and need not be repeated. On communal harmony, it maintained that the Alliance had in fact done a disservice to the country by encouraging its 'white-skinned masters' to implement racial discrimination and to 'deepen the contradictions among the various races in our country and seriously damage the existing unity'.[81] Concerning the Alliance's claim that it had preserved law and order, the SF retorted that the only kind of order which prevailed in the country was that which thrived on the indiscriminate use of preventive detention.[82] On foreign policy, it condemned the Alliance for its Defence Treaty with Britain and for being a 'mouthpiece of the Western *bloc*' as a result of which it had been isolated by the Afro-Asian nations.[83]

To some extent, the most interesting (and perhaps the bitterest) controversies seen during the campaign were those that were directly sparked off by the PAP's decision to participate in the election. The volume of debate was

[80] *Sunday Times*, 19 April 1964.
[81] *Sin Chew Jit Poh*, 10 April 1964.
[82] *Loc. cit.*
[83] *Ibid.* 6 April 1964.

quite out of proportion to the actual strength of the PAP's bid, and may be explained in terms of the fact that everyone concerned took the view that the party's performance in the seats it contested would be a strong indication of its *potential* strength in the urban areas.   Having apparently made a hasty decision to contest, the PAP was satisfied to restrict itself to eleven parliamentary and fifteen state seats. This was only a 'token' participation, but the party was careful to point out that such a participation would be sufficient, not only to indicate the amount of popular support that it commanded, but also to expose the public's dissatisfaction with the MCA and the SF.   Through its success in the seats it contested, the PAP hoped to show the UMNO that it was the party of the future in the urban areas, and thereby encourage the latter to accept it as its main partner. With this in mind, it followed a deliberate policy of wooing the UMNO and of making constant protestations of confidence in its leadership. It even went to the point of instructing two of its parliamentary candidates not to proceed with their campaigns once it was found that their opponents included UMNO candidates.[84]

The MCA and the SF were the two main targets of the PAP's attack. These were the chief parties in the urban areas, and confidence in them had to be destroyed if it was to make any headway in Malaya.

The campaign against the MCA was based on two main arguments. First, it was claimed that the party was effete and corrupt, and that it was led by self-seeking and ineffectual politicians who were described by one PAP speaker as 'fat-headed and fat-bodied' men whose 'chests and intestines [were] full'.[85]   The PAP, in contrast, was honest and dynamic as shown by its performance in Singapore. Malayan politics needed a shot in the arm, and only the PAP could provide it. Said Lee Kuan Yew at a rally in Penang:

[84] Although these candidates were officially declared to be non-contestants by the party, their names appeared on the ballot papers since their nominations had already been filed before the identity of the other candidates was known.

[85] *Sin Chew Jit Poh,* 25 March 1964.

The best result internally for our progress and for bringing about the winds of change in economic and social policies is to have the UMNO leadership returned, but the MCA discarded. A vote for the MCA is a vote for continued inactivity, complacency and decadence. To bring about this change, there must be a jolt on the leadership of the Government. That jolt can come about by voting for the PAP.[86]

The second argument used against the MCA was that dissatisfaction with it would cause more and more 'protest votes' to go to the SF. This augured ill not only for the future stability of the Alliance but also for that of the country. In this connexion, the PAP's election manifesto observed:

> Since the MCA cannot rally the masses in the urban areas...the danger of a pro-communist and anti-Malaysia party like the Socialist Front winning by default is considerable.... We must realise quickly that the Socialist Front, despite its facade of some respectable front men, is the advance guard of the Indonesian Communist Party just as the PMIP is the beachhead in Malaya of Indonesian racialism. The Socialist Front and the PMIP though anti-Malaysia for different reasons and though manipulated by different Indonesian groups are nevertheless jointly serving the interests of Indonesian expansionism in this region. The UMNO can deal with the PMIP in the rural areas. In the urban areas, because of the ineffectiveness of the MCA, the PAP has to help in the battle against the anti-Malaysia Socialist Front. The task of the PAP is to ensure that the protest votes in the urban areas do not become votes against Malaysia and for Soekarno.

The PAP thus argued that the urban voters should not be left in a cleft stick by being forced to choose between two unacceptable alternatives: the MCA which they neither liked nor respected and the anti-Malaysia SF whose cause they did not want to further. Only the PAP could

86 *Straits Times,* 20 April 1964.

stop the tide of dissatisfaction from benefiting the SF, and give the urban areas the leadership and political influence which they deserved. This was the main purpose behind its 'token participation'[87] — to deal with the SF while at the same time destroying 'the decadent political opportunists [in the MCA] who had relied on politics to become rich'.[88] As a partner in the Alliance the MCA had been able to hold its position only because its 'tycoons' had been able to 'nourish the UMNO financially throughout the existence of the Alliance'; their investment was redeemed through the use of influence gained in the Government.[89] In condemning this arrangement within the Alliance Mr. Toh Chin Chye, the Deputy Prime Minister of Singapore, told a rally in Penang:

> An effective government cannot be run by philanthropic patronage. Money is no substitute for ideas. It is in this outlook that the PAP differs from the Alliance. The PAP realises the overall importance of political stability and an effective central government in these perilous times. That is why we are prepared to work with the UMNO which still represents the rural base of the country so that Malaysia will survive the attacks of Indonesian confrontation.[90]

In countering the PAP's attack the MCA argued first of all that the former's participation in the election, although presented as an attempt to increase the pro-Malaysia vote, would in fact have the reverse effect. It was the pro-Malaysia vote that would be split, and the only party to benefit from this would be the SF. Thus if the PAP was really loyal it should have given its whole-hearted support to the Alliance and not launched a bitter campaign against it.[91]

[87] The PAP also pointed out that it had decided not to put up more candidates because such a move would have 'caused complications' with the Malay leadership of the Alliance with whom they had to co-operate in the interests of the country. *Straits Echo*, 25 March 1963.

[88] *Sin Chew Jit Poh*, 23 March 1964.

[89] *Straits Echo*, 23 April 1964.

[90] *Ibid.* 23 April 1964.

[91] *Malay Mail*, 16 April 1964.

The MCA also maintained that in talking about 'protest votes' the PAP was merely trying to find an excuse for its participation in the elections. In this connexion a statement issued by the Alliance Headquarters observed:

> The PAP says it is contesting the general election to ensure that the Socialist Front will not benefit from the 'substantial protest votes' against the MCA. These so-called 'protest votes' are a myth created by the PAP.[92]

Another argument used by the MCA was that, despite its claim to be a non-communal party, the PAP was in fact playing up to the communal sentiments of the Chinese community. In this connexion it was alleged that Lee Kuan Yew, while uttering non-communal slogans and praise for the Tengku when he spoke in Malay or English, said quite different things when he addressed his audience in Chinese. Said Tan Siew Sin:

> The greatest disservice the PAP is doing in its present election campaign ... is its blatant use of communalism as a vote-catching device. It is supposed to be non-communal but in practice it is communal in the extreme. While professing friendship for the UMNO and loyalty to the Tengku and Tun Razak in Malay and English, Mr. Lee Kuan Yew, the Prime Minister of Singapore and Secretary-General of the PAP, has made disparaging remarks about the Tengku in his speeches delivered in Chinese. For example, he said that the Tengku was not fit to be a national leader of high calibre. He is alleged to have said also that while the Tengku does not mind taking food with the poor, he does it not because he likes mixing with them but in order to spy on them.[93]

Using examples like these, the voters were reminded that

[92] *Straits Times*, 21 March 1964.
[93] *Straits Echo*, 30 March 1964.
These accusations were vigorously denied by Lee Kuan Yew, who claimed that the story had been made up by certain people in the MCA. The Tengku had to be saved from these 'so-called friends', who were exploiting his personal loyalty to them. *Sin Chew Jit Poh*, 30 March 1964.

the PAP had a history of treachery towards its friends, and that the overtures which it was making to the UMNO were only for the purpose of serving its immediate objective, which was the destruction of the MCA. Once successful in this it would then turn on the UMNO itself, since power was the only thing that the PAP was interested in. In a press statement the head of the MCA's Youth Section declared:

> Lee Kuan Yew's political power has always been built over the dead bodies of his friends and allies. With his present pro-UMNO and anti-MCA policy he hopes to isolate the Alliance and weaken the anti-invasion, anti-Soekarno, anti-Aidit and anti-infiltration forces of the Alliance party. ...Lee Kuan Yew's hop-step-and-jump political line ... is only a means of capturing political power to satisfy his power-mad intentions.[94]

The upshot of the PAP's campaign, it was argued, would be to drive the Chinese into communal politics. This was unsavoury in itself, but it would also cause the Malay leaders in the country to become distrustful of the Chinese community. This argument was carried to its limit when the President of the MCA observed that, judged in terms of its disruptive influence, the PAP could be classified as an 'anti-Malaysia' party.[95]

Just as the PAP tried to enhance its reputation by pointing to its achievements in Singapore, the MCA did its best to discredit that party by belittling these achievements. It was often pointed out that it was relatively easy for a government to achieve seemingly dramatic progress (for example in public housing) in a territory the size of Singapore, and that achievements there were not a proper indication of what a party could do in Malaya. Malaya was not only much larger but, unlike Singapore, was mainly rural. The magnitude of the problems differed in the two territories, and so did the priorities which any Government would have to follow. The emphasis in Malaya was,

94 *Sin Chew Jit Poh*, 19 March 1964.
95 *Malay Mail*, 16 April 1964.

and had to be, on rural development, and this was not a field in which dramatic success was possible in a short period of time. In reply to the PAP's claim that, unlike the Malayan Government, it had dedicated itself to the task of bettering the lot of the common man, the MCA pointed out that this simply could not be true since the Singapore Government was paying only 2½ per cent. interest on employees' contributions to the Central Provident Fund while the Malayan Government was paying 5 per cent. Much of the development in Singapore was financed by depriving the common man of the money to which he was entitled. Said Tan Siew Sin:

> If [the PAP] professes to have more acute social conscience than the Alliance, that has, however, not prevented it from depriving the contributors to Singapore Central Provident Fund of something like $250 per worker in earned interest alone. If you multiply this $250 by the tens of thousands of contributors to the Fund it is clear that they have been deprived in the aggregate of a sum which must run into hundreds of millions of dollars. Let us remember that the people affected are not the rich, they are the salaried employees who earn their livelihood by the sweat of their brow.[96]

To minimize the importance of the PAP's achievements, the MCA (helped by the UMNO) also pointed out that the PAP Government had survived in Singapore only because the Malayan Government had used its powers[97] and influence to prop it up and defeat its opponents. At the same time, the MCA also took pains to convey the impression that the PAP, while posing as a champion of national interests and an effective opponent of communism, was in fact a party that was prepared to co-operate with the communists when it suited its interests. The public was reminded of how the PAP, before it came to power in

[96] *Straits Echo*, 30 March 1964.

[97] Particularly in respect of internal security. Before the formation of Malaysia, the Malayan Government was jointly responsible with the Governments of Britain and Singapore for the island's internal security.

Singapore, had worked with the communists. The suggestion was also made that, despite its respectable front, the party continued to be an agent of communism. Said Mr. Lee San Choon, the leader of the MCA's Youth Section, at a press interview:

> Nobody knows what medicine [Lee Kuan Yew] is selling. He is singing the high notes of democracy, imposing Hitler's dictatorial measures and harbouring the ill intention of socialism, but he has not made it clear to the people whether his socialism is the same as the ultimate aim of communism. During the formation of Malaysia he went to pay homage to Moscow. Before he went to Africa he wrote to Chou En Lai. . . . But now he has started to sing anti-communist tunes. What can Lee Kuan Yew and his fellow-travellers do for the people and for the society? Can we be assured that when he captures political power he will not establish a second Cuba in Asia?. . .[98]

To drive home this point, the MCA put up a large number of posters which were solely confined to asking the PAP such questions as: 'Why did the PAP Secretary-General go to Moscow?' 'Why did the PAP allow [the] Communist Plen[99] to operate safely under their Government?' 'Why did the PAP allow the Communist Plen to return to Indonesia safely in 1963?' 'Why did the PAP make Lim Chin Siong[100] a Political Secretary to their Government? and 'Why did the PAP Minister for Labour go to Peking?' Through these questions the MCA clearly insinuated that

[98] Sin Chew Jit Poh, 19 March 1964.

[99] The 'Plen' (abbreviation for 'plenipotentiary') was an alleged communist agent whom Lee Kuan Yew (in the course of the PAP's earlier campaign in Singapore) had claimed to have met over a period of a few years. Lee Kuan Yew had given accounts of his meetings with this person in order to show the extent to which the Barisan Sosialis in Singapore was controlled by the communists. The MCA was now accusing Lee of having allowed the 'Plen' to exist freely instead of arresting him as a known communist.

[100] Lim Chin Siong was once in the PAP, but later led the group which broke away from the party to form Barisan Sosialis. He was under detention at the time of the election.

the PAP was a security risk and that its professed intentions should not be taken at face value.

Finally, the MCA warned the electorate that if the PAP ever succeeded in gaining control of the Central Government, it might impose a dictatorship. Reference was often made to the use of intimidation and other unsavoury methods by the PAP Government in Singapore. The President of the MCA also revealed that a year earlier Lee Kuan Yew had gone to the extent of trying to introduce a law which would make a member of the Legislative Assembly forfeit his seat the moment he ceased to be a member of his party, and which provided that his seat would be filled not through a by-election but by nomination by the party concerned.[101] 'This', the MCA President declared, 'is what I call a PAP brand of guided democracy. You can imagine what [Lee Kuan Yew] will do if he is the Prime Minister of Malaysia.'[102]

Although the PAP's attacks on the MCA had started some time earlier, it was not until a few days after the campaign had officially begun that the UMNO came firmly to the defence of its partner. In addition to repeating many of the charges made by the MCA, the UMNO leaders also stated quite categorically that the PAP was an unwelcome suitor and that they had no intention of abandoning the MCA in its favour. To them it made no sense for the PAP to claim that it was opposed only to the MCA and that it was keen to co-operate with the UMNO. Any attack on the MCA was an attack on the Alliance and hence on the UMNO as well. In attempting to split the Alliance, the PAP was contributing to nobody's victory except Soekarno's, and this was precisely what the Indonesians were hoping for.[103] With reference to the PAP's intention of contributing to the emergence of an enlightened leadership in co-operation with the UMNO, the Tengku declared: 'The PAP wants to teach us what is good for us. We know what is good for us, and what is

101 *Sin Chew Jit Poh*, 30 March 1964.
102 *Straits Echo*, 30 March 1964.
103 *Ibid.* 6 April 1964.

bad. What the PAP really wants is to displace the MCA.
They say they want to join the UMNO, but we don't want
them'.[104]   On one occasion the Tengku went to the extent
of saying that the UMNO would stick by the MCA even
if only five of its candidates were returned because of its
achievements and its 'commendable objectives'.[105]   But
there were also less temperate comments from UMNO
leaders.   In accusing the PAP of being anti-Malay, Syed
Ja'afar Albar (the Secretary-General of the UMNO), for
example, warned that party 'to stop being aggressive to the
Malays and instigating them; otherwise the Malays would
abandon democracy and use fists to teach the PAP the
meaning of democracy'.[106]

Despite these rebuffs, the PAP continued to refrain from
attacking the UMNO and its leadership.   But there was
one change of tactic.   Having originally emphasized that
the UMNO was itself not too enthusiastic about its association with the MCA, it now began to argue that whatever
its sympathies the brute facts of politics would soon compel the UMNO to accept the PAP's offer of co-operation.
In this connexion, Lee Kuan Yew observed:

If all the nine [Parliamentary candidates] win, an
agonizing reappraisal will have to be made.   In the heat
of the elections, it is said that even though there are
only five MCA M.P.s left, UMNO will carry on with
the MCA.   That may well be.   But can UMNO leaders go through the awful predicament of pretending for
the next five years that these five MCA M.P.s really
represent the urban Chinese — five men who have won
by UMNO's leave and licence in Malay rural areas?
The Tengku knows that good leadership is the reconciling of ideal solutions with the realities of life.   If the
urban areas, constituting more than half the people of
Malaya, give their verdict for the winds of change, no
leader can afford to ignore it.   Parliamentary democracy . . . will work only if people choose rationally from

104 *Sunday Times,* 15 March 1964.
105 *Malay Mail,* 24 April 1964.
106 *Sin Chew Jit Poh,* 4 April 1964.

the alternatives they are offered in an election. The ideal is never offered.[107]

The Tengku, Lee argued, had said many things against the PAP in the course of the campaign because he was hurt by its attacks on the MCA. After the heat of the elections had worn off, and when there was a 'more sober, cooler climate', he and the other leaders of the UMNO would 'reappraise the situation' and decide to co-operate with the PAP.[108] It did not matter whether the Tengku liked or disliked him; future developments would be determined by 'basic political factors'.[109]

While continuing its relentless attack on the MCA, the PAP also argued that there was really no need for it to spend any effort on destroying that party since it had discredited itself through its own actions. As stated by Inche Othman Wok, Singapore's Minister for Social Affairs, 'If the MCA loses this election it will be their own fault and not the fault of the PAP, because since they were elected in 1959 they have done nothing for the people in the urban areas. Their leaders were only interested in making easy money.'[110] The real battle in the urban areas was therefore between the PAP and the SF.

The PAP's attack on the SF was based mainly on the argument that the latter was heavily infiltrated, if not controlled, by the communists and that it was working hand-in-glove with the PKI (Indonesian Communist Party) to bring about Malaysia's downfall. In an attempt to incriminate the SF the PAP repeatedly posed questions for it to answer,[111] questions which plainly suggested that the party was the tool of the PKI and that it was working closely with the Barisan Sosialis and with known communists in Singapore.[112] The PAP, in contrast, was not a

107 *Straits Times*, 25 April 1964.

108 *Sunday Times*, 12 April 1964.

109 *Straits Echo*, 25 March 1964.

110 *Straits Times*, 27 March 1964.

111 On one occasion a list of twenty questions was posed for the SF to answer, and this was followed by another list of seven. See *Sin Chew Jit Poh*, 31 March and 1 April 1964.

112 Barisan Sosialis speakers in fact addressed some SF rallies.

communist front but a genuine socialist party which had
a realistic appraisal of the country's economic problems.
Voters were warned not to fall for the glib talk of the SF
simply because they could not get social justice by supporting the MCA. The SF's main interest was not the achievement of social justice but the creation of chaos and dissatisfaction which would undermine democratic values in
the country. Just as leaders of the MCA were held up
as examples of the political bankruptcy of their party,
those of the SF were taunted as being mere puppets of
ruthless behind-the-scene operators. The latter were said
to be the main enemy, and the MCA was given the back-
handed compliment of being the lesser of the two evils.
Observed Lee Kuan Yew in this connexion: 'Where the
choice is between only the MCA and the Socialist Front,
out with the Socialist Front. For while the MCA has
been a bane on our society, the Socialist Front will be a
blight on Malaysia'.[113]

In the course of emphasizing the dangers of supporting
the SF, the PAP also explained why it was the most appropriate party to deal with the communists. It had waged
a life-and-death battle against them in Singapore and knew
the way they worked. Unlike the MCA, it was able to
win the battle for the hearts and minds of the people not
only through open argument and debate but by following
the type of social and economic policies which could remove the source of basic dissatisfaction.[114] 'The PAP',
declared Lee Kuan Yew, 'has withstood the fire of the
Communists and survived because of a consistent and practical policy implemented by a whole group of effective
leaders, tried and tested.'[115] Although the situation in
Malaya had not reached the same proportions, every effort
had to be made to prevent a repetition of what had earlier
happened in Singapore. But this would be difficult as
long as the Government did not handle its problems intel-
ligently. In elaborating on this, Lee Kuan Yew observed:

[113] *Straits Times,* 25 April 1964.
[114] *Sin Chew Jit Poh,* 6 April 1964.
[115] *Straits Times,* 25 March 1964.

What Malaysia wants is a policy which can keep the
Malay mass base from communist influence and can win
back the support from the cities and towns, and wipe
out fury and dissatisfaction .... The long-term policy
should be to use persuasion and evident improvement
in the cities to win over the support of the people ....
The UMNO has got the support of the rural Malay
masses and the PAP has an effective and wise policy to
counter-attack communist sabotage in the cities and
towns. A government with a combination of these two
good qualities is the best answer to the communist challenge. It is the best way to maintain peace and security, to accelerate economic and political development
and to raise the living standards of the people.[116]

Continuing, Lee pointed out that the UMNO was then
having to counter Indonesian propaganda aimed at the
Malay masses and that it was quite possible that racial and
cultural chauvinism would turn many Malays into Indonesian sympathisers. It was therefore essential that the
UMNO should form a government that reflected the
strength of the Malay population. It had to win the
battle for the loyalty of the Malay community but, in
order to do that, it had to 'learn the methods of the PAP,
the methods [it] used skilfully in counter-attacking the sabotage activities of the communists in the urban areas'.[117]

In attacking the SF, the PAP also accused it of playing
up to Chinese chauvinism by using language, education
and other cultural issues to encourage dissatisfaction and
thereby to increase its support in the urban areas. Unfortunately, the Malay leadership in the country was
unable to differentiate between communists and Chinese
chauvinists, and hence attacked them as one. This had
complicated matters in the urban areas because hostility
to the communists had easily become translated into hostility towards those who wanted to improve the position of
the Chinese.[118]

116 *Sin Chew Jit Poh*, 6 April 1964.
117 *Loc. cit.*
118 *Loc. cit.*

Like the MCA, but with greater vigour, the SF accused the PAP of being a dictatorial party which would use every opportunity to erode democratic practices and institutions if it came to power. It was said to have ruthlessly and methodically eliminated all effective opposition in Singapore, and was plainly branded as a 'fascist party living on lies and deceit'.[119] To embellish the image, Lee Kuan Yew was described as being 'more like a Hitler or a Mussolinni, but with less polish and skill'.[120] Rajaratnam, Singapore's Minister for Culture, was compared to Goebbels.[121] It was pointed out that the constitution of the PAP was further proof of its undemocratic character, since control was virtually in the hands of a single person, the Secretary-General.

The SF also belittled the PAP's achievements in Singapore by pointing out that although the problems there were relatively easy to handle the progress which had taken place was insufficient. The Government's achievements in low-cost housing (for which the PAP had gained a considerable reputation) were dismissed as unimpressive, since nothing but 'skyscraper slums' had been built.[122]

Finally, the SF denounced the PAP for being a 'bogus socialist party' which was bent on 'disrupting the unity of the working class and small businessmen'.[123] The only genuine socialist party in the country was the SF. The PAP claimed to be a socialist party, but followed policies which bore no resemblance to socialism. It also preferred

119 *Straits Times*, 26 March 1964.

120 *Malay Mail*, 28 March 1964.

Lee Kuan Yew's character was a subject for comment by the other parties as well. Zulkiflee bin Muhammad (PMIP) described him as 'a bee which, when touched, tended to sting'. (*Straits Times*, 1 April 1964.) Dato Haji Hassan bin Yunos, the Mentri Besar of Johore, compared him to 'a hungry dog. You feed him out of pity when you see his pathetic look. But when he is well fed, he turns around and bites you.' (*Straits Times*, 3 April 1964.) Tan Siew Sin felt that he was more reminiscent of 'a chameleon, a remarkable creature which can adjust its colour to its surroundings'. *Sunday Mail*, 29 March 1964.

121 *Sin Chew Jit Poh*, 28 March 1964.

122 *Sunday Gazette*, 29 March 1964.

123 *Sin Chew Jit Poh*, 27 March 1964.

to see the right-wing Alliance win rather than the left-wing SF, and devoted a great deal of its energy to maligning genuine socialist leaders. It maliciously used false propaganda to frighten people away from the SF, and had conjured up fictitious enemies in order to justify its participation in the elections. Even the Alliance Government by abolishing the Emergency Laws in 1960, had recognized that there was no such thing as a 'Red menace'; but the PAP had chosen not to believe this. Said Lim Kean Siew in this connexion:

> The PAP ... has to create this bogey in order to make itself useful; otherwise what excuse has it got to come to Malaya to attack democratic socialist parties like ourselves, whilst pretending itself to be democratic and socialist? In fact, it is beating the drums of hysteria that will lead to militarism and dictatorship which will give rise to oppression, discontent and finally to revolution. The creation of the PAP bogey-man is what, in fact, will give rise to the ultimate revolution and chaos and bloodshed.[124]

Since the present study is limited to the parliamentary election, it is not the intention in this chapter to give any special attention to issues which were specifically related to the state elections. However, there were some areas where such issues featured prominently in the contest for parliamentary seats. This was most evident in Kelantan and Penang.

In Kelantan, one of the main arguments used by the Alliance was that the preceding five years of PMIP rule in the state had brought nothing but misery and economic stagnation. In contrast, the other states had prospered under Alliance rule. The case of Trengganu, a neighbouring state where the PMIP had been in power between 1959 and 1961 before being replaced by the Alliance, was the one most frequently brought up to heighten this contrast between Alliance and PMIP rule. Since assuming control, the Alliance had poured in a great deal of money

[124] *Sunday Gazette,* 29 March 1964.

into that state, and the attention of voters in Kelantan was constantly drawn to this fact with the promise that they could expect similar things if they returned the Alliance to power. Experience had also shown that the PMIP, which had come to power in Kelantan by posing as the champion of Malay rights and 'Islamic principles of administration', had been able to promote neither. It was the Malay community, the Alliance argued, which had benefited most from the vast development schemes in the other states, since the emphasis was always on rural development. This would be even more apparent in the case of Kelantan if the Alliance were to be returned to power, not only because there was more room for development in that state but because the vast majority of the population there was Malay. Thus it was the Malay community which suffered most as a result of PMIP rule.

Five days before polling day the Alliance caused a sensation by exposing an alleged PMIP plan to lease 375,000 acres of fringe jungle land in Kelantan, one-fifth of the total acreage of the state, to a Chinese company from Singapore interested in logging and mining.[125] The last days of the campaign saw the Alliance make a frantic attempt to topple the PMIP government on this single issue, attention being focussed on the fact that it was a *Chinese* company to which the PMIP had 'mortgaged' one-fifth of Kelantan. It was also emphasized that the land was being given away tax and rent free for a period of thirty-three years, and that the only financial arrangement was that substantial contributions would be made to the PMIP's own coffers. Leaflets exposing this 'treachery' were quickly distributed throughout the state, and in them the Alliance maintained:

> The PMIP has been forced to mortgage Ulu Kelantan[126] because the party wants money for its election expenditure . . . . Because of this PMIP treachery the Malays of Kelantan will suffer humiliation for 33 years. The

[125] *Straits Times*, 21 April 1964.

[126] The land in question was in Ulu Kelantan, the state's largest district.

> PMIP has committed the greatest treachery in Kelan-
> tan's history, against the Malay race, Malay land and the
> Islamic religion.... Because of money and because the
> PMIP is power-mad, it is willing to leave the Malays
> in poverty and hand over Kelantan to the Chinese.

In addition to the normal methods of distribution, the
Alliance air-dropped half a millon copies of this leaflet in
Kelantan two days before the elections.

The tail end of the PMIP's campaign was understandably taken up in refuting the various charges concerning
this alleged 'land deal'. It was argued that the plan in
question was for the purpose of developing new land in
Kelantan, and that there was absolutely no question of
the Malays being betrayed. In any event, nothing had
been finalized and it was therefore absurd for the Alliance
to suggest that there had been a deliberate attempt at
secrecy. This issue aside, a point frequently emphasized
by the PMIP was that Kelantan was the last remaining
stronghold of the Malay community, the only state which,
by refusing Alliance rule, had averted Chinese domination. Only the PMIP could continue to keep Kelantan a
'pure' Malay state, and save it from being exposed to ex-
ploitation by the Chinese. The voters were also reminded
that they had a wider responsibility in this respect, because it was only by keeping the PMIP in power in their
own state that they would be able to fight a rear-guard
battle on behalf of the country's entire Malay community.

Thus the campaign in Kelantan was to a very large extent dominated by the struggle for the control of the State
Assembly. The parliamentary and state compaigns were
even less differentiated than they were in the other states,[127]
and it was very common for the parliamentary candidates
of both parties to base their appeal on the desirability of
having their own party returned at the state level.

With the creation of Malaysia, the Central Government
had begun making plans for the creation of a common

[127] In most of the other states, however, this was the result of the
dominance of national over state issues.

market and this implied, among other things, the loss of Penang's free port status. The future of this status thus became an important issue there and featured prominently in the state as well as the national campaign. The SF was the most outspoken critic of the Central Government's proposals, and set out to establish itself as the main defender of Penang's rights. The chief purpose of the common market proposals, it argued, was to save Singapore's economy from collapsing. Penang was being deprived of its free port status merely to encourage the growth of industries in Singapore.[128] It was also alleged that the Alliance had undertaken in its 1959 manifesto to protect Penang's free port status. This promise was now broken and the Government, instead of holding a referendum on the subject, was riding rough-shod over the wishes of the people.[129] 'If the Socialist Front is voted into the State Government', one of the party's leaders declared, 'we will immediately hold a referendum with a simple "yes" or "no" answer as to whether or not the people of Penang want to lose their free port privilege. We will also strive for a proper and adequate guarantee from the Central Government that it [will] not change the wishes of the people of Penang.'[130] As a concrete measure, the SF suggested applying 'the principle of zoning and bonded areas' whereby Penang Island could remain a free zone while Province Wellesley (the mainland component of the state of Penang) remained within the common market area.[131]

The UDP also emphasized the importance of protecting Penang's free port status, and maintained that the state's chances of making industrial progress ultimately depended on it. Indonesian confrontation and falling rubber prices had already hurt Penang considerably, and the proposed common market would only worsen the situation. The party dissociated itself from the SF's proposals on the subject, and its leader, Dr. Lim Chong Eu, called the principle

---

128 *Malay Mail,* 4 April 1964.
129 *Straits Times,* 31 March 1964.
130 *Ibid.* 20 April 1964.
131 *Ibid.* 28 March 1964.

of zoning 'a shameless betrayal' of the people of Penang.[132] Addressing a rally, he told his audience that every vote for a UDP candidate was a vote for the retention of Penang's free port status. 'I am quite certain', he declared, 'that if 100,000 voters in Penang vote for the UDP in order to show the Central Government that we want to retain the free port status, then the Central Government must accept the will of the people.'[133]

For its part, the Alliance argued that no firm decision had been made by the Central Government on this question, and that in any event no attempt would be made to force the people of Penang into accepting a change in their island's status.[134] It was also pointed out that, by shelving the matter temporarily, the Alliance was in fact giving everyone a chance to understand the implications of the common market. Further, the stand taken by the SF was not necessarily in Penang's interests, because there was every possibility that the common market might prove successful, and the acquisition of a permanent free port status might therefore only deprive the state of the opportunity of joining it at a later stage.[135]

Both in Kelantan and Penang, a common strategy adopted by the Alliance was to warn the voters of the dire consequences which would follow if they chose to elect another party, since by doing so they would inevitably incur the hostility of the Central Government. Those in Kelantan were constantly reminded of the difficulty which the Central Government had had in co-operating with the PMIP state government and how this had prevented the extension of Federal land development schemes into that state. This was accompanied by promises of vast sums of

---

[132] *Straits Echo*, 7 April 1964.

The SF in turn accused Dr. Lim Chong Eu of 'shamelessly betraying' the people of Penang on the question of the island's free port status. 'This very able champion of our free port status', revealed the Chairman of Penang SF, 'voted against its retention at a meeting of the then Settlement Council on 5 December 1956.' *Sunday Times*, 12 April 1964.

[133] *Straits Echo*, 7 April 1964.

[134] *Ibid.* 24 March 1964.

[135] *Ibid.* 16 March 1964.

money from the Federal purse in the event of an Alliance victory. The argument in Penang was that the preservation of its free port status depended on whether or not a 'friendly' Government came into power. While state Alliance leaders argued that they were the only ones who could gain the co-operation of the Central Government, national leaders made it quite plain that they would not have much sympathy for Penang's interests if they had to deal with a hostile state government. Said Tan Siew Sin:

> It is open to the Federal Government by a short amendment to the Customs Ordinance to abolish the [free port] status with one stroke of the pen. We will take into account the wishes of Penang, but, if there is a hostile State Government in Penang, the position might be quite different. This does not constitute a threat but I am only stating the facts of life.[136]

Penang voters were further warned that Federal grants might be cut off if the SF were to come to power in their state. This and other similar warnings also came from the PAP. Lee Kuan Yew, for example, observed at a rally:

> No Central Government of Malaysia can afford to have Penang or any other State Government used as a base for Communist subversion, particularly at a time of pressure and crisis as a result of Indonesia's confrontation.... The revenue of the State Government of Penang is negligible, and like Kelantan and Trengganu, it must depend on Federal grants for all development projects.... Eventually a State Government at loggerheads with the Central Government will find itself suspended just as the Indian Government suspended the State Government of Kerala.[137]

136 *Straits Times,* 31 March 1964.
137 *Straits Echo,* 20 April 1964.

VII

The Campaign

ALTHOUGH the campaign did not officially begin till March 21 (nomination day) the parties had spent the best part of the preceding five or six months preparing themselves for the elections. The battle for voters was thus already a few months old by the time the campaign was formally launched; but, naturally, there was a marked difference in both the volume and style of party activity before and after nomination day.

In discussing the campaign, it will be helpful first of all to look at the way in which the parties organized themselves for the elections. The three major parties, the Alliance, the PMIP and the SF, will be discussed first. Differences between their organization and that of some of the other parties will be mentioned later.

Both the Alliance and the PMIP had a functioning local organization during the inter-election period; but this organization was primarily geared to the 'normal' working of the parties. With the approach of the elections, new and more elaborate structures had to be created, aimed at turning the party into a 'fighting force'. However, especially at the lower levels, this did not mean that a totally separate organization was set up: the permanent structure in many ways formed a basis for the new allocation of power and responsibility.

The Alliance election machine was under the general control of an Election Committee of four members, assisted by seven secretaries.[1] Heading this Committee was Inche Senu bin Abdul Rahman, who had earlier been the

---

[1] The seven secretaries were made up of the Political Secretary of the Deputy Prime Minister, the Political Secretaries of the Ministries of Education, Agriculture and Health, and representatives (one each) from the UMNO, MCA and MIC.

Ambassador to Indonesia and West Germany.[2] While this Committee was the highest policy-making authority for the election, responsibility for administration was entrusted to a central 'Operations Room' in Kuala Lumpur, headed by the Assistant Minister for Rural Development, Inche Abdul Rahman bin Ya'akub.[3] Under him were six secretaries, each in charge of a different function: 'legal affairs', 'transport', 'rallies', 'publicity', 'police liaison', and 'election machinery'.[4] The Operations Room, described as the 'nerve centre of the party's election machinery',[5] came into full operation on 1 March, and was the scene of feverish activity throughout the campaign period. Aimed primarily at co-ordinating the party's election effort, it was here that plans were worked out for the speaking tours of national leaders,[6] the printing and distribution of posters, etc. As the campaign progressed the Operations Room also received estimates of party support in the various constituencies, on the basis of which charts were prepared depicting fluctuations in support. This information was of considerable help in deciding on the priorities which were to be given to the different states and constituencies; most of it (particularly the details of constituencies where the party was reported to be weak) was kept secret.

At the next level were the various State Election Committees, with their own directors and secretaries.[7]

2 Inche Senu was himself a candidate, and was later made the Minister for Information and Broadcasting.

3 Inche Abdul Rahman was from Sarawak, and had earlier helped to organize the Alliance election effort there. He was also a member of the Election Committee.

4 The total staff of the Operations Room, however, numbered more than thirty. Some of these were volunteers.

5 And said to have been modelled on the Operations Room of the Ministry of National Development.

6 There was a constant demand from all the constituency organizations for visits by the party's national leaders, and careful planning was necessary (based, to a large extent, on an assessment of 'need') in preparing the itineraries for important figures, especially the Tengku, Tun Razak, Mr. Tan Siew Sin and Syed Ja'afar Albar.

7 Each state also had its own Operations Room, run on lines similar to the one in Kuala Lumpur.

Each committee had under it individuals who, like their counterparts at the national level, were in charge of separate functions.[8] These secretaries in turn had their equivalents at the constituency level, with whom they were to liaise directly.[9] Each parliamentary and state constituency also had its own election committee ('Action Committees') to take charge of the campaign in its own limited area. At a yet lower level a 'supervisor' was appointed for each polling district, whose duties included the mobilization of all party branches (and hence election workers) in his district.

At the base of the Alliance organization was a huge work force[10] which was relied on for such duties as putting up posters (and sometimes tearing down opponents' posters), establishing and maintaining links between the party and the electorate, and submitting reports concerning the distribution of support. Because of its size, this work force was probably also useful in conveying to the electors the impression that the Alliance was by far the strongest and the most widely-supported party in the country.

A distinction should be drawn, however, between the rural and urban areas. First of all, there were on the whole far more workers for each rural constituency. To some extent, this might be explained by the fact that the Alliance had more supporters in the rural areas, but such factors as the presence of fewer competing attractions (to political activity) in the rural areas, and the greater availability of the self-employed rural population for party work, were also important. Further, because more people were illiterate in the rural areas, there had to be a greater concentration on personal contact than on written propaganda, and this meant that more ground had to be covered. In addition, the cost of workers was consider-

[8] There were committees for 'Finance' and 'Election Procedure' in addition to those on the national list.

[9] In other words, the secretary in charge of, say, transport at the constituency level would communicate directly with the person in charge of transport at the state level.

[10] Estimated at about 100,000 by one of the party's national organizers.

ably higher in the urban areas, where the party often found it necessary to compete with more employment opportunities, and hence was forced to offer more money.[11] It was conceded by party officials that in some cases there was only an employer-employee relationship between the party and its workers; other workers were influenced both by party loyalty and the offer of money. Given a 'market' situation where the different parties were to some extent competing for a limited number of workers, this was almost inevitable. Finally, there was also some difference — related to the differences in the number of workers — in the nature of the work done by party workers in the rural and urban areas. In the former, a systematic attempt was made to group the houses in each constituency into units of about ten, and to place a worker in charge of each unit. It was the duty of every worker to visit the households in his charge as often as possible (at least twice a week) so as to create and keep alive an interest in the party. Each worker had also to submit a weekly report on how support was distributed between the different parties in his own area.[12] These reports were pooled at the constituency level, and a graph was kept depicting support (in the parliamentary and state constituencies) at the end of each week.[13] These estimates were transmitted to the state headquarters and thence to the Operations Room in Kuala Lumpur.

Due mainly to the relative insufficiency of workers, organization along these lines was hardly practicable in the urban areas; further, while in the rural areas, where most

11 In fact, there was seldom any payment of wages in the rural areas, and most of the money spent on workers was in the form of small allowances, where necessary, for food and transport.

12 The usual procedure was to designate households (stating the number of voters in each) as 'white' (i.e. safe Alliance voters), 'grey' (those classified as doubtful) and 'black' (those firmly committed to other parties). It was generally the practice not to spend too much time in trying to convert 'black' households. The effort was concentrated mainly on the 'greys', although brief visits were frequently made to 'white' households so as to keep interest alive.

13 It was a common practice, in preparing these graphs, to deduct 10 per cent. from the estimates submitted by party workers. It was claimed that this usually represented the degree of error, resulting from optimism.

people could be contacted at home in the evenings, part-time workers were quite adequate, similar methods would not work in the urban areas. Given the more compact nature of urban constituencies, the greater cost of workers there, and the relative convenience of holding rallies in them, the emphasis in such areas was placed on brisk tours of constituencies by the candidates and by groups of workers.

Certain other campaign preparations should perhaps also be mentioned. A few months before nomination day, the Alliance conducted a course in Kuala Lumpur for the chairmen, secretaries and/or publicity officers of all the divisions in the country. This was aimed at familiarizing these officials with the broad features of the party's campaign; indirectly, it must also have been hoped that a 'get-together' of this kind would help to work up enthusiasm in each constituency organization and so initiate some activity before the official commencement of the campaign. In some states (notably Perak) steps were also taken to employ or train professional speakers who could address smaller rallies. There was apparently a great demand for those with ability and, from one account, this offered temporary employment for youths who had left school but had been unable to find jobs.[14] In some cases the training scheme was quite elaborate, involving the use of tape recorders and the making of extempore speeches on given topics. In Perak, those selected to be speakers were given mimeographed booklets which explained the party's stand on all the issues that were likely to become prominent and also drew attention to the dishonesty and/or poor policies of other parties. It was, however, often necessary for these speakers to address their audiences 'off the cuff' on topics which had a purely local flavour.

With the approach of nomination day, each branch was supplied with 'polling cards' which were to be sent to the

[14] One of those hired in Perak, a youth who had finished his schooling, impressed the party so much that funds were raised after the election (mainly from successful candidates) to send him to Formosa for higher studies.

voters conveying such details as their registration numbers and polling stations. These cards were perforated in the middle and one half, kept in the party files, contained the relevant details of each voter, such as whether he was literate or illiterate, and, in the case of a Malay voter, whether he read *Rumi*[15] or *Jawi*,[16] and whether, on the basis of reports submitted by party workers, he was 'white', 'grey' or 'black'.[17] Since these cards were sent to voters essentially to help them to vote, those who were classified as 'black' were not generally sent their cards.

Alliance officials were agreed that the party was much better organized in 1964 than it had been in 1959. Generally, those involved in the party's election organization did not feel that it was either unwieldy or confusing. However, there were some who often found it more expedient not to adhere to the hierarchical channels of communication which had been formally established. In part, this was caused by the natural tendency to deal directly with individuals who were personally known, even if this meant by-passing established procedures. In the case of those who were prominent within the party but who were involved in directing operations at the state, rather than the national, level, there was also the obvious temptation to ignore the bureaucracy that had been set up in Kuala Lumpur and to attempt to get things done from the top — that is, by making requests direct to people like Tun Razak and Tan Siew Sin, who, although they were not members of the Election Committee, were important enough within the party to 'push' things if they felt so inclined. Some of those in charge at the state level probably also resented the implied superiority of the Election Committee and the Operations Room in Kuala Lumpur, especially when, as individuals, they considered themselves to be more important members of the party. The view was also expressed that it was the 'men on the spot' who were really in the thick of the battle and hence played a more

15 Romanized script.

16 Arabic script.

17 See footnote 12 of this Chapter.

important role, and that it was they who should decide
how the campaign was to be conducted; the national
bodies should exist more for their convenience (that is,
giving them financial and other help when they needed
it) than for the purpose of exercising control.[18]

Despite its highly centralized control, an interesting feature of the Alliance campaign was that when it came to
projecting the party's image, the emphasis was placed
largely on the *member* organizations. Thus to a very significant degree the spotlight was on the UMNO, the MCA
and the MIC. No doubt their different images were influenced by the fact of their common partnership in the Alliance and by the inter-communal slogans uttered, especially
by the national leaders; but there was no mistaking the
separate themes — the UMNO appealed as a Malay party,
the MCA as a Chinese party, and the MIC as an Indian
party. The fact that the different communities were to
some extent concentrated in different areas of the country
must have made this easier, but the need to adopt different
emphases was clearly a result (and an indication) of the continuing relevance of communalism in Malayan politics.
The Alliance must have realized that it was only through
the medium of its member organizations that support could
most effectively be channelled. Even the actual structure
of the election organization, as will be seen, was to some
extent influenced by this.

Although the Operations Room was meant to co-ordinate the entire Alliance election effort, the MCA operated
a modified version of it for its own purposes. During the
campaign period its headquarters in Kuala Lumpur was
converted into a semi-independent co-ordinating centre,
with interest limited to those constituencies where MCA
candidates were contesting. Many of the activities here
were similar to those in the Operations Room, itineraries

[18] One of those interviewed, a person who directed operations in one of
the states, complained that the Operations Room in Kuala Lumpur was 'all
bullshit', and that it had not been able to supply speakers when required
except for a few Ministers. He felt that it served no purpose to keep
charts and maps indicating support. These refinements were of no immediate benefit for the campaign.

being prepared for speaking tours by prominent members of the MCA, and up-to-date details kept of support in constituencies where there were MCA candidates. As with the Operations Room, there were maps depicting vital information about constituencies, such as the names and parties of the various candidates contesting, and the racial breakdown of the electorate for each seat.[19] Unlike the Operations Room, however, the MCA centre displayed some of the cartoons put up by the MCA attacking opposition parties and candidates; there was also a collection of opposition propaganda, presumably to keep party organizers reminded of the issues raised by their opponents.

Considering that the Operations Room was not meant to be limited to any particular section of the Alliance, one might be tempted to regard the MCA's parallel effort as superfluous. However, it is worth noting that the management of the Operations Room was predominantly in the hands of Malays. Although there was no reason to believe that this was the result of a deliberate move on the part of the UMNO,[20] there might have been some uneasiness in MCA quarters that the activities of the Operations Room might (perhaps only inadvertently) be biased in favour of concentrating on winning the Malay votes in the country, and hence on bolstering up the political future of the UMNO. It was thus safest for the MCA to make a special effort of its own, even if only to satisfy its supporters that it was in charge of its own affairs, since the mere

19 Since no racial breakdown was officially made available, the Alliance had compiled its own figures, employing people to go through each electoral register in detail. Although laborious, this presented no serious problems, since Malay, Chinese and Indian names are easily distinguishable.

20 There might have been some political advantage for the whole Alliance in this, since there was probably more to be gained from Malay voters by giving them the impression of a Malay-dominated effort than from non-Malay voters by giving them the reverse impression, or even the impression that the Malays were not in control. The UMNO, it must be remembered, was recognized by all as the 'senior' partner in the Alliance.

location of the Operations Room in the UMNO head-quarters might have cast some doubts on this.[21]

Although it may not specifically have influenced the decision to set up a separate Operations Room, there is no denying that the MCA had a compelling reason in 1964 to make a special effort over and above that of the Alliance as a whole. In addition to the obvious desire to win seats and thereby be a fairly strong partner in the Government, the MCA was in a sense also fighting for its own political survival as the main representative of the Chinese community. Admittedly these two factors must have been inextricably linked, but the threat posed by the PAP, particularly its hope of replacing the MCA as the UMNO's chief partner, led to a general feeling in the MCA that the outcome of the election would not be satisfactory merely if the Alliance won a good majority. It was also vital that the MCA should show no signs of a decline in support, since this might have been interpreted as a further step towards its demise. The PAP had repeatedly maintained that the MCA was already discredited, and that those who disbelieved this had only to wait for the outcome of the elections. Furthermore, a certain amount of disaffection had always been endemic in the MCA, and it was perhaps only the absence of an alternative[22] which had held it together. There was now some indication that many of the party's members, including some who were fairly prominent, welcomed the PAP's intervention and might have crossed over to that party the moment it showed strength at the expense of the MCA. Under these conditions, the MCA leaders probably decided that there was an urgent need to augment the *Alliance* effort with a special *MCA* one, directed

[21] For the Malays, it certainly seems to have been a matter of some satisfaction that the Alliance election machine was Malay-dominated. For example, in describing this machine a Malay newspaper commented: 'The Alliance Election Secretariat is situated on the third floor of the UMNO Malaya headquarters....Except for a Chinese and an Indian all the members of the Alliance Secretariat are influential UMNO personalities.' *Utusan Zaman*, 15 March 1964.

[22] That is, as the party in the Government which represented the Chinese.

specifically at the Chinese voters. The UMNO, recognizing the facts of the situation, and perhaps also mindful of the greater scope this offered for the Operations Room to concentrate its efforts on the Malay constituencies, obviously had no serious objections.

The first point to note about the PMIP's campaign organization is that it was influenced by the concentration of the party's efforts in the rural areas where the Malays are in the majority. Partly for this reason, and partly because, unlike the Alliance, the PMIP was not made up of different member organizations, there was much more uniformity in the way in which the party's campaign was both organized and conducted.

As early as the second week of October 1963, a Central Election Committee was formed, 'to give guidance and direction on election matters' to the state and branch levels of the party.[23] As a first step, this Committee requested all State Commissioners[24] to study in some detail the constituencies in their respective states and to make recommendations which the party could take into account in deciding where its candidates should be put up. The Commissioners were asked specifically for their estimates of the percentage of Malay voters, and the strength of the PMIP, in each constituency.[25]

Following the instructions of the Central Election Committee, State Election Committees were also set up throughout the country. As in the case of the Alliance, there was a functional allocation of responsibilities in these committees, although some of the functions appeared vague. In addition to a chairman, secretary, and treasurer, each of these committees had different individuals in charge of 'information' and 'research', and two persons — one from the party's women's section and the other 'pref-

[23] 'Communication from the Chairman of the Central Election Committee to all State Commissioners and Branch Secretaries'. (Mimeographed.)

[24] The Commissioners were the heads of the party organization in each state.

[25] *Loc. cit.*

erably' from its youth section — in charge of 'effort'.[26]
The Central Election Commitee's directive had drawn
special attention to the importance of the effort required
from the women's and youth sections. In this they were
no doubt influenced by the invaluable contributions to the
election effort made by similar sections in the Alliance,
particularly the UMNO. The directive read: 'As we
know, our women's section is still behind that of the opposition parties, particularly the UMNO. Therefore it is
imperative for us to make an immediate effort to rectify
our backwardness. . . . The duty of the members of the
women's section during the elections will be to explain
things to the voters, particularly through house-to-house
canvassing, until they are able to attract the womenfolk in
each constituency to support PMIP candidates.'[27] Concerning the youth effort, the directive stated: 'The Youths
should be a driving force no less important than the
women, because with the Youth's effort lies the success. . .
of any election. Therefore organize the youth force very
carefully.'[28]

Each parliamentary and state constituency also had its
own election committee, organized exactly along the same
lines as the state committees. The chairmen of the Parliamentary Constituency Committees were automatically
members of their respective State Committees,[29] and those
of the State Constituency Committees automatically belonged to the parliamentary ones.

What has just been described represents merely the minimum requirements laid down well in advance by the
national organizers. As the campaign approached, steps
were taken (possibly influenced by knowledge of the Alliance organization) to allocate more specific duties to individuals. Thus, by the time the campaign was actually in

26 The word *tenaga,* translated here as 'effort', usually means 'power'
or 'energy'.

27 *Loc. cit.*

28 *Loc. cit.*

29 The Chairmen of State Constituency Election Committees were also
included if the party was not contesting the parliamentary constituency to
which the state constituency belonged.

progress, it was common practice for each constituency committee to have sub-committees to look after functions like transport, food and drinks for workers, meetings, posters, and security.[30] There was also a further decentralization to the polling district level: each district had its own committee, and party branches were placed under its control for the duration of the campaign. Where more than one branch existed in any polling district, they were merged for the purposes of the election effort.

The PMIP also had a large number of workers, performing duties similar to those of their Alliance counterparts. However, each PMIP worker was given responsibility for a larger area; this was understandable since, from all accounts, the party had a smaller number of workers per constituency than the Alliance. The PMIP also kept graphs depicting support for the party, based on reports submitted by workers.

In comparison with that of the Alliance, the PMIP's election organization was less extensive and elaborate, in that there were fewer functions and a smaller number of workers; refinements like the Alliance Operations Room were also lacking. The PMIP's organization also seemed not to provide for functions to be allocated as specifically as in the Alliance. From actual observation of the way in which the campaign was conducted, however, the really significant difference appeared to lie mainly in the functioning of the organization and in the importance given to it by the party.

Through the setting up of new committees and the allocation of new responsibilities, the PMIP obviously sought to convert its existing structure into one aimed at turning the party into a 'fighting force' for the elections. Despite this, there was some evidence throughout the campaign that a major share of the responsibility for projecting the party's image lay with people *outside* this structure. Of particular significance were the various groups of religious

[30] It was the duty of the sub-committee for 'security' to report all incidents to state headquarters. It was up to the latter to decide whether or not a formal complaint was to be made to the police.

leaders and officials, to whom the party turned for the 'authoritative' exposition of its Islamic orientation. Being important opinion-leaders in many of the rural areas, these persons in many ways constituted the nucleus around which party support was built.[31]   This did not, however, mean that the formal election organization served no useful purpose; but, compared to the Alliance, the party seems to have relied less heavily on it.   During the campaign period, there seemed to be very little activity in many PMIP constituency headquarters: in one which was visited on the eve of polling day, although there were many supporters on the premises, almost all of them sat around doing nothing while some lay fast asleep on the floor. Alliance offices, in contrast, were invariably bustling with activity.

From a different viewpoint, and given the PMIP's reliance on the authority of traditional opinion leaders and the immediate appeal of its highly emotional religious and pro-Malay slogans, it is possible to argue that the very fact that the PMIP thought it necessary to have a 'rational' election organization on a fairly large scale is significant.   In this respect, the situation in 1964 was considerably different from that in 1959, and could be interpreted as representing a weakening of traditionalism.   Such an interpretation would not be wholly invalidated even if the new 'structure' was nothing more than a façade aimed at keeping up with the Alliance and giving the rank and file of the party's membership some sense of participation.

Of the other parties, the one that was best organized for the campaign was probably the SF.   This was only to be expected since, in terms of the number of candidates, it was the second largest party in the country.   Compared to the Alliance, however, a significant feature of the SF's election organization was the extent to which the state level operated independently of the national headquarters. This decentralization could perhaps be best explained in terms of the SF's apparent intention to concentrate on

[31] For an account of their activities in a selected constituency, see Chapter IX (a).

gaining power in some states. From most accounts the party's chief concern seems to have been the outcome in Penang, Selangor, Malacca and Johore.[32] Each of these states had a fairly vigorous organization of its own, and there was thus no advantage in a centralized election organization. Financially, too, the state and constituency levels were by no means as dependent on the national headquarters as were their Alliance counterparts; the fact that voluntary help by supporters was often more important than money, must have been partly responsible for this. This relative decentralization must also have been facilitated by the fact that each of the states mentioned had within its own organization some of the party's national leaders. Thus there was no risk that, at least in those areas where the party made its strongest bid, the absence of central control could lead to the projection of an image inconsistent with that preferred by the national leadership.

As part of its preparation for the campaign the Labour Party (one of the two partners in the SF) organized, during the third week of January 1964, a 'Leadership and Public Speaking Course' for delegates from all parts of the country. Papers were presented on a variety of subjects, most of them aimed at instructing those attending the course on certain aspects of government and elections, and on familiarizing them with issues which the party felt should be emphasized during the elections.[33] Said the Chairman in his opening address:

> Comrades, you must be able to convince the common people...that our Party possesses aims and plans that are better than those of the other parties including the Alliance. Victory in the coming general elections will

[32] Penang and Malacca were in a sense 'special' cases, since the party, by being in control of the municipal councils there, already had a 'base' in these states.

[33] Most of the papers were read by the party's own leaders. The two non-party speakers were Professor Ungku Aziz (Professor of Economics at the University of Malaya) who read a paper on 'The Rural Economy' and Mr. Ong Kah Seng, an official from the Election Commission, who spoke on 'Election Procedures'. There were also some speakers from the Barisan Sosialis in Singapore.

depend greatly on your knowledge, experience and tact-fulness. Our party speakers should change the old me-thod that is of just blindly attacking the opposition par-ties in public rallies without having any explanations, substantiation and proofs that are clear, to one that is more subtle and clear. You must also be able to answer clearly questions from the people about our manifesto, our objectives and our desires of establishing a society that is just and prosperous in our nation.[34]

Although it was very much in the limelight during the campaign, the PAP in fact had an unimpressive election organization. This was perhaps the result of the party's last-minute entry into Malayan politics, in consequence of which it had neither the branches nor the workers so valuable during elections. Hurried efforts were made to obtain premises and establish branches in those areas where the party put up candidates, but these were, in the main, of symbolic rather than real value. The adminis-tration of the campaign was controlled almost entirely by leaders from Singapore. Circumstances had made this in-evitable; but perhaps it was also felt that the projection of its 'Singapore' image might in fact prove advantageous since it was on the basis of its performance there (as well as the national fame of its leaders) that the PAP hoped to win support. Even party workers were frequently brought all the way from Singapore; this might have been made necessary because there was no time to recruit work-ers locally, but there was probably also a preference for 'trusted' or 'known' people who, under the circumstances, could only come from Singapore. The opinion was some-times expressed that the prominence of those who had been brought from Singapore had been resented by some poten-tial local supporters who otherwise might have come forward in larger numbers.

Some attention will now be given to the way in which the parties went about establishing contact with the voters.

[34] Labour Party, Malaya, 'Leadership and Public Speaking Course, held at the Training Camp, Morib, Selangor, on 16-18 January 1964'. Open-ing address by Inche Ishak bin Haji Mohammad, Chairman, Labour Party and SF, Malaya. (Mimeographed.)

Attention will, however, be confined to organized meetings and house-to-house visits; the mass media will be discussed in Chapter VIII.

Compared to 1959 there was a much greater emphasis on house-to-house canvassing in 1964, and there was general agreement among those interviewed that this was the most effective way of getting in touch with the voters. The Alliance in particular was convinced that it had not used this form of campaigning sufficiently in 1959 and, in some measure, attributed its defeat in Kelantan and Trengganu to this fact: the PMIP, it was claimed, had succeeded in building up its support in these states mainly through establishing close contacts with the people by visiting them in their homes.

For reasons already mentioned, such as the availability of more workers and the greater likelihood of contacting people in their homes, house-to-house campaigning was both easier and more effective in the rural areas. The problems faced by party workers were reduced by the fact that *kampongs* (villages) were usually fairly compact units. This kind of canvassing gave party workers more scope, not only to discuss local problems but also to fit their approach to the educational level of the persons they were talking to; it was also possible for them to give more detailed instructions on voting procedure, which was more complicated in 1964 because both parliamentary and state elections were being held simultaneously. Since visits of this kind were not feasible in the urban areas, parties were usually quite satisfied if each candidate could make a token visit to homes and shop-houses in some areas of his constituency merely to introduce himself and to shake hands with a few people.[35] They thus had to rely more heavily on rallies than they would probably have preferred.

All parties held regular rallies during the campaign period. These fell into three categories. First, there were a few mammoth rallies held in big urban areas, which

35 One of the SF organizers, however, felt that it was often necessary to spend some time in the homes of educated people, since they were interested in hearing the party's stand explained to them.

were perhaps intended as much to be shows of strength as means of contacting voters in the mass. There was usually a great deal of planning and organization behind these rallies, publicity being given to them by party workers in advance. Second, there were those rallies which, although they were aimed at particular constituencies, were addressed by 'national' speakers. These were usually arranged through liaison between the state and national levels of the parties. Finally, there were the rallies which were organized mainly at the constituency level, at which only the candidates concerned and/or local speakers were present. These were naturally the most frequent, although they were the least significant in terms of attendance.

The PAP was the party which most consistently attracted huge crowds. While at first glance this might appear surprising in terms of the party's eventual performance, there generally appeared to be no correlation between the size of rallies and actual performance at the polls. In the case of the PAP it is of course possible that a large number of people turned up merely out of curiosity to see and hear people (particularly Lee Kuan Yew) whom they had heard so much about, and who had been given so much publicity in the press. Attendance at Alliance rallies was certainly much less impressive. In fact, apart from its 'spectaculars' (at which twenty to thirty thousand people were present), the Alliance did not even succeed in attracting as many people to its rallies as the SF. The situation was similar to that witnessed in Singapore a few months earlier (see Chapter XI): there it was the Barisan Sosialis which quite clearly attracted the biggest crowds, although it was the PAP which won the election.

This phenomenon could perhaps be best explained by the evaluation of rallies made by the parties themselves. References to the size of rallies were quite frequently made by party workers and officials in the course of interviews, and a big turnout was always given as evidence that the prospects of victory were good. At the same time there was also agreement that it was only the supporters of each

party who usually turned up at its rallies.[36]   PMIP leaders, for example, felt that the main value of rallies (especially when they were well attended) was that they helped
to stir up enthusiasm and self-confidence among party
supporters, and encouraged them to feel 'strong' and 'boast-
ful'; in listening to his leaders, the average supporter could
also learn all the arguments he could use in discussing
politics with others.   Thus (except in the case of the PAP,
for reasons already given) the size of rallies was probably
more indicative of the number of dedicated supporters a
party had than of its electoral prospects, although the two
bore some relation to each other.

With a few exceptions, the absence of audience participation — even in the form of asking questions — was a
feature of rallies throughout the country.   There was
hardly any heckling or booing, and speeches were usually
completed without any interruptions.   This need not be
surprising since, according to the parties, it was their supporters who usually made up the audience at their rallies.
There may, however, be other implications of this aspect
of rallies which need to be discussed.

In reviewing an election in another country, one writer
has observed: 'More sinister was the fear of physical violence, illustrated by the absence of members of the rival
party at political meetings, and in a reluctance to ask

---

36 There were, however, a few cases where parties sent their own supporters to rallies held by their rivals in an attempt to disrupt proceedings
through organized heckling. The PAP seemed to be the party against
which such attempts were most frequently made, and, from all accounts,
this action was SF-inspired. When, following his earlier tactics in Singapore, Lee Kuan Yew invited hecklers to share the microphone with him
individually to debate things in the open, the police intervened and made
it clear that only authorized persons were allowed to speak at rallies.
A similar incident in Kota Bharu (in Kelantan) took a different course.
At a huge rally held by the PMIP towards the end of the campaign, at
which about 20,000 people were present, groups of Alliance supporters
(who had arrived in lorryloads) began hooting and heckling the moment
the first speaker started addressing the audience. Raising his voice, the
speaker informed the police who were present that if they did not put
a stop to the disturbance they would have to take responsibility for what
might follow. This was sufficient to take care of the situation.

hostile questions'.[37] In Malaya, too, as indeed in many other countries, there was some fear that rallies could in certain cases spark off violence. For this reason it was not uncommon for pleas to be made that it was always wise to have certain limits to the enthusiasm displayed at rallies. In warning of the danger of violence erupting at rallies one newspaper observed:

> Barracking is by no means a harmless pursuit. By its provocative and infectious nature it has a built-in capacity for violence. . . . Many of the ugly incidents of the past probably had their source in displays of unduly clamorous partisanship. . . . At the various political rallies, for instance, heckling in the true sense of the term is virtually unknown. Not that we consider it a particularly desirable development in the electioneering process. But the booing and slogan shouting that goes on is in actuality an inarticulate, degenerate form of heckling. It is a negative approach, vulgar, meaningless and destructive of the spirit of give-and-take which should underline political campaigning.[38]

Although there were in fact very few cases of violence during the elections, the fact that this fear existed was itself significant. But such fears need not be the only explanation for the relatively inactive audiences at rallies. If, as seems quite possible (especially with party prompting), attendance at rallies was in fact taken to be an indication of support, this situation need not have had sinister implications. It could, however, have been indicative of a lack of political sophistication.

Just as heckling and violence were generally absent, so were any extravagant exhibitions of support and enthusiasm, as witnessed, for example, in Nigeria and Sierra Leone. There were certainly no equivalents to the shouts of 'Zee-ee-k' and 'Awo-o-o' (by supporters of Azikwe and Awolowo, in Western Nigeria) or to audience participation in the form of chanting slogans (Sierra Leone).[39]

---

[37] Mackenzie and Robinson, *Five Elections in Africa*, p. 100 (Chapter on the Western Region of Nigeria).

[38] *Straits Echo*, 29 March 1964.

[39] See especially pp. 65 and 210 of Mackenzie and Robinson, *op. cit.*

There were no jingles and no provocative political songs. With a few exceptions, there was also very little showmanship on the part of speakers. It was, however, not uncommon for prayers to be said at the commencement of rallies in Malay rural areas, particularly in areas where the PMIP was strong.[40] The Alliance and the PAP often ended their rallies with shouts of 'Merdeka' (freedom).

No party could hold a rally without first obtaining permission from the police. The number of rallies per night in each constituency was always strictly controlled, and steps were taken to ensure that rallies were not held too close to each other. These arrangements were no doubt aimed at minimizing the likelihood of incidents and at making sure that the resources of the police, who were always in evidence at rallies, would not be stretched beyond certain limits. Whenever important ministers were present, detachments of the police force and often the riot squad were in attendance.[41] All speeches made at rallies were tape-recorded by the police, and this procedure, in addition to keeping records of the proceedings of each rally, was probably also aimed at discouraging rash statements; inflammatory communal statements, for example, were forbidden by law. Naturally this was not very popular among opposition parties, and often, in the course of speeches, speakers made a point of saying that they were not afraid to speak their minds — despite the presence of tape-recorders. One might perceive in this situation some restrictions on the freedom of the campaign, since the freedom both to hold public meetings and to speak freely at them are prerequisites of a free campaign. This freedom, however, must always be measured against the preservation of law and order. While it is likely that some of the opposition parties felt an inhibiting influence in the official scrutiny of their activities, it would be unrealistic to con-

40 In areas where the PMIP was strong, the Alliance took every opportunity to show that it was every bit as concerned with Islam as the PMIP.

41 Detachments of the riot squad had been sent to all parts of the country during the campaign period. Kelantan and Trengganu — the former in particular — appeared to receive the biggest share.

clude that they were denied effective means of communicating with the voters.

In the Malay rural areas it was also a common practice to hold small meetings (*cheramahs*), for which no police permission was necessary. These were usually held in the homes of party supporters and, where possible, in those of people with some standing in their respective *kampongs*. Attendance was usually between 50 and 200. Each meeting had a speaker (either the candidate or, if he was not present, some party worker) whose speech was usually followed by a discussion during which questions were asked by members of the audience. Refreshments were always provided, usually from party funds.

Both the Alliance and the PMIP placed great emphasis on the value of *cheramahs*. As social occasions, they served to tighten the bonds between the party and its supporters.[42] As political meetings they provided a better opportunity than rallies for detailed exposition of policy.[43] Unlike rallies, they also offered some scope for audience participation.

During the campaign period, the entire country was flooded with posters. In a frantic attempt not to be outdone by their rivals, all parties went in for some extravagance in this respect.[44] Most common were the posters which merely depicted party symbols, and every available surface — walls, tree trunks, lamp posts, bridges, milestones, windscreens, and in some cases, even traffic signs — was subjected to decoration. Banners were extremely common, especially in the rural areas, and arches were also

[42] As in the case of rallies, it was commonly felt that only the supporters of a party (and perhaps some undecided voters) turned up at its *cheramahs*. Often prayers were said at the commencement of these meetings. The experience of praying (and eating) together might also have helped to create and strengthen bonds.

[43] Some Alliance candidates also claimed that they used their *cheramahs* to explain the broad features of the country's Constitution — presumably to show that the special position of the Malays was guaranteed.

[44] The PPP, which contested only 8 (out of 104) parliamentary and 26 (out of 282) state seats, was said to have used more than 500,000 stickers (depicting the party's symbol), 600,000 posters of the candidates, and 350,000 voting cards. *Straits Times*, 4 April 1964.

frequently erected. There were also several huge displays, mainly of cloth or metal (the latter rather like outdoor advertising boards), depicting party symbols — e.g. sailing boat (Alliance) and star and crescent (PMIP).   In the case of the Alliance, there were a few neon signs as well.

The Alliance benefited a great deal through the co-operation given to it by the Department of Information, both at the national and state levels.[45] A few weeks before the campaign had officially begun, thousands of posters were put up throughout the country, saying: 'UNITE! Support Tengku'.   These were put up by the Information Department, supposedly to counteract Indonesian prop-aganda and to encourage unity at a time of national crisis. But there was no denying their relevance to the impending elections.   After the campaign had begun, the Informa-tion Department also published several other posters and leaflets, which were even more clearly of value to the Alliance election effort.   These usually took the form of conveying to the citizens broad details of the Government's achievements and expenditure in various fields—for exam-ple, religious education and pilgrimages, the telephone service, health, rural development, electrification, educa-tion, the building of mosques and prayer houses, and the promotion of 'Koran reading competitions'.[46] Some of these posters and leaflets also contained preambles aimed at evoking a favourable response, and all of them con-tained the words 'Support Tengku', with additions like 'Peace, Prosperity and Happiness'.   That devoted to the telephone service, for example, was headed 'The Excellent Telephone Service' and carried the words: 'The telephone service that is provided by the Alliance Government in Malaya is the best in Southeast Asia, comparable to that of any other country in the world.   More telephone booths have been built in the rural areas for the people's conve-

45 The state Information Departments are branches of the national Department, and hence do not come under the control of state govern-ments.

46 It could, of course, be claimed that these posters were aimed at instilling pride and confidence in the nation and thus at making the people more resistent to Indonesian propaganda.

nience.' The one on health, headed 'A More Healthy People', stated: 'A rural health centre is something that was unheard of before Independence. But now many are found in the rural areas. These centres have become an important branch of the Rural Health Service .... Since the Alliance came to power in 1955, as many as 138 Health Centres have been established in *kampongs* all over the country. More such centres have been planned by the Alliance Government. In the immediate future, a sufficient number of rural health centres will be built to serve the whole country.' The one on rural development, headed 'New Land — New Life', claimed: 'The Alliance Government has carried out a great effort to wipe out the poverty of the people. Thousands of acres of land in several areas have been opened up by the Federal Land Development Authority for farming. The people in the rural areas, who are landless or have little farming land, are now being given land sufficient for farming and settlement. Schools are being built for their children, and clinics are being set up to look after the people's health. Water and electricity are also provided.' The one on electrification, entitled 'A Bright House — A Happy Life', had the words: 'Since the Alliance Government gained power in the year 1955, the output of electricity in the country has increased by leaps and bounds. More people, in rural areas and in towns, now receive a supply of electricity.'

There were also leaflets which set out in greater detail the Government's achievements in particular areas, such as towns; these were obviously meant for circulation in limited areas. Because they were published by the Information Departments, all these posters and leaflets were entitled to be put up on official notice boards, such as those found in front of Government offices.

In terms of the need to establish firm foundations for representative government and, generally, of building confidence in it, this apparent collaboration between the governing party and a Government department was no doubt unfortunate. What was most surprising, however, was not the fact that the Information Departments had printed posters which quite obviously had the effect of augmenting the Alliance election effort, but that none of the opposition parties made any explicit complaints about this — not even in the course of interviews. It is, of course, possible that they had not bothered to find out who was responsible for publishing these posters. Should this have been the case, it certainly reflects poorly on their vigilance. What is more disturbing is the possibility that the opposition parties (or even only some of them) may have considered that the party in office should normally and properly enjoy such advantages.

There were also indications of other links between the Alliance and the various Information Departments during the campaign period. It was, for example, a not uncommon practice for Alliance organizers in the different states to contact the Information Departments for various kinds of information and help. There were even some complaints (made during interviews) by leaders of opposition parties that on some occasions the Information Departments had arranged free film shows in the vicinity of opposition rallies, allegedly in an attempt to lure away people who otherwise might have attended these rallies.

While a great deal of time and effort was spent by party workers in putting up large numbers of posters, some energy was also expended in pulling down those of rival parties. In some areas, workers had to be sent around twice or thrice during the campaign to replace posters that had been mutilated or removed. In places where this 'poster war' was most intense, there were even occasions (especially towards the end of the campaign) when party workers kept up all night patrolling areas where they had displays or an impressive collection of posters.[47]

In addition to posters and leaflets, some use was also made of cartoons. Perak was undoubtedly the scene of greatest activity in this respect, and here the Alliance (in actual fact the MCA) conducted a fierce 'cartoon war'

47 This claim was made in the course of interviews.

aimed primarily at the PPP. Fresh cartoons (in the form of leaflets) were issued almost every day during the last couple of weeks of the campaign, and thousands of copies were freely distributed throughout the state. Many of the cartoons merely depicted the high living of the Seenivasagam brothers, while others showed them as ruthless or devious politicians. From MCA accounts, these cartoons appear to have scored a great success, and their contents were claimed to have constituted a daily topic of conversation in coffee-shops and other public meeting places. It was also claimed that the PPP had tried very hard to reply with cartoons of its own, but that it had been unable to find a good cartoonist.[48]

Many of the cartoons clearly contravened the *Election Code*,[49] and the PPP therefore announced that it saw no reason why it should continue to honour that code.[50] This led to a considerable amount of verbal mud-slinging in Perak, particularly in Ipoh, where the Seenivasagams were based.

Some comment should also be made on the importance of candidates in the total campaign effort. As might have been expected, this was generally inversely proportionate to the degree of organization and centralized financial control[51] attempted by each party. It was therefore not surprising to find a large number of Alliance candidates being totally 'managed' by the organization which surrounded them. Prominent candidates were of course not subjected to the same amount of direction, although some of them (especially Ministers, who were involved in campaigning throughout the country) were unable to spend sufficient

48 It was also explained that the MCA cartoonist was the subject of major security precautions. Elaborate steps were apparently taken to keep his identity and whereabouts secret, to prevent attempts either to bribe or abduct him.

49 The *Election Code* was essentially a 'gentlemen's agreement', designed to discourage certain unsavoury forms of campaigning, which included personal abuse.

50 *Straits Times*, 14 April 1964.

51 The financial aspect of the campaign will be discussed later in this Chapter.

time in their own constituences to be able to take personal charge of their own campaigns. Especially in the rural areas, where the level of education and wealth among candidates was relatively low, the extent to which the party organization ran the show was indeed quite striking. While he was no doubt active in his campaign, the average candidate in these areas (like the one in Pasir Puteh, see Chapter IX (a)) often did not control it. It was clearly the party that was in the limelight throughout the campaign, and the attention of the electorate was constantly drawn to it. This question of the relative importance of candidates and party organization is not one which has received much attention in election studies, but the situation in Malaya was certainly unlike that in Ceylon, concerning which one writer has observed:

> In the absence of a well-developed party organization in the country, functions normally performed by agents and organizers in Britain have to be performed by the candidate . . . . The number of election committees which UNP and MEP candidates formed was often a function of their own personal financial strength. . . . One might even say that the candidate was the pivot of the campaign organization in a constituency. This is one of the reasons why the individual candidate still continues to play a far more important role in Ceylon than in, say, Great Britain.[52]

Although its selection of candidates indicated an emphasis on certain personal attributes,[53] the PMIP did not give the impression of having relied heavily on the initiative of its candidates for success. As in the case of the Alliance, the organization which surrounded the candidate was determined not by him but by the party. Although the party appeared not to depend as much on its formal structures as the Alliance, this did not imply a corresponding increase in the responsibilities of candidates. As has already been pointed out, it was to the traditional

---

52 I. D. S. Weerawardana, *Ceylon General Election, 1956*, pp. 213-14, 217.
53 See Chapter V.

religious élites that the party turned for the success of its campaign.

So far as the other parties were concerned, only candidates of national prominence were returned — Devan Nair from the PAP, Lim Chong Eu from the UDP, Lim Kean Siew and Tan Chee Khoon from the SF, and the two Seenivasagams from the PPP.[54]   In all likelihood this was more than mere coincidence: with the possible exception of the SF, none of these parties had constituency organizations comparable with those of the Alliance and the PMIP, and a great deal was therefore left to the resourcefulness of individual candidates.[55]   Except perhaps for Devan Nair, these candidates also spent much more than the average for their parties, and stood in outstandingly promising seats.   Three of them (the exceptions being Lim Chong Eu, Devan Nair and Tan Chee Khoon) were also sitting members.

In the vast majority of cases, there was little doubt that the primary objective of the campaign was the projection of the party's image rather than that of the candidate. The allocation of a single symbol for all candidates of each party no doubt enhanced this. All parties were also agreed that the holding of parliamentary and state elections simultaneously had increased the need for party identification, and hence the importance of symbols.[56]   Despite this it is worth emphasizing that, by and large, symbols did not assume an importance of their own as they appear to have done in other newly independent countries. Although the PMIP's symbol (the star and crescent) had an obvious religious *motif* (and probably encouraged some support),

54 Except perhaps for the two from the SF, they were in fact the most prominent candidates of their respective parties. In the case of the Seenivasagam brothers (PPP) and Dr. Lim Chong Eu (UDP), the claim might also be made that they *were* the party.

55 Although relevant in this context, this comment should not be interpreted to mean that issues did not play a significant role in the outcome of the elections.

56 Considering that each parliamentary constituency contained between two and six state constituencies, attempts at candidate identification might well have led to a great deal of confusion.

there were no equivalents to the attempts at extolling or condemning the qualities of symbols as such, or the elaborate ceremonies involving them, reported in other studies.[57]

Although it was earlier observed that none of the opposition parties had seen fit to comment on the use which the Alliance had made of the Information Department during the campaign, complaints on other matters were made in the course of interviews. It was claimed, for example, that electoral registers had in some areas been tampered with, and that the names of those who were known to be active supporters of opposition parties had been struck off under the pretext that they had moved from their polling districts. While some mistakes must no doubt have occurred, there was no indication that any systematic tampering had taken place. In any case, even if there had been wilful omissions, there was no reason why any party or individual should not have made use of the 'claims and objections period' to rectify matters.

Another complaint was that Federal Ministers often used their official visits to the states to spread party propaganda. Understandably, this complaint was most bitterly made by PMIP officials in Kelantan. Allegations were also made that in some areas where the Social Welfare Department was handing out relief money, the actual payment had been made, not by the appropriate officials, but either by local Alliance officials or by Alliance candidates. There were also many complaints about politically-directed Government expenditure, the one most frequently referred to being Mr. Tan Siew Sin's (the Minister of Finance) tours immediately before and during the campaign for the purpose of giving money (as part of a supplementary budget) to Chinese schools for furniture and renovations. This was seen as an obvious attempt to convince the Chinese community of the Government's concern for

[57] For some examples see R. L. Park and S. V. Kogekar (eds), *Reports on the Indian General Elections, 1951-52*, pp. 175-6, 285-6; K. W. J. Post *The Nigerian Federal Election of 1959*, p. 230; Weerawardana, *op. cit.* pp. 172-3.

Chinese education. In addition to questioning the ethics of this expenditure, opposition parties also argued that it was nothing but a glorified form of bribery, and that it merely showed that the Government was conscious of not having promoted the 'true' interests of Chinese education through the adoption of more favourable policies. This latter argument was probably aimed at minimizing the tactical advantage which the Alliance (the MCA in particular) might have gained through making the grants.

A similar complaint, made by the PMIP in Kelantan, alleged that a large portion of Federal aid to Trengganu since the Alliance came to power there in 1961[58] was essentially of a 'showmanship' kind, aimed at demonstrating to those in Kelantan what they were missing by not having an Alliance state government. A disproportionate amount had apparently been spent on the border area between Kelantan and Trengganu, to emphasize further the contrast between the rates of development in the two states.

There were also some allegations that police, especially in the rural areas, had helped the Alliance by being hostile to supporters of other parties and by not giving a sympathetic hearing to those who had complaints to make about Alliance tactics.[59]

Certain other complaints were also made against the Alliance but these did not involve accusations of the party's unfair use of official channels or organs. They included giving supporters of other parties money to go away on polling day (so that they could not cast their votes), and also paying people for the surrender of their identity cards on that day. The latter device, it was said, enabled Alliance workers to impersonate those whose identity cards had been procured.

There was also one other disadvantage which all opposition parties suffered, but for which no one could be blamed. Because they did not have many sitting members, none of these parties knew well in advance whether or not

58 Through defections, the PMIP having been in power since 1959.
59 This complaint was reiterated by a PMIP speaker when the new Parliament was convened. *Straits Times*, 8 July 1964.

it would be contesting certain constituencies, and this apparently made it difficult to arouse sufficient enthusiasm in some branches so that early foundations could be laid for the campaign. The Alliance, on the other hand, knew that it would be contesting every seat in the country, and each branch was therefore aware that it would be actively involved when the elections came along.

The Alliance, for its part, had a few complaints to make about the tactics of some of its opponents. The most serious of these concerned the PMIP, especially the various means adopted by that party to play on the superstitions and religious fears of the rural voters. In Kelantan and Trengganu, for example, it was alleged that covert use was being made of talismans, chain letters and even love charms. These love charms were apparently being sold to *kampong* women with the warning that they would not work in the case of those who voted for the Alliance. In attacking the PMIP for this, the Mentri Besar of Trengganu, Inche Ibrahim Fikri, urged his listeners at a rally to 'go home and check up on your wives for these love charms', and further advised them that 'such dirty tactics can only cause disharmony in homes'.[60] The PMIP was also accused of being connected with the circulation of certain 'seditious' pamphlets during the campaign. Believed to be printed in Hong Kong, these were long strips of paper[61] on which were printed quotations from the Koran and Hadith, to serve as 'guides for Muslims during elections'.[62]

Another accusation made against the PMIP was that some of its men had gone around spreading the word that it was *haram* (forbidden) for Muslims to vote for parties which had non-Muslims in them, and that for this reason those who supported the Alliance would be regarded as infidels who, in addition to suffering various other

60 *Straits Times*, 23 April 1964.

61 7 ft. 8 ins. long and 2 inches wide. This apparently made it convenient for them to be concealed in the lining of *songkoks* (fez-like caps commonly worn by Malays).

62 *Loc. cit.*

calamities, would also have their marriages annulled in heaven.[63] The local religious élites were claimed to have played an active part both in this 'whisper campaign' and in the distribution of talismans and love charms.

The Alliance also hurled back many of the accusations that were made against it: vote buying, intimidation, impersonation, etc. The UMNO in Penang claimed after the election that it had prevented some people from voting twice at a certain polling station. In a statement to the press, it went as far as criticizing the Election Commission for its 'lack of vigilance', and claimed that it had 'clear proof that fifteen people would have been allowed to vote twice but for the check made by our own polling agent'.[64] Another strong attack came from the Assistant Minister for Rural Development, who accused opposition parties of paying people for their identity cards. He said:

> I have heard rumours that all sorts of tricks are being used by certain unscrupulous people during the present election period. One of these is an attempt... to collect identity cards, in some cases on promise of payment, so that voters will not be able to cast their votes on polling day. One of the reasons given for taking away identity cards is that they are required to register people for land. This is a mean trick, calculated to deprive the voters of their legitimate right to vote.[65]

Some account must be given of the role played by individuals and groups who, although not a part of formal party organization, nevertheless exerted considerable influence during the campaign and thus helped to supplement the effort of party machines, particularly at the con-

[63] As mentioned in Chapter II some PMIP men were in fact arrested for their part in this propaganda, under a law which prohibits incitement to communal hatred.

Three of those arrested contested the state election in Kelantan. In the course of campaigning on their behalf, their supporters carried the *songkoks* worn by them to the houses in their constituencies, with the message that they represented the candidates who were unable to come personally because the Alliance Government had detained them. *Straits Times*, 7 April 1964.

[64] *Ibid.* 29 April 1964.

[65] *Ibid.* 22 April 1964.

stituency level. In this connexion three broad groups
may be discerned: (a) local administrative élites; (b) local
traditional élites; and (c) secret societies and gangsters.

In the first category, the most influential group were
undoubtedly the District Officers (D.O.s). With the exception of the major urban areas, each state is administratively subdivided into a number of districts, under the
control of individual District Officers. These officers are
invariably a crucial section of the State Civil Service.
They are the ones on whom the state governments depend
for the execution of their policies, and it is through them
that the average citizen comes into contact with his state
government. Since the colonial period, the influence
exerted by the District Officers in their respective areas,
and the high esteem in which they have been held by the
people, have been beyond question. One of the people
interviewed, a State Alliance Secretary, felt that this position of the D.O.s often made it difficult for the party in
power to explain to the people that it had been responsible for such improvements as the building of bridges. Not
having an adequate comprehension of democratic government, they often felt that it was the D.O. who had been
responsible for these improvements. Each district also
has Assistant District Officers (A.D.O.s), who are directly
responsible to the D.O. and who also belong to the higher
echelons of the local administrative élite.

There was little doubt that the vast majority of D.O.s
and A.D.O.s supported the Alliance in preference to the
other parties in the country. Since the main contestants
in the rural areas were the Alliance and the PMIP, the
Alliance had little competition for their support: their
status and educational background, if nothing else, would
have made it unlikely that their sympathies could be won
over by the PMIP.[66] Although claims were often made
that D.O.s openly campaigned for the Alliance, they do
not appear to have abused their official status to any significant extent. It was, however, commonly known that

[66] In some cases, the fact that the Alliance was the party in power must
also have helped.

most of them implicitly favoured the Alliance, and this in itself could have been important.

There was no evidence that it was directly influential. But the fact that the political allegiances of the D.O.s and A.D.O.s were commonly known, usually meant that many of those who came below them in the administrative hierarchy, especially the *penghulus*[67] who had much closer contacts with the people in the *kampongs* and who were generally less scrupulous about keeping clear of politics, also felt encouraged to support the same party. In the final analysis, it seems likely that it was the known allegiances of this latter group which most directly influenced some voters, if not into actually supporting the same party, at least into not openly campaigning for another.

The second category of 'influencers', the local religious élites, were most active in Kelantan. There were three main groups in this category: the *gurus*, the *mubhalirs*, and the *imams*. In Kelantan the PMIP clearly had the active support of the majority of these groups, and its success there was considerably influenced by this.[68] In the other states the Alliance often had the upper hand; this, however, was not of equal signficance since in these states the religious élites were both less active and less politically influential. This difference is perhaps best explained in terms of the more traditional nature of Kelantan society, a fact which has helped to sustain the influence of traditional opinion-leaders. Helped by the continuance of traditional values and relationships, there was also proportionately a greater number of religious leaders in that state.

Complaints of the use of thugs and gangsters by rival parties were universal, and some of those interviewed frankly admitted that their own party used them, although only 'defensively'. Particularly in the case of rural areas, the term 'gangsters' would perhaps be a misnomer. Most

---

[67] Kelantan has an administrative hierarchy somewhat different from that found in the other states. Here there is an additional group — the *penggawas* — similar to the *penghulus* in the other states. The *penghulus* in Kelantan are thus much less important than their counterparts in the other states.

[68] For a more detailed discussion of these groups, see Chapter IX (a).

of those involved were merely layabouts and unsavoury characters who probably took some pleasure (although they were, naturally, given other inducements as well) in such activities as stoning vehicles used by opposition parties, destroying opposition posters, and so on. Apparently they did not always receive detailed instructions from their 'retainers', and often used their own initiative in deciding how best to use their talents. Where the use of thugs was admitted, the explanations usually given were that they were necessary to restore the balance because other parties used them, and that they were required to ensure the safety of speakers and party workers in areas where threats had been made. In many cases these 'toughs' also seem to have been used for certain normal duties like putting up posters. It was also maintained that in some areas parties had successfully used them in intimidating voters who did not fully appreciate the secrecy of the ballot.

In the urban areas, secret societies appear to have profitably extended their normal 'protection' work to include parties and candidates. From what was said in the course of interviews, they did not seem to have really influenced the outcome in any constituency; they had merely offered their services, for past or anticipated favours, or for money, and many of the candidates and party officials they approached had naturally preferred to 'play safe' by not antagonizing them, although there was often no indication that they were going to be of much value. According to one disillusioned party organizer, leaders of gangs who had been paid money on the basis of their claim that they could influence votes had apparently just taken the money and shown no further interest in the party.

In view of their widespread use by parties and candidates, it might however be unrealistic to dismiss gangsters and secret societies altogether, and to pretend that they were of no significance during the campaign. Although it would be impossible to measure their effect, it is most likely that some of the allegations regarding attempted intimidation were true. If nothing else, some voters seem at least to have been prevented from casting their votes. In one area an official of one of the parties confided that his men, having previously asked known supporters of their own party to cast their votes early, had got a few thugs to stage mock fights late in the afternoon in order to discourage others from voting. As expected, the word had apparently spread quickly that there was 'some trouble' in the vicinity, and people had therefore been reluctant to take the risk of leaving their homes at dusk to go and vote.

Although all those interviewed had something to say about the use of thugs and gangsters by parties, this aspect of the campaign was never raised in public. This could indicate either that all parties used them or that their importance was known to be only minimal, perhaps both.

In the rural areas there was frequent mention of the payment of varying sums of money to village headmen on the understanding that they would be able to influence voting in their own villages. While it is possible that some headmen were able to do this, it also seemed evident that, as in the case of leaders of secret societies, payment was often made simply for fear of antagonizing them since opponents who were willing to pay might otherwise gain an advantage.

There was general agreement that communications posed no special problems during the campaign. The vast majority of voters were easily accessible by road, although there were some remote settlements which could only be reached by boat or by travelling on foot.[69] Especially in the rural areas, the contesting parties were quite satisfied that almost all the voters had been contacted by their workers during the campaign period. Considering the large number of workers used by the Alliance and the PMIP, this is not surprising. As already mentioned, it was not, however, possible to make a similar effort in the urban areas where rallies therefore assumed a greater importance as a means of contacting the voters. This probably meant that the proportion of voters contacted in the urban areas was smaller.

[69] The situation was markedly different in Sarawak and Sabah. See Chapters X and XIII.

In some areas it was the state rather than the parliamentary elections that were really in the limelight. In Kelantan, for example, the Alliance effort was aimed primarily at gaining control of the State Assembly. In the opinion of its officials, the party was bound to win a majority in Parliament from the seats it gained in the other states, and a few additional successes in Kelantan were not going to make much difference one way or the other. But the enemy was in power at the state level, and this was where he had to be defeated. The reverse argument also led the PMIP to concentrate on state seats. Even if it had won all the Parliamentary seats in Kelantan, there was not the slightest chance that the party could assume control at the national level; what it really stood to lose was its control of the State Assembly. It was thus not surprising that the heart of the campaign in Kelantan lay in the contest for the state seats. As shown in Chapter VI, this was also evident in the unmistakable emphasis given to state issues. The situation in Trengganu was not very different.

A similar situation, but at a less competitive level, also developed in Perak. By not putting up candidates against each other, the PPP and the UDP hoped to unseat the Alliance at the state level and, next to Kelantan and possibly Trengganu, it was in Perak that the Alliance had to face most seriously the possibility of its rivals coming to power. Unlike the situation in Kelantan, however, the parliamentary contest in Perak did not appear to have assumed a secondary importance. Among other things, local issues in that state were less separate from national issues.

On the basis of the number of seats contested by the different parties, it might seem that bids for power were made by opposition parties in most of the other states — certainly in Penang,[70] Malacca,[71] Selangor,[72] Kedah[73] and

70 By the SF and the UDP, which contested 24 and 21 seats respectively out of the 24 state seats.

71 By the SF, which contested all 20 state seats.

72 By the SF, which contested 26 out of the 28 state seats.

73 By the PMIP, which contested 21 out of the 24 state seats.

Perlis.[74] With the exception of Penang, it would however have been unrealistic to believe that there was any real threat to the Alliance in these states.

The 'safest' Alliance state, both on the above criterion and more generally, was probably Pahang. Of the twenty-four state seats there, no other party contested more than seventeen. In fact some Alliance leaders seem to have found it almost scandalous that other parties should have even contemplated challenging their dominance in that state. For example, a few weeks before nomination day, the Chairman of Pahang MCA observed:

> There have been instances where non-Alliance political parties' members visited several areas in the state to try to convince the people that they were genuinely interested in fighting for a better deal for the Chinese. Some of them have even attempted to set up branches in Pahang so that they could intensify their campaign against the MCA.[75]

A few words should be said about the money which went into the campaign. Even in countries where there are no legal limits to expenditure, it is usually difficult to get accurate information on how campaign funds were procured, how much was spent, and what the different items of expenditure were.[76] This is partly the result of the difficulties faced by the parties themselves in keeping comprehensive accounts of all aspects of their campaign finances. But in some situations (particularly, of course, where there are legal limits to election expenditure) parties also commonly take the attitude that it is somehow more creditable, and in some ways even more 'moral', to win votes without spending much money. For this reason there is frequently an attempt to quote low figures for one's own party and high figures for one's opponents.

While these difficulties were certainly present in Malaya, it was nevertheless possible to make approximate estimates

---

[74] By the PMIP, which contested 11 out of the 12 state seats.

[75] *Straits Times*, 4 March 1964.

[76] See, for example, *The Journal of Politics*, Vol. 25, No. 4, special issue, 'Comparative Studies in Political Finance'.

of some basic items of election expenditure. These were arrived at not only by considering the evidence of those interviewed, but also by costing the main items of expenditure.

To begin with, there was no doubt that the Alliance spent several times as much as any of the other parties, and perhaps a little less than three times their combined total. What was most significant, however, was not so much the volume of Alliance expenditure as its very centralized administration. Roughly two-thirds of the total Alliance expenditure was provided by the party's headquarters in Kuala Lumpur. The remainder was made up of money raised at the state level, and, in varying degrees, by the candidates themselves. On the whole the percentage of the expenditure which came from party sources was in the region of 75 per cent. of the total. Most of this money came in the form of donations made to the party by business firms and by individual businessmen. As a rule donations were made direct to the national headquarters; this was encouraged by the party, and made possible the high degree of centralization in the management of its campaign funds. It could perhaps also be assumed that those giving money would generally have preferred that their contributions should be known by those who really counted, namely those at the top. Where there was any anticipation of rewards (for example, in the form of business concessions), this would only have been natural. But there were also cases where substantial donations were made to the state level or to individual candidates (especially members of State Executive Councils) when this seemed the most advantageous: on mining rights and the granting of sites for industrial development, for example, the state governments have considerable powers.

Like the Alliance, the other parties also seem to have relied heavily on donations for their campaign expenses. There was no evidence that any of them had relied to any extent on membership fees even in respect of normal (that is, non-election year) expenses.[77] Compared to the Alliance, opposition parties seemed a little more secretive about the sources of their funds, and merely referred to donations by 'supporters' and 'well-wishers'. There were, however, indications that where some of these parties were in power either at the state or the municipal level, anticipated benefits or gratitude for past favours played a significant role. In these situations, some businessmen had apparently contributed both to the Alliance and to the parties in power, by way of 'insurance'.

The total amount spent by all the parties in fighting the parliamentary and state elections was probably around M$11,000,000.[78] The main items of expenditure seem to have been transport,[79] posters,[80] and payment to party workers. Compared to the Alliance, opposition parties seem to have had more dedicated workers, and for this reason were generally able to pay them less; to some extent this must have helped to balance the Alliance's financial supremacy.

The campaign was generally free of major disturbances. All parties seemed very concerned that violence should be avoided, and this must have helped. But the seeming omnipresence of the police must also have been a factor. The only clash of any significance, involving supporters of rival

[77] This was certainly true of the Alliance. (See R.S. Milne and K.J. Ratnam, 'Politics and Finance in Malaya', *Journal of Commonwealth Political Studies*, Vol. III, No. 3, November 1955.)

[78] It was estimated, in the case of the Alliance, that the total cost would probably have been about 50 per cent. higher had the state and parliamentary elections not been held simultaneously.

[79] The Alliance headquarters provided a new station wagon for every parliamentary constituency. These vehicles were purchased from a dealer on the understanding they could be resold to him at $2000-$3000 less than the original price, to cover depreciation. The PMIP had at least one land-rover per federal constituency in Kelantan. It was claimed that these vehicles had been bought when they were auctioned by district offices. In addition to these vehicles, the Alliance and the PMIP also had a large number of cars, either hired or loaned to them. The other parties had only vehicles belonging to the second category.

[80] In the case of the Alliance, almost all posters were provided by the headquarters in Kuala Lumpur.

parties, occurred in Kelantan on election eve. A truck-load of Alliance supporters returning from a PMIP rally had apparently been ambushed by a group of PMIP supporters, and a *mêlée* had ensued, during which two persons were stabbed. Twenty-four persons were subsequently arrested and charged with carrying offensive weapons.[81]

Despite the relative absence of major incidents, there was a constant fear of disturbances in some party circles. This was particularly so in areas where competition was keenest, each party claiming that its rivals were continuously provoking violence. There were also frequent complaints of intimidation both of voters and of party workers. As was perhaps inevitable, there were in fact some minor incidents involving party workers.[82] There were also stories of how clashes which seemed imminent had been averted (each party claiming that it had saved the situation while its opponents had engineered the trouble) and, in some cases, of how individuals had been beaten up by hired thugs. It was not possible to verify any of these stories.

Although some canvassing was permitted on polling day,[83] the main activity consisted of the frantic effort to convey voters to their respective polling stations. This involved careful planning, and the driver of each party vehicle had his duties and his area of operation explained to him in detail. Voters were given instructions on the various points from which they would be picked up, and the people whom they should contact in the event of any delay or confusion. Planning of this kind was necessary in order to put the available vehicles to the most economic use. However, things did not always go according to plan, and vehicles sometimes failed to appear at the appointed time

81 *Straits Times*, 26 April 1964.

82 In Kelantan, for example, the state where competition was perhaps keenest, there were some isolated cases of fighting between PMIP and Alliance workers. In addition to the general atmosphere of tension caused by the highly competitive situation, the fact that party workers were likely to have their paths cross frequently in the course of their door-to-door canvassing must have added considerably to the likelihood of these incidents.

83 See pp. 74-5 above.

and place. But the parties had prepared for all eventualities, and instructions were given to voters that when this happened they should without any hesitation use the vehicles provided by rival parties. Indeed, in many cases, parties which had a relatively small number of vehicles in particular areas solved their problem simply by using those of their opponents. The 'host' in most cases was, not surprisingly, the Alliance.

Another service provided by the parties on polling day was the operation of information booths in the vicinity of polling stations. It was fairly common for voters to use these for last-minute confirmation of voting procedure and their registration numbers By setting up these booths, the parties made sure that they would be at hand to help voters who might get into difficulties either because they had gone to the wrong polling stations or because there was some doubt about their identity.

VIII

The Press, Radio and Television

The Press

As in many other countries, the opposition parties in Malaya have frequently complained that the Press favours the Government. Certainly greater newspaper space is devoted to the Alliance than to any single opposition party, but this does not conclusively 'prove' that there is bias or that the Alliance is being unduly favoured. What a government party does is *news* to a far greater degree than what opposition parties do; this results simply from its being the Government party, with a power of making effective decisions which is denied to the other parties. The fact that the opposition is fragmented into several parties also means that, even if the opposition as a whole were given as much Press space as the Government, no single opposition party would receive anything like as much space as the Government.

Of course, it could be argued that, even if there were bias in favour of the Government over and above what was due to it by virtue of its having greater news value because it was the Government, this would be only 'natural'. One state leader of an opposition party had such a point of view. The Press was biased in favour of the Alliance, but this was natural. He would expect it to be similarly biased towards his own party, if it came into power. This reflects traditional ideas of the support which is due to a government, which apparently have persisted into an age in which there are elections which may possibly change the government.

Another consideration is relevant to the treatment of the election in the Press; the legal powers which the Government has over the Press in Malaya. Freedom of the Press is not explicitly mentioned in the Federation Constitution.

But, subject to certain specified restrictions, it is included in a general form in Article 10 (1): '. . . every citizen has the right to freedom of speech and expression'. The main legal control over the Press consists in the requirement that a permit from the appropriate Minister is necessary before any person may print or publish a newspaper.[1] The permit must be reviewed annually and conditions may be attached, for instance that the paper must be published in a particular language. An additional restriction is that, under the Internal Security Act (1960), the printing, sale and circulation of documents (including newspapers) may be prohibited, if they are 'likely to promote feelings of hostility between different races or classes of the population', or if they incite violence or civil disobedience or are prejudicial to the national interest. There are also restrictions on the import of publications from abroad.[2]

Some government statements have said that only limited use has been made of such powers. When Inche Mohamed Sopiee left his post as Director of Information Services in March 1964 he said that, as far as he knew, the Government had cancelled the licences of only two publications in the last few years.[3] He did not specify which papers he had in mind. However, the Socialist Front has complained that two of its publications *Nyala* and *Berita Buroh* were refused licences just before the elections.[4] On one occasion in 1960 an issue of the *Nanyang Siang Pau* was seized, scrutinized and then released.[5] More important than the actual instances quoted, the existence of such powers, particularly the need for annual permits, could

[1] The Printing Presses Ordinance, 1948, as amended by the Printing Presses (Amendment) Ordinance, 1957. The term 'newspaper' is widely interpreted, and has included publications of public interest produced at regular or irregular intervals, for instance the permission given to publish the *Biddy Basketball Handbook* (in English and Chinese).

[2] On other restrictions see H.E. Groves, *The Constitution of Malaysia*. Singapore, 1964, pp. 207-9.

[3] *Straits Times*, 16 March 1964.

[4] Dr. Tan Chee Khoon, speech in the *Dewan Ra'ayat*, 5 March 1965. (Mimeographed.) Dr. Tan added '. . . our printers were closed down'.

[5] Mr. D. R. Seenivasagam, reported in *Dewan Ra'ayat Debates*, II, No. 30, 5 December 1960, cols. 3334-5.

possibly 'create a subservient and uncritical press'.[6] Mr. D.R. Seenivasagam, for instance, has argued that on the *Talib Education Report* the Government attitude to the Press appeared to be, 'We tell you politely to do this . . . . Remember that we have the power to take away your licence'.[7] Mr. Lim Kean Siew has alleged in Parliament that 'in renewing licences for newspapers the Government had informed these newspapers not to touch on "certain subjects" in their publications. For example, the Press never reported statements by certain politicians who had a right to make their views known'.[8]

The Government's answer to such charges has been that the freedom of the Press has in fact been maintained. 'Since the Alliance party came into power, the Government has preserved this freedom and will continue to do so.'[9] The two points on which the Government has been sensitive and on which it has intervened have been communism (subversion) and communalism. The purpose of the Printing Presses Ordinance, said the Assistant Minister of Information and Broadcasting, was to safeguard the printing industry from being used by subversionists and their communist masters.[10] Restrictions on Socialist Front publications have been justified by drawing attention to an allegedly subversive pro-communist Socialist Front Community Song Book.[11] And the refusal to grant permits to the Socialist Front Party newspapers in 1963 has been explained by referring to the subsequent arrests of some Socialist Front members on the ground of collaborating with Indonesia.

The dangers of communalism have also been stressed by the Government. According to an Assistant Minister a few years ago, the Press was free, but liberty was not licence.

[6] R.H. Hickling, *Sunday Mail*, 8 September 1963.

[7] *Dewan Ra'ayat Debates*, II, No. 30, 5 December 1960, col. 3335.

[8] *Straits Times*, 6 March 1965.

[9] 'Tengku Abdul Rahman', *ibid*. 6 February 1965. See also statements by the Minister of Information and Broadcasting, *ibid*. 14 October 1964; and *Sunday Times*, 30 August 1964.

[10] Government Statement PEN 5/65/304 (INF), 30 May 1963.

[11] Inche Mohamed Ismail, Assistant Minister of the Interior, *Dewan Ra'ayat Debates*, II, No. 31, 5 December 1960, col 3487.

It was not free to sabotage the building of a Malaysian nation or to 'perpetuate ties of loyalty (or emotional ties of interest and affection which are indistinguishable from loyalty) to countries from which the ancestors of some of our citizens have come'.[12] Since the emergency following 'confrontation', which has placed a strain on loyalty to Malaysia among some sections of the population, this consideration has become even more important. In December 1964 the Minister of Information and Broadcasting referred to the critical period which Malaysia, a multiracial society, was going through. 'The Press have a very sacred task in helping to mould our national heritage by assisting our people to attain a sense of solidarity transcending considerations of mere race, religion, language or cultural origin. I have always been gratified by the sense of responsibility and patriotism which the Press as a whole have displayed towards our national problems.'[13] This, of course, represented a tribute to the 'built-in' restrictions which the Press imposes on itself, as contrasted with controls imposed from outside.

The titles, language and circulation details of some major newspapers are given below.[14] Newspapers published

[12] *Ibid.* col. 3486.

[13] Inche Senu bin Abdul Rahman, *Sunday Times,* 27 December 1964.

[14] The figures given are as at approximately April 1964; figures were obtained in most cases from the newspaper concerned. All daily papers with a circulation of 20,000 or more in Malaya have been included. Some with a lower circulation than 20,000 have also been included because they represent minority views which are of particular interest. Some of the circulation is outside Malaya and Singapore (for instance, in the Borneo territories), but in Table VII this has been disregarded. *World Press; Newspapers and News Agencies.* Paris, 1964, quoted by P. Lim Pui Huen, 'Malaysian Newspapers Currently Published', *Perpustakaan Malaysia,* Vol. 1, No. 1 (1965), p. 57, estimated that there were 28 dailies in Malaya (circulation 466,000) and 8 in Singapore (circulation 351,000).

Historical references on the Press in Malaya and Singapore include: P.L. Burns, *The English Language Newspapers, 1915-51.* (Singapore, University of Malaya B.A. Honours thesis, 1956-7); Nik Ahmad bin Hassan, *The Malay Vernacular Press.* (Singapore, University of Malaya B A. Honours thesis, 1958); W.R. Roff, *Guide to Malay Periodicals, 1876-1941.* Singapore, 1961; Linda Tan, *The Early Chinese Newspapers of Singapore, 1881-1912* (Singapore, University of Singapore M.A. thesis, 1962).

by the parties themselves were relatively unimportant. As mentioned above, two Socialist Front papers had recently been unable to have their licences renewed. Even inside the Alliance the MCA *Malayan Mirror* had ceased publication some years before. UMNO's organ, *Merdeka*, was still in existence, but its circulation was only a few thousands at the time of the election. *Petir*, the organ of the PAP, had an even smaller circulation in Malaya.

TABLE VII
MAJOR NEWSPAPERS PUBLISHED IN MALAYA AND SINGAPORE AND THEIR CIRCULATION

TITLE	LANGUAGE	WEEKDAY CIRCULATION	DISTRIBUTION OF CIRCULATION BETWEEN MALAYA AND SINGAPORE
Utusan Melayu	Malay (Jawi, non-romanized script)	49,000	85 per cent. in Malaya, 15 per cent. in Singapore
Berita Harian	Malay (Rumi, romanized script)	24,459	80 per cent. in Malaya, 20 per cent. in Singapore
Warta Negara	Malay (Jawi)	2,175	Nearly all in N.W. Malaya
Straits Times	English	142,824	55 per cent. in Malaya, 45 per cent. in Singapore
Malay Mail	English	23,799	Half in Malaya, Half in Singapore
Malayan Times	English	8,000	Nearly all in Malaya
Nanyang Siang Pau	Chinese	94,425	60 per cent. in Malaya, 40 per cent. in Singapore
Sin Chew Jit Poh	Chinese	70,000	Slightly higher in Singapore than in Malaya
Tamil Nesan	Tamil	14,369	Two-thirds in Malaya, one-third in Singapore
Tamil Malar	Tamil	5,000	Half in Malaya, Half in Singapore
Malai Nadu (now ceased publication)	Tamil	3,000	Mostly in Malaya

These newspapers have either Sunday editions or Sunday counterparts under a different name. These tend to give relatively more space to features than to news and generally have a larger circulation than the daily version. Some of the daily papers publish more than one edition, for instance there may be separate editions for Malaya and for Singapore.

A number of factors might be responsible for differences in the treatment given to the election by various newspapers. Among them are the ownership and direction of the paper, although the names of the directors are, by themselves, often uninformative, and no thorough analysis of the subject exists. Also relevant are the linguistic and ethnic groups who read each newspaper and the areas in which its circulation is greatest.

The column-inches devoted to various parties were measured for a sample of six days during the election period for a number of newspapers. The results are given in Table VIII.

TABLE VIII[a]

PERCENTAGE OF COLUMN-INCHES DEVOTED TO PARTIES
ON SIX DAYS DURING THE CAMPAIGN

	ALL.	SF	PAP	UDP	PPP	PMIP	PN
Utusan Melayu	73	11	8	2	–	6	–
Berita Harian	81	8	1	–	1	6	3
Warta Negara	52	10	3	1	1	33	–
Straits Times	58	13	20	2	1	2	4
Malayan Times	51	6	36	1	4	2	–
Malay Mail	65	11	18	–	5	1	–
Nanyang Siang Pau	60	19	19	1	1	–	–
Sin Chew Jit Poh	59	12	27	–	2	–	–
Tamil Nesan	72	11	15	–	2	–	–
Tamil Malar	68	8	19	–	1	4	–

a References in which there is material on several parties which could not be easily separated are not included. A tabulation of references to various parties in the *headlines* of the newspapers during the election period showed very similar percentages.

Note: PN = Party Negara.

It would be naïve to suppose that Table VIII by itself offers any conclusive information about the campaign. The six days chosen were at eight-day intervals between 18 March and 28 April. Some peculiarities resulted where smaller parties were concerned. For instance, the amount of space the *Straits Times* gave to Party Negara is exaggerated, because there happened to be a long story on the party on one of the six days chosen. Moreover, the amount of space given did not entirely reflect news value as modified by editorial policy. Some parties, particularly the PAP and the Alliance, were more efficient than others in 'feeding' material to the Press in a form in which it could be easily used. Also, the fact that a party is given attention in the Press, as measured by column-inches does not mean that it is necessarily given *favourable* attention. For instance, the space given the PAP by the *Utusan Melayu* consisted almost entirely of attacks on the PAP and refutations of its arguments. Nevertheless, taken in conjunction with examples of what particular newspapers said, the Table gives a general view of the focus of political interest of each paper. The Table does not include political advertisements by the parties in the newspapers. These were hardly used at all, the main exception being a large Alliance advertisement which appeared in most papers.

The two Malay papers with the largest circulations, the *Utusan Melayu* and the *Berita Harian*, showed the largest proportion of references to the Alliance. This was not remarkable as far as *Utusan Melayu* was concerned. Before Independence the paper had supported Malayan nationalist aspirations, but after 1957 it became increasingly critical of the Government. Individual members of the Alliance had bought up shares in the paper and in 1961 the editor was removed and an UMNO man installed, resulting in a strike by some of the editorial and production staff. Opposition members regarded the change of editor as harming the freedom of the press.[15] Later the Tengku

15 *Straits Times*, 8 August 1961. As early as 1950 Inche Abdul Aziz bin Ishak, then on the *Utusan Melayu*, wrote that Tengku Abdul Rahman

linked the episode to Indonesian designs to gain control of Malaya. Indonesia had used the paper 'by bribing the frustrated and unsuccessful employees who were also disloyal to the country'.[16]

Utusan Melayu criticism of the PAP was particularly marked in the editorials. In the six weeks before the election there were more editorials (all of them hostile) on the PAP than there were on the Alliance's own policy or on 'confrontation'. On 5 March the PAP was said to have the same policy as the PPP, in opposing Malay rights, hardly an attractive identification for Malays. The opposition candidates must not succeed in breaking the unity of Malay votes. This theme was repeated on 25 March.

On 30 March it was said that recent speeches by the Tengku and Mr. Tan Siew Sin had exposed Mr. Lee as a possible future dictator and a man who did not honour his promises. On the next day an editorial warned Mr. Lee Kuan Yew not to play with fire in alleging that the Tengku was not a leader of high calibre, an allegation that Mr. Lee later denied having made. This attack was kept up in April, until, after the election, the result was hailed as a glittering victory for the Alliance. The PMIP did not feature much in the editorials, but there were a large number of news items, aimed not so much at its policy as to convey the image of a divided and untrustworthy party. PMIP quarrels over candidate selection were featured in a news item from Kota Bharu on 19 March. On 6 April wide publicity was given to an Alliance speech attacking the PMIP, saying that one of its prominent members had outraged the modesty of a midwife and another had been caught in close proximity (*khalwat*) with a waitress.

The *Berita Harian* is owned by the same group as the *Straits Times*. Curiously, however, it gave as much space,

---

and Tun Razak 'had on various occasions condemned *Utusan Melayu* for its unfair criticism of them as the decadent feudal class which exploit the ra'ayat ! ! !' (*The Architect of Merdeka, Tengku Abdul Rahman.* Singapore, 1957, p. 87).

[16] *Straits Times*, 10 February 1965. The former editor had been arrested early in 1963 for complicity in the Azahari rebellion in Brunei.

probably more, to the Alliance than the *Utusan Melayu*.
One explanation which has been suggested is that, just
because it is known to be aligned with UMNO, *Utusan
Melayu* is almost immune from criticism by most Malays.
But the *Berita Harian* has to *prove* that it is really a pro-
Malay paper and it does this on occasion by being more
pro-UMNO than the 'UMNO paper'.   Certainly, in conversation, some Socialist Front supporters have claimed
that their party receives somewhat better treatment in the
Utusan Melayu than in the *Berita Harian*.   During the
election *Berita Harian* consistently supported the Alliance
and attacked the Socialist Front and the PMIP.   After the
election (27 April) its reference to the 'shining' victory of
the Alliance paralleled the *Utusan Melayu*'s mention of
a 'glittering' victory.   But, significantly, there was a relative absence of comment about the PAP.   There were no
editorials mainly on the PAP, and one of the few headlines
which mentioned it also mentioned UMNO: 'Rajaratnam:
UMNO only can control the danger of communalism'
(17 April).   In Singapore politics the *Berita Harian* had
usually supported the PAP Government, in sharp contrast
to the *Utusan Melayu*'s support of the UMNO.   In the
face of the PAP entry into politics in Malaya *Berita
Harian* apparently took refuge from the cross-pressures
to which it was subjected by cutting references to the
PAP to a minimum.

As a contrast to both these papers the *Warta Negara*
gave the PMIP almost two thirds of the space it gave the
Alliance.   In announcing the results *Utusan Melayu* and
Berita Harian headlines gave prominence only to Alliance
successes.   The *Warta Negara* headlines were much more
balanced: they included, just after the election: 'PMIP in
power again in Kelantan but their Deputy Mentri Besar
defeated'; 'Mentri Besar of Perlis happy.   Defeated in one
constituency because of rain — he said'.   In 1963 the
Warta Negara was owned by a small group of persons,
each of whom had invested several thousand dollars in it.
A few months before the election it was bought by some
PMIP sympathizers including a PMIP office-holder who

was one of the party's key men in north-west Malaya. However *Warta Negara* was not turned into an out-and-out PMIP propaganda vehicle; it gave a fair and balanced treatment of the election. Its editorials were very general and showed goodwill to both the Alliance and the PMIP; 'the Alliance has the intelligence to rule and the intelligence to oppose is with the PMIP' (8 April). On 22 April it featured a speech by a former head of PMIP youth, urging PMIP and UMNO to unite for the interest of the Malays and the Islamic religion. Several months after the election it was sold to *Utusan Melayu*.

The *Straits Times* has by far the largest circulation of the newspapers in Malaya. It has been frequently attacked on the ground that it is largely European-owned and European-controlled. Its relations with the Alliance Government have generally been good. The PAP, before it formed the Government of Singapore, violently attacked the paper on several occasions, but after it came to power in 1959 friction has been much less.[17] During the election the *Straits Times* unmistakably supported the Alliance. From the beginning of the campaign it took the line that an Alliance win was certain, and that the only doubt concerned the size of its majority. Its support for the Alliance gained in emphasis as the campaign progressed. On 24 April the Tengku's radio broadcast was reproduced almost complete, the only one to be so reported. On the same day an editorial, 'The Plain Choice' indicated that the choice should be the Alliance. It claimed that the Alliance slogan, 'A vote for the Socialist Front or the PMIP is a vote for Soekarno' contained much less exaggeration and much more truth than political rallying-cries usually did. The possible cross-pressures arising from the entry of the PAP into the elections were met in a rather different way from the *Berita Harian* solution. The PAP was given good coverage, considering the small number

[17] Ronald McKie, *Malaysia in Focus*. Sydney, 1963, p. 99; *Straits Times*, 29 May, 9 and 11 June and 15 September 1959 and 15 June 1963. The issue of 15 September 1959 gives an account of the International Press Institute Report on the Singapore Press by M. Armand Gaspard.

of seats it was contesting, and very fair treatment in headlines and presentation. The treatment of the PAP, as
compared with the SF, is exemplified in the headline of
16 April referring to a University Political Forum, 'Rajaratnam [PAP] confronts Miss Lim [SF] but she evades the
issues'. But in its editorials the paper was studiedly non-
committal on the PAP. It set the tone when the PAP
decision to contest the elections had been announced. 'A
particularly absorbing detail is how far the PAP will
succeed in establishing its influence north of the causeway'
(2 March). During the campaign this attitude was maintained. The PAP was given coverage, but it was neither
recommended to the electors nor was it denounced. The
Malay Mail, which also belongs to the *Straits Times* group,
adopted a very similar policy on reporting the election,
but its political coverage on Malaya was less thorough and
it devoted much space to 'feature articles' of general interest. It kept off the election in its editorials most of the
time. But on 2 March and 24 April it questioned the
desire and capacity of the opposition parties to deal with
'confrontation'. In a post-election editorial on 27 April
it specifically mentioned the SF and the UDP. The Alliance victory, it was said, was a rejection of these parties'
criticism of the Alliance handling of the Malaysia question. The tone of the headlines and news items towards
the PAP was friendly. The party was not mentioned in
editorials, except that on 13 March the choice of Mr. Lee
to head a mission to the United States was warmly approved. Other parties were not given much space, but
reports on them were quite fair.

The *Malayan Times,* although its Singapore circulation
is very small and although it is partly owned by persons
related to an Alliance Minister, Dato Sambanthan, gave
the PAP very good coverage. Editorially there was support for the Alliance, expressed in a reasoned manner. In
an editorial of 24 April it was assumed that the Alliance
would win and that only the size of the majority was in
question. Malaysia's most pressing problem was national
survival, and an overwhelming majority of the electors

would vote for the party most competent to deal with this problem. The PAP was scarcely mentioned in the editorials, even at the time when it entered the elections. However, in a post-election editorial on 27 April it was said that both the PAP and the SF had failed to understand that Malayans did not want a regimented economy. The PAP had won in Bungsar because the party appealed to educated young people who had no patience with traditional methods. The SF received hostile treatment in headlines. As the election drew nearer headline references to the Front became more unfavourable. Among the headlines on 17 April were: 'Socialist Front and PMIP leaders worked to bring in Japanese in last war'; 'Socialist Front leader denies Bung[18] has given $120 million [sic] for election costs'; 'Radio Indonesia calls for vote Socialist Front'. On 24 April, the day before the election, the headlines included: 'Eve of polls blast — Front's Treason. House to house bid to stop youths from defending country'; 'Socialist Front supporters of Bung threaten our way of life — Dato Sambanthan'; 'The Socialist Front clique is toeing Bung's line, Dr. Lim'.

Several Chinese newspapers circulate in Malaya, but the two with the largest circulations are the *Nanyang Siang Pau* and the *Sin Chew Jit Poh*. The *Sin Chew Jit Poh* was owned by a group which also owned two papers in Hong Kong, one in Bangkok and one in Penang. Both these newspapers also have large Singapore circulations. It may, or may not, be coincidental that the proportion of column-inches given to the PAP in the *Sin Chew Jit Poh* was higher than in the *Nanyang Siang Pau,* and that the former's circulation was proportionately higher in Singapore than in Malaya. Since Independence, Chinese newspapers have tended to be very 'correct' *vis-à-vis* the Government. However, a rather inaccurate impression is given by the following quotation, intended to refer to the Press about ten months after the election; '. . . the Malay-language paper *Utusan Melayu* continues to articulate the Malay point of view unchecked, while the

18 'Bung' Karno, i.e. 'Brother' Soekarno.

Chinese papers say virtually nothing, except on education and the place of the Chinese language in education'.[19] This estimate of the situation is misleading, because it has been precisely chiefly through agitation on the Chinese language and education issues that the 'Chinese view' has been expressed since independence. The controversy on this topic, which reached its climax at the 1959 elections and shortly afterwards, naturally received very full coverage then in the Chinese Press.

However, both the papers analysed were very fair as between the parties, although quantitatively *Sin Chew Jit Poh* apparently gave more space to the PAP compared with the SF, while the *Nanyang Siang Pau* gave them approximately equal space. In its editorials the *Nanyang Siang Pau* hardly discussed the election at all, although on 27 April it said that an important factor in the victory of the Alliance was the Tengku's having sought a mandate against Indonesia and it also referred to the people's 'wise choice'. The *Sin Chew Jit Poh* devoted a little more editorial space to the election than the *Nanyang Siang Pau*. At the time of the PAP entry, without explicitly attacking that party, it quoted the Chinese proverb on the inadvisability of changing one's boat in deep rapids or one's horse at the edge of a precipice (2 March). On election day it gave no direct advice on how to vote, but said that the elections were a test of ability to exercise the strength to resist aggression and elect a government which would defend the national freedom, independence and sovereignty of Malaysia (25 April). The headlines, which in Chinese papers tend to be fuller than in English-language papers, were impartial in the sense that they summarized what followed without giving any slant. The headlines in both papers on 25 April gave most prominence to Alliance statements and somewhat less prominence to the PAP. In the *Nanyang Siang Pau* the Socialist Front was given almost as many headlines as the PAP; in the *Sin Chew Jit Poh* it was given substantially less, but,

19 *Far Eastern Economic Review*, 4 March 1965, p. 372.

to balance this, one of the headlines read 'Subandrio says that Malaysia problem should be solved by Asians. There will be more tension if other countries interfere.' However, in both papers one of the headlines concerned the accusation, which had just been made by the Alliance and which was therefore 'news', that the PMIP Government in Kelantan had mortgaged state land and so made the people suffer.[20]   These were the only two headlines which concerned the PMIP during the entire campaign.

In the last year or so the Tamil papers have appeared discontinuously.   The *Tamil Nesan* was the main exception. But, among the other principal Tamil papers, the production of the *Tamil Murasu* was interrupted during the election period so that no analysis of its contents could be made.   The *Tamil Malar* was founded only a week or two before the election campaign began.   The *Malai Nadu* appeared throughout the election period, but ceased publication soon afterwards.

The *Malai Nadu* gave great prominence to news about political figures of Indian or Ceylonese descent.   When candidates were nominated, photographs of ten of them were printed.   Five were Indian or Ceylonese by racial origin; among the other five were the Tengku, Tun Razak and Mr. Tan Siew Sin.   There were editorials giving general advice about what kind of candidates were desirable. They should not be extremists, either of the right or the left; those who talked most were not necessarily effective. An editorial on 1 April attacked the SF leaders as being more desirous of fulfilling their own ambitions to come to power instead of serving the masses.   The 11 April editorial came out clearly in favour of the Alliance.   A feature, 'Here and There' attacked, on occasions, both the PAP and the Socialist Front.   On 2 April it prophetically foresaw that the PAP attack on the MCA might later be followed by attacks on UMNO and MIC.

The *Tamil Malar* asserted early in the campaign, in its editorial of 22 March, that the Tengku and his party would win.   Later it deplored the possibility that the

20 See Chapter VI.

Tengku might retire; this would be a misfortune for the nation, said its editorial of 3 April. However, at the founding of the paper in Singapore some weeks before, the chief speaker had been Mr. Toh Chin Chye, the Singapore Deputy Prime Minister. It would have been surprising, therefore, if the *Tamil Malar* had opposed the PAP. In fact it defended the PAP from attack by the MCA. Mr. Tan Siew Sin had said that 'without Malaysia Singapore would be a corpse', meaning that, without the help of the central government, Singapore could not have overcome its communists. An editorial on 4 April, entitled 'Why Whip Singapore?', replied: 'The people of Singapore feel deeply hurt by this unprovoked attack of the Finance Minister. Singapore is behind no other part of Malaysia in making it a success.'

The *Tamil Nesan* did not commit itself editorially on the conflict between the Alliance and the PAP, although it gave news coverage to some of the bitter exchanges between the leaders of the two parties. It did not, however, follow a general policy of remaining neutral. Its editorial of 26 March referred to some of the charges made against the SF and the PMIP by the Alliance, and challenged these two parties to remove all doubts about their loyalty to Malaysia and to show that they were not being used by Indonesia in its policy of 'confrontation'. Support for the Government was also implied in the editorial of 3 April, where the hope was expressed that the Tengku's leadership of Malaysia would continue for a long time to come.

There is as yet no such thing as the 'Malaysian Press'. This is not primarily because of external influences, although some of the Indian papers give great prominence to events in India and the English papers magnify the importance of the British 'social world'. The Chinese papers for some years have been very restrained in comments on what is happening in mainland China, and since confrontation the Malay papers have naturally ceased to be sympathetic to the government of Indonesia. The divisions which exist in the Press reflect the divisions between the various communities in Malaya and Malaysia. Not long after the elections the Finance Minister, Mr. Tan Siew Sin, referred to the well-known fact that each of the four main language groups in Malaya lived in a separate world. He thought that the newspapers could help to break down the barriers between these worlds. It would be a good idea if 'the *Straits Times* were to publish what is written in the *Utusan Melayu* and *Utusan Melayu* were to publish what is written in the *Nanyang Siang Pau* and so on'.[21] The recommendation may be debatable, but the diagnosis is certainly sound. Even the high degree of support which the Press in general gave to the Alliance Party did not obscure decided differences of approach in newspapers printed in different languages.

Radio and Television

At the time of the election there were approximately 350,000 radio licences in existence in Malaya. There was a small number of additional radio Rediffusion subscribers who paid licence fees on a monthly basis, and a larger number of 'pirates', perhaps approximately 50,000, who paid no licence fees at all. There are no figures available on exposure to election broadcasts specifically. However, generally, a Radio Malaya Listener Survey in 1961 included the following findings: 90 per cent. of the population were exposed to radio sometime during the week; the mean number of radio owners who had their radios switched on was 31 per cent; of those listening at any time 47 per cent. were on the Malay programme, 22 per cent. on the English, 21 per cent. on the Chinese and 10 per cent. on the Indian.

Until April 1964, the month in which the election was held, television in Malaya was new and was confined to the area round Kuala Lumpur; it was already well-established in Singapore. Not until February 1964 were special

21 *Sunday Times,* 16 August 1964.

licences required in Malaya to view television, in addition to ordinary radio licences.

Although there has been commercial advertising on the radio since 1962, it is not possible for political parties to buy time on the air. Political parties can explicitly appeal to the voters through the medium of broadcasting at election time only in programmes specifically allocated to parties for the purpose of political broadcasts. It is therefore not possible for a rich party to buy more radio time than a poor party. However, it is still possible that the allocation of time between parties for election broadcasts, particularly between the Government party and the opposition parties, could be unfair, although it is hard to define what might constitute 'unfairness'. For the 1964 election the Government started from the premise that it was 'privileged to command 50 per cent. of the total allotted airtimes for Party political broadcasts, and to start and end the series'. A formula was given out for the allocation of time among opposition parties, which depended on the number of candidates they put up for parliamentary elections. One of its provisions was that parties which put up fewer than twenty candidates, and Independents, would not receive any air time.[22] When the formula was applied to the parties with more than twenty candidates, the effect was to split the opposition time equally among the SF, PMIP and UDP. These three parties together were given the same total amount of time as the Alliance.

In terms of the votes cast in 1959, when the Alliance

[22] *Procedure on 1964 Parliamentary Election Campaign Broadcasts by Political Parties.* (Mimeographed, 1 April 1964.) At the 1959 election the Government did not enjoy such a preponderance. The number of broadcasts was based on the number of candidates. The Alliance Party was allocated five broadcasts; the PMIP, four, the Socialist Front, three and the PPP, one. Each broadcast could be given in up to four languages. While in 1964 the Alliance had 50 per cent. of the time allocated, in 1959 it had under 40 per cent. Another difference was that in 1959 ten candidates were enough to qualify a party for a broadcast, compared with twenty in 1964.

obtained just over half, the equal division of time between the Government and all opposition parties combined was not unreasonable. But while such an arrangement gives the opposition party equal time with the Government in a two-party system, in Malaya it reflects the fragmentation of the opposition and does not give any single opposition party nearly as much time as the Government party. In restrospect, the UDP, which was a new party, gained from the use of the number of candidates as the basis. In terms of parliamentary seats it did worse in 1964 than the PPP. Yet the allocation of time put the UDP on an equal footing with the SF and the PMIP, each of which won a much higher percentage of the vote in 1964 than the UDP.

The broadcasts were in four languages: Malay, English, Chinese and Tamil. Each individual broadcast was limited to thirteen minutes. For the Chinese broadcasts a party could select either Mandarin, Cantonese, Amoy or Hakka, but all its broadcasts had to be in the same dialect. The broadcasts had to be recorded in advance, and there were certain limits on their content. They were supposed to be on a party basis and not to refer to a particular candidate or constituency; however, reference could be made to a policy statement by a political opponent. The following were banned: material which might be construed as an incitement to the use of violence; statements which might be 'construed as a material or spiritual threat to induce an elector to vote or refrain from voting'; criticism which was 'vilifying or couched in unparliamentary language'; material criticizing or extolling the foreign policies of countries other than Malaysia.[23] These prohibitions are all intelligible in the light of the nature of politics in Malaya, which makes for extreme sensitivity to religious or ethnic references.

The broadcasts which were actually delivered were as follows:

[23] *Ibid.* The provisions closely followed those in force for the 1959 election. *Federal Government Press Statement*, D. INF. 5/59/59 (I and J).

TABLE IX
PARTY POLITICAL BROADCASTS, 1964 ELECTION[a]

ALLIANCE	OPPOSITION
	Broadcasts in Malay

	Socialist Front
Tengku Abdul Rahman (2)	Inche Hasnul Abdul Hadi
Tun Razak	Inche Tajuddin Kahar
Dato Syed Ja'afar Albar	Inche Ishak bin Haji Mohammad
Tuan Haji Mohd. Khir bin Johari	
Inche Senu bin Abdul Rahman	*PMIP*
Dato Dr. Ismail	Dr. Burhanuddin bin Mohd. Noor
Datin Fatimah binte Haji Hashim	Inche Mohammad Asri bin Haji
Inche Abdul Ghaffar bin Baba	Muda
	Inche Zulkiflee bin Muhammad

	Broadcasts in English
	Socialist Front
Tengku Abdul Rahman (2)	Inche Abdul Aziz bin Ishak
Tun Razak	Dr. Tan Chee Khoon
Dato Dr. Ismail	Miss P.G. Lim
Mr. V. Manickavasagam	
Mr. Tan Siew Sin	*PMIP*
Dr. Lim Swee Aun	Dr. Burhanuddin
Tuan Haji Mohd. Khir bin Johari	
Dato V.T. Sambanthan	*UDP*
	Mr. Ng Swee Kooi (2)
	Dr. Oh Siew Kheng

	Broadcasts in Chinese
	Socialist Front
Tengku Abdul Rahman (2)	Inche Abdul Aziz bin Ishak
Tun Razak	Dr. Tan Chee Khoon
Dr. Lim Swee Aun	Mr. Ng Ann Teck
Mr. Tan Siew Sin	
Mr. Chan Chong Wen	
Senator Khaw Kai Boh (2)	
Mr. Lee Siok Yew	

	Broadcasts in Tamil
	Socialist Front
Tengku Abdul Rahman	Mr. V. David (2)
Tun Razak	
Mr. V. J. Balasundaram	
Mr. V. Manickavasagam (2)	
Senator S.O.K. Ubaidulla	
Dr. P.T. Arasu	
Senator Athi Nahappan	
Dato V. T. Sambanthan	

[a] The names in the Table are those of the speakers in the 'original' language. In some languages the speeches were 'voiced' in translations by other speakers.

It is evident that parties which made a serious appeal to more than one ethnic group, such as the Alliance and the SF, had an advantage over others which could not make profitable use of the time allotted in some languages. For instance, there was little point in the PMIP making use of its broadcasting time in Chinese or Tamil, although it would have been an interesting challenge to have composed a PMIP script designed for Chinese listeners. More surprisingly, the PMIP gave only one out of three possible English broadcasts. The UDP did not use its Chinese, Malay or Tamil broadcasting time, nor did its secretary-general, Dr. Lim Chong Eu, give any of the broadcasts in English. The SF did not use one of its allotted Tamil times. In some cases the returns from giving such broadcasts might have been marginal, nevertheless it made some of the opposition parties' complaints about the small amount of time allocated to them superficially a little hard to justify.

In all four languages the Alliance made use of talks by the Tengku and Tun Razak. Their own voices were used in Malay and English; their speeches were read by others in the Chinese and Tamil translations. In Malay the other speakers were the Tengku, in a second speech, three present or future Cabinet Ministers (Dr. Ismail, Inche Khir Johari and Inche Senu), the secretary-general of UMNO (Dato Syed Ja'afar Albar), the leader (Datin Fatimah) of the UMNO Kaum Ibu (Women' Section) and the Chief Minister of Malacca (Inche Abdul Ghaffar bin Baba). All the English broadcasts were by present or future Cabinet Ministers, five by Malays, two by Chinese and two by Indians. In Chinese three of the Alliance broadcasts were by Malays, two by the Tengku and one by Tun Razak. Four were by Ministers (Mr. Tan, Dr. Lim and Senator Khaw (2)), one by the secretary-general of the MCA (Mr. Lee), and one by an M.P. (Mr. Chan).[24] The Tamil Alliance broadcasts included four which were also given in English, by the Tengku, by Tun Razak, by Mr. Manickavasagam

[24] Those by the Tengku, Tun Razak, Mr. Tan and Dr. Lim were 'voiced' by other speakers.

and by Dato Sambanthan (voiced by Mr. Manickavasagam). Another broadcast was also given by Mr. Manickavasagam, then an Assistant Minister and later a Minister. Two others were given by senators.

The SF English broadcasters were: Inche Abdul Aziz bin Ishak, a former Alliance Cabinet Minister, whose National Convention Party had recently joined the Front; Dr. Tan Chee Khoon, one of the Front's two successful parliamentary candidates; Miss P.G. Lim, sister of the other successful parliamentary candidate, Mr. Lim Kean Siew. In Chinese the talks given in English by Inche Abdul Aziz bin Ishak and Dr. Tan Chee Khoon were voiced by other speakers. The third talk in Chinese, by Mr. Ng Ann Teck, was original. The Front's three Malay talks were given by Inche Hasnul, President of the Malacca municipal council, Inche Tajuddin Kahar, secretary-general of the SF and Inche Ishak bin Haji Mohammad, former SF chairman. The two Tamil broadcasts were both given by Mr. David, a prominent trade unionist and member of Parliament, who was defeated at the election.

The PMIP chose its president, Dr. Burhanuddin to speak in both English and Malay. The other two speakers in Malay were Inche Zulkiflee, Deputy President of the Party, and Inche Mohammad Asri, a Vice-President, who later became Mentri Besar of Kelantan.

Two of the UDP English broadcasts were given by Mr. Ng Swee Kooi, the party's assistant secretary-general. The other was given by Dr. Oh Siew Kheng, who practises medicine in Malacca.

It is not proposed to examine the contents of the election broadcasts in detail. The themes were not markedly different from those which occurred in the other forms of election propaganda. Some speakers covered several topics in the time they had. Others, particularly Alliance speakers, who could afford to specialize because of their party's larger allocation of time, kept mainly to a single topic. Thus, Tun Razak talked mainly about economic development and Mr. Manickavasagam mainly about labour conditions, while Mr. Tan Siew Sin, Dr. Lim Swee Aun and

Tuan Syed Ja'afar Albar devoted most of their time to the Indonesian threat. Datin Fatimah made a special appeal to women. If there was a change of government it would be the women and children who would suffer. However, it is perhaps worth while to look at the broadcasts briefly from three points of view. What rival parties were chiefly attacked in a party's broadcasts? What allegations were made that other parties were not observing the 'rules of the game'? What appeals and references were made on communal themes and issues?

In his two broadcasts the Tengku hit out at all the opposition parties, including the PAP, and devoted a particularly scathing section to Inche Abdul Aziz bin Ishak without naming him. In the Alliance English and Malay broadcasts the SF and the PMIP were attacked most, because clearly they constituted the greatest threat to the Alliance. The SF was usually mentioned first. In the Alliance Chinese broadcasts, however, the PAP was given considerable, and unfavourable, prominence. It was attacked more fiercely than any other party in the broadcasts of Senator Khaw Kai Boh[25] and in the broadcast of Mr. Lee Siok Yew, that is, in three of the four original broadcasts in Chinese. The SF concentrated most of its fire on the Alliance; however, perhaps significantly, one of Mr. David's Tamil broadcasts contained a long and bitter attack on the PAP. An Indian PAP candidate was opposing Mr. David in his own constituency and in fact defeated him by a narrow margin. Inche Hasnul Abdul Hadi, speaking in Malay, also included the PAP in his attacks; so did Mr. Ng Ann Teck in Chinese. The PMIP's attacks were mostly on the Alliance, its chief rival for the Malay vote. However, Dr. Burhanuddin did not mention any other party but his own; most of his broadcast was devoted to the principles of Islam and included a quotation from the Koran. Most of the UDP attacks on other parties were aimed at the Alliance.

[25] Mr. Khaw, in the Special Branch in Singapore, had come into conflict with the PAP government before his early retirement in 1959.

In several of the broadcasts the 'rules of the game' were called in question. In their opening remarks several SF speakers made reference to the small amount of time allocated to the party, and also mentioned the detention of some of its key party workers by the Government and the refusal of the Government to licence its party organs. Inche Tajuddin Kahar said that without its own newspapers the party was like a boxer fighting with his hands tied behind his back. The Press in Malaya was owned either by British interests or by members of the Government, so the SF could not obtain space to answer the accusations against it. Regardless of the maxim, *qui s'excuse s'accuse*, Inche Ishak bin Haji Mohammad (SF) warned his listeners that the Alliance might spread slanders accusing him of having been a Japanese stooge, of being Soekarno's agent and of not being sane. Inche Mohammad Asri (PMIP) complained that the Alliance did not respect freedom of election, but was perpetually making arrests and threatening to make arrests. On the other hand half a dozen of the Alliance speakers accused the SF and the PMIP of collaboration with the Indonesians although the scope of the accusations varied. In his first talk the Tengku said that a good many of the PMIP and SF *leaders* were 'in constant contact with elements in Indonesia through Ibrahim Yaacob[26] and others'. He also said, however, that SF *members* feared domination by Indonesia because they knew of the sufferings of the Chinese in Indonesia. In his second talk he referred to the SF as 'openly siding with Indonesia', and described some of their pamphlets as treachery and treason. He said the PMIP was 'working hand in hand with Indonesia to topple this government by force of arms'. Inche Abdul Ghaffar bin Baba (Alliance), in Malay, said the SF and PMIP were agents of Indonesia, because they opposed the call-up. They would open the gates to communist soldiers led by Aidit, the Indonesian Communist leader or Mao Tse Tung.

26 A former Malay nationalist leader who was a member of a Malayan 'government in exile' in Indonesia.

The PMIP broadcasts were entirely 'communal' in the sense that they were addressed to one particular community. The emphasis was on Malay rights, particularly in education and language, and on Islam. The majority of the Alliance broadcasts were not beamed towards particular ethnic groups: this was particularly true of the English broadcasts which were obviously not intended for any single group. However, Mr. Tan Siew Sin's broadcast, which was given in both English and Chinese was explicitly directed to the Chinese: 'I speak to you tonight as one Malaysian Chinese to another Malaysian Chinese. This is not because I wish to take a communal approach, but because the Malaysian Chinese in this crucial election are in a critical position.' Mr. Tan's argument was that, if the Chinese voted for SF candidates instead of for the MCA and the Alliance, this might encourage some Malays who had previously been in favour of an independent Malaysia to revise their thinking and consider merger with Indonesia. Consequently, the stand of the UMNO leaders against Indonesia would be weakened. Mr. Lee Siok Yew, another Alliance speaker, who broadcast in Chinese only, took up the theme of the suffering of the Chinese in Indonesia. How could the SF, sympathetic to anti-Chinese Indonesia, fight for the interests of the Chinese in Malaysia? Two of the Alliance Tamil broadcasts, by Senator Ubaidulla and Mr. Balasundaram, made specifically Indian appeals. The former said that if the communists came to power they would try to execute the unpatriotic policies backed by the Indian communists when China invaded India. The latter devoted his entire speech to what the Alliance had done for Tamil education and the Tamil language. In the only SF broadcasts given exclusively in Chinese Mr. Ng Ann Teck devoted about a tenth of his time to the question of Chinese education. The Front's Malay broadcasts were not specifically communal, being devoted to the theme of poverty, to foreign control of the economy and to the Alliance Government's forcing through the creation of Malaysia and so creating trouble with Indonesia. At the start of an English UDP broadcast Mr. Ng Swee Kooi refuted the allegation that his party was 'Chinese'. In the broadcasts of all parties except the PMIP there were very few appeals and arguments that were openly communal.

The arrangements for recording the broadcasts did not work entirely smoothly. This was not the fault of the broadcasting authorities. Some speakers had not been briefed by their parties about avoiding personal references and were annoyed when the producers informed them about it. Some recordings were made only at the last minute; because of the pressure of the election campaign some speakers failed to turn up at the appointed time for making their recordings. On the other hand there were cases of persons trying to make arrangements for recording talks who had not been authorized to do so by their parties. The talks which were actually broadcast did not always correspond to the schedule of talks which had been planned.

The influence of broadcasting on party politics is not confined to party political broadcasts at election times. Between elections there are items in broadcast programmes which are of political significance. There are few of these in Malaya compared with some other places, such as Singapore. For example, there were few political talks or debates broadcast in Malaya between the 1959 and 1964 elections. For most of this period the main source of political information via the Radio was news broadcasts. However, starting several weeks before the election there was a series of about twenty ministerial broadcasts of about 800 words each on the work of the various government departments. These talks were given on radio and on television (which at that time was in an experimental stage in Malaya with reception limited to the Kuala Lumpur area). Ostensibly these broadcasts were not party political, but references in them to the achievements of the Alliance Government must have helped to create a favourable image of the Alliance Party.

Moreover, listeners and viewers in Malaya could be reached via transmitters outside Malaya. Quite apart from broadcasts from Indonesia, they could receive radio programmes, and also (particularly in the state of Johore and even as far north as Malacca) television programmes from Singapore. Radio Singapore repeated the series of ministerial broadcasts on the work of various government departments referred to previously. On Singapore television between 18 March and 23 April there were the following political items: talks by six Federal Government ministers, including the Tengku, and one assistant minister;[27] interviews with Mr. Lim Kean Siew and Dr. Tan Chee Khoon (SF); on 23 April, the eve of election day, talks by political leaders from six different parties.[28] In one respect the coverage was more complete than the radio coverage in Malaya; the PAP and PPP were included, while in Malaya they had been omitted.

In the same period on Singapore television there was also a news interview with the Tengku and five extracts from speeches by Mr. Lee Kuan Yew given to various bodies in Singapore.

[27] Perhaps significantly, in view of the PAP's overall strategy, all seven of these speakers were from UMNO.

[28] Tengku Abdul Rahman, Tun Razak, Mr. Tan Siew Sin and Dato Sambanthan (Alliance); Dr. Tan Chee Khoon (Socialist Front); Inche Zulkiflee (PMIP); Mr. Lee Kuan Yew (PAP); Mr. D.R. Seenivasagam (PPP) and Dr. Lim Chong Eu (UDP).

IX

Constituency Studies

(a) PASIR PUTEH (Kelantan)

PASIR PUTEH is fairly typical of the rural constituencies in north and north-east Malaya. Its population is relatively poor and predominantly Malay; rice cultivation is the main source of livelihood, together with some fishing and rubber production. Being situated in Kelantan it was particularly interesting for a case study, since there was every indication that local issues and federal-state relations would constitute an important part of the campaign.[1] Also, as in the majority of constituencies in that state, the main features of the traditional society in Malaya are well displayed in Pasir Puteh. A study of such a constituency thus provided an opportunity to observe in some detail the various pressures exerted by the traditional order on representative government.

Like some of the other rural constituencies in the country, the boundaries of Pasir Puteh coincide with those of a 'district'.[2] The geographic limits of the local administrative hierarchy's sphere of influence[3] thereby coincided exactly with those of the constituency. Further, districts constitute major units in the 1957 Census Report, and this made it much easier to get reliable information on some of the main features of the constituency.

Pasir Puteh was hardly affected by any population movement since the 1959 election, and the only changes in the

[1] Kelantan, it will be remembered, was the only state in Malaya which had a non-Alliance government at the time of the election.

[2] In this case the district of Pasir Puteh. 'Districts' are the main administrative subdivisions of each state, and have their own administrative hierarchy headed by a District Officer.

[3] For some discussion of the political influence of this hierarchy, see Chapter VII.

composition of the electorate were those caused by deaths and the inclusion of new voters who had attained the age of twenty-one during the intervening period. The net increase was just over 700, from 26,326 to 27,042. The communal breakdown remained almost the same, Malays constituting about 97 per cent. of the total.

As expected, only the Alliance and the PMIP put up candidates.[4] The PMIP candidate, Mohammad Asri bin Haji Muda, had been returned in this constituency in 1959, when he defeated his sole opponent, an Alliance candidate, by about 5,650 votes.[5] He was in his early forties, and had been involved in politics since 1945. He had joined the PMIP in 1953, having earlier been active in the Malay nationalist movement through the Malay Nationalist Party and a couple of small regional parties which he had helped to organize. Before making politics his career, he had been a teacher in a private Malay school. At the time of the election he was the national vice-president of his party, and was known to be one of its chief organizers and perhaps its best tactician. He also contested a state seat inside Kelantan, but not in Pasir Puteh.

In contrast the Alliance candidate, Haji Idris bin Ismail, was entering active politics for the first time. He was by no means unique in this, since, as pointed out earlier,[6] the Alliance had decided on a deliberate policy of putting up new candidates throughout Kelantan, being firmly convinced that its defeat in 1959 had in no small measure been caused by the 'bad reputation' of many of its candidates and the political capital which the PMIP was able to make of this. The emphasis was now on candidates with 'clean records', and earlier non-involvement in politics was taken to be one of the safest guarantees of this.

In his early fifties, Haji Idris was a retired teacher. Im-

[4] This was typical of Kelantan as a whole. See Chapter V.

[5] Asri had also contested the 1955 election as the PMIP candidate for Kelantan Timor, but had been defeated by 30,954 votes to 2,292 by an Alliance candidate. This was a three-cornered fight, the third candidate (from Party Negara) getting 4,019 votes.

[6] See Chapter V.

mediately before his retirement he had been a kind of supervisor of schools (*guru perlawat* — literally, 'visiting teacher') and, in this capacity, was thought to have established a good reputation, while also making some useful contacts.   There were, however, some who felt that a long career as a government servant had not failed to leave its mark on him, and that he was not sufficiently outgoing, and lacked the ability to relax and be informal in his relations with people — clearly not a politician!   But everyone was agreed that he was a 'nice man', and even his opponent, who had once been his pupil, thought highly of him as a person.   Thus, in terms of respectability and a 'clean record', Haji Idris was clearly a reasonable choice, although in terms of political skill there did not seem to be so much to recommend him.   But this was not considered a serious drawback by the state Alliance organizers, since they had every intention of making *the party* the main contestant in every Kelantan constituency.   It was enough that the candidate had a clean record and was prepared to work hard.   He was not required to have much initiative or any financial backing, since the party was going to organize and manage his entire campaign.[7]   The Alliance was throwing in everything in its bid to defeat the PMIP in Kelantan; it was not prepared to let the outcome depend on the relative merits of its candidates and their ability to run the campaign, although these were undoubtedly of some value. There was no doubt in the minds of officials and workers in Pasir Puteh that it was the party's image that had to be projected during the campaign, and that this would be the most effective means of winning votes.   As a result, the candidate came to be completely regulated by the party machine.   Every detail of the campaign, right down to the issues to be raised at meetings, the tactics to be employed,

7 Dato Nik Kamil, the party's candidate in Kelantan Hilir, was in many ways an exception to all this.   He was from a very well-known Kelantan family, and had had a most distinguished career which included being Mentri Besar of Kelantan, the Malayan High Commissioner in Australia, and the country's Permanent Delegate to the United Nations.   He was obviously expected to have a personal following.   He was also a man of considerable means, and did not require any financial help from the party.

the allocation of responsibilities among workers, and even the candidate's daily time-table, was laid down by the party organization. Each morning, before proceeding on his campaign tour, the candidate was required to spend about an hour being briefed at the party's divisional head-quarters.

Generally, it was also the PMIP's policy to emphasize the party more than the candidate. In the case of Pasir Puteh, however, the candidate's personal prominence and impor-tance within the party made it virtually impossible to distinguish between 'the party' and 'the candidate' in the management of the campaign. Being one of the party's chief policy makers, Asri automatically became the most influential person in his own election machine. This, however, only meant that he was not dominated by the organizers in his constituency; it did not mean that he per-sonally supervised all aspects of the campaign. There was, in addition, no evidence that the candidate's personal ap-peal was heavily relied upon to win the election.

As far as the election machinery of the two parties was concerned, there were no features peculiar to Pasir Puteh. The Alliance had an Action Committee for the consti-tuency, with secretaries to look after various functions.[8] A 'sub-centre' was established for each *daerah*,[9] and a 'super-visor' was placed in charge of each polling station. These supervisors co-ordinated the party machine in each polling district,[10] and were also in charge of the work done by the rank and file of party workers.

The PMIP's election organization was roughly similar. There was an Election Committee for the constituency as a whole, and sub-committees for each polling district. The latter co-ordinated the activities of party branches where

[8] One each for transport, relations with police, organization of rallies, finance, public relations, election procedures, and general supervision of the election machinery. There were similar secretaries for the state as a whole, and those in Pasir Puteh had direct links with them.

[9] The district of Pasir Puteh is subdivided into eight *daerahs*.

[10] There were 36 polling districts in Pasir Puteh, and 78 Alliance branches.

there were more than one in any polling district,[11] and were also in charge of party workers generally. Sub-committees were also set up to look after various aspects of the campaign: transport, food and drinks for workers, meetings, posters, and security.

Although there was some geographic sub-division of authority (in the sense that polling districts — and, in the case of the Alliance, *daerahs* as well — constituted distinct organizational units), the main devolution of authority seems to have been functional in the case of both parties. On the whole the Alliance machinery was the more elaborate of the two, and its ground workers, who numbered about 2,500, were almost twice as many as those of the PMIP.

Most of the issues raised in Pasir Puteh were either national ones or had a Kelantan-wide significance. These were: religion, Malay rights, Malaysia and confrontation, rural development, and, during the last couple of days of the campaign, the famous Kelantan 'land deal'. Since all these have been discussed in the Chapter on 'Issues', there is no need for further elaboration here: their treatment in Pasir Puteh was in no way different from that in the rest of Kelantan. To be sure, the PMIP also played heavily on the theme of fighting a rearguard action in Kelantan to avoid the fate which had supposedly befallen the other states, *viz.* Chinese domination. As against this, the Alliance kept emphasizing that Kelantan's only hope lay in having an Alliance state government because it was the only one that could co-operate with the federal government and thereby bring to Kelantan the benefits which the other states had been enjoying.[12] According to them, not only had Kelantan seen no progress under the PMIP, but it had become much poorer in relation to the other states; and, while Malays in other parts of the country were the ones benefiting most from the central government's develop-

11 There were altogether about fifty PMIP branches in Pasir Puteh.

12 Although this issue would have been strictly appropriate only in the case of state candidates, it also assumed considerable significance in the parliamentary campaign.

ment programmes, those in Kelantan were being left sadly behind.

But there was also one essentially local issue which assumed great importance in Pasir Puteh. This concerned the clearing and allocation of new land, and, connected to it but less important, the provision of better irrigation facilities. Land shortage was evidently quite serious, and had mainly been caused by fragmentation due to inheritance. The Alliance accused the PMIP of having done little to meet this problem, and promised immediate action if it came to power.[13] It also alleged that the PMIP had taken advantage of the land hunger in Pasir Puteh by making poor peasants pay excessive sums for new land, when in fact no charge should have been levied. It was further claimed that in most cases money had been collected merely on the promise that land would be allocated after the election. The Alliance also made capital of the Federal Government's $25 million irrigation project in Kelantan, which was well under way and which would benefit Pasir Puteh when completed.

For its part the PMIP claimed that these charges either had no foundations whatsoever or were grossly exaggerated. On the one hand it argued that a great deal had in fact been done to develop the rural areas and to make new tracts of land available for cultivation; on the other, it claimed that it was unfair to criticize the PMIP for not having done much when the Alliance had itself not done a great deal during its first term of office, between 1955 and 1959. However, PMIP election officials in the constituency admitted that most of the plans for the alienation of new land in Pasir Puteh would not materialize until after the election, since the work of surveying had only just

13 This too was essentially an issue for the state candidates. However, its importance made it a major item of party conflict, hence its inclusion in the parliamentary campaign. Furthermore, since both elections were held simultaneously and the main effort by each party was to discredit the other wherever possible, it was inevitable that there should have been little distinction between the parliamentary and state campaigns.

been completed.[14]   Both parties were agreed on the relative importance of the various issues.   They had no hesitation in identifying religion and land as the two most important; they were equally convinced that the issues connected with Malaysia and 'confrontation' would not play a significant role.

Although undoubtedly very important, the issues and the efficiency of the election machinery of the two parties were by no means the only important factors which helped to win votes.   A major part of the battle was fought behind the scenes, and involved competition for the support of the local élites.   To the observer, this was in many ways the most interesting feature of the election.   As far as the parties were concerned, they were thoroughly convinced that winning the support of these élites was the first step, and perhaps the most important, in a successful campaign; if nothing else, they were at least satisfied that a party that could not maintain a competitive position in this respect stood little chance at the polls.

In discussing the local élites there are several groups that need to be considered, not all of equal political importance.   To begin with, attention may be focussed on the structure of local administration, since some of the groups concerned derive their influence from the official or semi-official positions they hold.

14 According to official figures, about 800 acres of land had been cleared and settled in Pasir Puteh between 1959 and 1964. Peasants had to pay the following rates when new lands were alienated to them:

	Rate per acre	
	Minimum	Maximum
	($)	($)
Padi land	10	15
Village land	20	40
Rubber land	25	70

(Maximum rates were charged only when a person had illegally occupied state land before his application had been approved.)

One of the Alliance charges was that peasants often had to pay PMIP officials extra sums in order to have their applications favourably considered. This was not substantiated, however.

Each *daerah* in the district of Pasir Puteh is under the administrative control of a *penggawa*. These *penggawas* are directly responsible to the District Officer, and are appointed by the State Service Commission.[15] Like the District Officer, they are expected to remain above politics, although they did not as a group remain free of political involvement during the election. But this involvement was generally kept within limits: while no doubt they influenced people to support the party of their own choice, they did not go to the extent of campaigning actively or of allowing the parties to hold election meetings in their homes. Although, as individuals, the *penggawas* did not have as close contacts with the people as the *penghulus* who were directly below them in the administrative hierarchy, both parties placed a high premium on winning them over since it was generally felt that this was a good way of getting the latter's support.

The *penggawas* in Pasir Puteh seem to have split evenly between the two parties. The Alliance organization felt that four out of the eight supported their party and the other four the PMIP, and that two on each side were 'active' supporters. The PMIP on the other hand felt that two were in fact neutral and that, of the remaining six, three supported their own party and the other three the Alliance.

Each *daerah* is further subdivided into a number of *mukims,* and there are sixty-four *mukims* in Pasir Puteh.[16] For each *mukim* a *penghulu* is appointed, directly responsible to the *penggawa*. Both posts, although now bureaucratized, are a part of the indigenous political system and

---

15 In addition to carrying out all directives issued by the District Officer, the main duties of the *penggawas* are: (1) the overall supervision of the *penghulus* in each *daerah;* (2) acting as the representatives of the Registrar of Births and Deaths; (3) assisting all other government officials working in each *daerah,* provided such assistance is requested through the District Officer; (4) assisting the Land Office in its work as directed by the District Officer; (5) keeping separate registers of all cattle and boats in each *daerah;* and (6) giving assistance to the police, the armed forces and the Medical Department whenever required.

16 Each *mukim* covers a small number of *kampongs* (villages).

retain much of their traditional significance. The *penghulus* are only part-time officers, receiving a quarterly allowance for performing various official duties.[17] Although there are 64 *mukims* in Pasir Puteh, there were only 52 *penghulus* at the time of the election: some of the posts which had fallen vacant had apparently not been filled because of stalemates caused by political differences among those involved in the selection procedure.[18] In view of these vacancies, some *penghulus* had been required to extend their duties to neighbouring *mukims*.

Officially, *penghulus*, like *penggawas*, are expected to refrain from active participation in politics. However, they in fact played quite a vigorous role during the campaign, many of them to the point of doing house-to-house canvassing. Although the tendency was for *penghulus* to support the same party as their *penggawas*, there were certainly some exceptions. But when this happened there was usually little open conflict since the hierarchy was respected,[19] and the *penghulus* simply withdrew from active campaigning. According to Alliance records 21 out of the 52 *penghulus* were Alliance supporters, and most of them had agreed to do some open canvassing. At a rough guess, PMIP officials felt that about 60 per cent. of the *penghulus* supported their party, although no estimate was given of the number who would do active canvassing. Once again, there was hardly any variation in the estimates

[17] The *penghulus* are appointed by the District Officer on the recommendation of the District Committee which comprises the Senior Assistant District Officer as chairman, a locally elected member of the State Legislative Council appointed by the Mentri Besar, and a *penggawa* appointed by the District Officer. Appointments have to be confirmed by the State Secretary. In addition to carrying out instructions issued by the *penggawas*, the main duties of the *penghulus* are: (1) keeping peace in the *mukim*; (2) assisting the police and other government officials; (3) transmitting information to the people concerning land matters (for example, payment of rent, etc.).

[18] This point was not officially conceded, although no other explanation was offered.

[19] Self-interest apparently being the main motive: generally the *penghulus* did not wish to incur the disfavour of the *penggawas*, since the security of their position depended partly on the latter's goodwill.

made by the two parties, but this is not true of the other estimates which follow.

The Alliance headquarters in Pasir Puteh had made a very careful study of the local administrative and traditional élites, and, in the case of the more important groups, had compiled lists to show which individuals supported the Alliance and which the PMIP. This information was fortunately made available, and many of the figures given here are therefore not verbal estimates but the actual information contained in the party files. Moreover, the estimates are in all likelihood quite accurate, since they were not based merely on promises made before the campaign had begun. Although the initial lists had to some extent relied on promises, many amendments were made in the course of the campaign based on reports by party workers concerning the actual participation of individuals in the campaign. The PMIP on the other hand had either not followed similar procedures, or, if they had, chose not to reveal detailed information. Support among the various groups was often given in percentages, with the admission that they were only rough estimates. In some cases there were substantial differences between the estimates made by the candidate and those of his campaign organizers. The percentages given here are those provided by the latter, both because they were less ambiguous in their answers and because the candidate himself (since so much of his time was taken up by work outside his own constituency) felt that they should know more about these matters.

The *imams* formed another very influential group. Like the *penghulus*, they are also only part-time officials, receiving a small allowance for performing a limited number of duties connected with the work of the State Religious Council. There is one *imam* for each *mukim*, and he is elected by the residents of that *mukim*. These elections are conducted by the State Religious Council, and, although the candidates contest on their own merits and are not party nominees, both parties do a certain amount of house-to-house campaigning. Since the parties have no legitimate role in these elections, campaigning is kept at an informal level: there is certainly no place for posters and rallies.

Of the 64 *imams* in Pasir Puteh, the Alliance considered 26 to be their supporters. The PMIP, on the other hand, felt that about 50 supported their own party. Mainly because of the religious significance of many of their duties, both parties considered the support of the *imams* to be very important.

There was another category of officials representing the State Religious Council, who also had some political significance. These were the *mubhalirs,* of whom there were eight in Pasir Puteh, one for each *daerah.* They were also only part-time officials, and received an allowance for their duties. Both parties were agreed that all eight *mubhalirs,* and the supervisor who was appointed to co-ordinate their work, supported the PMIP. This was not surprising, considering that they had all been appointed by the PMIP state government.

The next group to be considered are the *tok gurus,*[20] who are private religious teachers. They provide religious instruction in their own huts, and are regarded by the community as its main spiritual guides. Unlike the *imams, mubhalirs* and religious school teachers (who are all government servants of one kind or another), the *tok gurus* are looked upon as men with a genuine spiritual calling who have dedicated their whole lives to unfolding the true meaning of Islam. It was inevitable in Kelantan that this group should play a most vital role, particularly since both the Alliance and the PMIP sought justification for many of their policies on the basis of different interpretations of the Koran. Although there were only ten *tok gurus* in the constituency, both parties were agreed that they were undoubtedly the most influential group among the local élite. In addition to being in much closer contact with the people than the other groups mentioned,[21] they also

20 Called *tuan gurus* in the other states.

21 Being the main stalwarts of the traditional society, they naturally had an easy *rapport* with the predominantly rural population.

had the advantage of not being government servants and therefore of being free to campaign as they pleased.

PMIP officials were confident that 'most' of the *tok gurus* in Pasir Puteh supported them. Alliance officials were more specific, and stated that only two supported them while eight were pro-PMIP. This meant that, issues and election organization aside, the PMIP started the campaign with a very definite advantage. The link between the PMIP and the *tok gurus* is perhaps not difficult to explain: if nothing else, there was at least the natural affinity caused by their common preoccupation with Islam. Since coming to power in 1959, the PMIP government in Kelantan had also made the additional gesture of giving the *tok gurus* a monthly allowance.[22]

Teachers constituted another group that was considered to be of some limited importance, mainly because of their contacts with parents. There were three categories of teachers: those who taught in standard government schools and *ra'ayat* schools,[23] those who taught in religious schools, and those who conducted adult education classes. There were 372 in the first category, and the Alliance felt that about 85-90 per cent. supported their own party, while the PMIP was of the opinion that the distribution was more or less even. The Alliance estimate in the case of religious teachers (of whom there were about 100) was that about 60 per cent. supported the PMIP;[24] the PMIP, however, considered 80 per cent. a more appropriate figure. As for the third category, the most pertinent fact is that adult education classes are organized and run by the

22 The official allowance was only $20 a month, but the view was expressed in Alliance circles that the PMIP was paying much more substantial sums, out of party funds, to those who supported it.

23 *Ra'ayat* schools literally means 'people's schools'. These are institutions where the salaries of teachers are paid by the Federal Government while the remaining costs are met by the school boards and parents.

24 It was the Alliance's view that the teachers in each school supported the same party as their headmaster. This meant that the entire staff of each school supported either one party or the other. Of the twenty religious schools in Pasir Puteh, eight were considered to be pro-Alliance by that party.

Federal Government; from various accounts, they are also aimed partly at making the rural population less amenable to the PMIP's appeal. Both parties were agreed that, not surprisingly, the PMIP had little support from those conducting these classes.

As far as the campaign itself was concerned, the Alliance effort appeared on the whole to be the more vigorous and methodical. In addition to its determined bid to capture Kelantan, the party was also making a 'special effort' in those constituencies (both state and federal) where the PMIP's top men were contesting; this seems to have been done without any reference to the size of the PMIP majority in 1959, and the assumption appeared to be that most of these seats were 'winnable'. Pasir Puteh thus became one of the Alliance's main targets, and a victory there was one of the cherished ambitions of the party's state organizers. Among other things, much more money was poured into the election effort in this constituency than was generally the case.

The Alliance held at least one rally a day during the entire campaign period, and its candidate addressed one each evening. The PMIP on the other hand held only twenty rallies during the five-week period, with its candidate appearing at no more than five. The Alliance effort was also augmented by addresses given by three national figures from other parts of the country; in the case of the PMIP, however, it was their own candidate who had to travel elsewhere, since he had duties as an important member of the party's national pool of speakers. As in the other Kelantan constituencies, both parties considered *cheramahs* (small meetings) and house-to-house canvassing to be more important than rallies; and once again the Alliance candidate had a potential advantage over his opponent due to the latter's inability to spend much time in the constituency.

In general, the campaign went off quite smoothly, without any major incidents. However, there was one area where there were frequent fights between Alliance and PMIP workers; but these remained localized, and in any case were nothing more than minor skirmishes. Apparently, most of these fights occurred towards the end of the campaign when the tempo had increased. In an atmosphere that had become quite tense, words were frequently exchanged between rival party workers engaged in house-to-house visits, and it had not always been possible to keep things at a verbal level.

It was felt by both parties that support was not distributed generally throughout the constituency, but rather tended to be in small pockets, often consisting of clusters of houses. If true, this could suggest that there was some coincidence between the social intimacy and the political affiliations of neighbouring families. It could also be an indication of the influence exerted by certain opinion leaders (for example, *imams* and *penghulus*) in their own immediate circles. Party workers on both sides felt confident that they knew which their strongholds were and which areas were 'enemy territory'.

One obvious way in which the parties ascertained the distribution of support was through the reports submitted by their workers. It was frequently claimed (particularly by the Alliance) that people in Kelantan, unlike those in the west coast states, were quite forthright about their political commitments, and that this made it comparatively easy to make estimates of support. Attendance at meetings (especially small meetings organized in the villages) was considered to be another valuable guide in identifying some[25] supporters, since both parties were agreed that only their own supporters attended their meetings.

A feature of the election in Pasir Puteh was the very large number of banners, posters and arches that decorated the countryside, almost giving the impression of a carnival. A substantial number of homes had posters displayed on them, and a voter's willingness to do this was often taken by both parties as some indication of support. In travelling through the constituency, one was also impressed by the tendency for groups of houses (or for a substantial ma-

---

[25] 'Some' in the sense that although all those who attended these meetings were assumed to be supporters, not all supporters attended them.

jority of houses in particular areas) to display the posters of the same party. This was perhaps an indication that support did in fact come in pockets. Only a very small number of houses displayed the posters of both parties. This was true of Kelantan as a whole, and was certainly far more pronounced in that state than elsewhere. What was really interesting, however, was not this alone but the additional fact that houses displaying the posters of both parties also seemed to be concentrated in particular areas. Both parties had the same explanation for this, namely that the voters in these areas supported one party while their *penggawa* or *penghulu* supported the other — and that both posters were displayed so as to avoid friction. It was also pointed out that many people avoided putting up posters altogether for the same reason, and that even some of those who displayed the posters of only one party did so merely because they had felt intimidated.

Both parties were certain that all the voters in the constituency had been contacted in the course of the campaign, both by their own workers and by those of their opponents. Considering the elaborate election machinery and the large number of workers involved on both sides, this was certainly quite plausible. Things were no doubt also made much easier by the fact that communications in Pasir Puteh were among the best in Kelantan, almost the entire constituency being quite accessible by road. There was, however, some disproportion in the percentage of voters contacted by the candidates themselves. By the end of the campaign, Alliance officials were confident that their candidate had come into contact with about 80 per cent. of the electorate through rallies, small meetings and house visits. The PMIP candidate, having less time for his own campaign, was not quite as successful, and party officials felt that he had contacted no more than half the voters. In addition to his extra duties as a national leader of his party, he was also handicapped by not living in his constituency; further, since he was contesting the state election in another area, the amount of time he could spend in Pasir Puteh was considerably reduced.

As the campaign drew to a close, PMIP workers were generally much more optimistic about the outcome of the election than their Alliance counterparts, although there were many indications that the Alliance, mainly by having increased its 1959 effort,[26] would make substantial gains. Those in the Alliance merely felt that it was enough encouragement to be still in the fight, and that their candidate stood a reasonable chance of a narrow victory.

Both parties kept a graph to depict the level of support at the end of each week of the campaign.[27] Steps were taken to keep these graphs concealed, since it was thought that the information they contained should not become known to the opposition. The PMIP took particularly strong precautions, claiming that an Alliance 'spy' had during the early part of the campaign succeeded in gaining access to certain confidential records, including the graph, which had been kept in the party office. The graph was thereafter kept under lock and key in the home of an official, and not made available to anyone outside a very restricted group. One thus had to rely on verbal statements made by the candidate and his officials concerning the level of support. Both claimed (at different interviews during the last week of the campaign) that the graph showed 80 per cent. support for the PMIP, but, judging from answers to various other questions,[28] this was quite obviously an exaggeration.

On the eve of the election the Alliance graph showed

26 The PMIP candidate, for example, felt that the Alliance was working 'at least twice as hard' in 1964.

27 As stated in Chapter VII, the parties had individual workers to look after small groups of houses (in the case of the Alliance, usually groups of ten), both to canvass for support as well as to keep the party constantly informed of the number of people (that is of those in their 'care') who supported it. The graphs were based on these reports, after the figures had been totalled for the whole constituency.

28 It was, for example, conceded that the Alliance (which received 36 per cent. of the votes in 1959) would do better at this election. One of the officials also agreed at an interview that a good way of sustaining morale among party workers was to avoid giving them the impression that there was any doubt about the candidate's chances of success.

that 57 per cent.[29] of the electorate in Pasir Puteh supported that party. This was arrived at by averaging the figures for the three state constituencies which together made up the parliamentary constituency: 60 per cent. in Pasir Puteh Utara, 58 per cent. in Pasir Puteh Tengah and 53 per cent. in Pasir Puteh Tenggara. There had been a sharp rise during the last two weeks of the campaign, the graph having stood at around 45 per cent. during the first three weeks. The increases had been most substantial in Pasir Puteh Utara (during the fourth week) and Pasir Puteh Tenggara (during the fifth and final week). However, despite the careful procedures followed in compiling these figures, Alliance officials continued to feel that their chances were just about even. They perhaps took the view that the sudden increase in support reported during the closing stages of the campaign was to some extent caused only by increased enthusiasm among their workers. The reports from Pasir Puteh Utara in particular appeared to be somewhat suspect, since that constituency had all along been considered the most difficult: the PMIP's religious appeal was thought to have been particularly strong in that region, and four out of the eight pro-PMIP *tok gurus* were based there.

On polling day, 23,208 voters (roughly 86 per cent. of the electorate) cast their votes. The PMIP candidate received 11,798 votes against his opponent's 10,393 — 1,017 votes being spoilt. As in all the other seats retained by the PMIP, the majority this time, when compared to that of 1959, was a substantially reduced one. Of the three state seats in Pasir Puteh, the PMIP won two; perhaps not surprisingly, the Alliance fared worst in Pasir Puteh Utara, where its candidate received only 41.7 per cent. of the votes cast.[30] By and large, the estimates made by the

29 After 10 per cent. had been deducted for error — a practice followed by the Alliance throughout the country.

30 The other state seat lost by the Alliance was Pasir Puteh Tenggara, where its candidate received just over 46 per cent. of the votes cast. In Pasir Puteh Tengah, the Alliance candidate received 53 per cent. of the votes.

Alliance during the first three weeks of the campaign were shown to have been reasonably accurate.

To conclude, a very significant feature of the election was the simultaneous functioning of elaborate and highly rational party machines, and the 'influencers' of the traditional society. On the one hand, there was great preoccupation with maintaining election organizations with well-demarcated hierarchies and an efficient devolution of power; on the other, there was the realization that no campaign could be successful without some support from the *tok gurus*, *penghulus*, etc. There seemed to be no question of incompatibility between the two, and the parties considered both to be indispensable. Here was the interpenetration of the traditional and the modern, almost in their extremes. They became, during the election, a part of the same process. The Alliance on the whole appeared to be stronger in the area of strict 'party' activity. This advantage was obviously not sufficient to offset the effects of the closer links which the PMIP had with the traditional 'influencers'.

(b) BATU (Selangor)
R. K. Vasil

The parliamentary constituency of Batu is one of the four parliamentary constituencies into which the city of Kuala Lumpur, the capital of Malaysia, is divided. The constituency is not untypical of urban constituencies in the country, even though a large part of the voters live outside the city limits in the small townships and *kampongs* around the town. It is definitely not a rural area: its proximity to the city of Kuala Lumpur makes it more urban than rural. A very large part of the population in these areas work in the city. Also, it is a typical urban constituency in that a very high percentage of the voters are non-Malays, mostly Chinese.

The parliamentary constituency is divided into two state constituencies — Kepong and Penchala. Table X gives a breakdown of the voters according to race and sex.

TABLE X

BATU CONSTITUENCY: BREAKDOWN OF VOTERS BY RACE AND SEX

Registration unit	Chinese	Malays	Indians	Male	Female	Total
KEPONG						
1. Segambut	286	704	155	671	474	1,145
2. Batu Village	1,480	759	409	1,494	1,154	2,648
3. Batu Caves	751	859	582	1,261	931	2,192
4. Jinjang	8,291	59	13	4,183	4,180	8,363
5. Kepong Selatan	1,085	66	118	705	564	1,269
6. Kepong Utara	2,959	145	58	1,598	1,564	3,162
7. Sungei Buloh Settlement	1,160	210	160	1,069	461	1,530
Total	16,012	2,802	1,495	10,981	9,328	20,309
PENCHALA						
1. Kampong Semarang	2,795	304	262	1,913	1,448	3,361
2. Kolam Ayer	3,143	149	468	2,116	1,644	3,760
3. Lake Gardens	1,710	1,582	686	2,429	1,499	3,928
4. Damansara	290	331	316	447	460	937
Total	7,938	2,316	1,732	6,935	5,051	11,986
Total for Batu Constituency	23,950	5,118	3,227	17,916	14,379	32,295

The registration unit, Segambut, consists mainly of two villages — Segambut Dalam and Kampong Pasir. The village, Segambut Dalam, is predominantly Malay with a handful of Chinese and Indians. Most of the people here work in the city as drivers, gardeners, and lesser employees in the Government. Some of them are rubber tappers, and a very small number have their own smallholdings in rubber. The other village, Kampong Pasir, consists primarily of Tamil estate workers and a small number of Punjabi and Pakistani families. They depend mostly on employment in the city.

The unit, Batu Village, is composed of the villages of Kampong Hailam and Kampong Selayang. The former is a predominantly Chinese village, most of these Chinese being Hainanese and Kheh. They work as cooks and run small coffee shops in the city. The latter, Kampong Selayang, consists predominantly of Malays, many of whom are of Minangkabau origin. These too work in the city as gardeners, drivers and in the Government services. Some of them are workers in the neighbouring tin mines.

Batu Caves has the following three villages in the area — Kampong Sungai Tua, Kampong Lalat and Kampong Melayu Batu Caves Baru. Kampong Sungai Tua is largely Malay. Kampong Lalat has an Indian as well as a Malay settlement. Kampong Melayu Batu Caves Baru, as the name itself indicates, is predominantly Malay.

Jinjang is the largest 'new village' in the country. It is almost entirely Chinese, and has a local council[31] which administers the affairs of the village. The name 'village' is not a very exact description of Jinjang. It is, in fact, a small town on the outskirts of Kuala Lumpur, which has a network of metalled and laterite roads. All modern facilities are available: it has a large cinema hall, showing Chinese movies imported from Hong Kong; beauty parlours abound; there are one or two maternity homes and several private medical practitioners. There are also shops

[31] Until 1962 the Socialist Front had held all the 12 seats in the Jinjang Local Council. But in the 1962 elections it lost control of the council. capturing only 5 seats, the remaining 7 being won by Alliance candidates.

selling T.V. sets (newly introduced to Malaya), refrigerators, cosmetics, and the latest fashion in dresses. A very large part of the population consists of ordinary Chinese workers — estate workers, masons, carpenters, hawkers and other manual, semi-skilled or skilled workers. At the same time it has a sizable number of small traders and a small number of middle-class business families. The working-class groups live mostly in the shabby houses built at the time when the new village was started. The others, who later were to become more affluent, have completely reconstructed their houses.

Kepong consists of the two registration units of Kepong Selatan and Kepong Utara. The town is about a mile from Jinjang, further away from the city. It is almost entirely Chinese and is very much like Jinjang except that it is not a new village and does not have a local council.

About seven miles from the city is the Sungei Buloh Leper Settlement, where modern medical facilities and treatment are available to the lepers. The settlement mainly consists of Chinese. It is, once again, more in the nature of a small town than a village. The population consists of a few hundred lepers, Chinese, Indians and Malays, and a large number of people, who have been completely cured of leprosy but do not have the courage or inclination to face the outside world and so have chosen to settle down in the settlement on a permanent basis. They have been drawn from all over the country and are largely of working-class origin.

These areas mentioned together form the large constituency of Kepong. The other state constituency is Penchala, which has only 11,986 voters, as against 20,309 in Kepong. It is more urban than Kepong, the bulk of its population living within the city limits of Kuala Lumpur. Unlike Kepong, which is largely homogeneous in class composition, the Penchala constituency consists of people with very different class origins. Ministers, senior Government officials, highly prosperous Chinese business families, small Chinese and other traders, trishaw drivers, ordinary workers, Chinese and other squatters living on the low muddy land in some of the worst slums in the country, together make up the electorate in the state constituency of Penchala. However, it does include two areas — Damansara and Sungei Penchala — which are not strictly urban. But the number of voters in them is very small.

As can be seen in Table X, Batu parliamentary constituency has a large predominance of Chinese voters, accounting for about 74·1 per cent. of the total. Malays account for only about 15·8 per cent. of the total. No further statistics about its economic and social characteristics can be quoted. Such statistics are given by administrative districts in the 1957 Census, and the boundaries of this constituency do not coincide with district boundaries.

1959 Elections

The following are the results of the 1959 elections for the parliamentary constituency of Batu and the two state constituencies of Kepong and Penchala.

Batu (Parliamentary)

Ng Ann Teck (Socialist Front — Labour Party)	8,737
Lim Hee Hong (Alliance — MCA)	6,408
Total number of electors	20,819
Percentage of electorate voting	73·5 per cent.

Kepong (State)

Chan Keong Hon (Alliance — MCA)	5,305
Ng Ann Teck (Socialist Front — Labour Party)	4,576
Total number of electors	13,566
Percentage of electorate voting	74.4 per cent.

Penchala (State)

Lim Jew Siang (Alliance — MCA)	2,299
Y.P. Liu (Socialist Front — Labour Party)	2,133
Total number of electors	7,291
Percentage of electorate voting	61.5 per cent.

It will be remembered that the general elections in 1959 were held in two stages — state, in the months of May and

June 1959, parliamentary, on 19 August 1959. Between the two elections occurred the very serious crisis within the Alliance, which at one time threatened to break it.

In the 1959 state elections in the state of Selangor, held on 30 May, there were 'straight fights' between the Alliance (MCA) and the SF (Labour Party) in the two state constituencies of Kepong and Penchala. Both were won by the Alliance candidates by a small margin. In Kepong the Alliance fielded Chan Keong Hon and the SF, Ng Ann Teck. Chan Keong Hon is a prosperous businessman from the state of Selangor. He, along with his family, owns several tin mines in the state and one large tin mine within the area of the Kepong constituency. His contact with the area is very old, and many of the tin mines were earlier owned by his father. His elder brother, Senator Chan Kwong Hon, is a prominent member of the MCA and is the President of the all-Malayan Chinese Chamber of Commerce. Chan Keong Hon himself is an important leader of the MCA in Selangor. On the other hand, Ng Ann Teck was in 1959 a newcomer to party politics. He is from Pontian in Johore and was active in the Johore trade union movement. He was earlier associated with the Factory and Commercial Workers Union in Johore, which was declared illegal by the Government in 1958 for extreme left-wing sympathies. The union disbanded, Ng joined the Labour Party, and shifted to Kuala Lumpur to the party headquarters; at the time of the elections in 1959 he was a paid Executive Secretary of the party. At one time he was a student at the Nanyang University in Singapore, which he left for want of money before completing his studies. He is very fluent in a number of Chinese dialects and has the reputation of being a brilliant public speaker in these dialects and in Mandarin.

In the 1959 state elections Chan Keong Hon of the Alliance secured 5,305 votes against 4,576 polled by Ng Ann Teck of the SF. The election was won by Chan Keong Hon primarily because of the substantial influence that he and his family always had in the constituency, and because he was helped by the better organization provided by the Alliance. Ng Ann Teck was able to secure the solid left-wing vote, largely the Chinese-educated young men and women, in Jinjang and Kepong. In April 1959 the SF had won all the four seats in the Jinjang Local Council for which elections were held. The tactical mistake committed by Ng Ann Teck was that he depended entirely on the left-wing vote in Jinjang and Kepong. He completely ignored the not inconsiderable non-Chinese vote and about a thousand voters in the Sungei Buloh Leper Settlement. He made no effort in these areas and did not even visit them.

In the other state constituency, Penchala, the Alliance fielded Lim Jew Siang and the SF, Y.P. Liu. The seat was won by the Alliance candidate by a narrow margin of 166 votes. Lim Jew Siang is a prominent member of the MCA in Selangor. He is Hainanese, and has been associated closely with the country-wide Hainanese associations and therefore has considerable influence among them. There is a fairly large number of Hainanese in the Penchala constituency. On the other hand, the SF candidate, Y.P. Liu, was not at all well-known in the area. He was not even a resident of the constituency, being from the neighbouring town of Rawang. In spite of the fact that he was a newcomer to politics and an outsider in the constituency, he secured a large working-class vote and was beaten by only 166 votes.

Soon after the completion of the state elections the serious crisis in the Alliance occurred between UMNO and the MCA. Eventually many of the top leaders of the MCA, who were close to the masses of the Chinese in the country, resigned from the MCA and some of them contested the federal elections as Independents.[32] There was a great deal of dissatisfaction among the Chinese, particularly among the non-English-educated, who formed a large majority within the Chinese community. It was in the wake of this general dissatisfaction within the Chinese community that the federal elections were held on 19 August 1959.

[32] See Chapter V, p. 84 above.

The MCA put up its Treasurer, Lim Hee Hong, in the Batu parliamentary constituency and the SF fielded Ng Ann Teck, its defeated candidate in the Kepong state constituency. Lim Hee Hong, a prominent national leader of the MCA, is also a leader among the Hainanese here. He has considerable business interests, owns quite a few hotels in Kuala Lumpur, and has a contract with the Malayan Railway for railway catering all over the country.

The outcome of the elections was that the prominent Lim Hee Hong was defeated by Ng Ann Teck, a relatively unknown man who had himself earlier been defeated by an MCA candidate in the state elections. The victory of the unknown SF candidate was entirely a result of the crisis in the Alliance which has been referred to earlier. In fact, it was not the only SF victory. In the city of Kuala Lumpur the SF was able to capture three of the four parliamentary seats. The fourth was won narrowly by the MCA candidate against an MCA 'rebel' candidate who contested as an Independent, the victory being helped by an SF candidate who split the opposition vote. In effect Ng Ann Teck won in the Batu parliamentary constituency purely because of the great dissatisfaction within the Chinese community, not because of positive support for the SF.

1964 Elections: Candidates

In 1959, there was a straight fight between the Alliance (MCA) and the SF (Labour Party) candidates in the Batu parliamentary constituency. However, in 1964, the PAP fielded a candidate in the constituency. All the three parties had in their candidates persons who had never contested general elections before. The Alliance (MCA) fielded Yap Chin Kwee and the SF (Labour Party) put up Dr. Tan Chee Khoon. The PAP candidate was Dr. Too Chee Cheong.

Yap Chin Kwee is a newcomer to politics, who joined the MCA only at about the time candidates were nominated. In an appeal to the voters Yap Chin Kwee stated that he had been 'specially chosen by none other than our beloved Prime Minister, Tunku Abdul Rahman, and fully endorsed by Tun Abdul Razak, the Deputy Premier, Mr. Tan Siew Sin, the Finance Minister and National President of the MCA, and Dato V. T. Sambanthan, President of the MIC'. He is a young man in his late twenties. Although primarily English-educated, he had had a few years of education in a Chinese school. He was born and brought up in Selangor, and his own dialect is Hakka. He maintains that he is essentially of working-class origin as his grandfather was a tin mine labourer and his grandmother a rubber tapper. However, his father was a government servant and is a leader of the MCA in Selangor. By profession Yap Chin Kwee is a journalist, and since 1954 has worked on the *Straits Times* as a reporter.

Dr. Tan Chee Khoon, a medical doctor by profession, born in 1919 in a small village near Kuala Lumpur, was of 'humble beginnings'. His father had a small farm on which Dr. Tan had to work as a boy. He studied at some of the schools in Kuala Lumpur and Kajang, where he was considered a brilliant student. At the end of his studies at the Victoria Institution in Kuala Lumpur, he was awarded a scholarship to study medicine at the Medical College in Singapore. He graduated in 1949, and since then has been a private medical practitioner in Kuala Lumpur except for the first two years when he worked at the General Hospital in Kuala Lumpur. He has a large practice in Batu Road, within his constituency. Dr. Tan joined the Labour Party about ten years back and has been very active in the party since then. Today he is one of the party's senior leaders, having been national Vice-Chairman from 1959 to 1962 and Treasurer since 1963.

He is one of the most respected citizens of Kuala Lumpur and has been closely associated with many and varied organizations. In 1963, he was elected Chairman of the Central Branch of the Malayan Medical Association for the year 1964. Just before the elections he was elected Chairman of the Private Medical Practitioners' Association of Selangor for the year 1965. He is also very closely associated with a number of other professional organizations.

Since 1959, when Dr. Tan was elected by the Guild of Graduates to serve on the Council of the University of Malaya, in Kuala Lumpur, he has been closely associated with the University.   He has also been associated with a large number of schools in Selangor as Chairman or member of the Board of Managers.   He has been the Chairman of the Board of Managers of at least three large schools since 1958.

Further, Dr. Tan has had close contacts with trade unions since 1956. In 1956 he was appointed a trustee of the largest single workers' union in the country, the National Union of Plantation Workers, a position which he has held ever since.   From 1956 onwards he has represented the staff side in a number of arbitrations affecting government employees.

Dr. Tan is also a very active member of the Methodist Church and is associated closely with many of the bodies of the Church.   Since 1960 he has been the lay Leader of the Wesley Methodist Church in Kuala Lumpur, said to be 'the highest post for a member of the Church'.

Like the Alliance candidate, and unlike the SF candidate, the candidate of the PAP, Dr. Too Chee Cheong, was a newcomer to politics.   However, he had been associated with the MCA for a short time before 1959.   He left the MCA in 1959 — where he was a leader of the Youth Section in Selangor — for personal reasons some time before the 1959 crisis.

Dr. Too, who is in his mid-thirties, comes from Kuala Lumpur, where he was educated in both Chinese- and English-medium schools.   He can, as a result, speak several Chinese dialects, though his own dialect is Cantonese.   After finishing school in Kuala Lumpur he went to Hong Kong where he took a degree in medicine.   Since his return to Kuala Lumpur he has been practising in the Chinatown area outside the Batu parliamentary constituency.   He joined the PAP just before the elections and was later Vice-President of the party's Kuala Lumpur branch.

To turn to the candidates in the two state constituencies

of Kepong and Penchala, the Alliance parliamentary candidate, Yap Chin Kwee, did not contest either of the state elections. The Alliance fielded the two candidates, Chan Keong Hon and Lim Jew Siang, who had won the elections in the same constituencies in the 1959 elections. The SF parliamentary candidate, Dr. Tan Chee Khoon, participated in the state elections also, contesting the state constituency of Kepong. The SF's candidate in the Kepong constituency in the 1959 elections, Ng Ann Teck, was moved over to the Penchala constituency. It was felt by the party that Ng Ann Teck would be a weak candidate against the influential Chan Keong Hon in Kepong, and that he would have a better chance against Lim Jew Siang in Penchala. Even though Dr. Tan's dispensary is situated in the Penchala constituency and he is very well-known over the whole constituency, he was asked to contest the Kepong constituency for the reason that the party felt that he was the only person who could possibly defeat Chan Keong Hon.

The SF did not choose Ng Ann Teck for the parliamentary constituency of Batu which he had won in 1959. The main reason for this seems to have been Ng Ann Teck's lack of any activity, both in the Parliament and in the constituency since 1959; for this reason he was not acceptable to Labour Party branches within the constituency. The PAP parliamentary candidate, Dr. Too, also contested the Penchala state constituency. The PAP did not put up any candidate for the Kepong state constituency, because of a shortage of suitable candidates; this was a distinct disadvantage for the candidate for the parliamentary constituency.

Election Issues
In the Batu parliamentary constituency, as elsewhere throughout the country, the Alliance attempted to make Indonesian 'confrontation' the sole election issue. However, for several reasons Indonesian 'confrontation' and Malaysia did not become the dominant election issues in Batu to the same extent as elsewhere. Firstly, the SF candi-

date, Dr. Tan Chee Khoon, did not emphasize the issue of Indonesian 'confrontation' and Malaysia in his campaign.[33] His speeches in the election rallies in the constituency contained very little on 'confrontation,' but emphasized the services he had rendered to the people, both within the the constituency and outside, and the failure of the Alliance during the nine years it had been in power to look after the interests of the proletariat. However, it must be added that his workers from the Labour Party did put some emphasis on the confrontation issue, although the part played by them in the elections was not very substantial.

Secondly, the PAP, which participated in the elections with the primary object of fighting the SF, did not show the same vehement hostility to Dr. Tan as against other SF candidates. On 22 March, a day after the nomination, in a rally at the Suleiman Court (in the Batu constituency), Devan Nair, one of the top leaders of the PAP in Singapore, said that there were 'nice people' like Dr. Tan Chee Khoon in the SF and that the PAP was not worried about them. What worried them was the communist group behind them. Also, as indicated later, the PAP campaign in the Batu constituency was half-hearted and lacked zeal.

Lastly, the Alliance candidates soon realized that it would be impossible for them to beat Dr. Tan Chee Khoon on the basis of the 'confrontation' issue, that a negative approach would not do, and that they had to come out with positive promises of schools, roads and other facilities in the area. They were forced to put emphasis on the good work that had been done by them and the Alliance and on all they planned to do for the constituency during the next five years. The following is what Yap Chin

---

33 Dr. Tan belongs to the moderate wing of the Labour Party. His views on the question of Malaysia and the Indonesian 'confrontation' have been different from the party 'line', which is largely determined by the Chinese-educated extremists in the party. In fact, because of his moderate views, his candidature for the Batu Parliamentary constituency and the Kepong state constituency was opposed by the Pudu Branch of the Labour Party in Kuala Lumpur, which consists entirely of Chinese-educated members.

Kwee, the Alliance candidate for the Batu parliamentary constituency promised to the electors in an open letter:

> If elected I shall fight unrelentlessly [*sic*] to:
> Provide improved health facilities.
> Provide improved social amenities.
> Strive to get land for the tiller in co-operation with my Alliance colleagues: Chan Keong Hon and Lim Jew Siang.
> Provide more educational institutions (schools in the constituency in particular secure funds for the establishment of a Chinese secondary school to serve the people of Jinjang, Kepong, Sungei Buloh, Batu Village and Subang).
> Strive for low-cost housing in the constituency.
> Strive for other amenities like water, lights, metalled roads, telephones.

There was no mention of Indonesian 'confrontation' and the SF attitude towards it. Further, an attempt was made to suggest that Dr. Tan was rich and did not care for the poor people.

Election Campaign

Nominations were made on 21 March and the elections took place about five weeks later on 25 April 1964. During the night following the nomination day the whole constituency was flooded with posters of the candidates of the Alliance and the SF. However, no posters of the PAP candidate were to be seen at this time; they did not start to appear until about a week later. It took the PAP some time to organize itself for the elections, and its campaign, on the whole, was conducted from outside the constituency, as has been described elsewhere in this book. In the Batu constituency the PAP did not set up any election centre, except one which was established in Jinjang New Village. Almost the entire PAP campaign in the Batu constituency was conducted from the PAP headquarters or the PAP election centre in the neighbouring parliamentary constituency of Setapak. Even the one election centre that it had set up in Jinjang New Village was not very active. The PAP soon found that people in the village were largely committed politically, and that it was useless wasting time and effort there. As a result it soon 'gave up' its efforts in Jinjang New Village.

The Alliance and the SF campaigns were conducted through the many branches in the constituency. The MCA and the UMNO have a very large number of branches. Almost every part of the constituency has a branch of the UMNO or the MCA, depending on the racial composition of the population. However, the MCA has no branch in Penchala, and as a result, the Alliance candidate had to set up a temporary election centre, in Ipoh Road.

The campaign of the SF candidate was carried on by the branches of the Labour Party. However, the Labour Party does not have branches in some parts of the constituency.[34] The whole campaign was co-ordinated and supervised by Dr. Tan Chee Khoon himself from his dispensary in Batu Road.

The election campaign of Yap Chin Kwee, the Alliance candidate, was completely dominated by the party. Being a newcomer to politics and to the constituency, he had no contacts of his own and therefore had to depend entirely on the party machine. He also had to rely very substantially on the two state candidates of the Alliance, who had been elected from the same constituencies in the 1959 elections and who had considerable influence and contacts in the constituency. In the Alliance house-to-house campaign, Yap Chin Kwee played a secondary role. The dominant role was played by the two state candidates, Chan Keong Hon and Lim Jew Siang, and the local MCA leaders. Yap Chin Kwee invariably went from house to house along with a large group. The group, in Jinjang New Village, for example, would consist of Chan Keong Hon, the local MCA officials, some of the Alliance councillors of

34 The Party Rakyat and the National Convention Party, member parties of the Socialist Front, have no branches in the Batu Parliamentary constituency. The Labour Party has the following branches: Kuala Lumpur, Batu, Batu Village, Jinjang, Kepong, Damansara New Village.

the Jinjang Local Council and a number of other people. The group generally consisted of at least ten persons. There was a conspicuous absence of any women in the group. The group was always led by the local MCA leaders[35] in the house-to-house visits. All the talking was done by the local MCA officials or the two state candidates. Yap Chin Kwee's role, on the whole, was restricted to shaking hands with the head of the family. The pattern was the same in the house-to-house and shop-to-shop campaign in the city areas. In the city areas, such as Batu Road and Ipoh Road, the group would be led by some persons with local influence or by the state candidate, Lim Jew Siang. Here again Yap Chin Kwee played no important role in the campaigning. His participation was restricted to being introduced as the Alliance candidate for Parliament. In the Ipoh Road and Batu Road areas the group always included two young Chinese who were introduced to the author as locally influential people.[36] In this area the two would always move at the head of the group. They knew most of the people and would be the first to get into the shops and speak to the head of the family. The rest of the group and the candidates would follow them.

The Alliance candidates did not carry on the house-to-house campaigning with the purpose of converting the voters to their side through political argument. In the city areas the real purpose was to influence the uncommitted voter through men of influence and power in the area. In areas outside the city the intention was to inform the known supporters of the transport arrangements for carrying the voters to the polling stations on election day and also to influence the uncommitted. The local MCA officials, accompanying the candidates in Jinjang and Kepong

[35] In the two cases in Jinjang New Village when the author was present they were led by the Vice-President of the MCA Jinjang branch.

[36] On election day these two were seen to be the most active in taking charge of the voters brought by the Alliance vehicles and leading them to the Alliance booths outside the polling stations. As far as the author could ascertain they were not members of the MCA.

always carried with them details about the households: number of voters in the family, members of the MCA, supporters of the MCA and so on. They tended to leave alone houses where they knew they did not have any supporters. In Jinjang New Village it was noticed that they invariably visited the new and more prosperous houses. They rarely went into the old houses occupied by ordinary working-class families.

In house-to-house campaigning the MCA people never spoke to every member of the family. On entering a house or a shop they would ask for the head of the family and speak to him.

After the hand-shaking the MCA officials would open their note-books and check the names of the voters, their identity card numbers, etc. Then they would take out the details of the transport arrangements for the election day. The head of the family was told that on election day so and so was in charge of transport for them and that he would contact them on the day. The whole area was divided into small units, each under the charge of a local MCA member who was to look after the transport arrangements on election day.

In addition to the house-to-house campaigning the Alliance candidate held a large number of election rallies throughout the constituency. At the beginning of the campaign rallies were held at two or three-day intervals. But, as the election day drew nearer, rallies were held almost daily. Most of these rallies were addressed by the candidates and the local MCA leaders. Very few top leaders of the Alliance addressed the rallies in the constituency.[37] However, the rallies were never considered to be very important. The MCA, on the whole, put great emphasis on the use of personal influence and on the arrangements on election day. These were, to them, much more crucial than election rallies and house-to-house campaigning.

[37] Only once did an Alliance Minister come to address an election rally organized by the Alliance candidate. The Prime Minister, the Tengku, was expected to address a rally in Jinjang, but he never did so. During

In the predominantly Malay areas no special effort was made by the Alliance candidates to woo the Malay voters. Their support was taken for granted; it was never feared that the Malays would support the SF or the PAP candidates in large numbers. Consequently, the Alliance candidate did not do any house-to-house campaigning in the Malay areas. A few election rallies were considered quite adequate.

On the other hand, the campaign of the SF candidate, Dr. Tan Chee Khoon, was characterized by the great emphasis he put on the house-to-house campaign, by the small degree of dependence on the party machine during the campaign as well as on election day, and by the lack of financial support from the party. Also, Dr. Tan was the first SF candidate in the Batu constituency, a predominantly Chinese constituency, to have made a definite attempt to woo Malay voters.

However, the emphasis on a house-to-house campaign was restricted only to non-Malay areas. In the predominantly Malay areas Dr. Tan did not do any house-to-house campaigning. He had to rely entirely on election rallies. Most of the Malays live in their *kampongs*, separate from

---

the campaign period Mr. Tan Siew Sin, the Minister of Finance and the President of the MCA, visited Jinjang New Village to perform the opening ceremony of the new Community Hall for the village. It may be added that Chan Keong Hon in a letter to the voters of Kepong had mentioned that it was he who was responsible for getting the village a new Community Hall. This made Dr. Tan Chee Khoon immediately issue a letter to the voters giving 'a short survey of the work done by your representative Enche Chan Keong Hon in the Selangor State Assembly during the last five years'. It said that on 13 and 14 April 1961, Chan Keong Hon, speaking on a motion by a SF member of the Assembly requesting financial help for the construction of a new Community Hall for Jinjang New Village stated: '...I as representative from that area, on the Alliance ticket, can tell this House that there is already in existence a Community Hall.... As such, why should there be another Community Hall? Mr. Speaker, Sir, the present Community Hall in Jinjang is situated in the South Village, which is less than a quarter of a mile from where the present Local Authority wishes to build another hall. As I know, this hall built in 1955 has gone through renovations from the Council funds but up to now I like to say that the hall is not used by anybody at all. What is the reason behind it?' This was when the Jinjang Local Council was controlled by the SF.

the non-Malays. An outsider cannot just get into a *kampong* and start visiting people house-to-house. He has to go through somebody living in the village. All these villages had some sympathizers of the SF, but these people being in a small minority were not willing to take the risk of accompanying an SF candidate house to house and canvassing for him. In campaigning, he relied entirely on his own popularity, never using the party machine, as did the Alliance candidate. Thus, although in Kepong and Jinjang he was always accompanied by two or three local party members, these persons were rarely leaders of the local party branch. Almost always they were ordinary, young workers. Within such groups were usually one or two young girls.[38]

The pattern of campaigning was that Dr. Tan, accompanied by this group of some three or four young men and women workers, would enter a house. Dr. Tan initially would do all the talking. After the candidate had finished the hand-shaking and made the request for their votes, the others accompanying him would get to work. Their approach was extremely informal. For example, one of the girls from the group would go to a woman washing clothes at the public water tap and sit down. She would start to talk to the woman, in the meantime washing her own face and hands. One would have thought they were old friends. At another place a woman might have just finished boiling sweet potatoes. The girl would sit with the woman and help her to peel them; when she left she would take a few of the sweet potatoes with her and start eating them. All the campaigning was done in a completely relaxed way; there was a great measure of camaraderie and fellow-feeling.

In this 'kissing the babies' campaign, as Dr. Tan put it, he would always try to move over to the next house after

38 On several occasions the author met two young girls — an egg-seller in the Jinjang market and a rubber tapper. Others the author met were ordinary young workers in their early twenties. The author never met any locally influential people accompanying Dr. Tan in the house-to-house campaign.

a minute or two and avoid staying for too long at one place. His reason was that if he stayed for too long people would start asking him about Ng Ann Teck of the SF who had been elected from the constituency in 1959 and who, in their view, had done nothing for them and had rarely gone to them during the last five years. Dr. Tan had a special reason for considering house-to-house campaigning as the most effective method of vote-catching since he has practised in the constituency for the last twelve years and is widely known. In the city areas, for example, along Ipoh Road and Batu Road, almost every household has a member who has been to him as a patient. For this reason Dr. Tan did not do much campaigning in the city areas. He concentrated mainly in Kepong and Jinjang. In Jinjang every third or fourth household had known Dr. Tan as a medical doctor. In Kepong, however, a much smaller number of people knew him.

Dr. Tan also held a large number of election rallies. Towards the end of the campaign period rallies were held almost every evening, in areas with a concentration of Chinese as well as in Malay *kampongs*. In Chinese areas Dr. Tan was always the main speaker. He rarely had any of the top leaders of the SF to address his election rallies. These rallies were always addressed by him, by the candidate for the state constituency and by some of the local party leaders and workers. But in the Malay *kampongs* Dr. Tan always had some of the Malay leaders in the SF (none, significantly, from the Party Rakyat)[39] to address these rallies. Most of these rallies were addressed by Ishak bin Haji Mohammad, the Chairman of the Labour

[39] In Selangor at least there was no co-operation between the Party Rakyat and the Labour Party. The two parties worked entirely on their own. However, the National Convention Party, which joined the SF just before the elections, and the Labour Party co-operated with each other. The lack of co-operation between the Party Rakyat and the Labour Party was largely because of the very tough bargaining that took place before the nomination of candidates. The Labour Party felt that the Party Rakyat had unjustly demanded a very large number of seats and had secured them.

Party, and Abdul Aziz bin Ishak and Dato Kampo Radjo of the NCP.

In his speeches in Malay *kampongs* Dr. Tan always emphasized three things. First, he would point out that he had just passed the LCE Malay Language examination.[40] He would remind them that among all the non-Malay candidates he was the only one who spoke to them in the Malay language. Second, he would tell them that in the state of Selangor the SF was contesting a total of twenty-six seats out of the twenty-eight and they had a fair chance of forming the state government. If the SF came to power its chief pre-occupation would be to eradicate all poverty and to work to raise the standard of living of all the people. Third, Dr. Tan would emphasize that the SF was the only real non-communal party. He would tell them that the SF was fielding only one Chinese candidate out of four in Kuala Lumpur, a predominantly Chinese area. Two of the remaining three candidates were Malays and one Indian. The Alliance, on the other hand, he would emphasize, had all four Chinese as its candidates.

The campaign of the PAP, on the whole, was characterized by a definite lack of zeal; it was conducted in a half-hearted manner. There was no urge to win, but rather to see that the SF candidate was beaten. The aim was to gather as many non-Malay anti-Alliance votes as possible. In line with this dominant aim to beat the SF, whose main support was among the working people of Chinese origin, the PAP did not make any effort whatsoever to secure Malay support. By design they completely left out of their campaign all Malay *kampongs* in the Batu constituency.

The PAP candidate, Dr. Too, was completely dependent on the party machine, and did not have any political resources of his own. For holding rallies he was completely dependent on the availability of PAP leaders from Singapore. He held only one or two rallies during the five weeks of campaigning and only one of these was specially for his constituency. This was held in Jinjang New Vil-

[40] Malay at Lower Certificate of Education level.

lage and was addressed by the Singapore Prime Minister, Lee Kuan Yew, and others from Singapore. The reaction of the crowd was so discouraging that after that the PAP candidate made no effort to win support in Jinjang. He felt that people in Jinjang were already so committed that it was impossible to make any impact on them in a short time. Dr. Too did very little house-to-house campaigning; and what was done was only in the city areas. The whole of the state constituency of Kepong was completely ignored.

In the house-to-house campaigning the PAP candidate was accompanied by four or five PAP workers from Singapore. He very rarely had any local people with him, and all the talking was done by the candidate himself. The activity of the party workers from Singapore was, on the whole, restricted to the distribution of election literature. Dr. Too would request the voters to exercise their vote wisely. He would tell them: if you think the PAP is a good party then kindly vote for the PAP; on the other hand, if you think that the PAP is no good, then forget it. He would usually make no attempt to convince them. The impression was given that these people had a definite air of superiority about them. They took for granted that everybody knew about the PAP, what it stood for and what it had done in Singapore. Therefore, it was unnecessary to tell them anything about the PAP. They would get into a shop and just say, 'We are from the PAP' and move on to the next one. They behaved as if it was unfortunate that they had to work in a politically underdeveloped area, and did not appear to feel at home among the politically unsophisticated voters in Malaya.

Organizationally the PAP was very weak. Its candidate was given about half a dozen workers by the party headquarters. On election day in most of the polling stations the PAP did not have any polling booths, and they were not able to offer any transport to take voters to the polling station, whereas the Alliance and the SF candidates had a very large number of cars available.

Yap Chin Kwee, the Alliance candidate, reckons that he

spent a total of about M$10,000. He was provided with M$5,000 from the Alliance party funds and all the required posters and printed literature. The bulk of this money was spent on payments to workers (at the rate of $3 per person per day according to Yap Chin Kwee), food during the campaign period and on the election day, and petrol and diesel oil for the vehicles used to transport workers to the polling stations.

Dr. Tan Chee Khoon maintains that he was able to contest the elections with a total expenditure of about $5,000. According to him he did not have to pay any allowances to the workers, because these were members of the party and would not accept any money for working for it. Only towards the end did he have to pay some money to the small number of Malay workers who helped him in the Malay *kampongs*. The largest item of expenditure in his case was on printing posters and other literature, because the posters and other literature provided by the party were very inadequate. He also had to spend a large amount on petrol and diesel for the vehicles used on election day. The expenditure incurred by the PAP candidate was very small in comparison to the amounts spent by the Alliance and the SF candidates. Dr. Too was not given any financial help by the party and had to spend his own money on the elections. However, he was given all the posters and other printed literature by the party, and he did not have to spend any money on workers and transport on election day. On election day he had no vehicles to transport voters and only a very small number of workers. On most of the polling stations he had no polling booths of his own.

Election Results

The following are the results of the elections:

Batu (Parliamentary)

Dr. Tan Chee Khoon (Socialist Front — Labour Party)	10,122
Yap Chin Kwee (Alliance — MCA)	9,774
Dr. Too Chee Cheong (People's Action Party)	2,459

Kepong (State)

Dr. Tan Chee Khoon (Socialist Front — Labour Party)	7,487
Chan Keong Hon (Alliance — MCA)	7,485

Penchala (State)

Lim Jew Siang (Alliance — MCA)	3,065
Ng Ann Teck (Socialist Front — Labour Party)	2,894
Dr. Too Chee Cheong (People's Action Party)	1,409

The SF candidate, Dr. Tan Chee Khoon, won the parliamentary election by a small margin of 348 votes. However, in the Kepong state constituency he was able to beat the influential Alliance candidate, Chan Keong Hon, by only two votes. In Penchala, the other state constituency, the Alliance candidate, Lim Jew Siang, defeated the SF candidate, Ng Ann Teck, by a margin of 171 votes. An interesting point about the vote is that the two Alliance candidates for the state constituencies together polled a total of 10,550 votes, 169 more than the total number of votes polled by the two SF candidates. If the electors, who had voted in favour of the Alliance candidates in the two state constituencies, had voted for the Alliance candidate in the parliamentary constituency, the latter would have won the election. But it is probable that some of those who voted for the Alliance in the Kepong state constituency, which was not contested by the PAP, cast their votes for the PAP parliamentary candidate. Perhaps there were also some voters who voted for the Alliance candidates in the state constituencies, but voted for the SF parliamentary candidate. This could possibly be the result of the not very happy relations between the Alliance parliamentary candidate, Yap Chin Kwee, and his running mates, Chan Keong Hon and Lim Jew Siang in the state constituencies. The relations between Yap Chin Kwee and Lim Jew Siang were alleged to be particularly bad. Lim Jew Siang, an older person, felt differently and had a different approach, which was not appreciated by the younger Yap Chin Kwee. It has also been alleged that the state candidates went campaigning on their own and are even rumoured to have told voters to vote for them for the state and vote for anybody they liked for the parliamentary constituency. During the campaign period at one prominent place the workers of Lim Jew Siang had written in huge letters 'Please Vote Alliance, Penchala'; the Batu parliamentary constituency was not mentioned. Yap Chin Kwee considered this unfair, and promptly took a photograph of it. He forwarded a copy of the photograph to the Alliance headquarters and is said to have made a formal complaint about it.

The victory of Dr. Tan Chee Khoon was definitely a personal victory. It was not the result of a straight party vote. The result indicates that under some conditions a sufficient number of people may vote for a candidate with a record of personal service rather than for party men and men of influence. Dr. Tan did beat, though by only two votes, Chan Keong Hon, the Alliance candidate in Kepong, who is a man of great influence in the area and has very considerable business interests. He also defeated Yap Chin Kwee, the Alliance candidate in Batu, a party man 'specially chosen by none other than our beloved Prime Minister, Tunku Abdul Rahman'. Dr. Tan was successful against the general anti-SF trend in the elections, although he had the great disadvantage of belonging to a party which, during the elections and before, was branded as being anti-national and pro-Soekarno.

X

Elections in Sarawak and Sabah[1]

THE 1964 general elections in Malaya returned 104 of the 159 members of the Malaysian House of Representatives. The remaining 55 representatives came from Sarawak (24), Sabah (16) and Singapore (15). These fifty-five were chosen *indirectly* through the state legislatures of the three states as from the beginning of Malaysia on 16 September 1963. In April 1964 elections for the Federal Parliament were not held in these three states: with only minor changes the sitting representatives continued to sit. As far as Singapore was concerned, the indirect election of representatives to the Federal Parliament was 'accidental', as will be apparent from the next Chapter. But in Sarawak and Sabah the choice was deliberate. These states were so underdeveloped politically that by 1963 they had not yet had direct elections to their own state legislatures. Indeed, even at the lowest level of government, the district, direct elections in Sarawak were only a few years old: in Sabah they were even more recent, and in a few districts were not held earlier than 1964. Therefore this Chapter is not concerned with direct elections to the Federal Parliament from the two territories in 1964, because these never took place. It deals with the original direct district elections, which, through a tier system of indirect elections, eventually produced representatives for the Federal Parliament, and also for the state legislatures. These district elections were held in Sarawak in June 1963, and in Sabah in in-

1 This Chapter was not based on first-hand observation of the elections in Sarawak or Sabah, but was reconstructed from interviews with politicians and others carried out in October and November 1964 and a study of relevant documents and newspapers. It will be apparent that the Sabah elections, which were largely uncontested, were less susceptible to statistical treatment than the Sarawak elections.

stalments in December 1962, from March to May 1963 and in April 1964.

Sarawak

Sarawak was both politically and generally under-developed. The only apparent exception to this was that average per capita annual income was about $550, lower than in Malaya, but higher than in some of the neighbouring countries of South-East Asia. But otherwise, there were clear signs of underdevelopment in the high percentage of the population occupied in primary production, in the lack of communications, in backwardness in literacy and in education generally. It was also a multi-racial society, in which there was a large number of different groups, leading separate lives and meeting only tangentially from time to time. The Chinese constitute about 30 per cent. of the population, but even they are divided into several dialect groups and, economically, into at least rural and urban. Malays form 17 per cent. of the population, and for many purposes the Melanaus (6 per cent.), who are mostly Muslims, may be considered along with the Malays. Among the remainder the largest groups are the Sea Dayaks, or Ibans (32 per cent.), and the Land Dayaks (8 per cent.).[2]

The low degree of political development has an historical explanation. Sarawak was ruled from 1841-1946 by the famous 'White Rajahs', the Brookes.[3] Until 1905 they expanded their original territories many times. In 1888 Sarawak became a British protectorate, and this gave the

[2] Some useful statistics, relating to 1960, are summarized in Appendix B to the *Report of the Commission of Enquiry, North Borneo and Sarawak*, the *Cobbold Report*. Kuala Lumpur, 1962. On economic aspects, see T.H. Silcock, *Fiscal Survey Report of Sarawak*. Kuching, 1956; *Sarawak Development Plan, 1964-1968*. Kuching, 1963. On the Chinese, see Ju-K'ang T'ien, *The Chinese of Sarawak*. London, [n.d.]; Michael B. Leigh, *The Chinese Community of Sarawak, a Study of Communal Relations*. Melbourne, 1963. (Mimeographed.)

[3] Steven Runciman, *The White Rajahs*. Cambridge, 1960; S. Baring-Gould and C.A. Bampfylde, *A History of Sarawak under its Two White Rajahs, 1839-1908*. London, 1909; R. Payne, *The White Rajahs of Sarawak*. London, 1960.

British government some formal control over its external relations. But internally the Brookes were suspicious of 'development' and 'progress', and were determined to protect the natives as against the Chinese. Consequently, although ensuring 'justice' in the sense of preserving peace and order, the Brookes did little to provide social services, especially education. Sarawak became a British colony only in 1946: apart from dynastic intricacies in the Brooke family, the reason for the change appears to have been that only the British government had the resources to rebuild and rehabilitate the country after the Japanese occupation.

Constitutionally,[4] the Rajah was supreme in Sarawak's internal government. But he set up a Supreme Council (Executive) and Council Negri (Legislature) to assist him. On the eve of the Japanese invasion in 1941, the powers of these bodies were increased, at least on paper, in a new Constitution. When the British Government took over in 1946, they also adopted this Constitution, but with some alterations, such as the replacement of the Rajah by a British Governor. The British approach to developing Sarawak politically was via the 'grass roots', namely local government bodies. The intention was that these bodies, originally consisting of nominated members, some of them government officials, would gradually be replaced by directly elected members. But direct elections would not, in the near future, be extended beyond this bottom level. Representatives to the higher levels would be chosen indirectly via a tier system. This principle was embodied in the Constitution of 1956, which took effect in the following year. The District Councils were within a few years to be entirely directly-elected. They would elect the members of Divisional Advisory Councils for each of the five divisions of Sarawak. Twenty-four of the forty-five members of the Council Negri were to be chosen by the Divisional Advisory Councils, the Kuching Municipal Council and the Urban District Councils of Miri and Sibu. The Supreme Council was to have five of its ten members

4 Liang Kim Bang, *Sarawak, 1941-1957*, and Edwin Lee, *Sarawak in the Early Sixties*. Singapore. 1964.

elected from the Council Negri, three of the others being *ex officio* and two nominated. By 1959 the system had evolved further. The indirect principle had been retained except at the lowest, district council, level, but within that framework the process was mainly 'democratic'. In the 1959 district council elections all the members of the councils were elected. The successful candidates chose the members of the Divisional Advisory Councils. These members, in turn, elected some of the members of the Council Negri. In 1963 the system was to be the same except that *all* the members of the Council Negri would be indirectly elected in this way, apart from three nominated and three *ex officio* members, and that the Council Negri would now choose the twenty-four members from Sarawak to sit in the Malaysian Parliament in Kuala Lumpur.

The introduction of elections into Sarawak led to the formation of political parties. The first two were the Sarawak United Peoples' Party (SUPP) and the Party Negara Sarawak (PANAS). SUPP, founded in June 1959, was intended to be a non-racial party. But its original strength was in the towns, and its leaders and supporters were mainly Chinese. At one time almost half of its membership was non-Chinese, but after the Azahari rebellion in Brunei in December 1962, which was supported by some persons in Sarawak, many of its non-Chinese supporters deserted it. SUPP was also 'pro-Chinese' in that it attacked government education and land policies, which, it claimed, penalized the Chinese.[5] The open leadership of the party ranged from 'moderate' to 'radical', but the Government later produced evidence[6] to show that the party was informally linked with an underground subversive movement, 'the Clandestine Communist Organization'

[5] On education see *A Guide to Education in Sarawak,* Kuching, 1961; D. McLellan, *Report on Secondary Education,* Kuching, 1959. On land see Leigh, *op. cit.* pp. 23 ff.; *Sarawak Gazette,* 31 May 1955, pp. 97-101; *Straits Times,* 16 December 1963.

[6] *The Danger Within,* Kuching, 1963. See also Justus M. van der Kroef. 'Communism and Chinese Communalism in Sarawak', *The China Quarterly,* No. 20, 1964.

(CCO). It was also influential in Chinese Chambers of Commerce and in some Chinese clan societies: it controlled several Chinese trade unions, notably the wharf workers. The links were indeed informal and hard to detect. What appeared to be prominent positions in the SUPP, for instance chairmen of branches, were often held by moderates, while the actual key posts were held by CCO men. Certainly, specified raids on SUPP premises had allegedly failed to find any subversive material.[7] So the party, if viewed in conjunction with the CCO, was at the same time a pro-Chinese party and also a radical, communist-infiltrated, party.

On both these counts it could be expected to oppose Malaysia, which could be represented both as an attempt by the Malays to 'take over' Sarawak and also as a British imperialist plot. More moderately put, SUPP opposition was not directed against association with Malaya, Singapore, North Borneo and Brunei on the basis of equality. But it was opposed to jumping unreservedly on the 'Malaysia bandwagon', and it resented the idea of the Borneo territories being brought in to provide a racial balance to a Malaya-Singapore union.[8]

The second Sarawak party, PANAS, was founded in April 1960, and came out in favour of Malaysia shortly afterwards. This was not remarkable, because, although PANAS was non-communal, its leadership was largely Malay, and therefore predisposed towards a closer association. Because of the importance of racialism, however, the situation of having two parties only, one pro-Malaysia and one anti-Malaysia, could not, and did not, last. In quick succession four other major parties were formed: the Sarawak National Party (SNAP), largely Iban, in 1961; the Barisan Ra'ayat Jati Sarawak (BARJASA), largely Malay,

[7] *United Nations Malaysia Mission Report.* Kuala Lumpur, 1963, para. 89.

[8] Mr. Ong Kee Hui, *Council Negri Debates,* 8 March 1963, cols. 74-8. SUPP, along with the Party Rakyat of Brunei and the Pasok Momogun of North Borneo, proposed independence in the form of a Federation of Sarawak, Brunei and North Borneo in a joint memorandum to the UN Committee on Colonialism. (*Straits Times,* 2 October 1962.)

in December 1961; the Sarawak Chinese Association (SCA) in July 1962; the Party Pesaka Anak Sarawak (PESAKA),[9] mainly Iban, in August 1962. Where the existence of these new parties could not be accounted for ethnically, there were ideological, geographical, personal and historical reasons for their foundation. The SCA, like SUPP, appealed to the Chinese, but its ideology (or lack of ideology) was different. SNAP was strongest in the Second Division, PESAKA in the Third. PANAS leaders had supported the cession of Sarawak to Britain in 1946, while the BARJASA leaders included prominent opponents of cession. The foundation of each new party, by catering more precisely for certain ethnic types in existing parties, made it inevitable that the residual membership in the earlier parties became more 'communal'.

In the absence of the Malaysia question it is impossible to say what exact shape the party system would have assumed. It is almost certain that, even without Malaysia, the number of parties would still have increased. The principal effect of the Malaysia proposal was to give the Malayan Alliance Party an interest in ensuring that the fluid and rapidly-evolving party system in Sarawak would produce a majority in favour of Malaysia.[10] Consequently the Alliance leaders in Malaya worked hard, both by visiting Sarawak and by having Sarawak opinion leaders visit Malaya,[11] particularly with a view to their seeing what had been achieved in rural development. The precise way in which the Malayan Alliance set about its task

9 PAPAS is often used as an alternative name for PESAKA.

10 Some of the parties which were later pro-Malaysia were originally against. In December 1961, Mr. Stephen Kalong Ningkan (who later became Chief Minister) said that those who backed Malaysia seemed to have no loyalty to Sarawak and preferred to depend on other people (Straits Times, 19 December 1961).

11 For example, on a visit by Dr. Lim Swee Aun, see Straits Times, 18 October 1962. A comment on the visits to Malaya was: '... as the result of several hundreds of ulu [backwoods] people from the interior being invited to Malaya for sight-seeing tours, accommodated in large hotels, taken on tours in big expensive cars and given V.I.P. treatment, the ulu people were overwhelmed with gratitude and [changed] their stand'. (Mr. Charles Linang (SUPP) in the Council Negri, quoted in Sarawak by the Week, 36/63, 1-7 September 1963, p. 43.)

has not yet been fully described. But its efforts were helped by the parallel negotiations which were going on at governmental level, in which some of the original doubts and reservations of groups in Sarawak, and Sabah, were being overcome by concessions and assurances.[12] By January 1963, the five parties, apart from SUPP, had formed the Sarawak Alliance. The example which was followed was that already in existence in Malaya. A number of communal parties came together by setting up a superstructure, which provided an inter-communal bridge. So Temenggong Jugah anak Barieng (PESAKA) was chairman of the Alliance, Mr. Stephen Kalong Ningkan (SNAP) was secretary, and the other Alliance offices, for example, for Finance or Publicity, were distributed among leading figures of the five parties.[13] It is difficult to say what the unifying policy of the Alliance, as opposed to the communal concerns of the various members, was: it could be best described, perhaps, as pro-Malaysia, anti-communist and pro-economic development. The relative unimportance of 'policy', to say nothing of 'ideology', in the Alliance was shown by the departure of PANAS from the Alliance in April 1963. PANAS did not leave because it had become opposed to Malaysia: indeed one of the reasons it gave for leaving was that it would now be *better* able to fight SUPP. It seems that the split occurred simply because PANAS did not consider that it was getting its fair share of the cake inside the Alliance, as regards top positions in the organization, share of membership, and nominations of candidates for the forthcoming district council elections.[14]

The preparations for the 1963 elections were begun in 1961 when there was a debate on the subject in the Council Negri.[15] The use of the tier system was attacked by the

[12] See the *Cobbold Report*, Appendix F, 'Malaysia Solidarity Consultative Committee Memorandum on Malaysia'; *Malaysia Report of the Inter-Governmental Committee* (the Lansdowne Report). Kuala Lumpur, 1963.

[14] *Sarawak Tribune*, 17 April 1963; *Borneo Bulletin*, 27 April 1963.

[15] See *Borneo Bulletin*, 14 October 1961, for a statement of the Government's argument. The system proposed would ensure that those eventually elected to the legislature were persons having the widest support

SUPP. Mr. Stephen Yong, the SUPP secretary-general, maintained that Council Negri members would be too remote from the electorate to be answerable to it. The most convincing defence of the system was similar to that originally used to justify the creation of presidential electors in the United States — that the tier system offered a better chance than direct elections for the choice of Council Negri members who had a *national* and not a purely local outlook. The proposed legislation was passed, and was embodied in the Local Government Regulations published in 1962.[16] In brief, with certain disqualifications, any person who had been normally resident in Sarawak for seven of the last ten years, had attained the age of twenty-one, and, on the qualifying day (1 November 1962), was resident within the area of a district council, was eligible to be registered as a voter for that council. Registration of voters was not compulsory, but, in spite of heavy floods in certain areas and the Brunei revolt in December 1962, registration was carried out as planned. To save those persons living in remote rural areas from having to make long journeys in order to register, government registration teams were used to travel from house to house. It is estimated that 84.6 per cent.[17] of the potential electorate was registered, which was considered to be a very high figure. There was a perceptible difference in the proportions of male and female electors registered except among the Malays: among them the numbers registered for each sex were approximately equal. Malay (including Melanau) electors constituted 90 per cent. or more of the corresponding adult population for both males and females. But, whereas Chinese male electors constituted 90 per cent. of the corresponding adult population, the females were only about two-thirds of the adult population. Among other races registered electors were about

of the representatives of all communities. 'A system of direct elections might encourage the appearance of the worst type of political opportunist and this would be against the best interests of Sarawak.'

16 For a summary see *Report on the General Elections, 1963*. Kuching, [n.d.], pp. 2-3; *United Nations Malaysia Mission Report*, paras. 74-81.

17 *United Nations Malaysia Mission Report*, para. 79.

70 per cent. of the adult male population but only about 50 per cent. of the female.[18]

The SUPP made some criticisms of registration in certain areas on the ground that it had not been complete, but it did not press them very hard.[19] A qualification for *candidates*, that they should have reached the age of twenty-five, had some political significance, although it was not made the subject of public discussion. The choice of twenty-five, instead of twenty-one, could be defended by saying that, in the absence of any literacy qualifications for candidates, it was desirable to ensure a certain degree of maturity by fixing a higher age than twenty-one. But it could not escape notice that one effect of the higher age limit was to debar a number of rather radical young SUPP members from being candidates. This effect could not have been too displeasing either to the Government or to the moderate SUPP leadership.

The ballot papers could include a party symbol. SUPP used its badge of three interconnecting rings within a circle; the Alliance symbol was a sailing boat with five men representing the five constituent parties; PANAS had a stag's head on a background of the Sarawak flag. Independents could choose a symbol of their own design if they wanted to. Sixty-five out of 142 Independents did so; the remainder did not, much to the relief of the Government Printer. There remained the problem of what an illiterate voter should do if, inside the polling booth, he did not recognize a party symbol or wished to vote for an Independent who did not have a party symbol. In such a case he could ask the help of the Presiding Officer in marking his paper.

In principle the arrangements for voting were similar to

[18] *Sarawak Gazette*, 31 August 1963, p. 192, Table VII, '1960 Census Report'. Kuching, 1962, pp. 134-5. Note that the census figures are for the population over twenty as at 15 June 1960, and so are only approximately comparable. Also some of the 'other races' are not classifiable into male or female from the names on the electoral register. Nevertheless, the figures suggest comparatively low registration figures for Chinese women, men of 'other races' and, particularly, women of 'other races'.

[19] *United Nations Malaysia Mission Report*, paras, 80-1.

those in Malaya. But, because there were not enough experienced persons to supervise voting in several hundred wards simultaneously, outside the urban centres polling teams were set up inside each district who toured the various wards. Inside each district up to a month was allowed for the teams to tour the wards. 'Polling agents, that is, witnesses on behalf of the candidates, accompanied the teams and signed the sealing tapes that were put on the ballot boxes when they were sealed on moving from one longhouse or village polling station to another and also at the conclusion of polling in a ward. The sealed ballot boxes were stored under police custody until counting took place, when they were unsealed in the presence of the witnesses who had signed the seals.'[20]   One consequence was that in most of the Dayak longhouses instead of the voters having to go to a polling station, the polling station came to them.

Along with these plans for ensuring that voting would take place in a legal and well-organized manner, went a campaign to inform the electors on election procedures. Two pamphlets were distributed, each in eight languages (approximately 40,000 copies each), *The Countryman's Guide to Politics* and *What You Must Know About the Elections*. As well as dealing with actual procedures the pamphlets contained a simple account on the evils of vote-splitting.   This, in conjunction with the requirement of a $50 deposit per candidate, not returnable if he failed to poll one-eighth of the vote, was intended to discourage frivolous candidates.

From the administrative point of view the election went off smoothly.   In the contested wards 72.8 per cent. of the registered electors voted. This was only slightly lower than in previous district council elections, which had been held on a more limited franchise.   The number of spoiled or rejected ballots was only 2 per cent. of those cast. There was only one administrative error of any consequence. To avoid any possible 'bandwagon' effect from the announcement of the earlier election results in the

[20] *Report on the General Elections, 1963*, p. 4.

series influencing voters in the later elections, it had been decided that none of the results should be made public until polling had been completed in all districts. In one district, however, some of the results were announced prematurely by mistake. Only two election petitions challenging the results were submitted, both by defeated candidates, and in each case the original result was confirmed.[21]

However, the smoothness of the administrative arrangements did not necessarily guarantee that the elections were 'free'. In its submissions to the United Nations Malaysia Mission the SUPP claimed that they were not. Among the charges were: that key members of the party had been arrested;[22] that newspapers critical of the government had been suppressed; that administrative officials and Native Chiefs (who are paid by the Government) instigated and coerced SUPP members to resign; that there were official acts of interference and intimidation in rural areas; that the Government had spread malicious propaganda seeking to discredit the SUPP by associating it with a subversive clandestine communist organization. The general line of the Government's reply to these accusations was that '. . . There was no Government action against SUPP and no Government propaganda against the SUPP either before the election or at any other time. The Government's action was against Communist subversion, and if the SUPP has suffered from it, it is because of the Communists in the party . . .'[23] Curiously, one instance of Government 'non-party' propaganda was not referred to publicly in the SUPP complaints. Early in 1963 there was a series of educational non-party broadcasts on communism.[24] Because the SUPP was not mentioned by name, it had no

[21] *United Nations Malaysia Mission Report,* paras. 82-6, 100.

[22] *Ibid.* paras. 87-94. It is interesting in view of the argument about 'key' positions (page 270) that in a list of twenty-six leading members given by the SUPP as having been detained, there was only one branch chairman and one branch vice-chairman, but ten secretaries of branches or sub-branches. *Ibid.* para. 88.

[23] *Ibid.* para. 95.

[24] *Sarawak by the Week,* 7/63, 10-16 February 1963, p. 35.

obvious ground for complaint: indeed complaints would merely have enabled the Government to reply that the complaints 'proved' that the SUPP was pro-communist. Nevertheless, the timing of the broadcasts seems hardly to have been coincidental. In them communism was attacked: in official pronouncements the SUPP was linked with communism. The voters were left to bridge the gap in the argument for themselves.

The UN Mission declined to pass judgment on the necessity or desirability of the security measures introduced by the Government. There had been 'several instances of unwarranted (and in some cases illegal) manifestations of over-enthusiasm by local Government officials to further the interests of the political party supporting the Malaysia plan. . . .' But in general, the UN Mission Report concluded, the election was conducted as fairly and as freely as is possible in human affairs.[25] More particularly, the number of persons detained during the election period, 106, was too small to have affected the result, either directly, or by reducing the campaigning potential of the SUPP.[26] The UN investigation revealed two general limitations on free elections, which were also evident in different ways in the elections in Malaya. Governments faced with subversion must take countermeasures which inevitably harm parties which have been infiltrated by subversives. But how can parties be assured that they are not being victimized just because they are rival parties? One danger is that they will cease to operate on the parliamentary-democratic level and go completely underground, thus removing the advantage of having an open critical opposition.[27] The other limitation is that, in a society which is politically very underdeveloped, 'the Government' enjoys tremendous prestige, simply because it is the Government. The Alliance Party

25 *United Nations Malaysia Mission Report* para. 96.

26 *Ibid.* para. 126.

27 There is reason to believe that some of the radicals in the SUPP feared that Government action had so weighted the scales against the party that they seriously thought that the party should not contest the elections.

would often be identified with the Government and so would enjoy the consequent benefits. In addition there were probably isolated instances of pressure by minor government officials, such as village headmen: a common example quoted by opposition parties was that their Iban supporters were threatened with discrimination when government officers issued cartridges.

Although its conclusions were almost certainly correct, the UN Mission perhaps did not make sufficient allowance for the influence of opinion-leaders.[28] A mere numerical calculation of the effect of the detainees' votes, when allocated to the wards in which they were registered voters, would not indicate the full extent to which their removal damaged the SUPP's chances.

The Alliance, SUPP and PANAS all issued manifestoes. Their contents were not very specific. The Alliance stressed that racial problems should be settled first by the various political bodies representative of the various races, and after that reconciled within an alliance of such political bodies. This system had worked well in Malaya. Some emphasis was placed on education; it was hoped that free primary education would be possible, and that secondary education would be expanded and made cheaper. There should be provision for the study of indigenous and Chinese languages so that when children left school they would have a good command of their own languages in addition to English. There was some mention of land policy without any racial reference. Perhaps a little too eruditely for its potential audience the manifesto also quoted the Djilas thesis that communism led to tyranny. The SUPP manifesto blamed colonialism for 'the barrier between the races and the low standard of living of workers and peasants including small traders'. The SUPP advocated 'a programme of development based on socialism adapted to the needs of this country'. Private enterprise would be encouraged to play its proper role, but 'outside interests'

[28] B.R. Berelson, P.F. Lazarsfeld and W.N. McPhee, *Voting*. Chicago, 1954; E. Katz and P.F. Lazarsfeld, *Personal Influence*. Glencoe, Illinois, 1954.

would not be allowed to control the economic life of Sarawak. In education the curriculum should be such as to foster a common loyalty to Sarawak. However, the language and culture of all races should be encouraged, and learning should be through the mother tongue of the pupil. The land problem would be tackled immediately, but no specific measures were put forward. The PANAS manifesto was not markedly different from that of the Alliance. The only policy issue on which the parties really came to grips at the national level was Malaysia, the Alliance and PANAS being for and the SUPP opposed. This was evident in the radio broadcasts, one by each party (separate ones for the four parties inside the Alliance), which were translated into other languages.[29] Inevitably, although the national pronouncements of the parties were supra-communal, when the campaign came down to district and ward level it also came down to earth and to racial appeals.[30] One feature of the campaign was the rumour of a secret pact between PANAS and the Alliance. This was officially denied by both the parties. If believed, it could have been helpful to PANAS in suggesting that PANAS had not 'really' broken away from the Alliance completely, and that it would not be betraying the Alliance to vote PANAS. Also worth noting was the uncomfortable effect on the SCA of the Government's decision, in view of the border troubles with Indonesia, to withdraw arms from 'non-natives', that is, Chinese. As the election approached, the SCA, in effect, was forced to dissociate itself from the Government decision. Expressing regret, it claimed that the Chinese were in general loyal, and that it was just as easy for guns in the possession of Natives to

[29] Iban, Malay, Chinese, Bidayuh and English (*Sarawak by the Week*, 16/63, 14-20 April 1963, p. 44).

[30] Mr. Ong Kee Hui, *Sarawak Tribune*, 6 September 1963. Inche Abdul Rahman bin Yaakub also stated that young SUPP workers had been alleging that the Malays would become the ruling class in Sarawak (*Sarawak Tribune*, 7 June 1963). However, in spite of the system of indirect election, the Malaysia question prevented the election from being fought on purely local issues. Cf., on elections in British West Africa, James S. Coleman, 'The Emergence of African Political Parties', C. Grove Haines, ed. *Africa Today*. Baltimore, 1955, p. 241.

fall into wrong hands as it was for those in the possession of Chinese.[31]

The range of campaign methods was similar to that used in Malaya, but the emphasis on various items was necessarily different. A governmental view of the difficulties of distributing information in one district is revealing.

> It has been made apparent that the Dayaks do not, in the main, listen to news or to news features on their radios. . . . They listen almost exclusively to *bensanggai* and other forms of music, and tend to switch off or ignore the radio when more serious matters are discussed. That is emphatically not an argument for abandoning the radio as a source of information. The problem is more to educate the people up to using it properly . . . the radio cannot yet be relied upon. Nor, strangely, have people come to believe that what they hear on the radio is the truth. By the same token, written propaganda is seldom read, unless it is very short — two or three paragraphs at the most. This is probably due to laziness. Reading is an effort to the semi-literate. These media cannot now be relied upon to put over Government's policies and ideas to the people. The day will come; but at the moment the only safe way is by word of mouth — by constant touring by Administrative Officers and others concerned. Another point that the political agents of parties have learned to their cost is that the long-house Dayaks usually tend to remember the arguments of the last speaker they hear.[32]

These comments are also applicable to political campaigning. They do not suggest conditions completely different from those in developed societies,—except possibly as regards the scepticism about what is heard on the radio. But they do bring out the importance of personal contacts in order to achieve communication, and in Sarawak personal contact is made difficult by the lack of 'good

31 *Sarawak Tribune,* 27 April 1963.
32 *The Sarawak Gazette,* 31 August 1963, p. 201 (referring to the Simanggang District).

communications', in a physical sense. These considerations affected the distribution of expenditure among various items by each party. Thus, the Alliance used less printed material, relatively, than in Malaya. It also recognized the limited appeal of long stretches of printed propaganda: it printed some of its pro-Malaysia posters in Iban, but not its party manifesto. Travel costs claimed a big share of party expenditure. Many areas can be reached only by river, and the SUPP apparently spent more on fuel for outboard motors than anything else.

Compared with Malaya, less money was spent by the Sarawak parties.[33]   Of course the electorate in Sarawak is only about a tenth of that in Malaya, but, even allowing for this, the amount spent *per head* was almost certainly less. SUPP and PANAS spent less than the Alliance. This was partly because of the greater financial resources of the Alliance; but it should also be remembered that the effort of PANAS was confined almost entirely to the First and Second Divisions, and that most of the SUPP strength was in the towns where communications are easier and cheaper. Like the SF in Malaya, the SUPP benefited from the free services of a substantial number of dedicated workers who were motivated by ideology. As in Malaya, not much of the money spent came from membership fees.[34]   SUPP membership fees are collected only in the big towns: in the rural areas collection would be inconvenient, it was said, and might sometimes result in victimization of members. Fun fairs proved to be a very successful way of raising money (up to $10,000 each) for the SUPP. In the Alliance, PESAKA alone did not collect membership fees. The Alliance appears to have been

[33] No provision was enacted to make candidates submit returns of their election expenses. It was believed that some candidates would find difficulty in making up the return and that it would be impracticable to check all the amounts properly. *Sarawak by the Week*, 11/63, 10-16 March 1963, p. 10.

[34] Most of the parties' estimates of their own membership have been fantastic exaggerations. The SUPP estimate of 40,000 members at the end of 1962 was perhaps less exaggerated than most. Yet the party's total vote at the 1963 elections was only 45,500.

helped substantially by the Malayan Alliance: some opposition parties have alleged that a high proportion of its
total expenditure was financed in this way.

Help from the Malayan Alliance was not confined to
finance. Apparently at least a dozen party officials came
over to Sarawak to help with the campaign. Against the
expertise they brought must be set possible adverse reactions to them, and the party they helped, as outsiders.
The SUPP alleged that this reaction existed, and was itself
determined not to accept help from the SF in Malaya or
the Barisan Sosialis in Singapore. It is reported, however,
that SF representatives did visit Sarawak before the elections. Two other campaigning features may be mentioned. It was illegal to make use of school children as
helpers in the campaign. Nevertheless, there were allegations that the SUPP (which might naturally have wanted
to use the large number of available youngsters) and the
Alliance did in fact receive help from school children. It
was also alleged that the SUPP transported truckloads of
Ibans from rural areas to attend its rallies in Kuching,
a technique reminiscent of the Barisan tactics at the 1963
election in Singapore. There was no problem in securing
a large Chinese attendance in Kuching; the presence of the
Ibans was intended to project the image of a truly multi-
racial party.

Voting at the district council elections is summarized
in Table XI.

There were also 73 uncontested seats, as follows: 5
SUPP (electorate: 1969); 6 PANAS (4,489); 34 Alliance
(24,872); 28 Independent (16,246).

The general picture was that the Alliance polled more
votes than any other party, but only very slightly more
votes than the Independents. If the uncontested seats are
taken into account, its performance is improved, but it still
did not have anything like an absolute majority. By divisions, the SUPP had a plurality in the First Division, the
Alliance in the Second, and the Independents in the other
three. In the Third Division this Independent advantage
disappears when the Alliance majority in the uncontested

TABLE XI
ANALYSIS OF SARAWAK DISTRICT COUNCIL ELECTION RESULTS[a]

COUNCIL	SEATS	TOTAL ELEC- TORATE	NUM- BER OF VOTERS IN CON- TESTED WARDS	PER- CENTAGE OF VOTERS IN CON- TESTED WARDS	VOTES COUNT- ED	PER- CENTAGE POLL	PARTY DISTRIBUTION							
							SEATS GAINED				VOTES SECURED			
							SUPP	PANAS	ALL	IND	SUPP	PANAS	ALL	IND
FIRST DIVISION														
Bau	16	8,703	7,515	86.3	4,857	64.6	7	1	6	2	2,019	781	1,300	757
Lower Sadong	12	9,356	6,734	72.0	4,358	64.7	2	8	2	—	714	2,539	740	365
Lundu	12	4,423	4,053	91.6	3,148	77.7	2	5	3	2	732	1,032	992	392
Kuching Municipal	27	16,302	16,302	100.0	12,083	74.1	21	6	—	—	6,436	1,846	3,246	555
Kuching Rural	34	33,188	33,188	100.0	26,426	79.6	14	15	2	3	8,093	10,303	4,161	3,869
Upper Sadong	15	13,334	12,461	93.5	9,389	75.3	2	4	6	3	1,728	2,682	3,260	1,719
Total, First Division	116	85,306	80,253	94.1	60,261	75.1	48	39	19	10	19,722	19,183	13,699	7,657
SECOND DIVISION														
Batang Lupar	19	20,611	15,343	74.4	10,353	67.5	1	5	11	2	1,378	2,208	5,318	1,448
Kalaka	18	11,892	11,250	94.6	9,056	80.5	1	2	11	4	871	1,209	4,834	2,142
Lubok Antu	15	7,509	4,367	58.2	3,385	77.5	4	—	9	2	1,345	—	1,481	559
Saribas	20	14,349	12,252	85.4	8,360	68.2	2	7	9	2	393	2,036	3,290	2,641
Total, Second Division	72	54,361	43,212	79.5	31,153	72.1	8	14	40	10	3,987	5,453	14,923	6,790
THIRD DIVISION														
Binatang	15	7,618	7,163	94.0	5,913	82.5	7	—	7	1	2,646	290	1,848	1,129
Kanowit	24	20,927	13,116	62.7	9,938	75.8	3	—	16	5	1,172	46	4,894	3,826
Kapit	17	23,180	18,910	81.6	13,478	71.3	—	—	17	—	2,904	—	8,624	1,950
Matu/Daro	13	5,107	2,537	49.7	2,090	82.4	1	—	7	5	—	—	955	1,135
Mukah	19	17,929	17,929	100.0	10,822	60.4	—	—	—	19	—	—	—	10,822
Sarikei	17	9,539	7,870	82.5	6,538	83.1	8	1	1	7	3,014	256	2,062	1,206
Sibu Rural	22	17,174	17,174	100.0	14,217	82.8	12	—	4	6	4,639	—	2,571	7,007
Sibu Urban	21	9,500	9,500	100.0	7,478	78.7	16	—	4	1	4,143	409	1,855	1,071
Total, Third Division	148	110,974	94,199	84.9	70,474	74.8	47	1	56	44	18,518	1,001	22,809	28,146
FOURTH DIVISION														
Baram	17	13,746	7,610	52.1	4,709	65.7	—	—	—	17	—	—	—	4,709
Bintulu	14	11,756	9,989	84.9	5,860	58.7	2	3	8	1	579	1,442	2,366	1,473
Miri	19	8,839	8,839	100.0	6,407	72.5	10	2	6	1	2,687	1,163	1,922	635
Subis	13	5,371	4,049	75.4	1,947	48.1	1	—	2	10	—	—	264	1,683
Total, Fourth Division	63	39,712	30,037	75.6	18,923	63.0	13	5	16	29	3,266	2,605	4,552	8,500
FIFTH DIVISION														
Lawas	15	5,393	2,903	53.8	2,018	69.5	—	—	6	9	—	—	913	1,105
Limbang	15	7,040	4,606	65.4	2,863	62.2	—	—	1	14	—	—	—	2,863
Total, Fifth Division	30	12,433	7,509	60.4	4,881	65.0	—	—	7	23	—	—	913	3,968
GRAND TOTAL	429	302,786	255,210	84.3	185,692	72.8	116	59	138	116	45,493	28,242	56,896	55,061

a *Sarawak Gazette*, Vol. LXXXIX, No. 1266, 31 August 1963, Table IV (abridged). Note that the voting figures have been corrected here and in subsequent Tables by making deductions to allow for the existence of a few multi-member wards.

seats is allowed for.   But in the Fourth and Fifth Divisions the Independent plurality is clear.   These were the most remote, least urban divisions, and those least penetrated by the party organizations, except that SNAP was quite strong in Iban areas.   The percentage of non-voters was also highest in these two divisions.   This might be partly explained by difficulties of travel.   But it might also result from the relative absence of political interest and party controversy in some areas.

Both the Alliance and the SUPP stressed the fact that their multi-racial character was reflected in their choice of candidates from all races.   SUPP had 7 Malay candidates, 130 Chinese and 70 others (mostly Dayak).   The Alliance had 65 Malays, 66 Chinese and 141 others.   Even these figures convey the picture of the SUPP as being a slightly Chinese party, on balance, and of the Alliance as being, more than anything else, a Dayak party.   This impression is heightened when the figures[35] for *successful* candidates are considered.

TABLE XII[a]

SUPP SUCCESSFUL AND UNSUCCESSFUL CANDIDATES BY ETHNIC ORIGIN

	SUCCESSFUL	NON-SUCCESSFUL
Chinese	104	26
Non-Chinese	12	65
Total	116	91

a *Sarawak Gazette*, 31 August 1963, Table XI.

So an SUPP Chinese candidate was about four and a half times as likely to be elected as a non-Chinese.

The Alliance prospects were just the opposite.   Exact statistics cannot be given, because no breakdown is available of the parties, inside the Alliance, to which individual unsuccessful candidates belonged.   However, non-Chinese candidates can be divided into Malay (including Melanau) candidates and non-Malay Native candidates.   These figures can then be compared with the available figures for

35 See Table XII.

successful candidates for particular Alliance parties. There were 65 Malay candidates. Malay candidates almost always coincided with BARJASA candidates, and 35 BARJASA candidates were returned. There were 141 non-Malay Native candidates, almost all of whom were PESAKA or SNAP; 47 PESAKA candidates and 52 SNAP candidates were successful. There were 4 successful SCA candidates and 66 Chinese candidates. BARJASA and SNAP are constitutionally multi-racial, but the correspondence between these parties and particular ethnic origins is very strong.[36] An Alliance non-Malay Native candidate had roughly two chances out of three of being elected; a Malay had a slightly better than even chance; for a Chinese the chances were sixteen to one *against*.

Corresponding to this breakdown of candidates, it would be possible to make an analysis of the voting, which would show that in general Chinese support went to the SUPP, and non-Malay Native support to the Alliance, while PANAS benefited from the bulk of the Malay vote in the First and Second Divisions.[37] The general connexion can be seen by comparing the last three columns of Table XIII with the voting percentages of the parties. It remains true, however, that the generalization is only a broad one; '. . . the SUPP commanded considerable support in a few other districts which had no concentrations of Chinese population. It also appears that in most of the major urban centres in which such concentrations are most marked the SUPP failed to carry with it some 10-15 per cent. of the Chinese vote: the proportion probably includes those business elements in the Chinese population to whose conservative attitudes the SUPP would have no appeal'.[38]

Another qualification is that the Alliance's mainly-Malay party, BARJASA, although it did less well than PANAS in the First and Second Divisions, did substantially better in

36 But note the group of successful BARJASA candidates for the Lubok Antu District Council who were not Malays.

37 R. O. Tilman, 'Elections in Sarawak', *Asian Survey*, Vol. III, No. 10, October 1963.

38 *United Nations Malaysia Mission Report*, para. 112.

the other three divisions. Altogether, in the contested seats, it won 35 seats to PANAS's 59, and obtained about 16,000 votes compared with PANAS's 28,000.[39]

It might have been thought that the Alliance's slight advantage in votes would have been translated (by a Sarawakian echo of the cube law)[40] into a more decisive advantage in district council seats. But this was not so. The SUPP 'needed' 392 votes to win one seat, on the average: the Alliance needed 412 and PANAS needed 479. Indeed, if the uncontested seats are allowed for, the Alliance disadvantage in seats-obtained-in-terms-of-votes is even worse, because it should be 'credited' with more votes than SUPP for the seats it won without contests. In Table XIII votes and seats are compared, by divisions, for the three parties. Where a party won a seat without a contest it is credited with a vote equivalent to 60 per cent. of the electorate for that seat.

The SUPP enjoyed an advantage when votes were 'translated' into seats in three of the four divisions which it contested. In the other, it broke even. The Alliance came out less well, especially in the First Division where the pro-Malaysia vote was split between it and the stronger PANAS. 'Distortions' in the electoral system which worked against the SUPP were not present at district council level, but arose at higher levels.

It is desirable to look a little more closely at the role of the Independents. After the election, Mr. Stephen Yong, the secretary-general of the SUPP, said that the Independents were returned by the electorate on independent 'tickets', and that it would amount to fraud, and would be equivalent to treating the electorate with contempt, if Independents who had defeated Alliance candidates in the election joined the Alliance later.[41] Many such Independents did in fact do just what Mr. Yong advised them not

39 The breakdown of successful Alliance candidates analysed in the three preceding paragraphs was obtained from Alliance HQ, Kuching.
40 D. E. Butler, 'Appendix' in H. G. Nicholas, *The British General Election of 1950*. London, 1951, pp. 327-33.
41 *Sarawak Tribune*, 29 June 1963.

TABLE XIII

SARAWAK: VOTES AND SEATS FOR PARTIES, AND ETHNIC COMPOSITION OF ELECTORATE, BY DIVISIONS

DIVISION	SUPP		PANAS		ALLIANCE		INDEPENDENTS		ETHNIC COMPOSITION OF ELECTORATE		
	Percentage of votes won	Percentage of seats won	Percentage of votes won	Percentage of seats won	Percentage of votes won	Percentage of seats won	Percentage of votes won	Percentage of seats won	Percentage Chinese	Percentage Malay	Percentage Other Native
First	32	41	33	34	23	17	12	8	35	32	33
Second	11	11	17	19	51	56	21	14	9	24	67
Third	24	32	1	1	38	38	37	29	26	18	56
Fourth	15	21	11	.8	19	25	55	46	20	23	57
Fifth	—	—	—	—	22	23	78	77	10	50	40
All	22	27	14	14	34	32	30	27	24	25	51

This Table is based on the *Sarawak Gazette*, Vol. LXXXIX, No. 1266, 31 August 1963, Tables IV and VII. 'Malay' into do.   There seem to have been quite a number of reasons for persons standing as Independents.   *The United Nations Malaysia Mission Report* gives three of these.[42]   A man might have been accepted as a candidate by a party, but have failed to receive authorization to use the party symbol by polling day.   He might have wanted to stand for a particular party, but the party might have selected someone else.   He might have wanted to avoid inter-party jealousies and identification with particular political or racial groups; because party politics were still largely un-organized in many areas, it might actually give him a better chance of election *not* to have a party symbol.

In the event, a large number of Independents joined the Alliance after the elections, approximately eighty.[43]   A much smaller number joined SUPP, approximately seven-teen.   About half a dozen joined PANAS.   This was by no means principally a bandwagon effect.   The United Nations Mission was convinced that the bulk of those who switched had taken their stand in favour of Malaysia during the campaign.   But there is no doubt that with the prospects of a deadlock because of the existence of three major parties and the highly complex system of in-direct election for the higher tiers of government, a suc-cessful Independent could be a flatteringly sought-after man after election.   It was even rumoured that there could be some financial advantage in being in this situa-tion.

Table XIV shows the strength of the Alliance parties by divisions before and after Independents had switched to the Alliance.   Generally, Independents switched to the 'obvious' party from the ethnic or geographical point of view. But in the PESAKA stronghold, the Third Division, more Independents switched to SNAP than to PESAKA; on the other hand, in the Fourth Division, where PESAKA had been weak, it picked up as much strength from ex-Independents as did SNAP.

42 Paras. 106-8.
43 Information from Alliance Headquarters, November 1964.

TABLE XIV

SARAWAK: STRENGTH OF THE ALLIANCE PARTIES BEFORE AND AFTER INDEPENDENTS ELECTED TO DISTRICT COUNCILS SWITCHED TO THE ALLIANCE

DIVISION	BARJASA			PESAKA			SNAP			SCA			ALLIANCE TOTAL		
	Before Strength	No. of Independents who switched	After Strength	Before Strength	No. of Independents who switched	After Strength	Before Strength	No. of Independents who switched	After Strength	Before Strength	No. of Independents who switched	After Strength	Before Strength	No. of Independents who switched	After Strength
First	8	1	9	2	1	3	8	2	10	1	1	2	19	5	24
Second	8	1	9	1	—	1	31	6	37	—	—	—	40	7	47
Third	10	11	21	43	9	52	—	13	13	3	2	5	56	35	91
Fourth	4	2	6	1	8	9	11	8	19	—	—	—	16	18	34
Fifth	5	11	16	—	—	—	2	4	6	—	—	—	7	15	22
Total	35	26	61	47	18	65	52	33	85	4	3	7	138	80	218

In view of the general tendency for the Alliance Party to be equated with 'Government', it is perhaps worth pointing to the prominence of *penghulus* (headmen of small administrative districts) among the successful non-Malay Native Alliance candidates. Seven of the 31 successful SNAP candidates in the Second Division were *penghulus*, as were 12 of the 43 successful PESAKA candidates in the Third Division. About half a dozen other *penghulus* were elected, mostly as Independents. All the 3 *penghulus* who were unsuccessful were Independents.[44]

It would be tedious to attempt to trace the exact sequence of events by which the Alliance plurality, afterwards reinforced by Independents who switched, was translated into a majority in the Federal Parliament. The essence of the Alliance problem was to obtain as big a majority as possible in the Council Negri. This was desirable in itself in order to control the state government. The proportion of seats held there by each party would also determine the proportion it received in Parliament.[45] The number of seats in the Council Negri filled by the indirect elections from the Division Advisory Councils was not the same for each division. The First and the Third Divisional Advisory Councils returned the largest number to the Council Negri, 10 and 11, respectively. Unfortunately for the Alliance it was precisely in the other three Divisional Councils that, with some Independent support, it was able to win a clear majority, yet they returned only 6, 6 and 3 Council Negri members, respectively. Attention therefore became concentrated on the elections to First and Third Division Councils. In the First Division a number of combinations was possible: any two out of the three major parties could have come to an agreement to share the seats, although for some of the combinations the support of several Independents was necessary. A PANAS-Independent majority was possible, even a SUPP-Independent majority was conceivable. Every possible combi-

44 Of the twenty-three indirectly-elected Alliance members of the Council Negri, four were *penghulus*.
45 Described later in this Chapter.

nation seems to have been seriously considered by at least some persons — even an Alliance-SUPP combination. In the end, the almost equally surprising combination of the SUPP and PANAS was formed, although there were some prominent PANAS leaders who would have preferred a deal with the Alliance. A compromise policy statement on Malaysia was put out, saying that both the parties agreed to a referendum.[46] In fact PANAS did not alter its pro-Malaysia stand. The manoeuvre was essentially tactical. In the other critical division, the Third, there was, in turn, a critical district council, Binatang, where the balance depended on one Independent councillor who was inclined towards the Alliance. Arrangements were made for him to make a visit to Malaya, where he would be less likely than in Sarawak to be exposed to influences which might make him change his mind. In the event, he proved to be firm in his allegiance, the critical Binatang council had an Alliance majority, and this was translated into an Alliance majority, and eleven Council Negri seats, in the Third Division. So the only non-Alliance seats in the Council Negri were those resulting from the SUPP-PANAS agreement in the First Division. It can therefore be maintained that the peculiarities and possible in-equities of the electoral system were made tolerable only by this apparently odd compact between parties which had widely-differing objectives.

The results of the various indirect elections in Sarawak are summarized in Table XV.

The Council Negri contains three nominated mem-bers.[47] The persons from Sarawak in the Federal Parlia-ment are meant to 'reflect as nearly as may be the political composition of the Council Negri',[48] therefore each politi-cal group is to be given in Parliament a number of seats

[46] *Sarawak Tribune*, 2 July 1963.

[47] Sarawak Constitution, Article 14 (1) (d). The Council Negri also con-tains three *ex-officio* members, but they do not come into the following calculation.

[48] *The House of Representatives (Election of Members) Order, 1963* (made under section 94 of the *Malaysia Act*), 4 (1). It is stated, further, that for this purpose Independents shall not be deemed to be a political

TABLE XV

SARAWAK: PARTY STRENGTHS IN DIVISIONAL ADVISORY COUNCILS AND COUNCIL NEGRI

	DIVISIONAL ADVISORY COUNCIL SEATS					ELECTED COUNCIL NEGRI SEATS				
	Total	SUPP	PANAS	Alliance	Ind.	Total	SUPP	PANAS	Alliance	Ind.
First	25	10	14	1	—	10	5	5	—	—
Second	22	—	1	20	1	6	—	—	6	—
Third	27	9	1	17	—	11	—	—	11	—
Fourth	22	4	—	7	11	6	—	—	6	—
Fifth	12	—	—	—	12	3	—	—	—	3
Total	108	23	16	45	24	36	5	5	23	3

Sarawak Gazette, 31 August 1963, Table V (summarized). The figures for the parties given in these Tables include some previous Independents who had already switched to a party, most of them to the Alliance. There have been some other changes since.

proportionate to the number of the thirty-nine Council Negri seats which it holds. Each group may nominate its candidates. Accordingly, the original allocation, based on the elections just analysed, was: Alliance 17; SUPP 3; PANAS 3; Independent 1.

Since these elections, there have been minor alterations in party strengths. Independent representation in the Federal Parliament has disappeared, and Alliance strength has, correspondingly, increased by one. Also, SUPP has one seat more and PANAS one seat fewer as a result of defections from PANAS at lower levels and the foundation of a new party, MACHINDA.[49] There may be further changes. Apart from conflicts over personalities and jobs, one of the reasons behind the foundation of MACHINDA was the prospect that PANAS and BARJASA might join to become a single party.[50] This would have increased the Malay emphasis in PANAS, and it is significant that the leadership in MACHINDA is largely non-Malay. In May and June 1965 there was a crisis in the Alliance, and it seemed that a Government split would result. However, the upshot was that PANAS rejoined the Alliance and was given representation in the Government.[51]

There are certain obviously unrepresentative features about the composition of the twenty-four members from Sarawak in the Federal Parliament. The Alliance is over-represented in terms of the votes cast directly in the district council elections, and SUPP and PANAS are under-represented. This effect has been magnified by the inclusion of the three nominated members (all Alliance) in the Council Negri membership on which the calculation of the party strengths in the Federal Parliament is based. It may also appear to be anomalous that some of the members chosen for the Federal Parliament (about half a dozen, all

---

group (*ibid.* 4 (2)). The persons so elected to the House of Representatives by the Council Negri need not be members of the Council, but must be qualified so to be.

[49] *Straits Times*, 18 February 1964.

[50] *Ibid.* 17 October 1963; Borneo Bulletin, 18 January 1964.

[51] *Straits Times*, 15 and 26 June 1965.

Alliance) are also 'nominated', in the sense that some did not stand for the district council elections or were defeated in them. However, it can be argued that some of those who did not stand or were defeated would make better, and more successful, candidates in larger parliamentary seats, where the emphasis is more on state and national issues and less on local issues than in the district council elections. In any case, the system itself is temporary, because direct parliamentary elections will be held at the latest after 'the first dissolution of Parliament occurring after the end of August 1968',[52] so any defects it may possess are also temporary.

Sabah

The constitutional development of Sabah (previously North Borneo) was similar to that of Sarawak, in so far as it also did not become a British colony until 1946, having been previously administered by the British North Borneo Company.[53] From that time onwards development accelerated somewhat, but it did not catch up with that of Sarawak. There was both an Executive Council and also a Legislative Council, which came to include an increasing number of 'unofficial' members.[54] At the same time the foundations of a system of local government bodies were laid. But at the time of the Tengku's Malaysia proposal there had not yet been any elections held, not even at district level.

In spite of its political backwardness, North Borneo was in some respects better-off than Sarawak. Its economic position, based largely on timber and copra exports, was healthier and its national income per head was higher. For several reasons, perhaps partly because of the more favourable economic climate and partly because they had fewer grievances about education and land, the Chinese

[52] *Malaysia Act* (1963), 94 (2). This would place the latest possible date in April 1969.

[53] K. G. Tregonning, *Under Chartered Company Rule.* Singapore, 1958, p. 45.

[54] Michael H. Baker, *North Borneo, the First Ten Years 1946-1956.* Singapore, 1962, Ch. IV.

(23 per cent. of the population) were less subject to communist infiltration; there was no equivalent of the SUPP.[55]

By May 1961 there had been no elections in Sabah. There were also no political parties, although the largest native ethnic group, the Kadazans, had organizations which took some interest in politics. Yet by the time that the first district council elections were held, in December 1962, there were five parties. Two of these were, broadly speaking, the parties of the non-Muslim Natives, the United National Kadazan Organization (UNKO) and the United National Pasok Momogun Party. The UNKO, under its leader, Donald Stephens, had its strength mainly on the West Coast. The Pasok Momogun drew its support more from the interior tribes. It had been founded partly at the suggestion of an enterprising Chinese businessman, Mr. Peter Chin, who also founded the (Chinese) Democratic Party. Mr. Chin belonged to Jesselton; the other Chinese party, the United Party, was based on Sandakan — Jesselton's commercial rival. The fifth party, the United Sabah National Organization (USNO), was the largest, consisting mostly of Muslim Natives. Only the USNO was originally in favour of Malaysia. However, the UNKO, once its leaders had been convinced that Sabah, on entering Malaysia, would receive certain guarantees on such basic points as religion, immigration and so on, changed its stand and supported Malaysia.[56] The other three parties were all opposed to Malaysia and would have preferred independence for Sabah by itself. But they also changed their views on the issue, partly, no doubt, because they also were influenced by the safeguards which were offered to Sabah

[55] For a summary of comparative pre-Malaysia statistics, see the *Cobbold Report*, Appendix B; *Report on the Economic Aspects of Malaysia* by a Mission of the International Bank for Reconstruction and Development. Kuala Lumpur, 1963. During the elections Mr. Donald Stephens said that there was no prospect of a left-wing party winning in Sabah, because there was no economic discontent which could be exploited. (*Starits Times*, 24 December 1962.) Significantly, trade unionism is less prevalent in Sabah than in Sarawak.

[56] A summary on the foundation of the parties is given in the *United Nations Malaysia Mission Report*, paras. 144-8.

inside Malaysia and also by the persuasion of Alliance politicians, particularly members of the MCA.[57] Mr. Chin gave up his interest in the Democratic Party, and it and the United Party came together to form the Sabah National Party (SANAP), which declared itself in favour of Malaysia. This move isolated the Pasok Momogun, and after some hesitation and ambiguity it also came out for Malaysia.[58] In the meantime an institutional framework for a 'Sabah Alliance', which would unite all the pro-Malaysia parties, was taking shape. The USNO and the UNKO had started by forming a union, and in the end the Alliance comprised five parties, USNO, UNKO, SANAP, Pasok Momogun and the small Sabah Indian Congress. Its highest body, the Alliance Council, was composed of different numbers of representatives of the various parties, roughly according to their strengths, but, of course, it could not compel the obedience of the constituent organizations: each of the five bodies had a veto on its decisions.

By the time the first district council (and town board) elections were approaching towards the end of 1962, the Alliance was the only organized party (or combination of parties) in the field. Any opposition came from Independents. It was originally intended that the elections should be held in the areas of fifteen town boards or district councils that had already been established: Jesselton, Sandakan, Labuan, Tawau (town boards); Kudat, Tuaran, Kota Belud, Jesselton Rural, Papar, Beaufort, Sipitang, Tenom, Keningau, Lahad Datu, Semporna (district councils). However, there were two changes from what had been planned originally. At the request of the party leaders, who were in the process of negotiating to form the Alliance, the elections were postponed for four weeks. The elections in the Sipitang District Council area had to

[57] For example, an MCA delegation led by Dr. Lim Swee Aun, *Straits Times*, 13 October 1962. There was also a visit by the Tengku. *Sunday Mail*, 18 November 1962.

[58] *Borneo Bulletin*, 23 September 1961; *Straits Times*, 3 November 1961, 13 and 19 September 1962; *Borneo Bulletin*, 20 October 1962; *Malay Mail*, 9 November 1962; *United Nations Malaysia Mission Report*, paras. 144 (iii) and 215-16.

be postponed even longer, because the Brunei revolt had produced unrest there.[59]   Consequently the first district council elections were held in December 1962 in the areas of only fourteen local authorities.   During 1963 elections were held for Sipitang (March) and three more recently-formed district councils: Kuala Penyu (April), Tambunan (April) and Ranau (May).   The elections were completed in April 1964 in two other district councils where local authorities had been set up.[60]

Through a system similar to that in use in Sarawak the district council elections would, through a series of further indirect elections, elect the members of the Sabah Legislative Assembly and the sixteen Sabah members for the Federal Parliament.   Sabah election officials were convinced that it would have been administratively possible to have arranged for direct elections to these two levels of government at the end of 1962.   But politicians who had long experience of the less-developed parts of the Interior questioned the desirability of holding direct elections in such areas with so little preparation.   Age and residence were the basic qualifications for voting.[61]   It was originally intended that registration should be compulsory and complete, carried out via a 'census-like automatic registration of voters'.   But shortage of staff made this impossible

[59] There was also a postponement in one ward in the Kudat area, where there was an irregularity in the nomination papers of the only candidate. *North Borneo Annual Report, 1962*, 'General Review', p. 9.

[60] A summary of the sequence is found in the *United Nations Malaysia Mission Report*, paras. 158, 198-203 and in the *Malaysia Memorandum*, submitted by the Sabah government to the United Nations Reviewing Team and the 'observers' who accompanied it, August 1963 (unpublished), pp. 5, 11-12, 14-15. The areas covered by the 1962 elections contained about 75 per cent. of the adult population. For a few years more a minority of the members of each local authority were to be appointed, not elected.

[61] *Malaysia Memorandum*, p. 8. To be qualified to vote a person had to be 21 or more, to have been born in North Borneo or have lived there for 7 out of the previous 10 years and to have worked or lived in the appropriate local authority area for the previous 5 months. The requirements for a *candidate* were stricter. He had to be 25 or over, have been born in North Borneo or have lived there for the last 10 years and have lived or worked in the local authority area for the last 12 months.

in the time available, and the method actually used was to send round registering teams.   The response of the public was good.   It is estimated that, for the fourteen areas which polled in December 1962, about 90 per cent. of those eligible to vote had their names on the voters' rolls. It was theoretically possible for duplicate registration to occur under this system, but no instances of it came to light.[62]   The UN Mission showed some concern over the low proportion of Indonesians registered in areas where there appeared to be substantial numbers of Indonesians who satisfied the residence requirements.   It appeared that failure to register was at least partly attributable to advice *not* to register, given by the Indonesian authorities.[63]

The 'Instructions to Residents and District Officers' gave guidance on how to divide each local authority area into wards; as far as possible, each ward was to have equal numbers of population and also to follow obvious natural boundaries.   The UN Mission remarked that there were considerable discrepancies in the numbers of electors for different wards, and quoted in one local authority extremes of 1512 and 179 on the rolls of two different electoral wards, and in another authority, 2761 and 449.[64]

All candidates were required to have symbols, to be reproduced on the ballot paper, even the Independents: there was no equivalent of the Sarawak 'whispering vote'. If all the Independents had insisted on devising, and having reproduced on the ballot paper, a symbol of their own choosing, the administrative inconvenience would have been considerable.   Fortunately all the Independents were accommodating enough to accept one of the limited range of symbols which the electoral authorities already had available.   The political innocence of Sabah is suggested by the report that the Alliance originally proposed to adopt the sign of a clenched fist as an election symbol.[65]

[62] *Ibid.* pp. 9-10.
[63] *United Nations Malaysia Mission Report,* paras. 278-9.
[64] *Ibid.* paras. 159-60.
[65] *North Borneo News and Sabah Times,* 21 November 1962. 'It is understood that later it was found that a clenched fist had communist

The mechanics of voting, as in Sarawak, were adapted to the problems of communication in the country. In the rural areas there were travelling polling stations, which moved, complete with portable screens and other impedimenta of democracy, from ward to ward. The extreme case of a travelling polling station would have been in the Ulu Padas ward of the Sipitang District Council, where the travelling time would have totalled nineteen days. Fortunately the ward was uncontested.[66] Sometimes, however, the administrative officers responsible for the election arrangements seemed almost to regret the high proportion of members returned unopposed, which resulted in some of their preparations for the election not being tested. The success of the adminstrative arrangements was shown by the small proportion of spoiled papers (generally less than 3 per cent. of the votes cast) and the small number of election offences reported — only two minor ones. Further evidence of good organization was that, of the cards issued to each voter, bearing his name and electoral number, fewer than 1 per cent. were lost.[67] Part of the explanation for this success lay in the extensive publicity campaign undertaken to inform the voters about procedure, which was carried on through various media: press, radio, pamphlets and cinema, usually in four languages, English, Malay, Chinese and Kadazan.[68] The UN Mission looked into the question of how many persons who were eligible to vote were prevented from doing so by having been detained. They concluded that the numbers concerned were very small.[69]

Apart from the question of Malaysia, which was supported by all the organized parties, the only issues at the elections were local or depended on the personalities of the rival candidates. Mr. Khoo Siak Chiew (SANAP), for

connotations and it was therefore decided that the symbol should be changed.'

66 *Malaysia Memorandum,* pp. 10-11.
67 *United Nations Malaysia Mission Report,* paras. 196, 188 and 199.
68 *Malaysia Memorandum,* pp. 13-14.
69 *United Nations Malaysia Mission Report,* paras. 223-31.

of the Sim Sim Central ward (Sandakan Town Board) and would try to see that the road to Berhala Darat was properly constructed and that the people were supplied with water and electricity.[70]   Since the electorates were so small in rural areas, it was only to be expected that men of local influence would be sought after as candidates.   Eight candidates who were also *orang tua* (headmen) were successful, six being unopposed.   All these were either USNO or UNKO.   Two *orang tua* lost, one who stood as Pasok Momogun and one who stood as an Independent.

It is generally agreed that the parties spent very little money on the election, even less than in Sarawak: there was no SUPP to fight against.   SANAP costs were said to be especially low, because the party operated mainly in the towns where communications were easier and cheaper.   In general, compared with Malaya the costs of politics are small: even then, what little money has been spent has gone on building up party organization, and in making demonstrations in favour of Malaysia for the benefit of the UN Mission, rather than in fighting the actual election. The political leaders of all the parties were given equal, free, time on the radio.

To be sure, there was no organized opposition at the elections from parties outside the Alliance, but there was a good deal of unorganized opposition from Independents and some, partly disguised, opposition from within the Alliance itself.   Shortly before the elections in 1962 Mr. Donald Stephens, the leader of UNKO, said that there would be agreed Alliance candidates in only about one third of the wards.[71]   In fact there were inter-Alliance contests in forty-nine out of 137 wards.   There may have been other inter-Alliance contests concealed by one of the contenders posing as an 'Independent'.   These figures

70 *North Borneo News and Sabah Times*, 5 December 1962.

71 *Straits Times*, 28 November 1962; *North Borneo News and Sabah Times*, 22 November 1962.

indicate that the Alliance parties were far from being agreed on the allocation of seats.[72]

Table XVI indicates the total numbers of candidates

TABLE XVI
SABAH: COUNCIL ELECTIONS, 1962 AND 1963,
STRENGTH OF PARTIES BY RESIDENCIES

COUNCIL INTERIOR RESIDENCY	NUMBERS ELECTED FOR EACH PARTY					
	TOTAL	USNO	UNKO	PM	SANAP (BUNP)	IND
Beaufort	9	5	–	2	–	2
Keningau	8	–	4	3	–	1
Sipitang	8	6	–	1	–	1
Tenom	7	2	–	2	3	–
Tembunan	6	–	6	–	–	–
Kuala Penyu	6	1	2	3	–	–
Labuan (town board)	8	4	1	–	3	–
Total	52	18	13	11	6	4
West Coast Residency						
Jesselton (district)	8	2	5	–	–	1
Jesselton (town board)	8	2	1	–	5	–
Tuaran	7	3	4	–	–	–
Kudat	10	5	4	–	1	–
Kota Belud	10	6	4	–	–	–
Papar	8	4	3	1	–	–
Ranau	6	2	4	–	–	–
Total	57	24	25	1	6	1
Tawau Residency						
Lahad Datu	6	2	1	–	3	–
Tawau (town board)	7	1	–	–	6	–
Semporna	8	7	–	–	–	1
Total	21	10	1	–	9	1
Sandakan Residency						
Sandakan (town board)	7	1	–	–	6	–
GRAND TOTAL	137	53	39	12	27	6

Official figures amplified by information on membership of parties *within* the Alliance obtained from Alliance HQ, Jesselton.

BUNP (Borneo Utara National Party) is an alternative name for SANAP.

---

[72] Also, at the UNKO annual meeting, April 1963, there were complaints that in some district councils the party had been discriminated

returned for each party in the 1962 and 1963 elections, and shows where the strength of each was greatest.

In the West Coast Residency and the Interior Residency UNKO and USNO were of approximately equal strength. Pasok Momogun's strength was concentrated in the Interior Residency. In the Tawau Residency, on the East Coast, USNO was far ahead of UNKO. Successful SANAP candidates nearly all came from the towns, where there is a heavy concentration of Chinese. The pattern of the various contests is suggested by Table XVII.

TABLE XVII

SABAH: DISTRICT COUNCIL ELECTIONS, 1962-3

COMBINATION OF CONTESTING PARTIES	USNO	UNKO	SANAP (BUNP)	PM	IND	TOTAL
Candidate returned unopposed	22	14	18	1	3	58
USNO-UNKO	2	4	–	–	–	6
USNO-SANAP	1	–	–	–	–	1
USNO-PM	7	–	–	5	–	12
USNO-IND	17	–	–	–	–	17
UNKO-PM	–	12	–	2	–	14
UNKO-SAP	–	2	–	–	–	2
UNKO-IND	–	2	–	–	–	2
SANAP-IND	–	–	8	–	1	9
PM-IND	–	–	–	1	–	1
SAP-IND	–	–	–	–	1	1
USNO-UNKO-IND	1	–	–	–	1	2
USNO-UNKO-PM	2	3	–	2	–	7
USNO-SANAP-IND	–	–	1	–	–	1
USNO-SAP-IND	1	–	–	–	–	1
UNKO-PM-IND	–	2	–	–	–	2
USNO-UNKO-PM-IND	–	–	–	1	–	1
Total	53	39	27	12	6	137

Source is as for Table XVI.
SAP = Sabah Alliance Party.

against in the allocation of nominated seats (*North Borneo News and Sabah Times*, 30 April 1963). In 1965 UNKO (by now joined with Pasok Momogun to form UPKO) complained again of being discriminated against in nominated seats. *Sabah Times*, 11 February 1965.

Most of the direct clashes between the members of the Alliance were USNO against Pasok Momogun or UNKO against Pasok Momogun. SANAP did not often get involved in open contests with its partners. A high proportion of its candidates was returned unopposed.

But the Table is misleading, unless a warning is kept in mind. The party names and symbols were not always what they appeared to be. For instance, in the only contested election in the Jesselton Town Board area, Harris bin Salleh (USNO) later a Cabinet Minister, defeated by only eight votes a candidate described as 'SAP/BUNP'. But this candidate was no more an official Alliance candidate than Inche Harris. However, it is said, because the BUNP (SANAP) did not yet have a separate symbol of its own, Inche Harris' opponent fought under the Alliance symbol. More important, not all the Independents in the Table were 'genuine' Independents in the sense that they were completely unattached to any of the Alliance parties. Many of them were in fact so attached, but they stood as Independents, because they themselves had not received the Alliance nomination.[73] In such an event an 'Independent' could be really an UNKO (USNO) man standing against another UNKO (USNO) man. Or he might be an UNKO (USNO) man standing against a rival party man from USNO (UNKO). It is not possible to make any kind of numerical estimate of the various types of 'Independents'. But the fact that 'Independents' existed, who belonged to an Alliance party other than the party of the official Alliance candidate, and who had adopted the protective covering of an 'Independent', showed that even at this stage there was not complete harmony inside the Alliance. In contrast to Sarawak, the fact that a few candidates who were elected as 'Independents' later changed to an Alliance party was often not equivalent to a climb on to the bandwagon but rather to an open declaration of their true original allegiance. Another indication of friction was provided by the low turnout of voters in Kudat, township

[73] *North Borneo News and Sabah Times*, 1 January 1963.

ward.   The Alliance candidate was Datu Mustapha bin
Datu Harun, leader of USNO, who later became Head of
State of Sabah.   It is true that Datu Mustapha was faced
by a weak, apparently 'Independent', candidate.   But, although supporters of the Alliance who were not pro-USNO
did not vote against him, many of them did not vote *for*
him.   The turnout was only just under 60 per cent., the
lowest in all Sabah: the low turnout 'was due to the lack
of support in a certain ethnic community for an Alliance
candidate put forward by another ethnic community....'[74]

It is not always possible to tell the ethnic origin of a
candidate from his name; for instance the UNKO Cabinet
Minister, Mr. Richard Yap, is half Kadazan.   But a scrutiny
of the candidates suggests that nearly all the USNO candidates were Muslims; there appeared to be only one Chinese
and four non-Muslim Natives.   All the SANAP candidates appeared to be Chinese.   UNKO and Pasok Momogun had some Muslim Native candidates, some non-
Muslim Native and some Chinese.   But whereas in UNKO
those with Chinese names or who appeared to be non-
Muslim Natives were relatively more successful compared
with Muslim Natives, among the Pasok Momogun candidates it was the Muslim Natives who had the greatest
chance of success.

Recently, Glick made an attempt to analyse Chinese
voting at the Sabah 1962 and 1963 elections.[75]   A positive
correlation was found between the size of the Chinese
population in each district and the percentage of the vote
which went to Chinese candidates.[76]   The explanation of
these figures is simply that the Alliance very often put up
Chinese candidates in areas where a large proportion of
the population was Chinese and also that Chinese Independent candidates were relatively frequent in these areas.
In Glick's article some of the statistics are presented in a

[74] *United Nations Malaysia Mission Report*, para. 190.   The average
turnout at the 1962 and 1963 elections was approximately 79 per cent.
[75] Henry Robert Glick, 'The Chinese Community in Sabah and the
1963 Election', *Asian Survey*, Vol. V, No. 3, 1965.
[76] *Ibid.* p. 147.

form which could possibly mislead. It is said that BUNP (SANAP) ran candidates 'in only six of the seventeen districts'.[77] But each of these districts contained several wards. It would be more informative to state that SANAP ran candidates in only twenty-seven out of 137 wards and that eighteen of these candidates were returned unopposed. The material available for analysis of the Chinese vote is therefore a trifle slim. However, it would appear that party labels are of more importance than the above analysis would suggest. In the 1962-3 elections there were nine contests between a Chinese SANAP (BUNP) candidate and an Independent.[78] In eight of the nine the Independent was also Chinese. In seven of these eight the SANAP candidate won. Sponsorship by SANAP (and the Alliance) therefore seemed to be an important factor for success, quite apart from the candidate being of Chinese ethnic origin.

The 1962 and 1963 district council elections were to be the basis for the election of members to the Legislative Assembly and the Federal Parliament. This was to be done through four Residency Electoral Colleges, one for each residency, which were to be chosen by the recently-elected members of the district councils.[79] So the existing Legislative Council members resigned as from 25 June 1963 and their successors were all elected by 16 July. The Residency Colleges were not important, except as electoral devices. Seats on them were allocated on the basis of one seat for approximately 5,000 persons in the area of the local authority concerned. But the number of seats in the Legislative Council, *to which* the Colleges would elect

[77] *Loc. cit.*

[78] Excluding the Bukit Padang ward by-election (Jesselton Town Board area), held soon after the original election, where an Independent narrowly defeated the SANAP candidate.

[79] *United Nations Malaysia Mission Report,* paras. 139-41, 205-8; *Malaysia Memorandum,* pp. 16-18; *Colony of North Borneo Government Gazette,* Vol. XVIII, No. 31, 12 June 1963, Schedule to No. G.C. 101/38/1; *State of Sabah First Supplement to the Government Gazette,* Vol. XVIII, No. 8, 30 December 1963, No. 42 of 1963. Note that the non-elected members of the district councils, of whom some still remained, had no say in choosing members for the Residency Electoral Colleges.

members were on the basis of one for approximately 25,000 persons. To be eligible for the Legislative Council, a person, among other things, needed to have been resident in the residency for the previous twelve months and to have a knowledge of the English language. In the West Coast and Interior Electoral Colleges there was no contest.

In the Tawau and Sandakan Colleges, Independent candidates were proposed, but were defeated by Alliance candidates. The Electoral Colleges' choice of members for the Legislative Assembly is shown in Table XVIII. The last column indicates the members chosen to represent Sabah as a whole in the Federal Parliament, again by party.

The Alliance worked out, and agreed upon, the number of seats that each of the parties was to have in the Legislative Council and in the Federal Parliament. Each party then chose its names. In the case of Legislative Councillors, because of the requirements about residence in a particular residency, a certain amount of adjustment was necessary between the parties in order to reconcile each party's proposals with residence requirements.

A further series of district council elections was held in April 1964 for the rural district councils of Tawau and Sandakan.[80] There were no contests between Alliance candidates, an agreed candidate being entered for each ward. Two Independents stood (for two Tawau wards), but all the Alliance candidates for the two district councils won. Eight USNO candidates and 6 SANAP candidates were returned for Tawau rural district council and 5 USNO candidates and 2 SANAP candidates for Sandakan rural district council. There was a corresponding change, via the system of indirect elections previously described, in the composition of the Sabah Legislative Assembly, which became: USNO, 15; UPKO (formed by a union of UNKO and Pasok Momogun), 12; SANAP, 9; Sabah Indian Con-

[80] By this time elections had been held in all districts except three: Pensiangan; Kinabatangan; Lubuk and Sugut. In the first of the three there was a council but all the members were appointed. In the other two there were as yet no district councils.

TABLE XVIII

SABAH: PARTY STRENGTHS AT VARIOUS LEVELS OF GOVERNMENT

RESIDENCY	DISTRICT COUNCILS						LEGISLATIVE ASSEMBLY					FEDERAL PARLIAMENT				
	USNO	UNKO	SANAP (BUNP)	PM	IND	TOTAL	USNO	UNKO	SANAP (BUNP)	PM	TOTAL	USNO	UNKO	SANAP (BUNP)	PM	TOTAL
West Coast	24	25	6	1	1	57	4	3	1	—	8					
Interior	18	13	6	11	4	52	1	1	1	1	4					
Sandakan	1	—	6	—	—	7	1	1	1	—	3					
Tawau	10	1	9	—	1	21	2	—	1	—	3					
Total	53	39	27	12	6	137	8	5	4	1	18	6	5	4	1	16

Source is as for Table XVI.

gress, 1. Representation in the Federal Parliament was unchanged.[81]

A few comments, in the nature of an extended footnote, are necessary, not to show changes in the composition of individual district councils, but to indicate how long Sabah is likely to continue to be without an opposition. There has been some talk of a complete fusion of the parties. One step, admittedly the easiest, towards this was taken when the two Native non-Muslim parties, the UNKO and the Pasok Momogun joined together to form the United Pasok-momogun Kadazan Organization (UPKO), which held its inaugural meeting in June 1964.[82] But, beginning in 1964, a number of disputes between USNO and UNKO (later UPKO) were openly publicized: on the question of a merger of the various components of the Alliance into one single party; on the holding of direct elections for the State Assembly and district councils; on the appointment of a State Secretary. There were two Cabinet reshuffles, each preceded by mediation by Tengku Abdul Rahman, in the second of which Dato Donald Stephens (UPKO) lost the position of Chief Minister and became a minister in the Federal Cabinet, being replaced by Mr. Peter Lo (SANAP).[83] It is difficult to judge the depth of the differences which divide UPKO and USNO. Many of the leaders are still friendly socially, as they were for years before political parties in Sabah began. Allegedly, some of the excitement may be attributed to younger members of the two parties who find Alliance politics, as they were originally, a little too tame. But it cannot be concealed that there has been a drive for membership by the parties, accelerated by the prospect of early direct elections. While talking of 'peace' (merger), the parties sometimes appear to have been preparing for 'war'. Both USNO and UPKO have been opening new branches and expanding

81 Details from the Secretary of the Sabah Alliance Party and the Clerk to the Legislative Assembly. Of these thirty-seven members, 1 USNO, 1 UPKO, 2 SANAP and 1 Sabah Indian Congress members were nominated.
82 *Straits Times*, 15 June 1964.
83 *Ibid.* 13 June 1964.

their field organizations. The two parties are acquiring distinct images: USNO that of a pro-Federal Muslim party; UPKO that of a states' rights non-Muslim party. Each appears to be manoeuvring for an advantage. The USNO believes that there are some non-Muslims who have been antagonized by the wish of the UPKO to call all Dusuns 'Kadazans', and who still prefer to be known as Dusuns. The UPKO was heartened by reports that some of the Bajaus (the largest Native Muslim group) felt that they were under-represented in the USNO hierarchy and contemplated founding an 'organization' which might conceivably come to have political aspirations apart from USNO.

The SANAP was strengthened in June 1965 when it joined with the Sabah Chinese Association (SCA), a Chinese welfare organization. The new body thus formed was called the Sabah Chinese Association. Its first, temporary, president was Mr. Peter Lo, the Chief Minister. The merger is intended to secure more Chinese interest in politics and more support for the party.

There are to be direct elections to the Legislative Assembly, possibly at the beginning of 1967. There is some doubt whether the Alliance, in view of its lack of complete solidarity since 1963, can keep together until, and during, these elections, when it is subject to so many stresses.[84] The attitude of the SCA (the former SANAP) will obviously be important, if there is a complete break between UPKO and USNO. However, at the next state elections the Chinese vote will not be as important as it was at the last district council elections. At the state elections the vote will be based on citizenship, not residence. About

[84] Dato Stephens announced that the Alliance would contest the elections as one component party, but 'in areas where it cannot be decided which party nominee should stand, we might have a friendly contest'. (*Daily Express*, 21 December 1964.) He stated, however, that the party with most seats would have the right to the Chief Minister's portfolio. With such a prize at stake it would be remarkable if most of the seats were not contested by more than one Alliance party. Dato Stephens later said that, no matter how 'friendly' the contests, election fights would 'hotten things up' and might break up the Alliance. *Sabah Times*, 13 March 1965.

50,000 Chinese in Sabah had not registered as citizens by the start of 1965, and some of these may not have a vote at the state elections.[85]   UNKO's union with Pasok Momogun, in UPKO, may not be of much direct advantage. If the 1962-3 district council results are examined, a Pasok Momogun-UNKO fusion at that time would have made little difference to the results.   There was only one seat where another candidate was returned because of a split vote between UNKO and Pasok Momogun.[86]   If there is a split in the Alliance before the election, the way in which electoral boundaries are delimited by the Federal Election Commission might be a decisive factor.   Finally, the result will be influenced by the appearance, or non-appearance, of new parties, about which there are rumours from time to time.

[85] Dato Haji Mustapha Albakri, Chairman of the Election Commission, *Sabah Times,* 30 January 1965.

[86] Jesselton District Council, Menggatal ward.

XI

The Singapore Elections of 1963

F. L. Starner

Introduction

THE special significance of Singapore's 1963 elections lay in the fact that they coincided with Singapore's separation from Britain and her incorporation as a semi-autonomous state in the new Federation of Malaysia. This was to be the third time that Singaporeans would have a controlling voice in choosing their own representatives, but it would be only the second time that the electorate would choose the entire Assembly — and hence the Government.

Singapore's first popular elections were held in April 1955 under the Rendel Constitution, which gave the British crown colony its first measure of self-government. At that time, the Progressive Party was the only one with continuity in Singapore politics, and, because it had close ties with the colonial régime, it became the chief target for the other five parties competing for the twenty-five elective seats in the Assembly. (There were, in addition, seven non-elective seats.) Winning ten of the elective seats, the Labour Front, led by David Marshall, was able, with the support of the three Alliance members, to form a government.[1] (This early Alliance was made up of the United Malays National Organization (UMNO), the Malayan Chinese Association (MCA) and the Singapore Malay Union.) Opposing Marshall's government were four Progressives, two members of the Democratic Party (subsequently merged with the Progressive Party), three members of the People's Action Party, and three Independents.

Marshall resigned as Chief Minister in 1956, when the

[1] *Colony of Singapore Annual Report, 1955.* Singapore, 1956, pp. 1-3,

British refused to agree to his terms for Singapore's home rule, although the coalition he had once headed remained in power until 1959. In the meantime, however, the PAP had won control of Singapore's City Council, although it only actually controlled thirteen of the thirty-two seats. And, long before the 1959 elections, the Labour Front, and the coalition through which it functioned, were in the process of disintegration.

The 1959 elections coincided with the termination of Singapore's status as a colony and the grant of home rule which Marshall's successor, Lim Yew Hock, had negotiated in London in 1957. In these elections there were 194 candidates contesting in the fifty-one single-member constituencies which had been created. In addition to thirty-nine Independents, there were representatives of thirteen parties standing — all of these independently of each other except for the UMNO and the MCA. Financial scandals, which rocked the coalition government in the months before the elections, aborted the efforts of anti-PAP forces to organize a united opposition In consequence, the opposition to the PAP was both demoralized and fragmented and the PAP completely dominated the elections, in which it won forty-three of the fifty-one seats with 54.1 per cent. of the total vote.

One aspect of the Singapore political scene in the 1950's, then, was the prevalence of small impermanent parties, which at best would come together for election purposes, only to splinter and form new groupings or to disintegrate altogether. A more significant aspect, however, was the rapid growth, from 1954 onward, of the PAP and its dominance of the scene through the latter half of the decade. The PAP's spectacular rise — and its cohesion in this period — were the more remarkable in view of the circumstances of the party's first five years. From its inception, the PAP's leadership was divided internally, and this division was accentuated by the involvement of its militant wing — and of its labour affiliates — in the violence and unrest which marked Singapore in the mid-1950's. Additionally, both the leadership and the ranks of the party were decimated on several occasions by large-scale security arrests.

The weight of the above factors was overwhelmingly on the side of extremism. Perhaps the basic factor in Singapore's political development has been the proletarian nature of Singapore society, a condition conducive to the growth of extreme left-wing, and in this case of communist-dominated, labour activity. Reinforcing this was the historical fact that in the first half of the twentieth century, the political activities of the Singapore Chinese tended to mirror those of mainland China. Thus, the schism which split the Kuomintang and the Communists in China before the war divided also the Nanyang Chinese; and during the anti-Japanese war many of the same forces that strengthened the movement of Mao Tse Tung gave fresh impetus to the militant left in Singapore. Finally, the struggle against British colonialism, in Singapore as elsewhere during this period, added its own incitement to violence to the others present.

Two factors somewhat mitigated this trend toward militancy. The first was the British policy of moving, from 1955 onward, in the direction of self-rule for Singapore, thus reducing the significance of anti-colonialism as a political issue. The second was the reality that Singapore standing alone possessed no economic future, and no hope of merging with Malaya unless domestic peace was restored and the Federation's fears concerning Singapore's political proclivities alleviated. This latter factor loomed very large at the end of the decade, in contrast to four or five years earlier.

By 1963, these factors were still present. But merger — of a sort somewhat different from that sought in 1959 — was to be a reality before the elections were actually held. Singapore's radical left was to be joined by the Indonesians at the beginning of 1963 in its open hostility to the Malaysia scheme. And the PAP, minus the radical left, faced the voters on a new issue: that of its record of achievement in its more than four years of power.

The Shifting Political Alignments, 1959-63

In 1963, there were four major parties standing in the elections. What was unique about the 1963 contest was that two of the major parties standing had splintered off from the PAP subsequent to the 1959 elections. These three parties — the PAP, the Barisan Sosialis and the United People's Party of Ong Eng Guan — were, by their own assessment, all socialist — and, incidentally, by their own assessment also, they were all 'non-communist' rather than 'anti-communist'. As socialists, however, they differed in their degree of militancy, with the two off-shoot parties both claiming to represent the true left-wing in Singapore and both accusing the PAP and each other of betraying the left-wing movement through opportunism.

The fourth party, the Singapore Alliance, was a combination of four parties which had stood in the 1959 elections and which had constituted a working coalition since 1961. The largest in terms of its electoral strength in 1959 was the Singapore People's Alliance, which was formed in November 1958 by Lim Yew Hock from remnants of the Labour Front and a segment of the Liberal Socialists. However, the vulnerability of its leaders to the PAP's charges, aired shortly after its formation, of corruption in the Government prevented it from gaining a substantial following or from effecting a united front. It succeeded in electing only four of its thirty-nine candidates in 1959, although it was the second largest vote-getter among the parties, with 20.7 per cent. of the total vote. Joining with the SPA in the 1963 Singapore Alliance were the Singapore affiliates of the Alliance parties of Malaya: the UMNO, the MCA and the MIC. Of these three, only the UMNO had demonstrated any strength in Singapore. Of the thirteen candidates which the UMNO and MCA put up in the 1959 elections, three — all Malays — were elected. Although the National Council of the Singapore Alliance was not formed until three months before the 1963 polls, its top leaders had worked together in the coalition which governed Singapore from 1955 to 1959, and SPA and UMNO leaders voted together when they constituted the opposition. In spite of the moves in June and July to integrate the Alliance parties, it was apparent throughout the campaign that their efforts were not really co-ordinated and that no unified leadership existed. In fact, it was publicly acknowledged in the press that where top level decisions had to be made as, for example, on the final selection of candidates, these decisions would be made in Kuala Lumpur — a point which the PAP used with telling effect in the campaign.

The Politics of Merdeka

A division existed between the militant and the moderate wings of the PAP from its inception. In its early anti-British stage the militant wing led by Lim Chin Siong was dominant; from 1955 to 1957, large-scale violence, instigated by communist and pro-communist elements within the party, was a major characteristic of the Singapore scene. Adroit political manoeuvring by Lee Kuan Yew —which enabled him subsequently to disavow responsibility for the activities of his party on at least three crucial occasions — and the assistance, inadvertent or otherwise, of the Lim Yew Hock government, enabled the moderate wing of the party to assume control of the party organization from 1957 onward. Significant as this change was, however, it did not at that time signify a shift in the centre of gravity of the party's mass base. The wide-scale arrests of the extreme leftists which brought Lee Kuan Yew, Toh Chin Chye and others to control of the party machinery were not generally recognized at the time as evidence that a shift toward the centre would follow.

Nor did Lee Kuan Yew find it useful for some time to repudiate the postures of the radical left. Indeed, in the 1959 campaign he insisted that, if the PAP won the elections, he would refuse to form a government until the principal detainees were released. After the elections he did secure the releases of Lim, Fong and three other top-level leaders; and he employed Lim and Fong and two of the other ex-detainees as political secretaries. Moreover, as late as 1960, Lee accused Lim Yew Hock on the floor of the Assembly of mendacity because the latter had 'suggested that the PAP was keeping in their membership a number of communist sympathizers and activists'.[2] However, he did not call for new elections subsequent to the release of the top detainees, as some spokesmen for the party had earlier predicted that he would,[3] and he did not effect the release of the others under detention.   Moreover, he kept a firm hand on the party apparatus.   Even before the 1959 elections, however, the Central Executive Committee of the party, under Lee Kuan Yew (and in the absence of the ideologists of the radical left) adopted a policy statement in which it reaffirmed the party's earlier commitment to *merdeka* (independence) but went on to assert that in order to achieve freedom it was necessary to achieve merger with Malaya.[4]

From the time the Lee Government assumed office, then, there was evidence that the PAP would adopt a more moderate policy.   The responsibility for providing effective government undoubtedly exerted a sobering influence on the new PAP leaders as did their anxiety over Singapore's future.   The objective of finding a formula for merger acceptable on both sides of the Causeway dictated a course of action far different from that which the PAP had pursued in the early years of its existence.   What created the crises of 1959 to 1963 was the fact that many of the voters who swept the party to power in 1959 were far more sympathetic with the ideas of Lim Chin Siong and the militants than they were with the practical politics of Lee Kuan Yew.

The first challenge to Lee Kuan Yew's authority within the party occurred in June 1960 when Ong Eng Guan launched the so-called Hong Lim Resolutions.   These sixteen resolutions strongly suggested that the PAP Govern-

---

2 Singapore, Ministry of Culture, *The Socialist Solution, Towards Socialism Series*, Vol. I, 1960, p. 25.

3 Willard A. Hanna, *Singapore Prepares for Local Self-government*, American Universities Field Staff Report, WAH — 3, 1959, p. 24.

4 From the Fourth Anniversary Souvenir issue of *Petir*, 22 November 1958, quoted in *The Socialist Solution, op. cit.* pp. 17-18.

ment was failing to advance the cause of independence, moving to the right on specific issues of domestic policy and generally losing its revolutionary zeal. The party itself, it was suggested, lacked internal democracy. Ong, the ex-Mayor of Singapore, had undoubtedly suffered blows to his prestige, first when he was appointed to the relatively unimportant post of Minister of National Development in the Lee Cabinet, and subsequently when he was deprived of control over such functions as housing development. The Hong Lim incident was, therefore, dismissed generally by the party as opportunism, with the militant left as a whole unwilling to risk a rupture at that time on Ong's charges. There were indications that they regarded the charges as having some substance, but they were unlikely under any circumstances to follow Ong, with whom they had come into open conflict in 1957. For his 'challenge to the Party's collective leadership', Ong was expelled from the party and the Government, apparently with little threat to either. Six months later, however, Ong resigned his Hong Lim seat in order to seek vindication from his constituents. In the words of Lee Kuan Yew, the Government chose deliberately to 'underline the importance of Hong Lim', and it undertook a massive campaign to bring about the rebel's defeat. In April 1961, in a straight contest with the PAP's hand-picked candidate, Jek Yuen Thong, Ong, standing as an Independent, dealt the Government a stunning blow, polling 7,747 votes against only 2,820 for the PAP candidate. In June, Ong organized the United People's Party (UPP).

Two and a half months after the Hong Lim by-election, the Government lost a second one in the Anson constituency. This contest, which returned David Marshall as an Independent by a small margin, was far from decisive in the sense that Hong Lim was. What gave it more than passing significance were the differences between spokesmen for the Government on the one hand and the Singapore Trade Union Congress (STUC) leaders and left-wing assemblymen on the other, which erupted during the campaign and no doubt contributed to Marshall's victory.

Once the differences between the PAP's rival factions were out in the open, the irrevocable break between the Government and the dissidents of the left was not long in coming. The issue upon which STUC leaders first challenged the Government was its continued failure to secure the release of all political detainees. Subsequently, however, they raised two additional issues: first, that of 'merger or supermerger', and second, 'internal democracy in the PAP'. In the event, these two were tied closely together. Lee Kuan Yew had undertaken negotiations with Malaya's Prime Minister, Tengku Abdul Rahman on the question of merger through a Malaysian federation; and the rebels alleged that there was an attempt by the Government publicly to commit the party on issues on which 'serious intra-party disagreement' existed. When the Government took the initiative and removed the rebellious party leaders from positions of authority, the latter led their followers in a walk-out from the PAP, and a short while later organized the rival Barisan Sosialis (Socialist Front).

Initially, thirteen members of the Assembly crossed the floor to join the Barisan and subsequently they were joined by a fourteenth member. Since Lim Chin Siong and other top leaders of the new party held key positions in the Trade Union Congress and members of the militant left occupied strategic positions also in the mass organs of the party, the Barisan was able to carry with it a substantial portion of the PAP's mass following in labour and in community organizations such as the People's Associations, associations of hawkers and rural dwellers, Chinese school student and alumni groups and others.

Thus, by a process of erosion, the PAP lost its majority in the Assembly. From 43 seats in 1959, they had dropped to 26 by August 1961; and with the death of the Minister for Health a year later, the PAP retained control of only 25 of the 50 seats in the Assembly which were occupied. In spite of this precarious balance, the Lee Kuan Yew Government did not topple. On matters pertaining to the so-called referendum on merger or on support of his agreement with the Tengku, as indeed on most questions of public policy, Lee Kuan Yew could count on the votes of the parties of the right. The close ties which the UMNO maintained with its counterpart in the Federation were sufficient of themselves to assure its support for the Lee-Tengku agreement. But this support was not forthcoming on 24 July 1963, when the Government presented a bill to provide for the election of Singapore's fifteen members to the new Malaysian Parliament. The Alliance and Independent members joined with the leftist opposition, deadlocking the Assembly 23 to 23, with four votes paired.

At this point the opposition parties of both right and left joined in demanding that the Government resign. However, Lee challenged the Alliance parties, if they wanted to bring down the Government, to vote against his motion to welcome Malaysia. This of course the Alliance could hardly do. Nevertheless, the Alliance members did abstain from voting on the Prime Minister's motion, which was carried 25 to 17 with no support except from PAP members.

The Events of August 1963

The circumstances which surrounded the birth of Malaysia were inextricably intertwined with the political developments which culminated in the 1963 elections. In addition, there were at least two other chains of events which comprise a part of the backdrop for the campaign. The detention of a number of Barisan and trade union leaders, under the Preservation of Public Security Ordinance (PPSO), in 'Operation Cold Storage' in February 1963, cast its shadow over the election. So did the trial in August of twelve Barisan leaders, including ten assemblymen, on charges of rioting and attempted intimidation of the Government, which grew out of a City Hall demonstration three months earlier. Even the so-called 'Blood Debt' rally which the Chinese Chamber of Commerce organized to press for compensation from the Japanese government,[5] was coincidentally caught up in the political cross-currents of the period.

The Malaysia agreement was finally signed by Lee Kuan Yew and Tengku Abdul Rahman on 9 July 1963, in London. Even so, in Singapore partisan controversy continued on the issue of Singapore's concessions to Malaysia. Nevertheless, with political merger agreed upon and the basis for a future common market blueprinted, Lee Kuan Yew returned from London to undertake a triumphal tour of all fifty-one constituencies. The opposition parties, particularly those which were anti-Malaysia, resented the obviously partisan overtones of the Prime Minister's tour. As a consequence, it was marked by disturbances in some areas, particularly those in which unions of the Singapore Association of Trade Unions (SATU)[6] were strong. Anti-Malaysia and anti-PAP banners were prominently displayed on union premises, and youths, frequently with their faces covered, booed Lee's speeches in these places; in one instance, a shoving incident took place which sent the Prime Minister into a monsoon drain.

This pattern of organized booing and jeering by anonymous young men marked also the incident of the massive 'Blood Debt' rally held on the *padang* in front of City Hall on August 27. On the night in question, in spite of close police surveillance and the use of high-powered searchlights to spotlight the offenders, Lee was booed and jeered almost continuously when he attempted to address the rally. Three days after the rally the Government made good on its threat to retaliate against the unions when it served notice of intent to de-register seven SATU unions, including the three largest. The show-cause order charged that the unions in question had, in spite of prior warnings by the Government, tried to 'exploit the Rally for Communist purposes' and taken part in 'activities of a political

5 The 'Blood Debt' movement was prompted by a 'gesture of atonement' which Japan proffered to compensate for suffering inflicted on Singapore Chinese during World War II.

6 The left-wing successor of the STUC, closely allied with the Barisan Sosialis.

nature outside the normal functions of genuine trade unions'.[7]

The postponement of the inauguration of Malaysia necessitated by the delays in completion of the United Nations survey in the Borneo territories provoked another kind of political incident. The postponement was to be from 31 August, the anniversary of Malaya's independence, to 16 September. Lee Kuan Yew proclaimed unilaterally on the originally proclaimed date that his Government was assuming the powers of defence and external affairs, in addition to those already held, until Malaysia came into being. Predictably, the Alliance Government in Kuala Lumpur reacted sharply to the Singapore Chief Minister's assertion of *de facto* sovereignty.

The time element is worth underlining in three developments of major significance. First, the culmination of the SATU-PAP feud led to the cancellation of registration of seven SATU unions. Second, the trial of the twelve Barisan leaders ended on 29 August with four acquittals and eight found guilty on the single charge or rioting; the latter were allowed bail during appeal. And third, Lee proclaimed Singapore's independence and engaged in polemics with the Alliance over the proclamation. It was in this atmosphere that the Government on 3 September prorogued the Assembly and called for election. Nomination day, set for 12 September, would precede Malaysia Day, and the elections would necessarily follow it, although at what interval would not be known until after the nominations. Meanwhile, in the interval before nominations, the PAP Government kept the offensive both in its conflict with the SATU unions and in its dispute with the Federation over Singapore's interim status. On 3 September, the day of the Assembly dissolution, Lee publicly announced that Duncan Sandys (the British Commonwealth and Colonial Secretary) would be given until 12 September to iron out 'certain matters related to the Malaysia agreement' or 'face the consequences' of Lee's

[7] Singapore Government Press Statement, 29 August 1963.

proclamation of *de facto* independence for Singapore. And on the eve of nomination day, after renewed talks in Kuala Lumpur among the Malaysia signatories, he announced that the remaining differences with the Federation Government over the London agreement, including the common market provisions, had been resolved to his satisfaction. The SATU faced a fresh blow on 9 September when the Government froze the funds of its three largest unions, alleging that large sums of money were about to be withdrawn for purposes not consistent with their constitutions.

The Election Campaign

In a sense, the most remarkable characteristics of the campaign derived from the question of timing. By statute, candidates were required to present their papers in person at the appropriate nominations centre between 11 a.m. and 12 noon on nomination day, 12 September. Six hours after nominations closed the Government announced that the elections would be held on 21 September, or nine days later, which was the minimum interval allowed under the law.[8] The business of campaigning could not therefore start until Friday, 13 September. In the eight days nominally available for campaigning, the parties (at least those of the opposition) were hampered by the necessity of competing with the Malaysian festivities for the attention of the registered voters and by the lack of time in which to transact essential business in this particular period. Government offices and many businesses were closed one half day on Saturday, 14 September, as usual; a full day on Sunday (which was also the day on which festivities began); all day on Monday, Malaysia Day; on Tuesday, also proclaimed a legal holiday; and all day Saturday, 21 September, which was polling day. This left one and

[8] Under the law, as it stood in September 1963, nine days had to elapse between dissolution of the Assembly and nomination day, and another nine before elections. In December, however, even this period was shortened by allowing nomination day to be proclaimed only five days after dissolution. *Singapore Legislative Assembly Elections Ordinance,* as amended, 28 December 1963.

a half days at the beginning of the campaign period and three days at the end.

The opposition thus found themselves handicapped. They had great difficulty in reaching the registered voters at their homes, either in person or through the mail. They encountered further difficulties in securing sites and permits for rallies. And they found it virtually impossible to get printing work done, because local printers were so busy with Government orders for the Malaysia celebrations that they could not handle additional orders. (The PAP, however, the Barisan charged, had had its printing done in Hong Kong three months earlier.) None of the parties, however, showed any interest in joining with David Marshall in challenging the legality of the elections schedule in court, perhaps because they felt there was no time for anything but campaigning. Marshall's claim that there were not nine clear days between the elections proclamation and the holding of the elections, as the law required, was dismissed on 19 September.

The process of selecting candidates was accompanied by great secrecy on the part of the parties, each doing its utmost to keep the others from finding out who its candidates were and in which constituencies they would stand. It was predictable, of course, that all or practically all of the incumbent assemblymen would be standing, and this meant that there would be fewer surprises in the PAP line-up than in those of other parties. It was not known, however, whether PAP members would stand in their old constituencies, or not. In fact, eighteen of the twenty-five PAP assemblymen stood in their old constituencies, four were dropped and three, including one member of the cabinet, sought election in new constituencies. The newly-organized Alliance, faced with the delicate task of reconciling the conflicting demands of four member parties, took its problems to Kuala Lumpur to be ironed out. Reports from Kuala Lumpur indicated that probably neither the former chief minister, Tun Lim Yew Hock, who headed the SPA, nor Dato Abdul Hamid bin Jumat, the UMNO leader who had been Lim's Deputy Chief Minister, would appear in the Alliance line-up.

The Barisan Sosialis suffered from a major handicap in that some of their ablest men, including Lim Chin Siong, Fong Swee Suan, Sidney Woodhull and Dominic Puthucheary, were under detention. The non-English language press indicated that the party seriously explored the possibilities of nominating some of the detainees.[9]   These were persons held under preventive detention, without having been tried in a criminal court and they were not therefore ineligible to stand for election, as prisoners with criminal convictions were. Actually, however, there was no chance of any of these men being nominated while under detention, because the election law, as amended in April 1960,[10] required that the candidates present their nomination papers *in person* during the one hour that the nomination centres were open.

This peculiarity of the law was also responsible for another development. Early on the morning of 12 September, the Special Branch of the police moved in and picked up for questioning some seventeen persons described in the press as ex-detainees; it held them until the nominations centres closed at twelve o'clock. Although the Government insisted that these men were prohibited under the terms of their release under the Preservation of Public Security Ordinance from participating in political activities, they were not otherwise ineligible under the law from standing for the Assembly, or from taking their seats there if elected — provided they could get to the nominating centres at the time required.

The most frequent pre-nominations speculation concerned the number of candidates which each of the parties would put up. It was anticipated that the PAP and the Alliance would contest in all of the fifty-one constituencies and that the Barisan would contest in most. In fact, the Alliance did not put up candidates in some nine constituencies, which they conceded to the PAP or the Barisan.

9 *Tamil Nesan*, 6, 10 and 11 September 1963.
10 Sec. 29 (2).

The big surprise of the nominations, however, was the number of constituencies contested by the UPP. Ong Eng Guan and his colleagues put up forty-six candidates, equalling the number fielded by the Barisan. Only the PAP contested all fifty-one seats.

Four minor parties fielded from one to three candidates each. Of these, the Party Ra'ayat, an extreme left-wing, predominantly Malay, party, allied itself with the Barisan for election purposes. The United Democratic Party, with a single candidate, announced that it would co-operate with the Workers' Party. The fourth minor party contending was the Pan-Malayan Islamic Party (PMIP).

In all, 210 candidates contended for the fifty-one seats, or sixteen more than in the 1959 elections. However, it was the overall pattern of the 1963 contests which provided the most marked contrast with the previous ones. Whereas in 1959 there were seven straight contests, in 1963 there was only one. At the other extreme, while there were six or more candidates competing for each of four seats in 1959, there was only one contest in which six candidates were in contention in 1963. If the candidates of Party Ra'ayat are included with those of the Barisan, then one could say that representatives of all major parties opposed each other in three out of every four constituencies.

There were 164 Chinese standing in 48 of the 51 constituencies in the 1963 elections, and these made up 78.4 per cent. of the total candidates. This was higher than the figures for 1959, when the Chinese comprised only 68.0 per cent. of the 194 candidates. Of the 46 non-Chinese in 1963, there were 17 Indians distributed in 13 constituencies, and 25 Malays contesting in only 11 constituencies. This represented a drop both in absolute numbers and in percentages of the total candidates for both ethnic groups; the increase in the number and percentage of Chinese standing, however, was achieved chiefly at the expense of the 'Other' (chiefly Eurasian) category, in which there were only four candidates in 1963.

Although the re-aligned PAP in 1963 put up precisely the same ratio of Chinese to non-Chinese as the old party

had in 1959 — that is, 34 to 17 — both of its offshoots, the
Barisan and the UPP, put forward a very high proportion
of Chinese candidates. Of the former, 93.5 per cent. and
of the latter, 87.0 per cent. were members of the Chinese
community. Only twenty-nine, or 69.0 per cent. of the
Alliance candidates were Chinese. Among the minority
parties, the PMIP was, of course, exclusively Malay, and
Party Ra'ayat put up two Malays and one Chinese. The
UDP-WP candidates were all Chinese, and the Independents split thirteen Chinese to three members of other
ethnic groups.

Nowhere does the contrast between candidates of the
four parties show up more clearly than on age. Reflecting
the fact that it was a young man's party when it came to
power four and half years earlier, the PAP showed a heavy
concentration of candidates in the 30 to 35 age bracket,
although the median age was 37.5. The more conservative Alliance, although it had more candidates in the 35
to 40 than in any other, also had a number in the 55 to
60 bracket, and its median age was 43. The militant
Barisan together with its Party Ra'ayat affiliate put up 29
candidates below the age of 30, and the median age of the
Barisan was only 29 years. The United People's Party
also had a concentration of candidates in the 25 to 30 age
bracket. Unlike the Barisan, however, it had also a number of older candidates, who raised the UPP median to 34.
The median age of candidates from all parties for whom
age data were available was 35.

Regarding education, the evidence indicates that the
candidates were divided almost evenly between the English-educated and the Chinese-educated, with less than
5 per cent. shown as educated primarily in Malay. Although a high percentage were indicated as bilingual or
trilingual, only some 15 per cent. were shown as having
received education in both Chinese and English — and
hence able to both write and speak the two languages.
A few more were educated in combinations of English and
Tamil or Malay. Although the data are not complete on
the educational level attained by the candidates, it could

be established from the information that was available, that slightly over one-third of the 200 candidates had graduated from college or university, and of these some twenty-two candidates, or more than 10 per cent. of the total, had professional degrees.[11] Another one-third were indicated as having attained a secondary level of education, and the remaining one-third, for whom the level of education was not specified, appeared, on the basis of the vocational data given, to be somewhat lower generally on the education scale.

All those with professional degrees were educated in the English language stream, and a high proportion of these had degrees from England. The number of university graduates, exclusive of professionals, who were educated in the Chinese language stream was somewhat higher than that in the English language stream; this phenomenon was largely accounted for by the Barisan's active recruitment of Nanyang University graduates. And, among the secondary school graduates, there was a ratio of two Chinese-educated to one English-educated; among those where the level of attainment was unspecified, however, the English-educated slightly exceeded those with Chinese education.

An analysis of the education data on the basis of parties reveals significant differences among the parties comparable to the differences in age grouping. Three out of four Barisan candidates were educated in the Chinese language stream, and almost as high a proportion of the UPP candidates were Chinese-educated. This ratio was inverted in the cases of the PAP and the Alliance, with the latter indicating the smallest fraction of Chinese-educated of any of the parties. The Alliance also had the highest number of candidates with professional degrees (36 per cent. of the total) with the PAP second and the Barisan third. There were only two professionals on the UPP slate, although a third candidate was a medical student.

Surprisingly, it was the UPP which had the highest pro-

11 That is, holders of medical or legal degrees or doctorates.

portion of candidates born and educated in China. It
appears from the biographical sources that nine — almost
20 per cent. — of the UPP candidates were born and received some education on the Chinese mainland. There
were also a number of Alliance candidates who were
educated in China, although several of these were Federa-
tion-born. Two PAP candidates were born in China, but
only one of these was educated there. The PAP had three
candidates, however, who were born and apparently educated in India, and one born in Ceylon. (The Alliance
also had at least one candidate who was born in India.)
There was no evidence that any of the Barisan candidates
were born or educated outside of Singapore or the Federation, and only two or three had done any studying abroad.
Although the biographic data on the Barisan do not
include place of birth, it appears that Barisan candidates,
like those of the PAP, were most apt to be Singapore-born
and educated.

The data published on the occupational status of the
candidates affirm the continued importance of the labour
movement and of the educational profession as major
sources for political talent, and the lesser importance of
business and the legal profession. The data here complement those on age and education, completing the profiles
of the candidates of the various parties.

It is hardly surprising that organized labour continued
to be the primary source of political aspirants in Singapore
in 1963. In the Alliance as a party of the right, the number of unionists standing was negligible, and only six of
the UPP's candidates were involved in significant labour
activity. On the other hand, both the Barisan and the
PAP had high proportions of officials and former officials
of the labour unions on their slates. In spite of the leading role played by unionists in the Barisan's breakaway
from the PAP, the latter still claimed a higher proportion
of candidates with union connexions, current or past, than
the Barisan did. (Twenty-five of the PAP's fifty-one candidates were said to be present or past officials of unions,
compared with nineteen for the Barisan-Ra'ayat line-up.)

There was, however, a far higher degree of professionalization in the union activities of the Barisan candidates and a significant difference in the present labour activity between the two parties. In the case of the PAP, this pointed to an important aspect of the change which takes place within a political party when it assumes power. A large number of the PAP candidates who had risen to positions of leadership in the union movement no longer pursued labour goals because they were employed full-time in the business of politics and government. Of the entire PAP slate, approximately 65 per cent. were in the employ either of the party or the Government, and the majority of these held posts as ministers or as parliamentary or political secretaries. The Barisan slate included 11 paid unionists and 7 paid party workers; the PAP had 4 trade unionists and 9 party workers. In all, there were some 28 candidates employed in the teaching profession, and many more who had taught in the schools at one time. Of 15 businessmen or business managers standing in the elections for one of the major parties, 9 were with the Alliance and 5 with the UPP. Of the 12 lawyers standing, half were with the Alliance and 3 with PAP, although only 1 of the latter was a practising attorney.

In profile, the PAP candidates were moderately young, apt to be English-educated, frequently had union or teaching backgrounds, but were most likely to be working full time for the party or the Government at the time of the elections. The Alliance candidates were older, also tended toward English education, and a high percentage were businessmen or professionals. Both of these slates contained a substantial number of non-Chinese. The Barisan and the UPP candidates, on the other hand, were overwhelmingly Chinese and predominantly Chinese-educated. The Barisan candidate was most apt to be a union or a party worker or a teacher in the Chinese schools; he was also apt to be under thirty.

Bluntly, one can only say that the Government — and this meant the PAP — dominated the mass media in Singapore. Radio and Television Singapore were owned and

operated by the Government and much of their program-
ming originated with the Ministry of Culture, which functioned as a propaganda agency. Much of the newscast
time was devoted to reporting the speeches and other
activities of the members of the Government and commen-
taries were slanted to convey the PAP point of view.[12]
The Prime Minister himself indicated his estimation of
the significance of the media for the party in power when
he gave the Government's ownership of its own radio and
television station as a major reason why Kuala Lumpur
would not let the Barisan assume control of Singapore.[13]
And he indicated the scope of his own discretion when,
interrupting the moderator of a political forum on Radio
and Television Singapore on 18 September, he said:

> ... I think there is a misunderstanding about my posi-
> tion here. This forum has been allowed because I, as
> Prime Minister, instructed that there should be Radio
> and Television time for all, and I am Prime Minister
> until the next Government is formed after the 21st ....

On Monday, 16 September, the Government offered the
facilities of Radio and Television Singapore to the major
parties to present their policies to the people in a series
of forums and recorded talks; these were scheduled for
broadcast and telecast beginning on 17 September and
concluding on 20 September. Each of the four major
parties was given thirteen and a half minutes for a general
policy statement and four minutes for an eve-of-polling-
day summation, both to be presented in each of Singapore's four principal languages. In addition, there was a

[12] In the Barisan trials in August, F. Elwyn Jones, Queen's Counsel,
who came from London to assist the defence, formally protested to the
Court on the sixth day of the trial against what he termed consistently
one-sided and 'highly partial' reporting of the proceedings by Radio
Singapore. *Straits Times*, 15 August 1964.

[13] 'You see, the Central Government cannot allow a Communist-
controlled party to control Singapore — a State Government with a budget
nearly half that of the Central Government, with its own Radio Station
and Television Station, more powerful than the Central Government.'
Prime Minister's Broadcast Speech on Eve of Poll, Radio Singapore
Release, 20 September 1963.

45-minute forum in each language, in which the four parties were given the opportunity to confront each other.[14] Although the aggregate exposure of all four parties to the voters of a given language stream was thus slightly less than two hours, even these presentations undoubtedly put considerable strain on the opposition parties, who had to arrange for radio and television speakers in four different languages at this crucial time. (In the case of the Barisan, this proved impossible as far as the Tamil and Malay language forums were concerned.)

During this same period, the radio and television stations also presented at least two unannounced programmes of material from the rallies being held at mid-day in the city squares. According to a Radio Singapore official, on one evening thirty-four minutes was devoted to Lee Kuan Yew's appearance at a Raffles Quay rally and twenty-four minutes to Lee Siew Choh's speech at nearby Fullerton Square earlier that day; the former was edited at the studios, the latter was not. (The following evening the Prime Minister got twenty minutes and the Barisan chief seven.) Since the Ministry of Culture filmed and taped these presentations it was hardly surprising that the Prime Minister was photographed closeup by mounted cameras, and Dr. Lee only from a distance by moving cameras.

If the press was somewhat more objective in its coverage of the campaign than were radio and television, it was nonetheless under stringent enough control by the Government to afford little solace to the left-wing opposition parties. The Government had extraordinary power, to regulate printing and publication through its control of permits and licenses, and this was a power, the opposition

---

14 In these forums, the position of the moderator, employed by Radio and Television Singapore, but attempting to moderate a discussion in which the Prime Minister was apt to be a participant, was extremely ambiguous — as was that of the PAP itself. This was apparent both in the incident cited above, and in statistics derived from the transcripts of the forums. In the transcription of the English-language telecast, for example, Lee Kuan Yew's contributions to the discussion period totalled 191 lines, compared with 81 for Dr. Lee Siew Choh, 70 for Ong Eng Guan and 69 for Lim Yew Hock.

charged, which was used to inhibit criticism of the party in office and to suppress publications inimical to it. Dr. Lee, for instance, complained that not only did the Barisan not receive fair coverage in the daily newspapers but that much of the time it was also unable to find a printer for its own paper; the PAP, he alleged, had threatened to take away the licenses of printers who accepted the Barisan's work.

The Alliance was not, however, handicapped by the lack of a favourable press as the two leftist parties were. For one thing, several of the major newspapers in Singapore were published in the Federation and only distributed in Singapore, although the *Straits Times* publications — primarily English language but including one Malay language paper — had separate Singapore and Federation editions.

The most complete and accurate coverage of the campaign was to be found in the Chinese language press, and particularly in *Nanyang Siang Pau.* The issue of Chinese education received special attention in the Chinese press, as did the controversy which arose over the appeal by Nanyang University's board chairman, Tan Lark Sye, for electoral support for Nanyang graduates. The Chinese papers carefully refrained, however, from taking sides and from giving editorial support to individual candidates or to any of the political parties. Neither the Malay nor the Tamil papers reported the campaign with any thoroughness; for example, *Utusan Melayu,* published in Jawi script and therefore restricted in circulation to Malays, limited itself in the main to presenting the issues from the point of view of *kampong* Malays. It was openly pro-Alliance, while *Tamil Nesan* supported the PAP. Of the English language dailies, the *Malayan Times* offered the best coverage and it supported the Alliance editorially. The *Straits Times* papers, however, with far wider readership, opened their columns primarily to reporting the PAP position; releases of the other parties appeared, if at all, sharply abridged and in less prominent positions in the papers.[15]   Moreover, on polling day, the *Straits Times* editorially endorsed Lee Yuan Yew's warning of the dire consequences of voting for any party other than the PAP, including his threat of Central Government intervention in the event of a Barisan victory.   Significantly, the paper took no note of a statement issued by the Malaysian Prime Minister two days earlier, in which he denied that the Constitution would be suspended 'even if an extremist Government comes into power'.[16]

In Singapore, where voting was compulsory, symbols were important in identifying the parties on the ballot. Particularly for the opposition parties, all with symbols new in the present election, placarding was, therefore, important as a means of familiarizing voters with the party symbols and with their slogans.   All the parties vied to get their posters and banners up early and in the most conspicuous places and for this purpose hundreds of youths were dispatched through the constituencies at the beginning of the campaign period.

Under the circumstances, the parties of the opposition undoubtedly relied heavily on outdoor rallies and on house-to-house canvassing to get their programmes before the voters.   Again, this latter activity required large numbers of election workers to blanket the constituencies, and these were generally young men and women.   (By law, primary and secondary school pupils were prohibited from participating in election activities,[17] but it is doubtful if much checking of credentials was possible during this campaign.)   The rallies, which ranged from small neighbourhood gatherings to massive displays of statewide strength, were the responsibility chiefly of the party spokesmen and the local candidates, but they also required substantial

[15] Thus, on 14 September, the *Straits Times* devoted 42 column inches and used triple headlines on the PAP's first rally; one of the heads, five columns wide, proclaimed, 'BEWARE THE NEW BRAND OF REDS, WARNS LEE.' The Barisan's rally the same day received 16 column inches, including a three-column head and the Alliance rally received 14.5 inches in a single column story.

[16] *Malayan Times*, 20 September 1963.

[17] *Electoral Ordinance*, Section 73.

assistance of party workers in the organization phase. In addition, in the case of the PAP and the Barisan, large numbers of loyal supporters were apparently transported from rally to rally to demonstrate enthusiasm and to swell the crowds. The Barisan, in particular, produced organized cheering sections, generally dressed in white and some wearing dark armbands. Many of these were probably SATU unionists; at some of the larger rallies, such as Hong Lim, union banners were much in evidence. In addition, bus-loads of Nanyang University students reportedly participated in Barisan rallies, and, in all likelihood, there were also pupils from the Chinese middle schools attendant at these rallies. At one such rally, the writer estimated that from one-half to one-third of the organized 'inner circle' adjacent to the speakers' platform were probably not old enough to vote.

All the rallies were accompanied by varied displays of campaign propaganda. The PAP relied on a huge reproduction of the party circle and lightning flash to dominate its rallies, but it also made use of handbills and a large professionally-made sign which depicted the PAP triumphing over Lies, Corruption and other forces of political vice. The Barisan's banners were generally crudely prepared but they were numerous and they generally conveyed their messages quite imaginatively. The Tengku, wearing the Union Jack as a *songket* and waving a flag half-British and half-Malayan; Lee Kuan Yew girdled with swastikas; and Ong Eng Guan receiving American dollars from a leering Uncle Sam; all these depicted graphically the Barisan's major accusations against its enemies. The United States — portrayed by means of a tank, labelled 'U.S.', from which rose the Statue of Liberty holding aloft a missile in place of her familiar torch — received higher billing for the role of villain than did Britain. The Barisan also displayed prominently without comment huge photographs of their comrades under detention; and they distributed handbills which quoted 'Harry' Lee,[18] from the days when he was still a comrade, to prove his unreliability.

Neither the Alliance nor the UPP demonstrated the ability to stage public meetings with the effectiveness of the Barisan and the PAP. From the standpoint of audience turnout and response, the Barisan was generally conceded the advantage, at least in the massive evening rallies of the Hong Lim type. The PAP held their first rally of the campaign in Hong Lim and they scheduled one there for the final evening. However, their own disappointing turnout (estimated at only 2,000-3,000) compared to the subsequent crowds for the UPP (5,000-8,000) and the Barisan (estimated as high as 30,000 on the next to the last evening of the campaign) apparently caused them to reconsider and they substituted one hundred street corner meetings instead. However, PAP rallies — which were frequently addressed by the Prime Minister in English, Mandarin and Malay — drew responsive audiences particularly in the downtown areas. The UPP evoked little response and drew no audiences outside of the Hong Lim area; Alliance rallies were poorly attended and marked by apathy.

The campaign literature which the various parties put out reflected the various advantages and handicaps each possessed. The Government, for example, distributed both before and during the campaign a 64-page, profusely illustrated booklet entitled *Democratic Socialism in Action June 1959–April 1963,* which was prepared in the Ministry of Culture and lithographed by the Government Printing Office. Although this booklet was not ostensibly campaign literature, its contents constituted a virtual blueprint for the PAP campaign; and its intent was hardly left in doubt by assertions, sprinkled throughout, such as the following:

> It is now obvious to everyone in Singapore that the PAP Government is the only well-organised and coherent force which can give leadership to the broad alliance of the nationalist elements of our people.

[18] That is, the Prime Minister.

The PAP's campaign materials reflected the fact that the PAP had a corps of professionals to prepare them, a major advantage in timing and ample funds for quality reproduction. The Barisan, on the other hand, relied far more on mimeographed releases which, at least in the English language versions, frequently indicated a need for substantial editing. The Barisan's chief asset was the tremendous pool of ardent young assistants who were willing to devote long hours to the preparation and distribution of party propaganda.[19]   However, although it was seriously handicapped by lack of time, there was no evidence that the Barisan was hampered also by insufficient funds. Neither of the other parties had the same amount of assistance — professional and amateur — as the Barisan and the PAP.

Issues and Strategy

It was of necessity, of course, that the PAP Government should stand on its record, and in the field of civic achievement the Lee Kuan Yew team unquestionably had an impressive one upon which to stand. They could cite the construction of 24,000 public housing units, rapid expansion of educational facilities, building of new community centres, development of the new Jurong industrial site, and the addition of assorted facilities such as street lights, water mains and other utilities. And, with this, they could still point to a budgetary surplus of M$400,000,000. But at the same time it was obvious from the election schedule which the PAP chose that the Government intended to capitalize on the Malaysia issue and to base its chief bid for re-election on the success of its merger negotiations. This did not mean, however, that there was not still significant opposition in Singapore to Malaysia.

Without doubt the PAP did possess certain advantages at this time. No matter how little enthusiasm the Singapore Chinese had for Malaysia as it was constituted, few were willing to even contemplate Singapore's prospects as an independent state — the only likely alternative to Ma-

---

[19] Lee Siew Choh averred that the Barisan had from three to four hundred campaign workers in each of its forty-six constituencies.

laysia. And Lee's last-minute negotiations with Malaya seemed to affirm that Kuala Lumpur would not grant even minor concessions except under pressure and suggested that he had, after all, secured the best terms possible for merger. These events unquestionably enhanced the prospects of the PAP at the expense of the Singapore Alliance, since the resentment of many Singaporeans against the onerous terms imposed by the Federation Government was directed locally at the Alliance.

At the other end of the political spectrum, the fact that Malaysia was to become a reality before the elections actually took place created a dilemma for the Barisan and the UPP. On the one hand, the leftists could not readily abandon their long-standing opposition to the Lee-Tengku scheme; on the other hand, openly to advocate its abandonment after Malaysia Day posed far more serious consequences than it did before. The PAP was, of course, well aware of this and pressed their advantage, while the left-wing parties equivocated on the course they would pursue relative to Malaysia if they came to power.

The PAP's principal attack on the anti-Malaysia forces centred on the thesis that a communist conspiracy lay behind the opposition to merger. This thesis was certainly not new; Lee Kuan Yew had personally endeavoured to establish it as early as 1961[20] and continued to use it in his struggle for power with the Barisan in the intervening years. The 'pro-Communist Barisan Sosialis', the PAP's election manifesto proclaimed, was 'committed to the break-up of Malaysia ... their close association with the Indonesian Communist Party and *their advocacy of merger with Indonesia* are portents of what is likely to happen under a Barisan Sosialis Government.'[21] And it was not primarily the 'pro-Communist Barisan' against whom the PAP claimed to be fighting but a 'well-organised and dedicated Communist Party' which had 'mob-

[20] See *The Battle for Merger*. Singapore, 1961. A series of radio talks by Lee Kuan Yew.

[21] Emphasis added. Allegedly Lim Chin Siong did on one occasion advocate such a merger.

ilised [its] forces to give an impression of overwhelming strength by clever organisational technique'. However, the PAP propaganda frequently failed to distinguish clearly between the two.

Since communism *per se* was proscribed in Singapore, the Government found it necessary to justify, in a unique fashion, its own failure to suppress a movement allegedly known to be communist. According to the Prime Minister, he himself was responsible for the fact that the Internal Security Council, in which Singapore had a minority voice, had not proscribed the Barisan Sosialis. 'To have obliterated their symbol before the elections,' he argued, 'would have been to help build up this myth of Communist invulnerability – a myth we cracked in the Referendum last year.'[22]

While the arguments about the communist threat were directed primarily against the Barisan, they were also used by direction against the other parties. The communist strength, it was argued, was not of itself sufficient to win the elections; however, it was conceivable, if the anti-communist vote were split, for the Barisan, and hence the communists, to capture power. Since the other parties in the election were not capable of dealing with the communists – and since they could not win, anyway – the PAP was clearly the only choice for those who feared communist encroachment in Singapore, and for those who wanted to see Singapore retain its autonomy. Lee Kuan Yew in his final broadcast of the campaign charged that the MCA, having decided that the Alliance could not win, wanted to split the votes to promote a Barisan Sosialis victory and then take over Singapore by proclaiming an emergency.[23]

22 *Prime Minister's Broadcast Speech on Eve of Poll.*

23 'You know,' Lee said, 'The MCA are smarting from .the humiliation in London on the 9th July and again in Kuala Lumpur on 11th September when they were over-ruled because we stood firm on the rights of Singapore, and they would have shown quite clearly [*sic*] since they have no chance of winning, they prefer to see the Barisan Sosialis win so that they can really take over Singapore lock stock and barrel and perhaps later to give a State constitution like Penang and Kelantan where the State Government has to go begging for money to the Central Govern-

The Barisan chairman, Dr. Lee Siew Choh, denied privately that the party was communist or pro-communist; it was, he said, non-communist and non-Marxian socialist. Publicly, however, the Barisan leaders generally avoided committing themselves on the communist issues, their comments on it being limited to an occasional rebuke to the PAP and the Alliance for their anti-communist postures. The Barisan affirmed its determination to 'continue to oppose neo-colonialist Malaysia' and to 'continue to struggle for genuine reunification and for an independent democratic socialist Malaya [i.e. Singapore and the Federation] free of foreign troops and free of foreign control'. What they carefully avoided, even after Malaysia Day, was committing themselves on the form the continued struggle would take. With Malaysia a reality, many of the points raised by the Barisan — for example, with regard to internal security, foreign policy, federal citizenship and Singapore's parliamentary representation — were no longer subject to negotiation by Singapore. Nevertheless, the party continued to repeat its demands without specifying the weapons it would use in the 'long and arduous' struggle to achieve them.[24]

Paradoxically, the UPP, which was never itself accused of being pro-communist, attacked the Barisan not for alleged pro-communist activities but for having collaborated up to 1961 in the PAP's anti-communist activities. Thus, Chan Sun Wing, Leong Keng Seng, and Lau Por Tuck were said to have constituted a Secret Police Committee under the PAP which screened Nanyang graduates applying for government posts to determine 'whether they were Communist inspired'.[25] Another Barisan candidate,

---

ment where it can be controlled and emasculated from the centre.' (*Ibid.*)

[24] The paper on merger and Malaysia was entitled, 'Our Tasks in the Constitutional Struggle'. The paper, quoted here on the merger issue, appeared in *The Plebeian*, the Barisan official organ, on 16 September 1963.

[25] Report of a UPP mass rally, in *Nanyang Siang Pau*, 18 September 1963. Ong himself repeated this charge on the Chinese language forum on 20 September.

one of the Nanyang graduates, was charged with having been responsible for 'blocking Communist films'.[26]

On merger and Malaysia, Ong Eng Guan's party adopted a similar attitude. The Barisan had not been consistently anti-Malaysia, the UPP had. In spite of the quibbling over who were the patriots and who were the opportunists, however, the position of the UPP on the merger agreement differed little, even in the wording, from that of the Barisan: the UPP opposed the 'sell-out White Paper Merger proposals', and supported the 'principle of a full and complete merger'.[27] (The Barisan observed, however, that Ong attacked only the PAP but did not dare to expose the British as the 'behind-the-scenes plotters', or criticize the 'foreign capitalist clique', or expose Malaysia as an attempt by the neo-colonialists to 'bring the people in the area into the anti-Communist cold war'.)[28] Nevertheless, Ong was explicit during the campaign on the limits of the UPP objectives. The elections were only to elect a state government and, although the Singapore Government had been reduced to a 'secondary position' in Malaysia, it was still important who controlled it. The UPP would fight for Singapore's rights against 'unreasonable demands' from Kuala Lumpur, but showed no inclination for a showdown on Malaysia.[29]

The Alliance, handicapped from the outset because two of its top leaders chose not to contest the elections, was likewise disinclined to answer all the PAP's charges. On the communist issue, the Alliance was unequivocal. The Alliance was *anti*-communist, and all the other parties followed the communists. The PAP was the worst of all because it had come to power with the support of the Malayan Communist Party; although it tried to deceive the people with its claims of being non-communist, the voters had to anticipate that, with its record of opportunism, it

26 Ong Eng Guan's Chinese language radio talk on 19 September.
27 *Unity* (the UPP's official organ), August 1963.
28 Chinese language edition of the *Plebeian*, 19 September 1963.
29 Chinese Language Forum.

could again 'fall over to the Communist side'.[30] The Alliance, as could be expected, was unequivocal also in its support for Malaysia, and insisted that with its 'friendly relationship' with the Central Government it was in a better position to promote the interests of the people of Singapore under Malaysia than the PAP. The PAP, because of 'vain self-glorification and showing off', had clashed with the Central Government 'unnecessarily and unreasonably, causing bad feelings'.[31] 'If the Government wants to fight the Central Government every day', Lee Kim Chuan told the radio and television audience, 'the result will be that there will be bad feelings, and nothing can be done'.[32] But on the PAP's allegations that the Alliance's relationship with the Federation Alliance was one of subservience rather than friendly co-operation, the Alliance leaders were strangely silent.

On a question closely related to Malaysia and communism — policy regarding the detainees under the PPSO — the Alliance, surprisingly, joined with the leftist parties in calling for a review of the individual cases, but did not oppose the principle of preventive detention itself, as did the Barisan and the UPP. As was to be expected, it was the Barisan which made a major issue of the PPSO detainees.

Predictably, there was no issue upon which Barisan and UPP appeals were more emotional than that of the future of Chinese schools and Chinese school graduates. In rally after rally both the Barisan and the UPP attacked the PAP Government for its policies on education, which, they charged, ostensibly provided equal treatment for the four language streams but in actuality supported and assisted English education and suppressed Chinese education. And they insisted that Nanyang University was the object of deliberate discrimination on two levels: not only did it fail to receive the government assistance which the English-medium university did, but in addition, its degrees were

[30] Eve of polling day speech by Lee Kim Chuan (Chinese language).
[31] Loc. cit.
[32] Chinese Language Forum.

not recognized and its graduates were discriminated against in applying for government positions. The Barisan had ten Nanyang graduates on its slate, and the Party Ra'ayat had yet another, who commanded substantial organized support. And since no other party offered more than one or two Nanyang graduates, it was the Barisan who stood to gain the most from the issue of Nanyang University and Chinese education. Nevertheless, the UPP, which had put up one Nanyang student, charged repeatedly on radio and television and at its public rallies that it was the Barisan 'Chinese experts' who, as members of the PAP Government, had 'fixed' Chinese education, Nanyang University and Nanyang graduates.

It was no doubt inevitable that the issue of Chinese education should have been significant in the campaign. Nevertheless, it did not appear to rank as a major issue on the platforms or in the slogans of any of the parties, and might have remained an important but largely unacknowledged issue if the chairman of the Nanyang University Council, Tan Lark Sye, had not come out early in the campaign expressing gratification at the role of Nanyang graduates in the elections and urging the public to support them. Although he denied any partisan implications to his statement, he did suggest that Singapore's 'previous governments' had not fulfilled their promises of assistance to Chinese education, and expressed the hope that Nanyang graduates, if elected, would at least give equal treatment to it. Nanyang, he said, had received no official assistance since its opening in 1956.[33]

The PAP appeared to be stung more sharply on this issue than on any other of the campaign. It publicly deplored what it termed Tan's intervention in the campaign, and Lee and several of his ministers devoted considerable time to answering the charges of discrimination. Nanyang degrees were recognized and there were Nanyang graduates employed in the Government, they insisted; and the reason Nanyang did not receive financial assistance was

[33] Tan's statement was made in an interview with reporters. See *Nanyang Siang Pau*, 14 September 1963.

that it failed to raise its academic standards and comply with accounting and auditing procedures as demanded by the Government. Singapore students in attendance at Nanyang were heavily subsidized by the state even if the University itself was not. Nonetheless, and in spite of thinly veiled threats against him, the Nanyang Council chairman refused to retreat from his initial position and indeed re-stated and expanded it. Reacting particularly to critics who said he was stirring up communal strife, he retorted, 'When I call for support for Nanyang graduates, I am criticized as provoking racial disunity but when the MCA call for Chinese unity and UMNO and PMIP call for Malay unity, they are not regarded as provoking racial disunity'. Although Tan insisted that the university had no political bias and had forbidden undergraduates to participate in politics, there is ample evidence that Nanyang students were extremely active on behalf of the left. Indeed, the Nanyang University Students' Union and the Political Science Society issued statements which attacked the 'opportunists and colonialists' for the harm done to education of the local races, specifically accusing the PAP of a list of 'crimes' against Chinese education generally and Nanyang in particular.[34] In addition, the NUSU statement came out unmistakably on the side of the Barisan although it did not specify either of the left-wing parties by name.[35]

On the whole, the PAP remained on the defensive on questions relating to the particular interests of the Chinese community in Singapore. However, in one respect the Government did attempt to take the initiative in appealing to the Chinese. One of the PAP's election posters (in

[34] According to the NUSU statement published in the Chinese language edition of the *Plebeian* on 19 September, 'even if the Singapore river water was turned into ink we would not have enough ink for writing down the crimes of Lee Kuan Yew's government in damaging the education of the races'.

[35] It should be noted that this statement, together with that of the Nanyang political science group and those of two rural associations, thirty-seven trade unions and three hawkers' unions, was published in the Barisan Chinese language paper.

Chinese characters) proclaimed, 'A Vote for the Barisan Communists is a Vote in Favour of Merger with Anti-Chinese Indonesia', and many of the PAP's campaign speeches attempted to play heavily upon Chinese fears of persecution as a minority. Thus, the Minister for Education, Yong Nyuk Lin, told a street rally in his constituency:

> The Barisan advocates merger with Indonesia, which you know is a notorious anti-Chinese country. The Chinese in Indonesia are without any kind of protection. They have been robbed of their properties and their life is a misery. Yet the Barisan would want Singapore to merge with such an anti-Chinese country. Is this not enough proof that the Barisan intends to sell out Singapore?[36]

There were, of course, other issues raised by the various parties, and these reflected not only the preoccupations of the candidates but also the type of electorate to which a particular party was appealing. Peculiarly, the Alliance placed heavy emphasis on Singapore's water shortage for which it blamed the PAP. The Alliance and the Barisan both pledged to restore pay cuts imposed on civil servants by the PAP in 1959, although the Barisan's pledge was a qualified one. All the parties made promises to labour although the emphases differed greatly. The UPP, for example, put heavy emphasis in its Chinese language propaganda on appeals to the 'poor workers'[37] and the hawkers, but had little to say about organized labour. The Alliance, lacking ties with organized labour, nonetheless promised to strengthen it, and to free it from political

36 *Nanyang Siang Pau,* 19 September 1963.

37 In both the Chinese and English language versions of its 'analysis of the four major political parties battling for supremacy' the UPP noted that it had 'a broad mass base of workers, shop-keepers, hawkers, trishaw riders, taxi-drivers'. In the English version but not in the Chinese, it added that it also had 'professional people and intellectuals in the Party folds. The UPP is undoubtedly the most representative Party in Singapore'. On the other hand, the Chinese language version contained additional paragraphs on contributions to workers, rural people and hawkers not found in the English version.

manipulation. Significantly, the Barisan apparently found it necessary to issue a disclaimer in regard to their 'labour policy': although they were committed in the long run to a planned economy, 'for the present and for some time to come', a press release explained, they would have to work 'within the limits of a free enterprise economy'. In addition, the opposition parties attacked many aspects of the PAP's record in office, charging that housing rentals were too high, that industrial development lagged, and so on; and they attacked particularly the financial concessions which Singapore had granted to the Borneo territories and the Central Government. These, however, were peripheral issues and did not generally receive more than a passing enunciation in platform and campaign speeches.

The appeals made to Chinese-educated voters differed substantially from those made to the English-educated. This was not true of the appeals in Tamil and Malay, which in many cases were virtually identical with the propaganda material in English. Particularly in the case of the Malays, the inauguration of Malaysia — which carried with it the promise of special rights for Malays — loomed so large that it obscured all other issues.

Invective, much of it of a highly personal nature, was a major feature of the campaign. This was certainly not a new aspect of Singapore politics, although the relationship of the three left-wing parties to each other no doubt heightened the tendency to indulge in personalities. Thus, the PAP's election manifesto described the Alliance as 'a hotchpotch of bank compradores, unsavoury and corrupt politicians from the former Labour Front Government, agents for airport contractors and airplane firms,[38] touts who hope to get commissions from social welfare lottery tickets, friends of gangsters and others who hope to loot and plunder' Singapore. The radio and television forums among the top leaders of the parties were marked by constant interruptions, disorders,[39] and by a substantial

[38] An innuendo directed at Lim Yew Hock.
[39] At three points in the English language forum, the Radio Singapore transcript records simply 'Uproar'.

amount of personal invective as well.   In the Chinese-
medium debate, for example, this exchange was fairly
typical:

Lee Kim Chuan (All.):   All the other three political
                          parties ... are being mani-
                          pulated behind the scene by
                          foreign countries.   Lee Kuan
                          Yew receives orders from the
                          'Plen'.[40]   Only the Alliance is
                          a party representing all the
                          races.

Lee Siew Choh: Representing the 'purse.'

Lee Kim Chuan: You may say you are representing the
                 'purse' because you have received so
                 much money from foreign countries as
                 your election expenses.

Lee Siew Choh: Our money comes from the people.
                 One dollar, one dollar, like that.

Lee Kim Chuan: Money from Russia is also a dollar, a
                 dollar, like that.   A lot comes from
                 the PKI, too . . . .

In the English language forum this exchange took place:

Chairman: Let us have decorum please.   I have offered
            you time.

Lim Yew Hock: You asked me ... I was going to talk
                . . . . He chipped in . . . .

Chairman: Right, Tun Lim, please have the floor ...

Lim: Well, I have the floor ... it's mine . . . . It gets
       heated up because comrades have fallen out.   I
       would use a different word, but let it be 'comrades'.

Lee Kuan Yew: You never were my comrade, Mr. Lim.

Lim: Well, I said 1, 2, 3 — God forbid that I would ever
       be your comrade; but it was I who saved the PAP
       during the time when I was Chief Minister ...

[40] According to Lee Kuan Yew a top official of the Communist Party
with whom he had pre-arranged meetings on three occasions. See *The
Battle for Merger*, pp. 26-44.

In all of this batter of invective, none was more bitter than that which the Barisan leaders directed against the UPP and its head Ong Eng Guan. Not only did they caricature Ong repeatedly in rally banners and posters; they also devoted some 3,000 words in the Chinese language edition of the party organ, 'To Expose Completely and to Smash Radically the Pro-American Politician Ong Eng Guan'.[41] And they openly charged, without attempting to prove it, that the UPP was only able to wage its campaign because it had American money. The reason for this was not hard to find. Both Lee Kuan Yew and the *Straits Times* insisted that the Barisan and the UPP were fighting for the same anti-Malaysia votes,[42] and the Barisan made it clear that they believed that every vote the UPP won was a potential Barisan vote, and did their best, therefore, to discredit Ong and the UPP with left-wing voters. Similarly, the PAP saw the Alliance as the party with whom they would share the right-wing votes, and they directed much of their last-minute campaigning to an attempt to eliminate this threat.

The Elections

No scientific surveys of political attitudes were attempted. The PAP's chances were rated higher, it appeared, at the beginning of September than they were on the eve of the election. There were several reasons for this. A number of observers noted a decided lack of enthusiasm for Malaysia during the ceremonies marking the transfer of sovereignty and concluded from this that the PAP's support was less than they had previously thought. The heightening of tension between the new federation and Indonesia posed a threat to Singapore's substantial entrepôt trade with Sumatra which could have hurt the PAP. And for those examining the signs, there were also the tremendous crowds which the Barisan drew at its evening rallies, which led many observers to believe that the governing party was in extreme danger from this quarter. Indeed

41 *Plebeian,* 18 September 1963.
42 *Straits Times,* 21 September 1963.

there were indications that the PAP itself was distinctly worried, although this was, of course, not openly admitted.

The Poll Results

The PAP polled 273,500 votes, or 47.0 per cent. of the total vote cast, to win thirty-seven of the fifty-one seats. The Barisan, together with Party Ra'ayat, received 201,510 votes, or 34.7 per cent. of the total, to capture thirteen seats, and thereby become the only opposition group in the new Assembly.[43] The UPP, with 8.3 per cent. of the total vote, returned Ong Eng Guan in Hong Lim constituency and lost everywhere else. The Alliance, although it also succeeded in polling 8.3 per cent. of the vote, was completely shut out, as were the minor parties and the Independents.

Two highly significant trends are readily apparent. The first was the tendency for Singapore voters in 1963 to move in the direction of a two-party system. Significant from the standpoint of the two-party system is the fact that the PAP and the Barisan obtained the two highest votes in every constituency where they faced each other except in Hong Lim; in two other districts, the PAP and Party Ra'ayat stood first and second. Stated in a different way, there were only four constituencies where the principal contest was *not* between the PAP and the Barisan or its Party Ra'ayat affiliate.

The second major trend was a tendency for the PAP to veer to the right for its electoral support. If we examine the relative positions of the parties in the 1963 elections, one signal fact stands out, that the PAP, in terms of Singapore's political spectrum, was no longer a party of the left. There is some question where the UPP stood relative to the Barisan; Ong Eng Guan himself placed it to the left of the non-communists in the Barisan and to the right of the communists.[44] However, concerning the PAP's position there could be little quarrel. It

[43] Excluding the Party Ra'ayat candidates, the Barisan total was 193,251, or 33.2 per cent. of the aggregate vote.
[44] Interview with the writer.

was to the left of the Alliance and to the right of the anti-Malaysia parties. And if we compare its relative position in the spectrum in 1963 with that of 1959,[45] it is apparent that the loss of votes to the left — which totalled more than 40 per cent. of the party vote cast — was compensated for in large part by a gain of slightly more than 30 per cent. in votes from the right. A closer scrutiny of the distribution of the vote by constituencies confirms this trend.[46] The PAP showed a remarkable gain in those constituencies which were won by the UMNO and the SPA in 1959; indeed, in these 7 constituencies, the PAP vote in 1963 was 25.8 percentage points higher on the average than in 1959.[47] On the other hand, its losses were equally remarkable in the predominantly leftist areas; in 15 constituencies, the PAP suffered net losses of more than 20 percentage points, with losses of 43 to 45 percentage points in Hong Lim, Toa Payoh and Tampines.[48]

Partisans of the PAP were quick to note that three of the seats won by the Barisan might have gone to the PAP if the Alliance had not received a fraction of the right-wing vote.[49] In fact, however, the two left-wing, anti-Malaysia parties won an absolute majority of the vote in these three constituencies, as, indeed, they did in all of the constituencies won by the Barisan, in Hong Lim and in five won by the PAP as well. In two additional assembly districts, the Barisan-UPP vote exceeded that of the PAP, although it did not constitute a majority of the total vote.[50] Thus, in twenty-one constituencies the combined UPP-Barisan vote exceeded that of the PAP.

We noted earlier that the two left-wing parties were appealing for the same votes. Dr. Lee and other Barisan spokesmen went further and insisted that if the UPP had

---

[45] See Chart on the following page.

[46] See Table XIX.

[47] This figure is the more remarkable when considered with the fact that the PAP experienced an overall loss of 7.1 per cent. from 1959 to 1963.

[48] The average loss in these fifteen constituencies was 31.1 per cent.

[49] I.e. Bukit Merah, Bukit Panjang and Crawford.

[50] I.e. in Sembawang and Kampong Kapor.

CHART

A COMPARISON OF THE RELATIVE POSITIONS OF SINGAPORE'S MAJOR PARTIES
IN THE POLITICAL SPECTRUM IN 1959 AND 1963

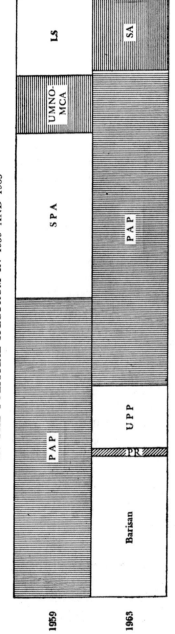

(Based on percentages of total vote received in the elections by each party)

not been in contention, its votes would all have gone to the Barisan candidates; Ong Eng Guan, on the other hand, told the writer that the communist issue had been built up to such proportions that the UPP voters would have been afraid to vote for the Barisan. It is impossible to say with any certainty what the effect of UPP vote-splitting was. We can, however, draw certain conclusions from the pattern of vote distribution and we can also project the effect of various divisions of the UPP vote on the principal contending parties.

In the first place, it should be observed that, of the fourteen constituencies in which Ong Eng Guan's party polled 10 per cent. or more of the vote, in all but two the combined Barisan-UPP vote constituted a majority. (In one of these two, the Barisan and UPP together outpolled the PAP; in the second, there was no Barisan candidate although there was one from Party Ra'ayat.) There was then a significant correlation between UPP strength and Barisan strength, but this applied chiefly in the urban areas. In the rural areas the picture was somewhat different. In the sparsely-populated constituencies in the eastern and northern portions of Singapore the UPP vote was generally negligible, although the Barisan captured a substantially higher proportion of the total vote than in the state as a whole. In the rural districts to the east, UPP strength again lay in the districts where the Barisan was also strong; here, however, the left-wing split did not result in victory for the PAP as it did generally in the closely-contested urban areas. How then would the outcome of the election have been affected if there had been no splitting of the left-wing vote? At the outset it should be stressed that the PAP would not have been beaten by the Barisan even if the latter had received *all* of the UPP vote; it would, however, have lost a total of eight seats. Moreover, presuming no other changes in the vote pattern, the PAP would have lost 7 of these constituencies if the UPP vote had been split between the Barisan and the PAP on a 70-30 basis in favour of the Barisan; projected on the basis of a 60-40 division, the Barisan would still have won 3 of these seats.

The most significant aspect of the left-wing split, was not, however, the number of seats which it may have given to the PAP but the nature of their occupants. Of 8 PAP ministers standing in the elections, only Lee Kuan Yew and Goh Keng Swee were returned by absolute majorities; 2, K.M. Byrne and Tan Kia Gan were defeated by the Barisan. The remaining 4 — S. Rajaratnam, Yong Nyuk Lin, Toh Chin Chye and Ong Pang Boon — were all outpolled by the 2 left-wing party votes combined, but retained their seats by narrow margins. In 2 of these constituencies, Rochore and Kampong Glam, where the only opposition to the PAP was from UPP and Barisan candidates, the margins of victory for Toh and Rajaratnam were 0.8 per cent. and 2.3 per cent., respectively.

Thus, the significance of the UPP vote in the urban areas was that it spelled the difference, potentially at least, between victory and defeat for half of the PAP Cabinet. For its part, the Barisan was understandably bitter against the UPP for the latter's role in the elections. Not only did the leftist, anti-Malaysia force lose roughly seven seats — and a psychological victory — which they might otherwise have gained; in addition, Dr. Lee himself was a victim of the close contest in Rochore in which Toh was returned with an 89-vote margin. It should be noted, however, that the large number of seats contested by the UPP had no apparent effect on the outcome, as Barisan leaders apparently feared that it would. All of the contests in which the UPP vote was crucial, except for Sembawang, were in the congested urban area where a large part of the UPP's main strength was located and where, therefore, it could reasonably have been expected to contest. In the absence of close contests in the suburban residential areas, where the PAP strength lay, and in the rural areas, where the Barisan had its strength, the UPP vote could not exert an influence on the overall results of the elections.

The evidence clearly indicates that communalism influenced the outcome of the 1963 elections but that it was not the determining factor. Lee Kuan Yew's governing party was significantly less strong in the all-Chinese constituencies than it was in the mixed constituencies, and it was strongest of all in the constituencies which were predominantly Malay. All 7 of the PAP's Malay candidates were successful, as were 8 out of the 10 Indians and Eurasians; out of 34 Chinese, however, only 22 won seats in the Assembly. But if Lee Kuan Yew's support among the Chinese had dropped heavily in comparison with 1959, he nonetheless retained sufficient support among some segments of the community to safeguard his margin of victory.

Briefly, of the 28 constituencies in which all of the contestants were Chinese, the PAP won 17 but was outpolled by the 2 leftist parties' combined vote in 16. Comparing the PAP record in 1963 in these 28 constituencies with that in 1959, we find that the PAP experienced an average decline of 12.5 percentage points, or from 58.5 to 46.0 per cent. of the total vote cast. It showed substantial gains in 5 of the constituencies, only 2 of which it had won — with pluralities — in 1959: its share of the total vote was 25.8 percentage points higher on the average in these 5 constituencies in 1963 than in 1959. On the other hand, in 17 constituencies in this category, the PAP's share of the total vote cast declined by no less than 10 percentage points, or 25.8 points decline on the average. Within the Chinese community, then, the PAP's gains in the middle- and upper-class constituencies compensated in some degree for, but could not offset, its losses in the lower-class constituencies. It was primarily in these constituencies, however, that the left-wing split was a decisive factor, and the PAP did not suffer the full effects of its alienation of a substantial part of the Chinese community.

In the three predominantly Malay constituencies — Geylang Serai, Kampong Kembangan and Southern Islands — the PAP won with gains of from 11.6 to 30.1 per cent. over 1959. Here the PAP's tendency to move towards the right and replace the Alliance parties was again apparent.

The evidence indicates that the vast majority of votes

TABLE XIX

A COMPARISON OF PAP VOTING STRENGTH BY CONSTITUENCIES, 1959 AND 1963.

CONSTITUENCY	PAP PERCENTAGE OF TOTAL VOTES CAST		INCREASE (+) OR DECREASE (−) (PER CENT.)	WINNING PARTY	
	1959	1963		1959	1963
(1) Aljunied	49.4	50.9	+ 1.5	PAP	Same
(2) Anson	60.7	46.3	−14.4	PAP*	Same
(3) Bras Basah	63.3	51.8	−11.5	PAP	Same
(4) Bukit Merah	59.1	39.0	−20.1	PAP°	Bar.
(5) Bukit Panjang	58.3	40.1	−18.2	PAP	Bar.
(6) Bukit Timah	61.2	42.3	−18.9	PAP	Bar.
(7) Cairnhill	20.7	66.5	+45.8	SPA	PAP
(8) Changi	35.1	44.2	+ 7.1	PAP°	Same
(9) Chua Chu Kang	56.3	31.5	−24.8	PAP°	Bar.
(10) Crawford	66.6	40.9	−25.7	PAP°	Bar.
(11) Delta	69.5	40.5	−29.0	PAP	Bar.
(12) Farrer Park	41.9	55.7	+13.8	Ind.	PAP
(13) Geylang East	51.9	47.3	− 4.6	PAP	Same
(14) Geylang Serai	30.5	47.9	+17.4	UMNO	PAP
(15) Geylang West	67.6	43.6	−23.0	PAP	Same
(16) Havelock	63.6	29.0	−34.6	PAP	Bar.
(17) Hong Lim	77.0	33.3	−43.7	PAP†	UPP
(18) Jalan Besar	62.5	51.9	−10.6	PAP	Same
(19) Jalan Kayu	62.5	30.7	−31.8	PAP°	Bar.
(20) Joo Chiat	39.6	65.9	+26.3	SPA	PAP
(21) Jurong	70.7	31.9	−38.8	PAP	Bar.
(22) Kallang	48.2	52.2	+ 4.0	PAP	Same
(23) Kampong Glam	65.3	44.8	−20.5	PAP	Same
(24) Kampong Kapor	54.3	41.9	−12.4	PAP	Same
(25) Kampong Kembangan	36.7	48.3	+11.6	UMNO	PAP
(26) Kreta Ayer	73.3	65.5	− 7.8	PAP°	Same
(27) Moulmein	47.3	58.0	+10.7	PAP°	Same
(28) Mountbatten	23.8	49.0	+25.2	SPA	PAP
(29) Nee Soon	73.3	34.8	−38.5	PAP°	Bar.
(30) Pasir Panjang	36.0	45.3	+ 9.3	PAP°	Same
(31) Paya Lebar	60.8	42.1	−18.7	PAP	Bar.
(32) Punggol	46.4	47.7	+ 1.3	PAP†	Same
(33) Queenstown	53.8	52.8	− 1.0	PAP°	Same
(34) River Valley	36.6	56.7	+20.1	PAP	Same
(35) Rochore	71.8	45.6	−26.2	PAP	Same
(36) Sembawang	54.7	42.2	−12.5	PAP	Same
(37) Sepoy Lines	58.4	52.2	− 6.2	PAP	Same
(38) Serangoon Garden	48.9	53.4	+ 4.5	PAP	Same
(39) Siglap	34.3	62.1	+27.8	PAP	Same
(40) Southern Islands	25.3	55.4	+30.1	UMNO	PAP
(41) Stamford	49.2	53.3	+ 4.1	PAP°	Same
(42) Tampines	73.3	29.1	−44.2	PAP	Bar.
(43) Tanglin	30.1	51.1	+21.0	SPA	PAP
(44) Tanjong Pagar	71.0	58.9	−12.1	PAP	Same
(45) Telok Ayer	67.4	44.0	−23.4	PAP	Same
(46) Telok Blangah	50.4	39.8	−10.6	PAP°	Same
(47) Thomson	54.6	39.5	−15.1	PAP°	Same
(48) Tiong Bahru	47.7	48.1	+ 0.4	PAP	Same
(49) Toa Payoh	77.7	33.9	−43.8	PAP°	Bar.
(50) Ulu Pandan	45.4	44.9	− 0.5	PAP°	Same
(51) Upper Serangoon	45.1	56.6	+11.5	PAP°	Same

* Independent as a result of 1961 by-elections.
° Barisan Sosialis since 1961.
† Later affiliated to United People's Party.

were cast for parties, not personalities.   Perhaps it would
be more accurate to say that the voter image of a particular party was influenced by its key personalities, but
that voters within a given constituency generally did not
choose from among the candidates on a personal basis.
There were exceptions, of course; Ong Eng Guan's popularity in Hong Lim certainly reflected little else than a personal following.   The personal factor undoubtedly had
some influence also in the cases of the PAP's two top
officials, Lee Kuan Yew and Goh Keng Swee. Both men
ran well ahead of their party. On the other hand, the
record indicates that PAP incumbents, including Cabinet
ministers, who were standing in their old constituencies
did substantially less well on the whole than non-incum-
bent candidates. Only two of the Barisan candidates returned to their old constituencies to contest, some of them
shifting constituencies in order to confront leaders of the
PAP.   Consequently, a comparison of the statistics on the
incumbents of the two parties would not be of significance.

Since polling day was an official holiday and since Singapore voters who failed to vote were subject to penalty, a
high percentage of the electorate, — approximately 95 per
cent. — did cast their ballots. The number of spoiled
votes was too insignificant to have possibly affected the
outcome of the election except in two constituencies.
One other aspect of the electoral statistics should be noted:
in sixteen constituencies, there was a decline in the number of voters from 1959 to 1963 and perhaps by coincidence, these included the constituencies of seven Cabinet
ministers and one parliamentary secretary. Because of
this element of coincidence and also because those contests involving the PAP Cabinet were in most cases extremely close anyway, the Barisan was inclined at one time
to demand a closer scrutiny of the electoral registers. In
fact, however, this phenomenon required little explanation, since the constituencies showing a decline were generally those located in the congested slum areas from which
public housing occupants were recruited, and the losses
in the electorate in these constituencies were more than

compensated for by gains in Queenstown and other constituencies which had major public housing developments.

The formation of Malaysia was undoubtedly the most
decisive single factor in the elections. However, their most
intriguing aspect derived from the split in the PAP which
created 3 parties where there had been 1 and the merger
on the right which produced 1 party where there had been
4. That this process resulted in victory for the PAP can
only be understood in terms of politics and not arithmetic.

XII

The Results

THE results of the election have been published by the Election Commission.[1] But results are not obtainable for votes cast in individual polling booths or precincts. This makes it impossible to use the classic method of electoral analysis by which the voting in such small areas is interpreted in the light of the known socio-economic characteristics of the areas.[2] The nearest approach to a breakdown of the voting for the parliamentary seats consists in the figures for voting for the state seats, which in 1964 (although not in 1959) took place on the same day as the voting for the parliamentary seats.[3] Fortunately for the student of elections each parliamentary seat is divided into two or more state seats, each state seat lying wholly within the boundaries of a single parliamentary seat. Fortunately, also, the boundaries for both parliamentary and state seats were the same in 1959 and 1964. Comparisons with the results of local elections are in general unrewarding. Local elections are not held at the same time as parliamentary elections; not all local elections are held at the same time;

[1] *Report on the Parliamentary (Dewan Ra'ayat) and State Legislative Assembly General Election, 1964, of the States of Malaya.* Kuala Lumpur, 1965. The corresponding reports for the 1955 elections (by T.E. Smith) and the 1959 elections were published in 1955 and 1960, respectively.

[2] Cf. André Siegfried, *Tableau Politique de la France de l'Ouest sous la troisième République.* Paris, 1913; Charles Morazé, *et al., Études de Sociologie Électorale.* Paris, 1947; François Goguel, ed. *Nouvelles Études de Sociologie Électorale.* Paris, 1954.

[3] This was probably partly responsible for the fact that in 1964 the Alliance percentage vote for a parliamentary seat was closer to the total Alliance percentage in the state seats which composed it than in 1959. The two percentages were closer in seventy-six instances and less close in twenty-two. Discrepancies between parliamentary and state percentages in 1964 were probably mostly the result of differences in the numbers and nature of the contesting opposition parties. In a few cases there may have been a 'personal vote' for a particular candidate.

most important, local elections do not cover the whole country, many rural areas being without elected local authorities. So the possibilities of comparison are very limited.[4]

Another source of information, available in some countries, was non-existent in Malaya in 1964. There were no opinion surveys to throw light on the attitudes of the electors.[5] The only way in which these could be ascertained, or guessed at, was by inference, based on the voting statistics.

The method used in this Chapter is therefore necessarily restricted to an analysis of the published voting figures. The treatment aims at simplicity and avoids attempts at high-powered statistical treatment. The approach is intended to be similar to the non-technical approach used in the Nuffield series of books on British general elections.[6]

Votes and Seats, 1959 and 1964

The broad picture of the votes and seats won by each party in the parliamentary elections in 1959 and 1964 is given in Table XX.

In both 1959 and 1964 the Alliance had an absolute majority of the votes, which was translated into a larger majority in terms of seats. Its average vote-per-seat-contested was not so very much higher than that of some other parties, such as the Malayan Party in 1959 and the PPP in 1964. But it should be remembered that in each year the Alliance contested *all* the 104 seats, while its opponents were able to concentrate on the areas where they were strongest. All the opposition parties which contested both elections did worse in terms of seats in 1964. They also did worse in terms of votes, except, apparently, the SF, which increased its percentage of the

[4] For an intelligent use of the opportunities for comparison that are available, see the analysis by T. E. Smith, referred to in footnote 49 of Chapter II.

[5] Two notable examples of this method of electoral study in the United States are: B.R. Berelson, *et al., Voting.* Chicago, 1954; A. Campbell, *The American Voter.* Michigan, 1960.

[6] See footnote 3 of Chapter I.

TABLE XX

SEATS AND VOTES, 1959 AND 1964 PARLIAMENTARY ELECTIONS

PARTY	1959						1964					
	CANDI-DATES	VALID VOTES	PERCEN-TAGE OF VOTE WON	AVERAGE VOTE IN SEATS CON-TESTED	SEATS WON	AVERAGE VOTES PER SEAT WON	CANDI-DATES	VALID VOTES	PERCEN-TAGE OF VOTE WON	AVERAGE VOTE IN SEATS CON-TESTED	SEATS WON	AVERAGE VOTES PER SEAT WON
Alliance	104	800,944	51.8	7,900	74	11,300	104	1,204,340	58.5	11,800	89	13,500
PMIP	58	329,070	21.3	5,700	13	25,000	53	301,187	14.6	5,700	9	33,500
SF	38	199,688	12.9	5,200	8	24,800	63	330,898	16.1	5,300	2	165,400
PPP	19	97,391	6.2	5,100	4	24,300	9	69,898	3.4	7,800	2	34,900
Party Negara	9	32,578	2.1	3,600	1	32,600	4	7,319	0.4	1,800	0	—
Malayan Party	2	13,404	0.9	6,700	1	13,400	—	—	—	—	—	—
Independents	29	74,194	4.8	2,600	3	24,700	8	13,509	0.7	1,700	0	—
UDP	—	—	—	—	—	—	27	88,223	4.3	3,300	1	88,200
PAP	—	—	—	—	—	—	11	42,130	2.0	3,800	1	42,100
TOTAL	259	1,547,269	100	—	104	—	279	2,057,504	100	—	104	—

Note: The calculations of average votes do not include the three seats in 1959 and the two seats in 1964 which the Alliance won without its candidates being opposed.
The 1959 figures include those for the Kedah Tengah constituency, where the election was postponed for six weeks.

vote from 12.9 per cent. to 16.1 per cent. However, on closer inspection, the improvement in votes is seen to be the result of a larger number of seats having been contested. The average vote in the seats contested actually dropped slightly, although the average number of electors in a constituency in 1964 was almost 30 per cent. larger than in 1959. The *percentage* of the vote won by the SF in contested constituencies actually dropped by 10 per cent., from 34.9 per cent. to 24.9 per cent. On the other hand it can be argued that the seats contested by the SF in 1959 were those where it was most likely to do well. To maintain almost the same vote per seat, when twenty-five extra seats were contested, even when the number of electors was larger, could not be reckoned a failure.

Between the elections the two parties which appealed almost exclusively to Malays, PMIP and Party Negara, dropped a total of 8.4 per cent. of the vote. The other non-Alliance parties (different at the two elections) together with Independents showed a slight average increase in their vote of 1.7 per cent.

The Alliance not only won most votes and most seats in 1964, its candidates' margins of victory were on the average higher than those of the winning candidates from other parties.

TABLE XXI

PERCENTAGE DIFFERENCE BETWEEN WINNING CANDIDATE'S
VOTE AND NEAREST RIVAL'S VOTE, PARLIAMENTARY
ELECTIONS, 1964

WINNING MARGIN	NUMBER OF ALLIANCE CANDIDATES	NUMBER OF OTHER CANDIDATES
Less than 1 per cent.	0	2
1 per cent. – 9.9 per cent.	4	5
10 per cent. – 19.9 per cent.	15	3
20 per cent. and over	68	5
TOTAL	87a	15b

a Two Alliance seats were won without a contest.

b Not all the winning opposition majorities were over an Alliance candidate. In three of the fifteen opposition seats the party with the second-highest vote was not the Alliance.

The larger size of Alliance majorities compared with those of the opposition parties tended to reduce its advantage in seats. Few of its candidates just squeezed in by a narrow majority. Many piled up huge majorities, comforting to the individual candidates who collected them, but not going towards winning any extra seats for the party.

In another respect, however, the Alliance benefited when votes were 'converted' into seats. A high proportion of Alliance wins were in the constituencies with the smallest number of electors. In the 20 with the highest number of electors the Alliance won 13 and the opposition parties won 7: in the 20 with the smallest number of electors the Alliance won 19 and the opposition parties won only 1.[7]

Geographical Distribution of Support for the Parties
Geographically, there were marked differences in support for the parties. The Alliance was strong in every state, but the other parties were regional, rather than national, parties. The strength of the PMIP is concentrated in Kelantan, Trengganu, Kedah and Perlis. The PPP is a Perak party and the UDP principally a Penang party. Even the SF, which of all the opposition parties has the strongest claim to be considered 'national', has areas of considerable strength, such as Selangor, Penang and Malacca, and of great weakness, Kelantan, Trengganu, Perlis.

The votes for the various parties, by states, are given in Appendix II. A feature of the 1964 election was that, although the number of parties had not diminished, there was more of an approach to a two-party system inside the individual states. At the 1959 parliamentary election in only three of the eleven states did the two parties with the highest vote share over 90 per cent. of the vote between them. In 1964 the corresponding number of states was six; in three other states the two top parties shared be-

[7] In the above analysis the opposition parties have been grouped together. But it may be noted that in the 20 seats with most electors only 1 of the seats won by the opposition went to the PMIP. The other 6 were 2 SF, 2 PPP, 1 UDP and 1 PAP.

tween 80 and 90 per cent. In nine of the states, something like a two-party system seems to be developing. In the four northern states, Kelantan, Trengganu, Kedah and Perlis the Alliance's main rival is the PMIP. In Johore, Malacca, Negri Sembilan, Pahang and Selangor the chief opposition party is the SF, although in Selangor the PAP has shown strength. In Perak 'polarisation' between the Alliance and the SF has been prevented by the existence of the PPP and UDP; in Penang by the UDP. Table XXII shows the division of *seats* between the parties, by states, for 1959 and 1964, and also attempts a division of the seats into three group: six 'urban', twenty-five 'quasi-urban' and the remainder.[8]

It is clear that at the 1959 elections, the Alliance Government did worst in the urban seats, better in the quasi-urban seats and best in the remaining 'rural' seats. In

[8] There is no official division of seats into 'urban' and 'quasi-urban'. Officially an urban area has been defined as a gazetted administration area with a population of 1,000 or over. (*Federation of Malaya Official Year-Book.* Kuala Lumpur, 1962, p. 36.) However, this seems to be too small a figure for the present purpose. The *Yearbook* gives a list of the urban areas with the largest populations. Those areas with a 1957 population of more than 20,000 according to the *Yearbook* were selected. They were then identified on a map of the parliamentary constituencies. Those constituencies which consisted entirely of these urban areas were counted as 'urban'. Those which contained only a portion of one of the urban areas were classified as 'quasi-urban'. One defect of this procedure is, of course, that while a constituency classified as 'quasi-urban' might have a portion of an urban area of over 20,000 inside it, another constituency, not classified as quasi-urban, might have a larger portion of an urban area with under 20,000 population inside it. Any procedure, including the one just described, is open to theoretical objection. The main difficulty is that the constituency boundaries hardly ever coincide with an obvious urban/non-urban division.

The six urban seats were: Bukit Bintang; Bandar Malacca; Ipoh Menglembu; Dato Kramat; Tanjong. The twenty-five quasi-urban were: Batu; Bungsar; Damansara; Setapak; Rawang; Klang; Johore Bahru Timor; Johore Bahru Barat; Malacca Tengah; Larut Selatan; Batu Pahat; Muar Pantai; Telok Anson; Kluang Utara; Seberang Tengah; Bagan; Kampar; Kuantan; Alor Star; Sungei Patani; Batu Pahat Dalam; Seremban Barat; Seremban Timor; Kota Bahru Hilir; Kuala Trengganu Selatan.

On urbanization generally see Hamzah Sendut, 'Patterns of Urbanization in Malaya', *The Journal of Tropical Geography*, Vol. 16, October 1962.

TABLE XXII

DIVISION OF PARLIAMENTARY SEATS, URBAN AND OTHER, BETWEEN THE ALLIANCE AND OPPOSITION PARTIES, 1959 AND 1964

STATE	1959 URBAN		QUASI-URBAN		OTHER		TOTAL		1964 URBAN		QUASI-URBAN		OTHER		TOTAL	
	ALL	OPP	ALL	OPP	ALL	OPP	ALL	OPP	ALL	OPP	ALL	OPP	ALL	OPP	ALL	OPP
Kedah	–	–	2	–	10	–	12	–	–	–	2	–	10	–	12	–
Perlis	–	–	–	–	2	–	2	–	–	–	1	–	2	–	2	–
Penang	–	2	2	–	3	1	5	3	–	2	2	–	4	–	6	2
Perak	–	2	3	–	12	3	15	5	–	2	3	–	15	–	18	2
Selangor	1	–	1	5	7	–	9	5	1	–	4	2	7	–	12	2
Malacca	–	1	1	–	2	–	3	1	1	–	1	–	2	–	4	–
Negri Sembilan	–	–	–	2	4	–	4	2	–	–	2	–	4	–	6	–
Johore	–	–	6	–	10	–	16	–	–	–	6	–	10	–	16	–
Trengganu	–	–	–	1	1	4	1	5	–	–	1	–	4	1	5	1
Kelantan	–	–	–	1	1	8	1	9	–	–	1	–	1	8	2	8
Pahang	–	–	1	–	5	–	6	–	–	–	1	–	5	–	6	–
TOTAL	1	5	16	9	57	16	74	30	2	4	23	2	64	9	89	15

ALL = Alliance,   OPP = Opposition Parties.

1964 it won a very high proportion of the quasi-urban
(92 per cent.), and the non-Alliance seats were revealed as
being nearly all of two quite distinct types.   In the urban
seats they were held by parties which were in essence 'non-
Malay communal parties';[9] the SF (Dato Kramat), the PPP
(Ipoh and Menglembu) and the UDP (Tanjong).   The two
quasi-urban seats lost by the Alliance in 1964 were also won
by this type of opposition party — Batu (SF) and Bungsar
(PAP).   The seats held by the Opposition which were
neither urban nor quasi-urban, were all won by the PMIP
and were all in Kelantan or Trengganu.   Significantly, the
two quasi-urban seats in these two states were both held by
the Alliance.

The distinction between 'urban', 'quasi-urban' and the
remaining rural constituencies is rather rough and ready.
The urban seats are in effect seats comprised entirely of
town areas.   The quasi-urban seats are those which include parts of larger towns with over 20,000 inhabitants.
As might be expected, the urban seats have some characteristics which are strikingly different from the rural seats.
However, the quasi-urban seats do not show such marked
differences.   For instance, the average Alliance percentage
of the vote in the urban seats was only 37 per cent. compared with 57 per cent. for the quasi-urban and 58.5 per
cent. for the electorate as a whole.[10]   The average number
of electors in an urban seat was 35,000; in a quasi-urban
seat, 30,000; in the remainder, 26,000.   In some respects,
however, the urban and the quasi-urban differed more
from each other than either differed from the remaining
rural seats.   The average *increase* in the Alliance vote,
1959-64, in the urban seats was only 1.9 per cent.   In the
quasi-urban seats it was higher (9.3 per cent.) than in the

[9] See the following section on 'Race and Voting'.

[10] The racial composition of the electorates is not published officially.
However, in 1959 it was published in the newspapers for most seats. For
the remaining seats and for 1964 it was obtained indirectly from party
sources. A more extended analysis of race and voting is given later in
this Chapter.

other, 'rural', seats (7.7 per cent.).[11] Also, the average percentage increase in the number of electors was high in the urban seats (32 per cent. compared with 27 per cent. for all seats): but in the quasi-urban it was higher still, 39 per cent. This difference is probably attributable to the fact that the centres of the big towns are already so crowded that expansion of population has been somewhat slowed down in comparison with expansion in the immediately surrounding, largely quasi-urban, areas.

The Alliance, then, did less well in urban seats than in the two other types of seats. Because urban seats, on the average, had more electors than others, it might have been expected that the Alliance would also have done worse in the seats with most electors. It has already been pointed out that the Alliance had a high proporion of *wins* in the seats with the smallest number of electors. This was also true about *votes*. In seats with under 20,000 electors the average Alliance vote was 67.3 per cent. In those with over 30,000 it was only 49.2 per cent. This difference also held good for the average percentage *increase* in votes for the Alliance between 1959 and 1964. In the seats with under 20,000 it was 9.2 per cent. In those with over 30,000 it was only 5.2 per cent.

However, although urban seats also tended to have more than the average number of electors, the decisive influence on the size of the Alliance vote seems to have been the urban factor, not the number of electors. All six urban seats were among the twenty seats with the largest number of electors. In them the average Alliance vote was only 37 per cent. The fourteen seats which were among the twenty with the largest number of electors, but which were *not* urban, had an average Alliance vote of 55 per cent., only just under the figure for the whole of Malaya. A prominent feature of the urban seats was the very small proportion of Malays in them, only 13 per cent.

11 The total percentage increase for the Alliance was 6.7 per cent. (58.5 per cent. — 51.8 per cent., see Table XX). But the increase was highest in the seats with fewest electors (see next paragraph). So the average (arithmetic mean) increase in the Alliance vote per seat was 7.8 per cent.

The other fourteen seats with the highest number of electors had an average of 43 per cent. Malays, much closer to the average number of Malays in all the seats (54 per cent.).

Race and Voting

Clearly, any analysis of voting is bound to consider the racial factor in Malayan politics. The Malays still hold a dominant position in the electorate, although their superiority has slightly diminished since 1959. In that year they constituted approximately 56 per cent. of the electors, the Chinese 36 per cent. and the 'Others' (mostly Indians) 8 per cent. In 1964 the proportion of the Others remained the same, but the Malays had dropped approximately two percentage points, and the Chinese had gained approximately two. The 1964 figures were: Malays, 54 per cent; Chinese, 38 per cent; Others, 8 per cent.[12] However, when individual constituencies were considered, Malay dominance was rather more evident.

TABLE XXIII

NUMBER OF PARLIAMENTARY CONSTITUENCIES WITH VARIOUS RACIAL MAJORITIES, 1959 AND 1964

	1959	1964
Malay absolute majority over all other races	60	59
Malay relative majority	3	3
Total: Malay majority	63	62
Chinese absolute majority over all other races	26	32
Chinese relative majority	15	10
Total: Chinese majority	41	42

Thus, although the Malays had only 54 per cent. of the votes, they had an absolute majority in nearly 57 per cent. of the seats. This magnification of Malay dominance in

12 Rather more precisely, the percentage of Malays for the two years was 56.5 per cent. (1959) and 54.3 per cent. (1964). But the raw figures are not sufficiently accurate to justify more than rounded-off percentage figures.

terms of seats results from the fact that rural constituencies, where the average number of electors is lower than average, contain a higher percentage of Malays than other constituencies.[13]

It is a truism to say that the racial composition of the electors is of vital importance to the parties. The word 'communal' as applied to parties is obviously capable of many interpretations. Only the PMIP might be prepared in some situations to admit that it was a communal party.[14] But, whatever the professions of faith and the aspirations of the other parties, it is undeniable that, *objectively*, they depend heavily on the votes of particular racial groups. The situation of the Alliance is a little more complex than that of the opposition parties, and will be considered later. However, the opposition parties' reliance on 'racial' votes is revealed in their decision to contest some seats rather than others and in the differ-

TABLE XXIV

PERCENTAGE OF SEATS OF DIFFERENT RACIAL COMPOSITION
CONTESTED BY THE OPPOSITION PARTIES,
PARLIAMENTARY ELECTIONS, 1959

PERCEN- TAGE OF MALAY VOTERS	TOTAL NUMBER OF SEATS	PERCENTAGE OF SEATS CONTESTED BY				
		PMIP	SF	UDP	PPP	PAP
0- 9.9	2	—	100	50	50	100
10-19.9	6	—	100	17	33	50
20-29.9	15	7	87	33	20	27
30-39.9	12	17	83	58	17	—
40-49.9	10	30	100	30	10	20
50-59.9	10	40	90	10	—	—
60-69.9	11	64	27	45	—	—
70-79.9	10	90	50	20	—	—
80-89.9	14	93	21	—	—	—
90-99.9	14	100	14	14	—	—

13 Reference has already been made to the above-average number of electors, and below-average percentage of Malays, found in urban and quasi-urban seats.

14 But sometimes it has identified Malay communalism with nationalism. 'The PMIP wishes to fight for the Malays in this country and make Malay the national language. This is a national issue, not a communal issue.' *Straits Times*, 10 December 1959.

ing degrees of success they had in seats of varying racial composition. Table XXIV amplifies the information given in Chapter V on the racial composition of the seats contested by the opposition parties.

It is evident that the PMIP did not attempt to contest seats with under 20 per cent. of Malays, while the PPP and the PAP did not attempt to contest seats which had over 50 per cent. of Malays. The SF and the UDP, however, expressed their non-communal professions in concrete terms by putting up quite a large number of candidates even in Malay-dominated seats.

The percentage of the vote won by the opposition parties in different types of seats is shown in Table XXV.

TABLE XXV

VOTES WON BY OPPOSITION PARTIES IN SEATS
OF DIFFERENT RACIAL COMPOSITION

PERCENTAGE OF THE ELECTORS WHO WERE MALAYS	AVERAGE PERCENTAGE OF THE VOTE WON BY OPPOSITION PARTIES IN SEATS CONTESTED				
	PMIP	SF	UDP	PPP	PAP
0- 9.9	—	32	45	6	19
10-19.9	—	30	32	53	13
20-29.9	3	30	17	41	20
30-39.9	8	27	16	14	—
40-49.9	7	28	10	26	3
50-59.9	16	23	12	—	—
60-69.9	19	18	10	—	—
70-79.9	22	17	9	—	—
80-89.9	33	10	—	—	—
90-99.9	47	6	5	—	—

The extent of each party's reliance on the Malay, or the non-Malay, vote is clear from Table XXV. The dependence of the PMIP on the Malay vote is particularly plain. The PPP seems to have stopped putting up candidates at an 'early' stage: it was still getting an average vote of 26 per cent. per seat when Malays constituted as much as 40-49 per cent. of the electorate, but it did not put up any candidates at all in the '50-59.9 per cent. Malay' range. The PAP pattern was influenced by its decision to contest only seats with a high proportion of non-Malay electors. The two Johore seats for which it entered candidates, and in which it received an average of only 3 per cent. of the vote, were an exception. Nothing can be inferred from the low level of the party's vote there, because it did not campaign in them. The UDP percentage of the vote declined very sharply when the proportion of Malays reached as high as 20 per cent. This apparently reflected its concentration on, and success in, Penang; its high average vote where the percentage of Malays was under 20 per cent. came from just two seats, both of which were in Penang. With the possible exception of the UDP, the SF would seem to have been the least dependent of the opposition parties on votes from a particular racial group. To a small extent, however, which could not be determined statistically, the relative success of the SF and the UDP in the Malay-dominated electorates might have been helped by the absence of PAP and PPP candidates in such constituencies.

Because of the weakness of Party Negara (which won only 10.5 per cent. of the vote in the four parliamentary seats it contested) the PMIP vote in Table XXV gives a good picture of the Malay communal vote. But the combined effect of the total non-Malay communal vote is not apparent from the Table. Its dimensions in the seats with most non-Malay electors were considerable. In all the eight seats with under 20 per cent. of Malay electors the combined vote of the non-Malay communal parties (SF, UDP, PPP, PAP) was over 50 per cent. In three of the eight it was over 70 per cent. The average combined non-Malay communal percentage in the eight seats was 63.7 per cent.

Table XXV showed the percentage of the vote obtained by the different opposition parties in seats of varying racial composition. Table XXVI indicates how the success of Alliance candidates was affected by this factor.

TABLE XXVI

ALLIANCE VOTE AND RACIAL COMPOSITION OF SEATS

PERCENTAGE OF THE ELECTORS WHO WERE MALAYS	NUMBER OF SEATS WHERE THE ALLIANCE VOTE WAS IN THE RANGE					Total
	20-39.9%	40-49.9%	50-59.9%	60-79.9%	80-99.9%	
0-19.9%	4	4	–	–	–	8
20-39.9%	–	6	9	12	–	27
40-59.9%	–	–	3	16	2	21
60-79.9%	–	–	2	14	3	19
80-99.9%	5	5	6	10	1	27
	9	15	20	52	6	102

The Alliance did best in seats where the racial composition was 'mixed', where it was neither overwhelmingly Malay nor non-Malay. The most striking way of stating the point is to look at the seats where the Malays made up between 40 per cent. and 79.9 per cent. of the electors. *In none of these 40 seats did the Alliance proportion of the vote fall below 50 per cent.* In the seats with fewer than 40 per cent. Malay electors there were fourteen where the Alliance vote fell below 50 per cent: in ten of those with 80 per cent. or more Malays the Alliance also failed to reach 50 per cent. of the vote. Without speculating deeply on the explanation for this, it may be suggested that in seats which are predominantly Malay or predominantly non-Malay, to vote for an appropriate communal party may simply be a way of expressing that one belongs to that community.[15] A Malay is more likely to vote 'Malay-communal' when he is surrounded by many other Malays; a Chinese is most likely to vote 'Chinese-commu-

[15] This seems to be most applicable to the Malays, and least applicable to the Indians who did not form as much as a quarter of the electorate in any constituency.

Conversely, it is the first maxim of Alliance Party organizers that the most solidly pro-Alliance voters are the Chinese and Indians in the seats with the highest percentage of Malay electors, likewise the Malays in the seats with the highest percentage of non-Malay electors.

nal' when surrounded by many other Chinese.[16] It would also appear that voters in 'mixed' seats who were apprehensive about communal parties based on a race other than their own would have good reason to vote for the inter-communal Alliance. To put this another way, a Malay in Kelantan could vote PMIP without any fear that, by his splitting the UMNO vote, a Chinese-communal candidate might be elected. A Chinese in one of the big towns could vote SF, UDP, PPP or PAP secure in the knowledge that there was no danger in such a seat of a Malay-communal candidate being returned. But in the mixed seats the safe course would be to vote Alliance.

The high Alliance vote in the mixed constituencies was accompanied by a high proportion of seats won. Of the eight constituencies where the Malays formed less than 20 per cent. of the electors the Alliance won two and the opposition parties six. The Alliance won all the sixty-eight seats where the proportion of Malays was between 20 percent. and 80 per cent. In the seats where the proportion was over 80 per cent., the Alliance won nineteen, while the opposition (PMIP) won nine.

The *increase* in the Alliance vote was especially marked in two groups of seats. For the contested constituencies in Kelantan and Trengganu it was 13 per cent; it was also very high, about 14 per cent., in the seats where Chinese Independents had stood in 1959 (Table XXIX, below). When these two groups of seats were excluded, the increase in the Alliance vote was highest in seats which had roughly equal members of Malays and non-Malays, next highest in seats with a high proportion of Malays, lowest in seats with a high proportion of non-Malays. The Alliance also gained heavily in terms of

[16] Cf. the findings of H. Tingsten (*Political Behaviour.* Stockholm, 1937, pp. 180 and 230-1) and others on *social class* and voting. Tingsten found (in Stockholm, 1932) that the adhesion of a particular group to the party which, in general, may be considered as best representing it, grows with the strength of the group in the area under consideration. Workers, for example, vote socialist more regularly in proletarian districts than in better-off districts.

seats in such 'racially-intermediate' constituencies, particularly where the proportion of Malay electors was over 20
per cent. but under 50 per cent. In 1959 the Opposition
held eight seats with this racial composition. After the
1964 election it held none.[17]

It is possible to make a rough estimate of the racial
composition of the total votes cast for the Alliance. The
basis of the calculation is that virtually *no* non-Malays
vote for the PMIP or Party Negara and very few Malays
vote for non-Malay communal parties. The crux of the
problem is to estimate the latter figure: how many Malay
votes did the non-Malay communal parties receive? This
was estimated at 10 per cent.[18]

The opposition percentage of the total parliamentary
vote in 1964 was 41.5 per cent. How much of this consisted of Malay votes? Presumably the entire vote for
PMIP and Party Negara plus, on the above assumption,
10 per cent. of the remainder of the opposition vote.[19]
Thus the percentage of the total vote cast for opposition

[17] The average increase in the Alliance vote in the eight seats was 22
per cent. Four of these had been fought by Chinese Independent candidates in 1959, which could explain the increase. But even in the other
four the Alliance vote increased by an average of 20 per cent.

[18] This figure was chosen on the basis of conversations with officials,
including field officials, of the parties and also by analysis of the percentage of the votes obtained by these parties in seats with varying ethnic
composition (Table XXV). Some parties claimed a higher proportion
of Malay votes than 10 per cent. But it was impossible to have any long
general discussion with officials from these parties without hearing about
the 'weakness' of the Malay side of the organization as compared with
the non-Malay. 10 per cent. is an average figure. A refined calculation
would take account of the fact that some parties, for example the SF,
might have a vote which was a little more than 10 per cent. Malay,
while others, such as the PPP, might have a vote which was less than
10 per cent. Malay. Ideally, also, where the Malays form a high proportion of the electors in a particular seat, it would be logical to assume
that the figure would be higher than 10 per cent. Even if it were
assumed that SF, UDP, PPP, PAP and non-Malay Independents won on
the average as many as 20 per cent. of their votes from Malays, the
broad conclusions reached would not be substantially altered (see footnote
to Table XXVII).

[19] The vote for Malay Independents (less than 0.2 per cent. of the
total vote cast) was ignored in the calculations.

candidates by Malays would consist approximately of 15 per cent. PMIP and Party Negara plus 10 per cent. of the remainder of the opposition vote (2.7 per cent.), a total of 17.7 per cent. approximately. The opposition non-Malay[20] percentage of the total vote would consist of the total opposition votes cast for parties other than PMIP and Party Negara, *less* the 10 per cent. figure estimated for Malay votes. The total opposition non-Malay vote would thus equal approximately 23.8 per cent. of the total vote (41.5 per cent. minus 17.7 per cent.).

The racial composition of the total electorate was approximately: Malay 54 per cent; non-Malay 46 per cent. Therefore, if roughly 17.7 per cent. of the 54 per cent. Malay vote was cast for the opposition, about 36.3 per cent. was cast for the Alliance. It follows that the Alliance vote which came from non-Malays amounted to about 22.2 per cent. of the total vote (58.5 per cent. minus 36.3 per cent.).[21]

Table XXVII is a reminder of the extent to which Alliance strength is still founded on UMNO and the Malay

TABLE XXVII

ESTIMATED ETHNIC SOURCES OF THE VOTE, PARLIAMENTARY
ELECTIONS, 1964[a]

	MALAY (Percentages)	NON-MALAY (Percentages)	TOTAL (Percentages)
Alliance	36.3	22.2	58.5
Opposition	17.7	23.8	41.5
Total	54	46	100

[a] If it were assumed that the opposition parties other than PMIP and Party Negara had gained 20 per cent. of their votes from Malays (instead of 10 per cent.), then the Alliance vote would have consisted of approximately 33.7 per cent. Malay votes and 24.8 per cent. non-Malay votes. The opposition percentages would have been 20.3 per cent. Malay and 21.2 per cent. non-Malay.

[20] In the electorate as a whole about 38 per cent. were Chinese; about 8 per cent. were Indians.

[21] The above calculations assume that turnout was approximately the same among Malays and non-Malays. This assumption is roughly correct (see pp. 397-8 below).

vote. On the above assumptions Malays split more than two to one in favour of the Alliance, while non-Malays slightly favoured the opposition. But the Table should not be construed to mean more than the figures show. UMNO may be dominant in the Alliance in terms of votes. But on Malay votes alone the Alliance could gather only just over one third of the total vote. Non-Malay votes, amounting to over a fifth of the total electorate, were vital to its securing a majority of the vote.

In the preceding calculation no attempt has been made to divide the 'non-Malay' vote into 'Chinese' and 'non-Chinese'. But rather over 80 per cent. of the non-Malay electors were Chinese, and a *prima facie* assumption may be made that findings about the non-Malay vote will also apply broadly to the Chinese vote. On such an assumption, it would seem from Table XXVII that the MCA did not have the support of as many as 50 per cent. of the Chinese voters. However, from Table XXVII and also from Table XX it appears that the MCA almost certainly received more of the Chinese vote than its strongest rival for that vote, the SF. If it is assumed that about 10 per cent. of the votes cast for the SF were Malay, it received approximately 300,000 votes from non-Malays, as compared with about 430,000 for the Alliance. So, if the Chinese proportion of the non-Malay vote corresponded roughly to these figures, almost one and a half times as many Chinese votes were cast for the Alliance as for the Front.

A calculation could be made, similar to that summarized in Table XXVII, to show the racial sources of the vote for 1959. This has not been attempted here. However, a reference to Table XX is suggestive. Between 1959 and 1964 the combined percentage vote for PMIP and Party Negara fell by 8.4 per cent. This must have been almost entirely a Malay vote, which in 1964 was transferred largely to the Alliance. On the other hand, the percentage of the vote cast for the other opposition parties and for Independents rose by 1.7 per cent. between the two elections. This was largely a non-Malay vote. Some of the gain could be attributed to the fact that there was a rise in the proportion of non-Malay electors, 1959-64 (2.2 per cent.). A broad conclusion would be that, although the Alliance won a higher proportion of the Malay vote in 1964 as compared with 1959, its percentage share of the non-Malay vote was roughly the same in the two years. There is no evidence to suggest that this conclusion does not apply to the Chinese vote as well as to the non-Malay vote in general.

The non-Malay vote for the Alliance was hit by the increase in the number of candidates put forward by non-Malay opposition parties in 1964, shown in Table XX.[22] In the next section, 'Changes in the Alliance Share of the Vote, 1959-64' it is argued that the Alliance vote was vulnerable when candidate from this type of party were put forward for the first time in 1964. However, the increase in the opposition non-Malay *vote* was not sufficiently concentrated on candidates with a good chance of winning to make the Alliance lose any *seats*. On the contrary, a remarkable feature of the election was that among MCA candidates (most of whom ran for predominantly non-Malay seats) the number of winners was twenty-seven in 1964 compared with nineteen in 1959. This success was partly due to the fact that four out of the eight gains were in seats where Chinese Independent candidates had run strongly in 1959, a type of seat in which the Alliance increased its share of the vote heavily in 1964.[23]

[22] Non-Malay parties, as defined above, put forward 110 candidates in 1964 compared with 59 in 1959. The number of non-Malay Independents, however, fell from 19 in 1959 to 5 in 1964.

[23] See Table XXIX. Three of the four had been contested by UMNO or MIC (not MCA) candidates in 1959: Bruas, Setapak and Seremban Barat. The fourth was Seremban Timor. In another of the eight seats won by the MCA in 1964 for the first time, Bandar Malacca, the sitting Malayan Party member became the 1964 MCA candidate. The other three seats gained in 1964 were two adjoining Perak seats, Ulu Kinta and Batu Gajah, both won from the PPP, and Damansara, won from the Socialist Front.

Changes in the Alliance Share of the Vote, 1959-64

In a mainly two-party system it is possible to calculate the changes in the vote between elections in terms of 'swing', which expresses, as a percentage of the total vote, the average of one party's gain in any seat (or group of seats) and the other party's loss. But in Malaya the Alliance was the only party to contest all the seats: none of the others contested as many as two-thirds of the seats. Also, different combinations of parties contested most of the parliamentary seats in 1959 and 1964. The distribution of the vote might be greatly affected by the withdrawal of a party which had contested in 1959 or by the addition of one which had not contested in 1959. So any increase or decrease in the percentage of the vote obtained by the Alliance in a particular seat would be only a very rough indication of whether or not its performance had improved between 1959 and 1964. An attempt was made to ensure some comparability by treating all the parties except the Alliance as 'communal', in the sense that they were more likely to attract either Malay voters or non-Malay voters. The PMIP, Party Negara and Malay Independents were treated as Malay communal. The SF, UDP, PPP and non-Malay Independents were treated as 'non-Malay communal'. The division between 'Malay communal' and 'non-Malay communal' refers to the party, not to the candidate. Thus, if the SF put up a Malay candidate, this would be classified as 'non-Malay communal' intervention. For the purpose of this calculation the PAP was treated separately. The seats were then divided into four broad categories. In the first were placed all the seats where the challenge to the Alliance was of the same communal nature in 1964 as in 1959. There were various sub-categories depending on the exact combination of opposition candidates: non-Malay communal at both; Malay communal and non-Malay communal at both; Malay communal at both. There were also separate subcategories to include cases where the communal party was the same one each time (for example PMIP 1959 and

PMIP 1964) or different (Party Negara 1959 and PMIP 1964). However, in this classification no account was taken of the *number* of communal parties contesting in each year. Opposition by the SF alone would be classified in the same way as opposition by the SF, the PPP and the UDP.[24]

The second category contained all those seats where Malay communal opposition had been withdrawn, where non-Malay communal opposition had been added, or where Malay communal opposition had been withdrawn *and* non-Malay communal opposition added, in 1964. The third category was the reverse of the second. It included seats where non-Malay communal opposition had been withdrawn, or where Malay communal opposition had been added, or where non-Malay communal opposition had been withdrawn *and* Malay communal opposition added, in 1964. Once again, in constructing these categories the *number* of parties of each communal description is ignored. A seat contested by the SF in 1959 and by the SF, the UDP and the PMIP in 1964 would be counted as 'Malay communal opposition added'. The fact that an additional non-Malay communal party had also been added would not affect the classification.

The fourth category included seats fought by the PAP in 1964.

However, there was one type of seat, which cut across the above categories — seats in which a Chinese Independent candidate had made a strong showing in 1959. To have included such seats under the headings just mentioned would have distorted the analysis. In these 'Chinese Independent seats' the swing to the Alliance, 1959-64, was much higher than average. Consequently the thirteen seats where the 1959 Chinese Independent vote was over 10 per cent. of the total valid vote are excluded from the present analysis and are discussed at length in the following section, 'Seats where a Chinese Independent

[24] In the following calculations any candidate who obtained a vote of under 2 per cent. is disregarded.

Stood in 1959'. The average swing to the Alliance between the two elections in these thirteen seats was 13.1 per cent.

Table XXVIII gives a condensed summary of the effect of changes in the type of opposition party on the Alliance percentage of the vote.

TABLE XXVIII

PERCENTAGE INCREASE OR DECREASE IN THE ALLIANCE VOTE IN CONTESTS AGAINST VARIOUS COMBINATIONS OF OPPOSITION PARTIES, 1959-64

CANDIDATES OF OPPOSITION PARTIES IN 1964 COMPARED WITH 1959	NUMBER OF SEATS IN WHICH THE COMBINATION OCCURRED	INCREASE (+) OR DECREASE (−) IN THE ALLIANCE VOTE (*per cent.*)
1. Communal nature of opposition unchanged, 1959-64.	50	+ 9.1
2. Communal nature of opposition had become 'more non-Malay', 1959-64:		
a) Malay and non-Malay opposition, 1959; only non-Malay opposition, 1964.	11	+ 7.6
b) Only Malay opposition, 1959; only non-Malay opposition, 1964.	2	− 4.1
c) Only Malay opposition, 1959; Malay and non-Malay opposition. 1964.	11	+ 3.4
Total, 2a), 2b), 2c)	24	+ 4.6
3. Communal nature of opposition had become 'more Malay', 1959-64.	6	+ 6.1
4. PAP opposition in 1964.	7	+ 3.9
Total, 1 − 4	87a	+ 7.2

a The total number of seats contested in both 1959 and 1964 was 100, the 13 'Chinese Independent seats' analysed in Table XXIX being excluded. If included, the average increase in Alliance vote, for 100 seats, was 47.8%.

The increase in the Alliance vote was slightly higher (almost 2 per cent.) than average for the first combination, that is where the communal nature of the opposition was unchanged. There was no great variation among the sub-categories of this combination, so they are not given separately. Where the communal nature of the opposition had become 'more Malay' (combination 3), the increase in the Alliance vote was about 1 per cent. less than average. There were too few cases in this combination to justify a breakdown into sub-categories. In the seats where the PAP intervened, the swing to the Alliance was well below average. However, this does not disprove the PAP claim that their intervention would, on balance, help the Alliance. PAP intervention may have taken away some Alliance votes, but it may have done more damage to the SF vote.

The second combination, where the nature of the opposition had become 'more non-Malay', needs to be looked at in more detail. Where Malay communal opposition was withdrawn in 1964 (2(a)), the increase in the Alliance vote was only just below average. But where a non-Malay communal candidate appeared for the first time (2(b) and 2(c)), there was a perceptible drop in the Alliance increase. Indeed in the two seats coming under 2(b) there was actually a decrease.

The same general pattern was found in the state seats. Where the communal nature of the opposition had become 'more non-Malay' the increase in the Alliance vote was smallest, 1959-64. Once again it was in category 2(b), where Malay communal opposition in 1959 had been replaced by non-Malay communal opposition in 1964, that the Alliance did worst of all.[25]

It would appear, then, that the Alliance was vulnerable to the effects of a candidate from a non-Malay communal party who contested the election in 1964 when there had not been such a candidate in 1959. This

[25] This finding was based on the figures for over twenty state seats in category 2 (b).

analysis may be taken a little further by considering those seats which were contested by the SF in 1964 but not in 1959. If all these seats are taken together, the increase in the Alliance vote was lower than average, only about 4 per cent. The Alliance increase was lowest, in other words the SF did best, in seats which had not been contested by *any other* non-Malay communal party in 1959. Many of these seats, where the Alliance had not faced competition from a non-Malay communal party in 1959, had a high proportion of Malays in the electorate. But it does not seem that the SF's success in these seats was due entirely to Malay votes; it did worse in those of the seats which had a *very high* proportion of Malay electors compared with the rest.

Other factors than racial ones may have affected changes in the Alliance percentage of the vote. Among these are: the size of the majority in 1959; the number of parties contesting in 1959 and in 1964; the number of electors in the constituency.

The size of the Alliance majority in 1959 did not seem to be related to the increase in the Alliance vote, 1959-64. The seats which were won in 1959 by less than a 10 per cent. margin of votes over the nearest rival party showed an average increase in the Alliance vote of 7.9 per cent. between the two elections, just about the same as the average increase for all seats. However, the seats which the Alliance lost in 1959 showed a higher-than-average increase in Alliance votes in 1964 over 1959. This held true even when the three exceptional seats which the Alliance lost directly through the 1959 MCA split, but regained in 1964, are excluded.[26] In the other seats lost in 1959, the average increase in the Alliance vote, 1959-64, was almost 9 per cent. Conceivably this might have resulted from a concentration of the Alli-

[26] Bruas, Seremban Timor, Seremban Barat. The seats lost by the Alliance in Kelantan and Trengganu were also excluded from this calculation. In them there was a 13 per cent. increase in the Alliance vote, 1959-64.

ance's considerable resources on these seats, or on the majority of them.

The number of parties fighting the Alliance in a seat made a big difference to the increase in the Alliance vote. In twelve constituencies there was a decrease in the number of opposition parties, and in these the average increase in the Alliance vote, 1959-64, reached the high figure of 16.8 per cent. In the twenty-nine where the number of parties increased between the two elections, the increase in the Alliance vote was only 3.9 per cent., about half the average increase. Apparently in a sense the Alliance is a party which picks up 'residual' votes when opposition parties withdraw and also loses votes if new parties contest which appeal to the voters' tastes more exactly than it does. However, there appears to be a limit to Alliance losses from such a source. In four seats there were *two* more opposition parties than in 1959. But in these the increase in the Alliance vote, 1959-64, was just the same as in the twenty-five seats where the number of parties increased by *one* between the two election years.[27]

The increase in the Alliance vote between the two elections was highest in the seats with fewest electors, lowest in the seats with most electors.[28]

Seats Where Chinese Independents Stood in 1959
Some of the large increases in the Alliance vote, 1959-64, occurred in seats where there had been a Chinese Independent candidate in 1959. Of the twenty-nine Independent candidates who stood in that year, eighteen were Chinese, and they obtained the major share of the votes cast for Independents. The seats where such a

27 In other words, it could be argued that, with exceptions, Alliance losses through an increase in the number of parties contesting arise mainly from the adverse effects of the first Malay communal party and the first non-Malay communal party contesting. This assumption lay behind the construction of the categories used in Table XXVIII.

28 See earlier section on 'Geographical Distribution of Support for the Parties'.

candidate stood in 1959, and received over 10 per cent. of the vote, are shown in Table XXIX.[29]

TABLE XXIX
SEATS FOUGHT BY CHINESE INDEPENDENTS, 1959 AND ALLIANCE INCREASE IN THE VOTE, 1959-64

SEAT	CHINESE INDEPENDENT VOTE, 1959 (per cent.)	UDP VOTE, 1964 (per cent.)	PERCENTAGE INCREASE ALLIANCE VOTE, 1959-64
Bagan	35.9*	5	16.7
Ulu Perak	26.4	15	13.6
Bruas	38.8	34	19.4
Sitiawan	39.3	40	18.7
Ulu Selangor	43.9	—	13.1
Bukit Bintang	34.7*	—	5.2†
Setapak	24.8	—	19.5†
Bungsar	28.4	—	4.6†
Seremban Timor	40.6	8	29.5†
Seremban Barat	38.9	11	26.0
Segamat Utara	39.8	15	4.4
Batu Pahat	26.2	12	−14.5 (decrease)
Batu Pahat Dalam	24.4	15	14.6

* Percentage is calculated from the total vote of *two* Chinese Independents.

† On these seats, contested by the PAP in 1964, see next section.

For these thirteen seats the average increase in the Alliance vote between the two elections was 13.1 per cent. compared with an average for all seats of about 7.8 per cent.

These Alliance gains reflected the decline in importance of the issues, notably Chinese education, on which the Independents had fought the 1959 election, and on which an Independent had actually won in three constituencies, Bruas, Seremban Timor and Seremban Barat. Many of the 1959 Independents who did so well were former prominent members of the MCA. But the 1964 performance of the UDP, which, in a sense, represented a continuation of the MCA 'rebel' tradition, was nothing

[29] Of the 29 Independent candidates in 1959, 18 were Chinese; 13 of the 18 won over 10 per cent. of the vote.

like as good as that of the 1959 Independents. Only in
Sitiawan did the 1964 UDP percentage exceed, fraction-
ally, the 1959 percentage obtained by the Independent.
The increase in the Alliance vote between the elections
did not seem to depend closely on whether or not the
UDP contested the seat in 1964, or, if it did contest, on
the size of its vote.

The four seats out of these thirteen which the SF
fought in 1964, but not in 1959, deserve some attention:
Bagan; Ulu Selangor; Segamat Utara; Batu Pahat. In
Bagan there were two Independent candidates (both
Chinese) and a PPP candidate as well as a PMIP candidate in 1959. The Independents and the PPP dropped
out in 1964, while the SF and the UDP came in: the
PMIP again ran a candidate. The benefit from the
withdrawals went to the Front and to a lesser extent to
the Alliance: the UDP hardly benefited at all. In Ulu
Selangor the 1959 straight fight, Alliance-Independent,
was replaced in 1964 by another straight fight, Alliance-
SF. Once again, presumably the Front received a large
share of the previous Independent votes, but the Alliance
received enough to produce a big increase in its majority.
In Segamat Utara and Batu Pahat,[30] both in Johore, the
combination of a UDP candidate and the addition of
a SF candidate since 1959 hit the Alliance hard. In the
former seat the increase in the Alliance vote was below
that for the whole of Malaya; in the latter seat there was
a substantial percentage *decrease* in its vote.

Effects of the PAP Intervention
The PAP intervention is of particular interest. Did it
indeed, as some PAP leaders claimed, work to the advantage of the Alliance by attracting votes which might
otherwise have gone to the SF? It would be too easy
just to assume that the effect was limited to taking the

30 The Batu Pahat division of UMNO was suspended in December
1963 '... following squabbles within its ranks. These squabbles caused
the Alliance defeat in the Batu Pahat Town Council elections'. *Straits
Times*, 31 March 1965.

Bungsar seat away from the SF. It would also be altogether too simple to say, with one commentator, that '. . . in five of the seats contested by the PAP (including its sole success) its intervention probably cost the SF a victory'. The number, five, seems to have been derived from the fact that in five seats, which were not won by the SF, the SF vote plus the PAP vote exceeded the Alliance vote. There is an implicit, unsubstantiated, assumption here that all, or nearly all, PAP votes would have gone to the Front in the absence of a PAP candidate. Details of the eleven seats fought by the PAP are given below.

TABLE XXX

SEATS FOUGHT BY PAP; PAP VOTE AND WINNING PARTY'S
MAJORITY

SEAT	PAP VOTE, 1964	WINNING PARTY'S MAJORITY IN 1964
1. Seremban Timor	5,410	4,194 (Alliance over PAP)
2. Bandar Malacca	3,461	3,131 (Alliance over SF)
3. Tanjong	778	4,412 (UDP over SF)
4. Batu	2,459	348 (SF over Alliance)
5. Setapak	4,214	4,404 (Alliance over SF)
6. Bungsar	13,494	808 (PAP over SF)
7. Bukit Bintang	6,667	2,440 (Alliance over PAP)
8. Damansara	3,191	546 (Alliance over SF)
9. Kluang Utara	1,276	2,464 (Alliance over SF)
10. Johore Bahru Barat	447	6,926 (Alliance over SF)
11. Johore Bahru Timor	773	7,257 (Alliance over SF)

In any statistical calculations it is difficult, in the absence of opinion polls, to take account of voters' reactions. It is quite likely, for example, that the entry of the PAP, by providing extra anti-SF propaganda during the election, may have resulted in a number of abstentions by electors who would otherwise have voted for the Front. However, such reactions have not been allowed for (and could not have been accurately allowed for) in the analysis which follows.

On this basis, in the seats where the PAP vote was smaller than the winning margin it may be concluded that the

PAP intervention had no influence on which party won, although, of course, it may have influenced the size of the majority. Seats 3, 5, 9, 10 and 11 (the last two of which were not campaigned for) come into this group. In 2, Bandar Malacca, the PAP vote was slightly more than the winning margin. But if the PAP vote were redistributed between the SF and the Alliance, the former would have had to receive an extremely high proportion of it in order to win, 94 per cent. to the Alliance's 6 per cent. Such a distribution would be plausible only if the SF and the PAP were parties with a closely similar ideology and appeal. Given the differences between the PAP and the Front and the *similarity* between PAP and Alliance policy on the key issue of Malaysia, it is highly unlikely that the PAP vote, in the absence of the party's intervention, would have split in this most unequal fashion.

In Bukit Bintang the PAP vote was over two and three-quarter times the Alliance majority over the SF. Looking at the 1959 figures, the Alliance won with 37.4 per cent. of the vote, while the SF obtained 28 per cent. and two Chinese Independents obtained 33 per cent. and 1.6 per cent. respectively. In 1964, the percentages were: Alliance, 42.6 per cent; PAP, 31.1 per cent; SF, 23.3 per cent; PMIP, 3 per cent. It has been shown that seats which in 1959 had a high vote for Chinese Independents nearly all had a swing substantially above average to the Alliance, 1959-64.[31] Without PAP intervention, the Alliance might have expected to increase its 1959 percentage lead over the SF. Even in the unlikely event that the former Independent votes had broken slightly in favour of the Front in 1964 (say, 60-40 per cent.) the Alliance would probably still have won Bukit Bintang. Seremban Timor was another seat with a high (and winning) Independent vote in 1959. If a PAP candidate had not contested it in 1964, the voting figures for seats with a high Independent vote in 1959 indicate that it also would have been safe for the Alliance.

[31] See Table XXIX.

Bungsar, the PAP's only victory in 1964, was another seat where a Chinese Independent had done well in 1959. The figures were: 40.5 per cent; Alliance, 21 per cent; Independent, 28.5 per cent; PPP, 10 per cent. In 1964 the seat was fought by the Alliance, the Front, the PPP and the PAP. If only the distribution of the former Independent vote is considered, then, other things being equal, without PAP intervention the Alliance would have needed to win about 85 per cent. of it, to 15 per cent. for the SF, in order to win the seat. But other things might not have been equal: from the experience of other seats a direct gain in votes from SF to Alliance might have been expected. Still, in order to win, assuming that there was no PAP candidate and that the PPP share of the vote stayed about the same, the Alliance would have had to increase its share of the vote by about 26 per cent. over 1959. This was a much higher percentage than the average Alliance increase in this 'ex-Chinese Independent' type of seat. On balance, it seems to be possible, but un-likely, that the Alliance would have won Bungsar in the event that the PAP had not contested it.

In Batu and Damansara the PAP vote was several times as great as the majority of the winning candidate. Batu had been a straight fight between the SF and the Alliance in 1959, when the SF had won by 2,329 votes, corresponding to about 15.4 per cent. of the vote. In Damansara in 1959 the Alliance had been 23 per cent. behind the SF vote. What assumptions can be made, on the basis of what happened in other parliamentary seats, about the probable outcome in Batu and Damansara in the absence of PAP candidates in 1964? In 1959 both Batu and Damansara had straight fights between the Alliance and the Front. There were only five parliamentary seats which had straight fights between the same two parties in 1959 and 1964. The increases in the Alliance vote in these five ranged from 3 per cent. to 13.4 per cent. The average percentage increase was 8.7 per cent. This was not a very different average increase from the average increase in the ten seats where in each of the two elections an Alliance candidate had fought the same non-Malay communal party, or combination of parties.[32] The average increase for the ten was 7.6 per cent. It seems quite likely that, from the experience of other seats, the Alliance, with no PAP candidate in 1964, could have won Batu. For its deficit of 15.4 per cent. to become a winning percentage, its vote need have risen by only 7.8 per cent. and the SF vote have fallen by the same percentage. The experience of other seats indicates that this would have been quite possible. Without the entry of the PAP the Alliance would have found it harder to win Damansara. The 23 per cent. SF lead of 1959 could have been overcome only by an Alliance increase, and a corresponding SF loss, of just over 11.5 per cent. This was possible, but on balance improbable. It would have been more difficult than to have won Batu.[33]

On balance, if the PAP had not contested any seats at the 1964 elections, three of the results could well have been different. Probably the Alliance would not have won Damansara. Alliance chances of winning Bungsar and Batu would have been better, at least on paper. An intelligent guess might be that PAP intervention probably gave the Alliance one seat, but possibly deprived it of one, maybe two, other seats.

Changes in Votes cast for Opposition Parties, 1959-64
To some extent fluctuations in the votes of opposition parties, 1959-64, could be attributed to the appearance or disappearance of other opposition parties with a similar communal appeal in particular seats. In the few instances where it occurred, there was a perceptible effect on the PMIP vote in 1964 when, compared with 1959, a Party Negara or Malay Independent candidate was added or

[32] The ten seats included the five straight fights with the SF, mentioned above. The ten seats comprised one of the sub-categories of combination 1 in Table XXVIII.

[33] In these calculations candidates' personalities are ignored. But in Batu the Front seems to have had an advantage on this score (see Chapter IX (b), above).

subtracted. This type of effect was most obvious in the competition to which the SF was exposed. In the seats in which it faced the same number (including zero) of non-Malay communal opponents in 1964 as in 1959, its percentage share of the total vote fell by 5.3 per cent. But where there were more non-Malay communal opponents in 1964 the average decrease rose to 13.3 per cent. In the three seats in which it faced fewer non-Malay communal opponents in 1964 than in 1959 the percentage drop in its vote was only 1.7 per cent.

Some of the damage done to the SF by the intervention of such competing parties came from the PAP. The number of instances, ten,[34] is too small to justify any generalizations about the effect on the SF vote, although the effect on particular seats was discussed earlier.

Where there was a contest between parties appealing to similar communal groups, some such parties habitually did better than others. In the four parliamentary contests between PMIP and Party Negara, PMIP won two-thirds of the two-party vote and Party Negara one third. There were sixteen contests between the SF and the UDP, which were not contested by any other non-Malay communal party. In these the SF won 66 per cent. of the two-party vote to the UDP's 34 per cent. Of six similar contests between the PAP and the SF, the Front won 70 per cent. of the two-party vote and the PAP 30 per cent. Where a third communal party was present, the two-party split between the SF and the PAP was still about 70-30 per cent. The PPP, because it was selective in the seats it chose to contest, did much better against the SF. Where these two were the only non-Malay communal parties involved, the PPP won 78 per cent. of the two-party vote to the SF's 22 per cent. In the small number of contests where there was an additional non-Malay communal party, the PPP did much less well compared with the SF.

The formation of a 'Convention' of opposition parties

[34] One of the eleven seats fought by the PAP had not been contested by the Front in 1959 (Bandar Malacca).

in 1965 prompts the question: what would have been the effect of such a combination of parties, if it had been in existence at the time of the 1964 election? The parties in the Convention which contested the election in 1964 were the PPP, the UDP, and the PAP. The indirect effects of such an alliance, for instance by improving morale in the parties concerned and by impressing the voters by a show of strength, cannot be calculated. But, from a purely arithmetical point of view, it is possible to calculate, very easily, what the effect would have been, if, in order to avoid splitting votes, these three parties had made agreements on which would contest which seats and had not fought each other. The effect would have been precisely nil. No seats were lost in 1964 through these three parties fighting each other and so splitting the non-Malay communal vote.[35]

Candidates and Race: Changes of Candidate: Personal Votes

It was pointed out in Chapter V that parties did not always choose candidates of the same race as the majority of the electors in a constituency. In 1964 the Alliance had three Indian parliamentary candidates, although no constituency had anything like a majority of Indian electors. It had ten Malay candidates in seats where the Malays were not the most numerous race and four Chinese candidates in seats where the Chinese were not the most numerous race. The choice of such candidates did not seem to have any perceptible effect on support for the Alliance. The Alliance Malay supporters in Malacca Tengah seem to have turned out just as loyally to vote for Mr. Tan Siew Sin, the Finance Minister[36] as they would

[35] Of course, any combination of opposition parties which had included the SF (particularly the Labour Party) would have had more chances of success.

[36] Mr. Tan had the highest proportion of Malays in his electorate (64 per cent.) of all the Alliance Chinese candidates. He obtained 74 per cent. of the vote. He had the support of five Alliance Malay candidates who stood in the five state constituencies which made up his parliamentary constituency. The Alliance Malay candidate who had

have to vote for a Malay candidate. In the seventeen seats where the Alliance candidate was not of the majority race the Alliance vote was above average, the percentage increase in the vote over 1959 was above average, and the vote of the parliamentary candidates did not seem to differ abnormally from the total vote of the corresponding state candidates for the same area. Indeed the high Alliance vote for these seats can be explained by saying that it was only in safe Alliance seats that the risk of putting up this kind of candidate could be taken.[37]

There were four instances in which the race of the Alliance candidate was changed, 1959-64. But, before considering these a more general question must be asked: what was the effect, if any, of a change of candidate, even if the new candidate was of the same race as the former candidate? If Kelantan and Trengganu (where there was a wholesale change of candidates by both Alliance and PMIP) are excluded, in the remainder of the country there was hardly any difference between the voting behaviour in seats where the Alliance candidate was changed and those where he was the same. If anything, the Alliance did slightly better where the candidate was changed. This was especially so in the seats won by the Opposition in 1959, in all of which a new Alliance candidate was chosen for 1964. However, the greater success of the Alliance in these seats might have been attributable to the greater effort called forth by the need to dislodge the Opposition. But, even in the Alliance-held seats, a change of candidate was followed by a slight increase in the Alliance vote over 1959.

---

the highest proportion of non-Malays in his electorate (79 per cent.) was Tengku Abdullah (Rawang), who won 67 per cent. of the vote.

[37] Cf. the statement attributed to Tengku Abdul Rahman after the 1955 elections for the Legislative Council: 'I had complete faith in victories for our Chinese and Indian candidates, who were in the strongest UMNO areas. Frankly we dared not put them anywhere else; we had to try to win the confidence of the people first.' H. Miller, *Prince and Premier*. London, 1959, p. 177. However, it is not quite clear what he meant by 'strongest UMNO areas', because no country-wide elections had been held previously.

The four seats where there was a change of race in the Alliance candidate were as follows.

TABLE XXXI

ALLIANCE SHOWING IN THE FOUR SEATS WHERE THERE WAS A CHANGE OF RACE IN ITS CANDIDATE, 1959-64

SEAT	RACE OF ALLIANCE CANDIDATE		PERCENTAGE RACIAL COMPOSITION OF THE ELECTORATE, 1964			PERCENTAGE INCREASE IN ALLIANCE VOTE
	1959	1964	MALAY	CHINESE	OTHER	1959-64
Seberang Selatan	Chinese	Malay	41	44	15	26
Bruas	Malay	Chinese	37	50	13	19
Setapak	Malay	Chinese	25	63	12	20
Seremban Barat	Indian	Chinese	27	56	17	26

In all four seats the increase in the Alliance vote was over twice the average increase for all seats. This large increase is easily understandable in Bruas, Setapak and Seremban Barat. All three were seats where a Chinese Independent had stood in 1959. In this type of seat the percentage increase in the Alliance vote, 1959-64, was exceptionally high.

However, there is no obvious explanation for the movement of the vote in Seberang Selatan. There had been no Chinese Independent candidate in this seat in 1959. The change in the race of the candidate was not even in the direction which calculations based on the racial composition of the electors might have indicated. A Chinese candidate was replaced by a Malay, although there were slightly more Chinese than Malays in the electorate.

No attempt was made to analyse the effects of changes in Opposition candidates in detail. However, as far as the seats won by the Socialist Front were concerned, there did not seem to be any perceptible differences between seats which were fought by the 1959 winner and seats which were fought by a new candidate. Comparison was made difficult because of the complications resulting from the intervention or non-intervention of UDP or PPP candidates in particular seats. A rather more definite indication as to the importance or non-importance of the candidate is provided by the voting figures for Kelantan and Trengganu. In 1959 the PMIP won thirteen parliamentary seats in these states. In 1964 they changed nearly all their candidates. However, of the few who stood again two were outstanding, Inche Zulkiflee, PMIP Deputy President, and Inche Asri, who became Chief Minister of Kelantan after the election, both men of outstanding ability, well-known throughout the length and breadth of Kelantan and Trengganu. In 1964 one of these two did slightly better than the average for the remainder of the seats held by the party in Kelantan and Trengganu, the other did decidedly worse. Taking the average for the two, the PMIP did rather worse than in the other seats. Even allowing for the fact that many other factors may have been important, the results indicate that in one sense there was little or no 'personal vote' for these two men.

Where opposition parties (SF, UDP and PAP) put up a Malay candidate in a seat with a non-Malay majority of electors or put up a non-Malay in a seat with a Malay majority, the party's vote did not seem to have been adversely affected. However, none of these candidates actually won.

Other evidence for or against the existence of a personal vote is hard to interpret. Probably there is hardly any personal vote for Alliance candidates, although there might be one for Alliance Ministers. But for some opposition parties' candidates, particularly in the smaller opposition parties, there may be quite a sizable personal vote.

The evidence already given about the consequences of changing Alliance Party candidates is perhaps the strongest indication of the lack of an appreciable personal vote for such candidates. If any Alliance *Ministers* had failed to contest in 1964, there would have been data on the

effects of replacing prominent personalities by persons
who were presumably less prominent. But there were no
such data, because all the Ministers stood in 1964. Ministers increased their vote, 1959-64, very slightly more than
other Alliance candidates (8.4 per cent. compared with
7.8 per cent.). But even if this increase had been more
marked, it would have indicated not the size of their
personal vote, but only, possibly, the increase in the size
of their personal vote.

In investigating whether or not there is a personal vote
for Ministers, another approach is to compare the Alliance
vote for each parliamentary seat contested by Ministers
with the total Alliance vote for the state seats which make
up that parliamentary seat. However, these totals are not
always strictly comparable, because a different combination of opposition parties may have contested the parliamentary seat from the combination which contested the
state seats. However, five parliamentary seats won by
Ministers *were* comparable in this sense with the corresponding state seats. In them the vote for the parliamentary candidate was on the average higher than the state
total vote by 1.7 per cent. In all seats the Alliance parliamentary total averaged only 1.3 per cent. more than
the state total. Of the five parliamentary percentages,
Tengku Abdul Rahman's was 2.7 per cent. higher than
the state total, Inche Khir Johari's was 4.5 per cent.
higher. Unfortunately, this analysis may not reveal the
full extent of the personal vote, because of the existence
of what in the United States has been called the 'coat-
tail' effect. For instance, the personal vote for the
Tengku may have been higher than the figure given,
because those who turned out at the polling station to
deliver that personal vote may also have exhibited their
support for the Tengku by voting for the Alliance *state*
candidate. The size of the vote for the state Alliance
candidates, who thus benefited from the coat-tail effect,
would be indicated only at the election after the Tengku's
retirement. So the personal vote for Ministers might be

appreciable, although it appears to be negligible for Alliance candidates as a whole.

Among the opposition parties' candidates there seem to be several instances of a personal vote, although its size is hard to measure. One possible instance was the vote for the former Cabinet Minister, Inche Abdul Aziz bin Ishak, who, after leaving the Government, founded a new party, the National Convention Party, which shortly before the election joined the Socialist Front. It might have been expected that in his long career as a Minister Inche Aziz would have collected a personal vote which would stay with him even after he changed his party. In 1964 Inche Aziz fought, as a SF candidate, the parliamentary and state seats to which he had been elected, as an Alliance candidate in 1959. The SF had not fought either of these seats in 1959. The Alliance percentage of the vote dropped in each of the two seats fought by Inche Aziz. In Kuala Langat (parliamentary) it fell by 6.9 per cent; in Morib (state) it fell by 6 per cent. This is quite a large drop when it is remembered that the average *increase* in the Alliance percentage of the vote was almost 8 per cent. These figures might indicate that Inche Aziz had a personal vote of about 15 per cent. However, the nature of the opposition parties which fought the seats in 1959 and 1964 must be considered. Kuala Langat and Morib were seats which had not been contested by a non-Malay communal party in 1959, but which were contested by the SF in 1964. In such seats it has been shown that the average increase in the Alliance vote, 1959-64, was very small. So it might be more correct to say that Inche Aziz's personal vote was about 8 or 9 per cent.

It was widely believed among politicians of all parties that Dr. Lim Chong Eu's victory in the parliamentary seat of Tanjong resulted from a personal vote. It was regarded as a tribute to his fight, first inside the MCA and then outside it, on behalf of the Chinese and particularly on behalf of Chinese education. The election situation in Tanjong was too intricate in both 1959 and

1964 to justify any inferences about a personal vote through a comparison of the two years. In 1959 Tanjong was fought by the Alliance, SF and PPP: in 1964 by the Alliance, SF, PAP and UDP (Dr. Lim). However, a comparison is possible between the figures for the parliamentary seat of Tanjong in 1964 and the three state seats which composed it. In 1964 each was contested by the same four parties. But the UDP vote for the parliamentary seat was 45.4 per cent., compared with a total percentage of 39.1 per cent. for the three UDP state candidates taken together. Because Dr. Lim himself was one of the state candidates, and because of the coat-tail effect referred to above, the full influence of his personal vote was concealed. But it was apparently at least 6 per cent. and may have been much higher.

There may also have been a personal vote for Mr. Devan Nair who won, narrowly, the PAP's only victory in Bungsar. In one of the two state seats which made up Bungsar, the PAP was beaten decisively by the Alliance. It did not even contest the other, which was won by the SF. Yet in Bungsar Mr. Nair defeated both the Alliance and the SF. It could be argued that the voters' greater support for the PAP in the parliamentary seat resulted from a desire to give the PAP a national forum in the Federal Parliament, while a PAP member in a state legislature would have obtained little publicity. But this argument ignores the fact that the PAP, through its twelve members from Singapore, was already assured of a 'forum' in the national Parliament.

At first sight it might appear that the two MCA 'rebels' who had fought and won as Independents in 1959 but who became Alliance candidates in 1964 had a large personal vote. The increase in the Alliance vote in the two constituencies they won in 1964 was certainly much higher than average.[38] But a large part of the increase is probab-

---

[38] Mr. Yeo Tat Beng (Bruas), increase in Alliance vote of 19.4 per cent; Mr. Quek Kai Dong (Seremban Timor), increase in Alliance vote of 29.5 per cent. Mr. Yeo had won Bruas in 1959. Mr. Quek had won the adjoining seat of Seremban Barat.

ly attributable to the fact that the seats concerned came into the category of seats fought by Chinese Independents in 1959 rather than to a personal vote.

Turnout

The average turnout for all parliamentary seats in 1964 was 78.9 per cent. as compared with 73.3 per cent. in 1959. The state elections turnout rose from 74.0 per cent. in 1959 to 78.9 per cent. in 1964.

When a large number of candidates contested a seat there was no apparent increase in turnout. Of the six parliamentary seats which had a turnout of under 70 per cent., two had two candidates, one had three candidates and three had four candidates. The average number of candidates per parliamentary seat was just under 2.7.

The turnout was slightly lower in Opposition-held seats than in Government-held seats. There did not seem to be any marked relation between size of turnout and narrowness of the winning party's majority at the 1959 election. The party organizers either did not concentrate on getting out the vote, or did not succeed in doing so, in seats where the election result had been especially close in 1959. However, Table XXXII does show that in the seats which had the smallest majorities in 1959, the turnout was less likely than in other seats to be *very low* in 1964.

TABLE XXXII

TURNOUT IN PARLIAMENTARY SEATS, 1964, AND SIZE OF MAJORITY IN 1959

	NUMBER OF SEATS IN 1964 WITH A TURNOUT OF:			
SIZE OF WINNING MAJORITY, 1959	BELOW 75 PER CENT.	75-79.9 PER CENT.	80 PER CENT. AND ABOVE	TOTAL
0-999	1	7	5	13
1000-1999	1	2	11	14
2000-4999	8	14	15	37
5000 and over	4	16	16	36
Total	14	39	47	100

Sometimes it has been suggested that non-Malays are less likely to vote, even when qualified to do so, than Malays. Such a failure might be held to reflect a failure of non-Malays to be integrated in the community, since one expression of being so integrated might be the act of voting. Whether or not these speculations are valid, there was in fact very little difference in turnout according to the racial composition of the constituency, although what differences existed were in the direction of higher Malay participation. In those seats with over 90 per cent. Malay electors the turnout was about 1.5 per cent. higher than in those with below 20 per cent. Malay electors.

Turnout was about 4 per cent. higher, on the average, for the six urban seats in spite of the fact that one of the six, Bukit Bintang had a turnout of only 65.7 per cent. In quasi-urban seats it was 1.2 per cent. higher than the average for all seats.

Spoilt Votes

In 1959 the percentage of spoilt votes dropped from an average of 2.5 per cent. at the state elections to 1.1 per cent. in the parliamentary election.[39] The state elections were held first, and the reduction in the percentage of spoilt votes at the parliamentary elections was generally held to reflect an improvement in the voters' capacity to handle the mechanics of voting. In 1964 the electors were called upon to vote for both parliamentary and state candidates on the same day, and this seems to have been too much for many of them. The average of spoilt votes for the parliamentary elections was 4.2 per cent; for the state elections it was 4.8 per cent. It is not obvious why there were more state spoilt votes than parliamentary spoilt votes.

The proportion of spoilt votes, in the 1964 parliamentary election, seemed to be lowest in the urban and quasi-urban seats.

There was some correspondence between a parliamentary constituency's having been high or low in spoilt votes

39 *Report on the Parliamentary and State Elections, 1959*, p. 6, para. 37.

in 1964 and its percentage of spoilt votes in 1959. When the seats with the highest and lowest percentages for the two years were compared, eight seats appeared among the twenty with the highest percentage in both years. Seven ap-

TABLE XXXIII

SPOILT VOTES IN DIFFERENT TYPES OF SEATS, PARLIAMENTARY ELECTION, 1964

	6 URBAN SEATS	25 QUASI-URBAN SEATS	REMAINDER	TOTAL
Twenty seats with the lowest percentage of spoilt votes	5	7	8	20
Twenty seats with the highest percentage of spoilt votes	0	2	18	20
Sixty-two seats with an intermediate percentage of spoilt votes	1	16	45	62
Total	6	25	71	102

peared among the twenty with the lowest percentage in both years. There was no instance of a seat's appearing among the 'high twenty' in one of the years and the 'low twenty' in the other.

A curious feature of the 1959 seats with the lowest proportion of spoilt votes was that seven of the twenty seats were in Kelantan. Kelantan is less-developed educationally than the rest of the country, and it might have been thought that the electors would have had more difficulty than most in mastering the operation of voting. In 1964 only one Kelantan seat appeared in the list of the twenty with the lowest percentage of spoilt papers. Either the electors there were particularly perplexed by the intricacy of casting state and parliamentary votes at the same time, or, conceivably, the standards of what constituted a 'spoilt vote' in Kelantan had been tightened since 1959.

In a few parliamentary constituencies the gap between the number of spoilt votes and the number of spoilt votes for the corresponding state seats was very high. The average difference for the whole of Malaya was 0.6 per cent., reflecting slightly fewer spoilt parliamentary votes than state votes. But in Kampar the percentage for the state constituencies taken together was 10.1 per cent. and the parliamentary was 4.0 per cent., while in Seremban Timor the state figure was 7.4 per cent. and the parliamentary was 2.9 per cent. On the other hand, in Batu Pahat Dalam the parliamentary percentage was 10.8 per cent., while the state percentage was lower at 7.3 per cent. These differences seem to be too great to be explained by chance or by difficulties in the mechanism of voting. Possibly they reflect some kind of protest on the part of the electors, for example because they did not have a chance to vote for a party's candidate in the state seat as well as in the parliamentary seat, because one had not been put up in the former, or *vice versa*. This type of explanation could apply to the three instances just cited.

A high percentage of spoilt votes seemed to be positively related to a low turnout. The twenty seats with the highest percentage of spoilt parliamentary votes in 1964 (those with over 5 per cent. spoilt votes) had an average turnout of about 2.7 per cent. less than the twenty with the lowest proportion of spoilt votes (those with under 3.2 per cent.).

XIII

Conclusions

NEEDLESS to say, the politics of any country – the way in which parties and pressure groups are organized and function, the extent of popular participation in political activity, and so on – must strongly be influenced by the communication facilities which exist. These would include not only the physical accessibility of the different parts of the country but also the variety of ways in which the people are kept informed of developments and in which parties, for example, co-ordinate their activities at different levels. For obvious reasons, literacy would be of great value in strengthening 'communication' in this broad sense. The extent to which politics is competitive may also have some influence, since it is likely that where there is keen competition there will also be more intense political activity and hence a greater volume of political propaganda.

Although not as well developed as in Singapore,[1] the communications network in Malaya may broadly be considered satisfactory, at least in the negative sense of not being a barrier to the effective functioning of democracy. Radios and newspapers may only play a limited role in the rural areas, and there is still an imbalance between urban and rural literacy.[2] But the administration has

[1] Singapore, it must be remembered, is compact and highly urbanized. It also has a relatively high rate of literacy, and its politics is extremely competitive.

[2] There has, however, been a strong drive to improve literacy in the rural areas. Between December 1956 and June 1963, the total enrolment in primary schools in the rural areas increased from 273,282 to 583,313 During the same period, the enrolment in rural secondary schools increased from 6,361 to 21,035. Malaysia, *Interim Review of Development in Malaya under the Second Five-Year Plan.* Kuala Lumpur, 1964, p. 65. In addition, a large number of adult education classes have also been started in many rural areas.

penetrated virtually every part of the country, through local councils and through the various District Offices from which a hierarchy of officials reaches down virtually to the village level. Further, almost all the inhabited areas are easily accessible by road.[3] This means that party workers do not have many problems in contacting voters, even in the rural areas. Because of the intense rivalry between them, it is usual for the Alliance and the PMIP to have a large number of branches in most of the rural constituencies, and these branches (along with those of other parties) perform the important function of keeping the average rural voter informed (even if only at a very rudimentary level) of changes in the political scene. There is thus always some awareness of what the Government is doing, and of the arguments for and against its policies. Due mainly to this interpretative function performed by the various party branches, but also because it is quite usual for party leaders to tour the different parts of the country addressing the people, the distance which is often believed to exist between the Government and the bulk of the population in developing countries does not quite apply in the Malayan case. Nor is there any reason to assume that Malaya is exceptional in this respect, and there may be grounds why the notion as a whole should be re-examined. In writing about Nigeria, for example, Sklar observed:

> The communal orientation of Nigerian politics, involving a high degree of mass participation in the evolution and implementation of public policies, has been noted frequently in this study. It is consistent with traditional political practices of major cultural groups, and it is reflected in party organization and activities at the local level. The assiduity with which members of the political elite, including ministers of

3 In Sabah and Sarawak, on the other hand, the communication problem is still an effective barrier to widespread political participation. Only limited areas in these states are accessible by roads and railways, and large sections of the population live in areas which can only be reached by boat and by travelling on foot.

state and parliamentarians, keep their ears to the ground and seek continuously to justify public policies to their constituents would seem to suggest that the hypothesis of a great psychological gulf between the 'elite' and the 'masses' requires re-examination.[4]

Some basic questions have not been investigated explicitly so far: to what extent were the elections 'free' and 'democratic'? In what ways did the contending parties imitate each other's political 'styles'? What kinds of political leaders are evolving in Malaya? What was the role of pressure groups in the election? What light do the results throw on the future course of politics in the country and on the prospects of the parties?

Where the Elections 'Free'?

To what extent were the elections 'free' and 'democratic'? In developing countries which adopt a Western pattern of government there is an obvious conflict between two opposing tendencies. On the one hand it is usually taken for granted that 'democracy' is desirable. On the other hand, the passions which might be aroused in an election which was really free-for-all and in which no holds were barred might encourage those forces making for divisions in the society which it was the Government's main concern to combat. Also, quite apart from any consequences resulting from conflicting objectives, there may be a general tendency for the system in ex-colonies to 'run down' by the standards of the former colonial power. The administration of elections in Africa, it has been said, is at first European; when the Europeans leave the system becomes more indigenous, politics may become dirtier and the interests at stake may become more open and vigorous in their tactics.[5]

There were several complaints by opposition parties about the conduct of the 1964 elections in Malaya. Some referred to inaccuracies which favoured the Government

4 R.I. Sklar, *Nigerian Political Parties.* Princeton, 1963, pp. 503-4.
5 W.J.M. Mackenzie and Kenneth Robinson, eds., *Five Elections in Africa.* London, 1960, p. 464.

in the electoral registers.[6] Others referred to intimidation by officials and police.[7] To these complaints the Chairman of the Election Commission replied with the challenge that the complainants could go to court if they were dissatisfied.[8] Such opposition complaints, which were reproduced in newspapers, were repeated and amplified in the course of several interviews. They were supplemented in interviews by circumstantial allegations that ballot boxes had been 'stuffed' by the Government party with ballot papers which had not been marked by the electors themselves.[9] The politicians who made the allegations were high-ranking members of their parties, and no doubt they sincerely believed that their charges were true. At the same time, the precautions taken to prevent this type of abuse were elaborate,[10] and no objections on this score were actually taken to court by opposition parties. Perhaps the most ingenious trick alleged to have been used by the Alliance was that the girls who counted the votes (in Kelantan) had spoiled ballot papers cast for the PMIP by marking them with pencils concealed underneath their long fingernails.

The verdict on these opposition allegations must, in general, be 'not proven'. It could be argued that the use of such 'dirty tricks' on any large scale is implausible, if only because, on a sober and cynical estimate, the Government was not in such a desperate situation that it *needed* to employ such tricks.

Concern about the freedom of the 1964 elections and the extent to which they were democratic should be focussed not so much on the mechanical devices which could be used to achieve fraud, such as 'stuffing' and the misuse of long fingernails, but on the wider context in which the elections were held. This may be considered

6 See Chapters IV and VII.

7 See Chapter VII, *Straits Times*, 29 April 1964.

8 Dato Haji Mustapha Albakri, *Straits Times*, 29 April 1964.

9 Mr. D.R. Seenivasagam raised the question of why extra ballot papers were printed but not issued. *Ibid.*

10 See Chapter IV.

under three headings: arrests of opposition leaders; Government advantages in propaganda; the use of personal influence by government officials for the benefit of the Alliance party.

The arrests of opposition leaders from the SF and the PMIP, before the election, were mentioned earlier.[11] There have been other arrests since the election.[12] The Government's stand on this point is understandable and defensible. At the time of the election the country was in effect at war with Indonesia, and the Government claimed that the persons arrested were in contact with, and working for, the enemy. At the same time, when extremists in a party are arrested the role of the moderate leaders who remain, such as Dr. Tan Chee Khoon in the SF, is hard, because the morale of the remaining party members is bound to suffer. Parties like the SF have probably also been weakened as a result of the Government's tactic of releasing middle rank activists *provided* they gave up political activity. It will be recalled that in Sarawak some of the members of the SUPP were so discouraged by the handicaps that the party had to face in contesting democratic elections in 1963 that at one time they thought that it was useless to put up a fight.[13] The damage inflicted on a party by the arrests of key workers cannot be measured solely by the numbers arrested, in spite of the pronouncements of the UN Mission on Malaysia.[14] Apart from arrests, opposition parties resented the fact that rallies required a prior permit from the police and also that tape-recordings were made of their speeches.

The Government party's advantage in the mass media is shown in Chapter VIII. It also benefited from the availability of Information Department services for party use.[15] A similar situation was revealed in Chapter XI

11 See Chapter VII.
12 See particularly *A Plot Exposed.* Kuala Lumpur, 1965.
13 See Chapter X, section on Sarawak.
14 *Ibid.* footnote 26.
15 See Chapter VII.

as regards the Singapore Government's advantages at the 1963 Singapore election.

Apart from any question of deliberate intervention by government officials, such as police, on behalf of the Alliance Party, the party benefited just because it *was* the Government. In the rural areas of Malaya society is still traditional. It is understood that the Government is meant to be obeyed, and to many no distinction is apparent between the Government and the Government *party*. Where the Federal Government does not benefit from this (as in Kelantan, where the PMIP has successfully challenged the authority of the Alliance), the advantages enjoyed by the Alliance as the ruling party have been counterbalanced only by the competing attraction to a traditional society of a party specifically committed to the preservation of traditional values and receiving the support of traditional religious élites. Perhaps the most extreme version of the failure to distinguish between the Government and the Government party existed in rural Sarawak, especially in the longhouses. In Singapore the authority of the Government is *not* based on tradition to the same extent. Consequently the Government itself has had to strive, rather obviously, to *create* an identification, in the minds of the electors, of the 'Government party', with the 'Government'.

On these last two points, the Government party's advantage in the mass media and through identification with government authority and government officials, the really astonishing thing is that the opposition parties seem not to have made any vehement public protests. It was only 'natural' for the newspapers to give more space to the Government, said an official from a rival party.[16] The opposition parties were surprisingly silent about the Alliance's use of Government information services, although just after the election Inche Ishak bin Haji Mohammad, SF, possibly made an indirect allusion to it when he said,' . . . the success of the Alliance has been

16 See p. 199 above.

the success of their use of party and State propaganda machinery'.[17]

In assessing the extent to which the Malayan elections were 'free' or 'democratic', abstract definitions need some amplification. W. J. M. Mackenzie's definition is short and pertinent, although subjective. Free elections are 'elections in which voters believe that they have a real though limited choice in some matter of importance to the state and to themselves'.[18] Another view of democracy, by Chief Obafemi Awolowo of Nigeria, runs as follows:

> The idea of democracy is not liable to modification or distortion, even though mankind has invented different methods for its realisation. In a democracy, the government must rule with the consent of the governed. The governed are inalienably entitled at periodic intervals to give this consent to the same or a different set of people who form the government. The expression of such consent must be free and unfettered; and must on no account be stultified or rigged. Furthermore, the consent must never be obtained by duress, threat or intimidation; by undue influence or fraud. . . .[19]

Persuasive and eloquent as the definition is, it is difficult to choke back the questions: What is *undue* influence? May a government party exercise influence so long as it is not 'undue influence'? If so, who is to say when it has exceeded the limit allowed?

Certainly, Malaya (Malaysia) is far removed from being a one-party State. It belongs, rather, to the group of 'dominant non-authoritarian party systems', found in countries where nationalist movements have been successful in gaining independence.

17 *Straits Times,* 27 April 1964.

18 W. J. M. Mackenzie, 'The Export of Electoral Systems', *Political Studies,* Vol. V No. 3, 1957, p. 255. See also: W.J.M. Mackenzie, *Free Elections.* London, 1958; R. S. Milne, 'Elections in Developing Countries', *Parliamentary Affairs,* Vol. XVIII No. 1, 1964-5.

19 Quoted in Robert O. Tilman and Taylor Cole, eds., *The Nigerian Political Scene.* Durham, N.C. 1962, p. 268.

Most of the significant interest groups, associational and non-associational, have joined in the nationalist movement around a common program of national independence. In the period following emancipation the nationalist party continues as the greatly dominant party, opposed in elections by relatively small left-wing or traditionalist and particularist movements. This type of party system is a formally free one, but the possibility of a coherent loyal opposition is lacking.[20]

To be sure, there is a tendency for a dominant party, anywhere, to push its opponents to the wall.[21] This tendency has been seen more clearly in the PAP as the Government Party in Singapore than in the Alliance as the Government Party in Malaysia. But the situation in Malaya, and Malaysia, is far removed from that in Ghana. The Alliance Party does not claim to *be* Malaya, or Malaysia, in the way that the Convention People's Party claimed to *be* Ghana.[22] Nor has the Opposition in Malaya/Malaysia been 'forced out of public life' in the way that the Ghana Opposition was, between 1957 and 1960.[23] Despite the advantages enjoyed by the Alliance, it is important that none of the opposition parties was denied the opportunity of communicating with the voters and of explaining their own policies in addition to publicly attacking those of the Alliance. Further, many of these parties were genuinely optimistic of making significant gains, and did not feel *beforehand* that their appeal would be significantly diminished because of the obstacles which they felt they had to overcome.

Dispassionate consideration of what constitutes 'democracy' or 'free elections' is not helped by a statement such as, 'Federation of Malaya democracy is a marriage of convenience between Malay aristocrats and Chinese big

20 Gabriel A. Almond and James S. Coleman, eds., *The Politics of the Developing Areas*. Princeton, 1960, p. 41.
21 R. I. Sklar, *op. cit.* p. 499.
22 Dennis Austin, *Politics in Ghana, 1946-1960*. London, 1964, p. 31.
23 *Ibid.* p. 48.

businessmen, with Hindu trade union leaders as the Number Two Wife'.[24] It is no more enlightening to say that the 'governments of South-east Asia [including, presumably, Malaya or Malaysia] are not democratic at the present time whatever they may become eventually', and that Malaya and the Philippines will be governed in the near future by oligarchies of the new Western-educated class.[25] Surely democracy and oligarchy have now been written about long enough for it to be plain that, in one sense, there are always oligarchical tendencies in democracies, whether in South-East Asia or anywhere else. In Malaya, as in other countries, effective political decision-making may be concentrated in the hands of a few. It is quite permissible to say that those who wield power may be solicitous in advancing certain interests. But if the existence of such a state of affairs rules out the possibility of democracy in Malaya, it rules out the possibility just about everywhere else. The proper test of the existence of a democracy, which Mills himself applies when he quotes Rupert Emerson,[26] is whether or not there are periodic elections at which opposition parties are allowed to function freely. By and large the Malayan elections of 1964 fulfilled this requirement, making allowance for the restrictions necessitated by Indonesian aggression.

About a year after the election, the continuance, and stepping-up, of Indonesian attacks led to an announcement that the local elections due to be held in Malaya in the middle of 1965 would not take place. The suspension would be lifted 'the moment peace is declared'.[27]

Innovation and Imitation by the Parties
Duverger, discussing the features of party organization, observed that right-wing parties in Europe which had originally been based on parliamentary caucuses gradual-

24 Lennox A. Mills, *Southeast Asia*. London, 1964, p. 9.
25 *Ibid*. p. 15.
26 *Ibid*. pp. 284-5.
27 Tengku Abdul Rahman, *Straits Times*, 2 March 1965.

ly adopted some of the organizational characteristics of
socialist parties, especially by making 'branches' (which
were a socialist invention) their 'basic units'.[28] They felt
compelled to do this because, with the advent of universal suffrage, it became evident that more efficient ways
had to be found to recruit new members and generally
to broaden the base of party activity; and 'branches' suited
this purpose ideally. This, according to Duverger, represents a 'contagion from the left', and was caused
by the attempt by élitist parties to compete more effectively with socialist parties by adopting an organizational
framework which was characteristic of the latter and
which was more efficient for electoral purposes.[29] More
recently another writer, Theodore Lowi, has maintained
that it was not the 'leftness' of socialist parties which enabled them to be a channel of innovation, but rather
their minority status in the electorate at a time when
the old élites continued to hold sway.[30] His argument,
based on the contention that in a party system 'innovation is a function of the minority party, that is, the
"government in the making" '[31] is aimed at showing that
it is a 'dominance-minority' rather than a 'left-right'
distinction which is relevant as a stimulus to innovation.
By 'innovation' he means not merely the adoption of
new organizational techniques but also the identification
of new problems and the advancing of radically different
solutions to old problems.

If on the one hand Duverger's 'law' is too influenced
by Western European experience and is basically nothing
more than 'an acute observation of a few important historical facts',[32] Lowi's reformulation of it would seem
to be applicable only in well-established societies where

[28] M. Duverger, *Political Parties*. London, 1959, p. 25.
[29] *Loc. cit.*
[30] T. Lowi, 'Toward Functionalism in Political Science: The Case of Innovation in Party Systems', *American Political Science Review*, Vol. LVII, No. 3, p. 577.
[31] *Ibid.* p. 575.
[32] *Ibid.* p. 578.

political alignments are relatively 'stable'. In countries where elected governments and competitive politics are still only of recent origin there would not tend to be much likelihood of a consistent, let alone a predictable, pattern of 'contagion' or 'innovation'. This would be so for a variety of reasons,[33] not all of which may be applicable in every case. To begin with, the main parties in these countries are themselves often not very old and are therefore still in the process of crystallizing their identities and of making adjustments to accommodate important internal pressures. They have, so to speak, yet to find their own 'internal rhythm'. For this reason, when they modify their styles, policies and structure, often they may not be reacting to the activities of their competitors. Furthermore, as leaders of their respective nationalist movements, many of these parties (e.g. the Congress Party in India, the AFPFL in Burma and the Alliance in Malaya) originally integrated a wide variety of interests, some of which were held together only by their common dedication to the struggle for independence. With the withdrawal of the colonial power, the binding quality of this shared goal could no longer promote the same unity, and many groups became alienated because their own particular interests could not be absorbed to their own satisfaction in the post-independence formulation of policies. Most of the parties which initially came to power in the newly independent countries also enjoyed a degree of support which was considerably in excess of that enjoyed by successful parties in the older democracies. Many of them continue to hold a position of unchallenged dominance, and this enables them to be innovative (in forestalling their actual or potential enemies, and also in preserving unity within their own ranks) without being unduly concerned about losing their majori-

33 Lowi does not in fact maintain that there is such a pattern and indicates that there are certain exceptional circumstances under which majority parties may tend to be innovative (*ibid.* p. 581). But the circumstances outlined here are not included in his analysis.

ties.[34] The opposition parties, on the other hand, often do not have sufficient strength to regard themselves truly as 'governments in the making' and for this reason are not always innovative in the sense conveyed by Lowi. Some appear satisfied to represent narrow interests, and do not appeal to a wide enough section of the electorate in order ever to be able to form the Government. Although they may be innovative in the course of their attempts to monopolize the loyalties of a limited section of the electorate, their general political style may tend to be primarily consolidative. The PMIP in many respects belongs to this category.

There are also some opposition parties which, while not having limited horizons, are nevertheless too weak to feel that slight readjustments in policy or minor changes in organization are all that they need in order to be able to come to power. These parties often attempt to assume sensational or revolutionary postures because what they need is not a slight tilting of the balance in their favour but a dramatic change of political fortunes. They may therefore tend to be innovative[35] in an exaggerated fashion, and may resolutely repudiate everything that their opponents (particularly the ruling party) stand for. To this extent their 'innovative' behaviour may merely be a manifestation of their counter-suggestibility, since they tend to be extremely preoccupied with sharpening the contrast between themselves and their opponents. The SF, to some extent, falls within this category. It misses no opportunity to denounce the Government for virtually everything that it stands for, and is the party which advocates the widest area of change in the coun-

34 In simple form, Lowi's argument is that innovation implies an element of risk, and that majority parties are disinclined to attempt innovation because they have more to lose and less to gain than minority parties.

35 'Innovative' in the extra-organizational sense mentioned earlier, that is in identifying new problems and in suggesting radically different solutions to old problems.

try's political and economic life.[36]   The issues it has concentrated on have not on the whole induced the other
parties to reformulate or adjust their own policies.   This
has been so mainly because these issues are not specifically related to the dominant theme in Malayan politics
which has to do with promoting and safeguarding communal interests.   Although it attacks the Alliance (and,
for that matter, every other party) for perpetuating communalism in the country, the SF has not made itself
attractive by offering properly formulated alternatives to
Alliance policies.

Of the parties in Malaya, the Alliance is the one which
has been most influenced by its rivals into making periodic adjustments.   Because it attempts specifically to represent the interests of all three major communities in
the country, it has had to lean in different directions in
order to prevent its support from being undermined by
parties which are more exclusively dedicated to representing the interests of particular communities.   Faced with
increasing competition from the PMIP, the UMNO has
had to give greater emphasis to its Malay identity, while
the MCA, periodically confronted with the threat of de-
clining support, has had to find ways and means of showing that it is a dedicated and effective spokesman of the
Chinese community.   Needless to say this need to lean in
different directions at the same time has produced certain
strains within the Alliance, each partner wanting to improve its salience in the overall party image.

In its effort to regain losses, or to prevent further loss,
of support, the Alliance has resorted to copying some of
the styles and techniques of its nearest rivals.   In this
sense there has indeed been a certain amount of 'conta-

---

[36] It should, however, be pointed out that although the constitutions
of its component units advocate large-scale nationalization, the SF has
not given much prominence to this issue during elections.   But it has
been the severest critic of the role of foreign capital in the country,
and has condemned the Government for supporting Western 'neo-
colonialism'.   The party has also focussed a great deal of attention on
the various injustices which it has allegedly been made to suffer,
through having its activities circumscribed.

gion', although not always in the strictly organizational
sphere. Especially in the north and north-east, the
UMNO, faced with a growing challenge from the PMIP,
has adopted some of the latter's methods of appeal. Having come to realize the enormously important role played
by religious issues in the more traditional Malay areas
of the country, it has, particularly since 1959 when it was
beaten in Kelantan and Trengganu, decided that the
PMIP can best be defeated or forestalled not by raising
other issues as a counterbalance to religious ones but by
catering to the religious sentiments of the electorate. The
UMNO has therefore made a determined effort in these
states to show the population that it is at least as interested as its rival in the welfare of Islam and that it
has in fact done far more to protect and further the interests of that religion. This change of tactics has been
clearly reflected in the vastly increased religious content
in its propaganda. Being aware of the valuable role
played by religious élites in enhancing the PMIP's popularity, the UMNO has also made resolute attempts to
compete for the loyalty and support of these élites by
using financial and other inducements. It is also likely
that the decision (made in 1959) to set up a special *ulama*
(religious scholars) section within the party was not un-
related to the attempt to persuade religious leaders to
participate in its activities, and to offer them a counter-
attraction to the PMIP.[37] Finally, the UMNO's more
formal methods of campaigning have also undergone some
changes as a result of PMIP influence. In 1964 there
was a definite shift of emphasis from rallies to house-to-
house tours, particularly in the rural areas.[38] It was apparently felt that the PMIP's success in Kelantan and
Trengganu in 1959 had to some extent been the result of
the efficacy of its house-to-house campaign, at a time when
the Alliance had relied more heavily on rallies.

[37] Both in the UMNO and in the MCA, the process of internal re-
adjustment has to some extent been directed at preventing defections to
more communal parties.
[38] See Chapter VII.

Faced with new competition from the PAP, the MCA has also made some efforts to alter its style of politics. Although the actual electoral threat posed by the PAP was not great in 1964,[39] the MCA was fully aware that its future strength in the urban areas would depend on its ability to counteract the PAP's appeal. The PAP had entered Malayan politics as a new dynamic force, and everything would be lost if the MCA appeared, in contrast, to be a tired old party which had little life left in it and which had survived only because it had access to money and patronage, and was prepared to 'play along' with the UMNO. It was therefore not surprising when, towards the end of 1963 and in early 1964,[40] the MCA took various steps to revitalize itself. This period of reappraisal culminated in internal reforms which were aimed at giving the party a more vigorous and youthful image.[41] Its leaders showed a new keenness to dispel all suspicion that they were self-seeking or that they were remote from the people, and some of them (particularly the party's President, who was also the Finance Minister) undertook frequent constituency tours which were vaguely reminiscent of those of Lee Kuan Yew in Singapore. This sudden enthusiasm for internal reform and for a new orientation showed that the MCA, like the UMNO, considered that by moving in the direction of its nearest rival it would render it less effective. Even before the PAP threat had become a factor to be considered, there had been some agitation for a new orientation, inspired by the growing competition from the SF. This agitation was spearheaded by the MCA's Youth Section, which felt that the party had to have a

39 It will be remembered that the PAP fielded only eleven parliamentary candidates.

40 Although it was not known until the very last moment that the PAP would be contesting the elections, there had been bitter rivalry between it and the MCA from the time the Malaysia Agreement was being negotiated. Each expected that the other would be its main rival in future Malaysian politics.

41 See Chapter III.

more dynamic image, and possibly also an ideology, if it were successfully to counteract the SF's appeal.

Although it has constantly had to adapt itself to new pressures, the Alliance has not had to face the agony of having to abandon any of the essential features of its identity, or of compromising its principles. This has been so, mainly because it is essentially a pragmatic party without a strict ideological base. It has thus not been constrained by any specific policy commitment, except perhaps its commitment to inter-racial partnership, which in any case is sufficiently broad to leave ample scope for adjustment.[42] Further, having always enjoyed a dominant position in the country, it has more room in which to manoeuvre, feeling satisfied that its position cannot be undermined by any slight shift in support.

Despite the fact that its popularity depends almost entirely on religious propaganda, in which it has little to learn from the other parties, the PMIP has in one important respect followed the Alliance's lead. This concerns the way in which its campaign organization has been influenced by that of the Alliance. Although its formal election organization has not been crucial to its success, the PMIP has apparently been sufficiently impressed by the organizational superiority of the Alliance to want to have an elaborate structure of its own. It would seem that this has been inspired partly by the desire to boost the morale of its members by giving them wider scope for active participation, and partly by the wish to offset any advantage the Alliance might have if it were the only well-organized party in the rural areas.

The Malayan example would thus tend to suggest that contagious political styles and forms of party organization do not necessarily emanate from left-wing or minority parties. In the case of the Alliance there has been contagion from the left (PAP) as well as from the right (PMIP); and a minority party (the PMIP) has adopted some of the

[42] The PMIP and the PPP, for example, cannot afford to make concessions to the non-Malays and Malays respectively, without sacrificing the core of their appeal.

organizational techniques of the country's dominant party, the Alliance. A realistic conclusion might therefore be simply that styles and techniques which are believed to be politically rewarding tend to be contagious[43] and that, in societies which lack an established pattern of party politics, neither 'leftness' nor 'minority status' may solely determine the source of innovation.

Elites and Leaders

In discussing political élites, one may begin by drawing attention to a basic difference in the social framework of the Malay and non-Malay communities. Being the indigenous community, the Malays are the only ones who possess a traditional aristocracy and a hierarchy of traditional ruling élites, headed in their case by the various sultans. However, ascriptive criteria are no longer the main determinants of effective political authority, although the Tengku, for example, may owe some of his influence to the fact that he belongs to a royal family. In the case of the non-Malays, on the other hand, traditional institutions have never been of any relevance. These institutions were left behind in China and India and, consequently, there have been few (traditional) barriers to social and occupational mobility. There have been no fixed social ranks, and no hierarchy of traditional ruling élites.

Although traditional institutions were formally sustained through a policy of indirect rule during the colonial period, the rulers and the Malay aristocracy had lost their effective authority long before the nationalist movement got into full motion. For this reason, the rise of mass parties was not accompanied by any conflict between the rulers (and the traditional élites generally) and the new group of political leaders. The former had already accepted their purely 'constitutional' status, and therefore did not regard the rise of popular leaders as a threat to

[43] Provided, of course, that the party which chooses to adopt the techniques of its rivals does not thereby have to abandon the essential features of its identity or sacrifice its basic policies.

their own power. They were not in competition with the politicians, and were not concerned as long as their existing prerogatives were not threatened. The latter saw no advantage in attacking those trappings of traditional authority which had survived, because these did not in any way hamper their own pursuits.

It would, however, be misleading to assume that the political and traditional élites have become mutually exclusive groups. Members of the aristocracy have for a long time been successful in finding a new prestige and influence through recruitment into the bureaucracy. From the bureaucracy a few of them have gone into public life and have become prominent members of the new political élite. The best examples of this are the Tengku and Tun Razak, who are Prime Minister and Deputy Prime Minister, respectively.[44]

The politicians who rose to prominence during the pre-independence period are still, by and large, the main leaders of the Malay community. The national leadership of the UMNO, for example, has broadly remained within the hands of this group. Almost all of them are English-educated, and were originally either professional men or had been members of the bureaucracy. At the time of independence, any study of Malay political élites would have concentrated heavily on this group. Since then however, as active participation in politics has become more widespread, the circle of political élites has grown larger and different groups of power-aspirants have emerged. Two such groups may be discerned at first sight. The first, and so far the more menacing to the old leaders, is the group of politicians (for example, those in

[44] Before embarking on a full-time political career the Tengku, who belongs to the Kedah royal family, was a District Officer in Kedah and later Deputy Public Prosecutor in the Federal Legal Department. Tun Razak is a member of the traditional aristocracy in Pahang. In 1950 he became a Major Chief of Pahang, inheriting from his father the title of Orang Kaya Indera Shahbandar. Before going into full-time politics he was successively a member of the Malayan Civil Service attached to the Pahang State Secretariat, the State Secretary of Pahang, and the Acting Mentri Besar of Pahang.

the PMIP) whose orientation is almost exclusively communal and who have sought to popularize a new basis of legitimacy for Malay political leadership. The present 'establishment' has so far legitimized its position by emphasizing its dual function of fighting for Malay interests and at the same time avoiding communal conflict by working in partnership with the other communities. The emergent group of communalists, on the other hand, by operating solely as champions of the Malay community and by emphasizing the conflict between that community and the others, seeks legitimacy on grounds which are less complicated and which are calculated to evoke a more immediate emotional response. Although referred to as 'emergent', this group is not essentially made up of individuals who have only recently entered the political arena. Many of its leaders (for example, Dr. Burhanuddin, the President of the PMIP, and Inche Mohammad Asri, the PMIP Mentri Besar of Kelantan) have been actively involved in politics since the early post-War years, and have for a long time been associated with the same cause. Their main vehicle has been the PMIP, with its appeal based on religion and special Malay rights. The significant gains made by the PMIP in 1959 showed the seriousness of the threat posed by this group (the majority of whom are educated only in Malay and Arabic, and speak little or no English) to the 'accommodationist' UMNO leaders. The UMNO, without having any direct links with the traditional Malay élite, has probably benefited from the loose alignment between its leadership and that élite. Where the PMIP has undermined the advantages conferred by this alignment, it has done so only by harnessing another traditional force, Islamic 'ideology'.

Even *within* the UMNO, a new group of popular leaders is coming into prominence. Those belonging to this group have not as yet made any serious attempt to oust the old leadership, although their influence has affected the formulation of national policies. Many of them enjoy considerable power at the state and lower levels. Their main characteristic is that they are more exclusively dedicated than the others to promoting Malay interests, and as such they have a certain amount in common with their rivals in the PMIP. Unlike their rivals, however, they have not chosen to emphasize religion and have preferred to concentrate on language and special Malay rights. Many of them are Malay-educated, and view their responsibility as being primarily to the Malay electorate. The party's Youth Section, which has always shown a certain amount of impatience at the accommodationist outlook of the national leaders, has often been used by this group to enhance its strength within the party. Realizing the growing popularity of this group and the emotional appeal of the stand taken by it, some of the national leaders have shown a willingness to identify themselves, at least partially, with the trend it represents.

It would therefore appear that there has been a gradual diversification of the sources from which Malay political élites are recruited. Those with an English education and a background in the Government bureaucracy or the professions no longer enjoy the same pre-eminence as before independence, and their influence is being challenged by men who are closer to the grass roots and who are less compromising in promoting Malay interests. This trend may well reflect changing conceptions of legitimacy. During the colonial period, the main role of political leaders was the attainment of independence. It was therefore natural that support should be given to those who could make the best impression on the colonial government. The first group of leaders, because of their education and occupational background, were clearly the best suited for this role. With the attainment of independence, however, there was no further need to have leaders who could effectively negotiate with the colonial power. The main task was now to protect and further the interests of the Malay community, so that its political supremacy could firmly be established. Although the legitimacy of the original leaders was not confined to their role as spokesmen of the nationalist movement (in that they also championed communal interests), this consideration was bound to give added prominence to those who most emphasized their Malay identity and who were more exclusive in wanting to promote Malay interests.

Similar changes have also taken place within the non-Malay communities, for very much the same reasons. But in their case (for reasons that will soon be explained) even the emerging political élites are recruited primarily from the ranks of the English-educated. In discussing non-Malay political leadership it may be worth recalling that the MCA, the largest non-Malay party, began as a welfare organization. In the early years it was therefore inevitable that wealth and social standing should have been the most important criteria in the selection of leaders, since fund-raising was one of the organization's main preoccupations. Partly because of this background, businessmen have continued to play a prominent role in the MCA's activities, and there are still close ties between the party and the Chinese guilds and chambers of commerce. However, especially since independence, there has been a growing body of opinion which has sought to replace the old leaders with new and more dynamic ones, feeling that the criteria which enabled the former to come to power are irrelevant if not damaging to the party's present interests. There have been periodic crises, resulting in the replacement of many of the older leaders by men less obviously associated with wealth and social status but who can claim to be of greater value to the party by being 'closer to the people'. But the older leaders have not all been replaced, and there are some within the party (especially in the Youth Section) who feel that their influence is still too great and that their presence has served to limit the MCA's popular appeal.

The post-independence period has also seen the rise of new leaders who have set out more specifically to represent and promote non-Malay communal interests. They are critical of the MCA's accommodationist policy within the Alliance, and resent the Government's pro-Malay bias. Although the chief spokesmen of this group are found among the leaders of the PPP, UDP and PAP, there are also some sections within the MCA which have been advocating a 'tougher' line in their party's dealings with the UMNO, with a view to defending more vigorously the political and cultural interests of the Chinese.

It should, nevertheless, be noted that the emerging political élites within the non-Malay communities do not include within their ranks a group comparable to the Malay-educated leaders who have been coming into prominence. Non-Malay leaders continue to be recruited from among the English-educated (or at least the English-speaking), although the ability to speak fluent Chinese is an undoubted asset when appealing to Chinese voters. The main explanation for this would lie in the fact that Malay and English are the only official languages,[45] but some regard may also be given to the 'defensive' character of non-Malay communal politics. In promoting their communal interests the non-Malays are not on the whole attempting to establish the superior claims of their own communities. They do not regard the attainment of a dominant status for their own languages and cultures as one of the goals of Malayan nationalism, and do not feel that their languages have any special claims to constitute the 'base' for cultural unification or for the promotion of a single national identity. Their main concern is that they should not be compelled to abandon their own languages in favour of Malay. Thus, even among intra-party élites (who are not affected by any language requirements) there has been no noticeable increase in the proportion of those educated only in Chinese or Tamil.

45 This means that any non-Malay who gets into Parliament or a State Legislative Assembly must be able to speak in one of these two languages. Since only a very small number of non-Malays are Malay-educated or are fluent in Malay, the English-educated have tended to have a virtual monopoly of non-Malay political leadership. (English will enjoy an official status at least until 1967.)

Almost all the national leaders of the Labour Party, the UDP, the PPP and the PAP are primarily English-educated. Even in the case of the MCA, the only *specifically* Chinese party in the country, the proportion of national leaders whose educational background is basically Chinese has not increased meaningfully over the years. Table XXXIV shows the percentage distribution of English-educated, Chinese-educated, and English-and-Chinese-educated members in the MCA's Central Working Committee (CWC) for the period 1956-65. In reading the Table it will have to be borne in mind that those belonging to the last category (that is, the English-and-Chinese-educated) would not, as a rule, have had much formal education in Chinese. Further, even those described as 'Chinese-educated' are often reasonably proficient in English.

TABLE XXXIV

EDUCATIONAL BACKGROUND OF MEMBERS OF THE MCA
CENTRAL WORKING COMMITTEE

	TOTAL MEMBERSHIP OF THE CWC	ENGLISH-EDUCATED (%)	CHINESE-EDUCATED (%)	ENGLISH- AND CHINESE EDUCATED (%)
1956-7	22	36.4	22.7	40.9
1958-9	22	27.2	13.6	59.2
1959-61*	18	27.8	11.1	61.1
1961-3*	31	45.2	9.6	45.2
1963-5	31	25.8	25.8	48.4

* The decline in the strength of the 'Chinese-educated' group between 1959 and 1963 might conceivably have been caused by the victory of the accommodationist group during the 1959 party crisis.

The Role of Pressure Groups

Although an established pattern of pressure group activity is yet to emerge in Malaya, there are certain important groups which have identified themselves with specific political goals. In most cases it is not too difficult to ascertain the political alignments of these groups, but there are few *expressed* links between them and political parties.

Compared to its counterpart in Singapore, the Malayan

trade union movement is less well organized and exerts very little political influence. There had been a considerable amount of political activity among the unions soon after the war; but this was suddenly changed following the declaration of the Emergency in 1948, when the Government took firm steps to circumscribe union activities on the grounds that the trade union movement had become heavily infiltrated by the communists. Although many of the restrictions then imposed have since been removed, resulting in the revival of some trade union activity, the experience of the immediate post-war years must have contributed to the continuing reluctance on the part of most unions openly to express any political commitments. The wider implications of this need not be discussed at any length here. It may, however, be worth pointing out that there are some people who feel that by taking an active interest in politics the trade union movement might be able to foster communally neutral allegiances among the working classes, and thereby make a positive contribution towards the eradication of communal conflict. Theoretically, this is quite possible. But it might be more realistic to assume that, at least for the present, even an otherwise influential trade union movement will have little success in moulding the attitudes of the working classes on major communal issues, because communal interests clearly override economic interests. It is even possible that any attempt by the trade union movement to express its views on communal issues might only result in conflict among its members or at least give rise to the emergence of different communal wings within the movement, each with a different party affiliation.

Because of its limited influence in politics, the labour movement has not on the whole provided a channel for the recruitment of new political leaders. This is in sharp contrast to the situation in Singapore, where many of the political battles are fought as much within the unions as in the more general political arena and where many of the leading figures in the PAP and the Barisan Sosialis acquired their political influence through participation in union activity. At no time has there been more than one trade union leader in the Malayan Parliament or, since 1963, from a Malayan constituency in the Malaysian Parliament. V. David of the SF, a well-known trade union figure who had been returned in Bungsar (Selangor), was defeated in his constituency in 1964 by the prominent trade union leader from Singapore, Devan Nair, who contested on a PAP ticket.

The compact and highly urbanized character of Singapore might partly account for the greater prominence of the trade union movement in that state. Also, industrial and salaried workers form a much higher percentage of the population there than in Malaya. Because Singapore is small, it is much easier for the trade union movement to make its influence felt throughout the island. The fact that the island had developed as a separate political entity must also have been of some relevance, because this meant that there were no effective counterweights to urban pressure groups, of which the trade union movement has been the most prominent. In Malaya, on the other hand, the main electoral strength lies in the rural areas and even a strong trade union movement can therefore have only a limited political influence. However active the unions might be during elections, their influence will not be felt in the majority of constituencies.[46]

A certain amount of pressure group activity is carried on by various interest associations which exist within each community. The best examples of this in the case of the

[46] At the end of 1964 Malaya, with a population of about 7.81 million, had 278 registered unions with a total membership of 322,544. Singapore, with a population of only 1.82 million, had 106 unions with a total membership of 157,050. In terms of its potential influence in politics, a significant feature of the trade union movement in Malaya is that about 40 per cent. of its total membership belongs to the National Union of Plantation Workers, whose members live in the various plantations which are scattered throughout the country and who therefore cannot easily be mobilized for political action, particularly as party workers during elections.

Chinese community would be the guilds, chambers of commerce and educational organizations (for example, the Chinese Schools Management Committees and the United Chinese School Teachers Association). Especially during periods of major constitutional change (for example, in 1947, when the Federation of Malaya Agreement was being drawn up, and in 1957, when the Constitution of the independent Federation of Malaya was being decided) the guilds and chambers of commerce have made vigorous attempts to secure favourable treatment for the Chinese, and to this end have exerted a great deal of pressure either on the Government as such or on the representatives of their community in the Government (in 1957, the MCA). The educational organizations have, understandably, confined themselves to matters concerned with the Government's language and education policy. A good example of their role as a pressure group was seen in 1959, when they launched a public protest against the policies of the Government which were allegedly inimical to the interests of Chinese education. This protest, coming only a few months before the 1959 Parliamentary Election, helped to precipitate a serious conflict between the Government and influential groups within the Chinese community, and contributed to severe dissension within the MCA which culminated in the resignation of some prominent leaders from that party.

Within the Malay community, teachers and religious leaders constitute the groups which exert the greatest political influence. This is not surprising, since between them they represent the areas of Malay culture (language and religion) which have the greatest political significance. Their grievances and demands are readily recognized as being symbolic of those of the Malay community as a whole, and the UMNO (and hence the Alliance) cannot afford to ignore them for fear of making it easier for the PMIP to pose as the true champion of Malay interests. Of the two groups, the teachers are by far the better organized, formally. They have always been an important pressure group within the UMNO, but, although the party now enjoys good support from them, relations between the two have not always been harmonious. In 1958, for example, several members of the Malay School Teachers Association (which was openly pro-UMNO) who had been members of the party resigned from it in protest against the alleged insincerity of the Government in promoting the interests of Malay education. Although many of them have since abandoned their opposition and become once again sympathetic to the UMNO, this rift must have had some influence in enhancing the PMIP's popularity during the 1959 elections.

From the foregoing, if one were to generalize about pressure group activity in the politics of Malaya, an obvious comment would be that the bulk of this activity is closely interwoven with the more general attempts by each community to promote its interests.

The Results and the Future
If asked to account for the result of the election, the man in the street, or the man in the *kampong*, in Malaya would almost certainly answer with the single word, 'confrontation'. By the time of the election the threat from confrontation was serious enough to provide a patriotic rallying-point to the Government; it was not serious enough to have led to disillusion or defeatism.[47] opposition parties, such as the SF and the PMIP, which seemed to be lukewarm in their condemnation of Indonesian aggression, could not effectively repel the Alliance charge that they were unpatriotic. The Alliance, in effect, succeeded in dictating what the main election issue should be — whether the parties were pro- or anti-Indonesia. Some opposition parties, notably the SF, were mesmerized by this issue and unable to shake them-

[47] There was no substantial movement of the vote in the parliamentary by-elections held soon after April 1964. In Bachok (June 1964), the Alliance vote was up 2.5 per cent. and the PMIP vote was down by the same percentage. In Seberang Selatan (November 1964) the Alliance vote went down by about 4.6 per cent. and the Socialist Front rose by about 7.3 per cent.

selves free of it. On the other hand, parties which advocated resistance to Indonesia, such as the PAP, had to explain why, if defence of Malaysia was the prime issue, they were fighting the Alliance instead of supporting it. Was it not apparent that the persons who could be best trusted with Malaysia's defence were exactly those Alliance politicians who alone in Malaya had had experience of government and international negotiations? Basically, this was the PAP's difficulty. The PAP was indeed 'too subtle'[48] in claiming to support UMNO while obviously attacking the MCA. It is difficult to believe that the PAP could really have thought that the Tengku, known to be loyal to his friends even to excess, would ever have agreed to 'desert' the MCA. Their whole argument collapsed as soon as the Tengku gave forthright support to the MCA. If the Tengku was the man to be trusted and followed in resisting Indonesia, it was clearly up to him, not the PAP, to say who his political allies should be. From another point of view, however, PAP strategy was the reverse of subtle. In late 1963 quite a number of observers, including some MCA officials, expressed the opinion privately that, if the PAP fought the election in Malaya, it would make serious inroads on the Chinese vote. But such expectations were based on the assumption that the PAP, according to its own claims a 'calculating' party, would conduct the 'invasion' operation rationally. Instead, it gave itself only just over seven weeks to set up an organization in Malaya and fight the election campaign there. Some of its candidates and helpers aroused hostility because they were not local men, but had been 'imported' from Singapore. The PAP also gave the impression of half-heartedness by running only eleven candidates. If the PAP intervention was only a 'token intervention', why should the party be surprised that the electors should give it only 'token support'? Its candidates' difficulties are illustrated in Chapter IX (b), on the Batu constituency

48 Mr. Lee Kuan Yew, *Straits Times*, 27 April 1964.

elections, where there was no time for propaganda in depth; in effect all the PAP was able to do was to announce its presence and *ask* the electors to vote for it without having any opportunity to tell them at any length *why* they should vote for it. One might even argue that the most puzzling question about the PAP intervention is not why it did so badly, but why it did well enough to win one seat, Bungsar.[49]

It would also appear that the PAP erred in carrying too far its attacks on the MCA. These attacks had commenced some months before the election, and the point had already been made that the MCA was effete and corrupt and that the Alliance would have a much brighter future if the UMNO accepted the PAP as its chief non-Malay partner. The UMNO, perhaps half-convinced of the validity of this argument, had all along refrained from taking any firm stand on the PAP-MCA conflict, and this had had a damaging effect not only on the MCA's own morale but also on its public image. Had the PAP stopped, or even moderated, its criticisms of the MCA after the campaign had officially begun, it is conceivable that the UMNO might have chosen to continue watching from the sidelines. But, if anything, these criticisms were intensified after the commencement of the campaign, and the UMNO (no doubt under pressure from the MCA) felt compelled to come publicly to the defence of its partner. Even at this point the PAP could have decided to alter its tactics, but decided not to. The more it attacked the MCA the more firmly the UMNO supported its ally, and soon a new battle was being waged between the UMNO and the PAP. The UMNO's decision to remove all confusion about where its sympathies lay had two important consequences. First, it provided a much-

[49] Partial explanations are: a personal vote for the PAP candidate, Mr. Devan Nair, a well-known trade union figure in Singapore and Malaya; a weak, 'unwesternized' MCA candidate who failed to attract the middle-class 'Mini-minor' vote; rain about 5 p.m. on polling day which prevented a high working-class SF vote, but did not have the same effect on middle-class electors who tended to vote earlier.

needed fillip to MCA morale, and helped that party to become far more disciplined and energetic than had earlier been thought possible. Second, it must also have made it clear to the Chinese voters that voting for *the Government* meant voting for the MCA. Indonesian 'confrontation' had given a special reason for supporting the Government. It was no longer possible for anyone to believe that he could do this by voting for the PAP.

Confrontation, then, was indeed broadly the explanation for the 7 per cent. increase in the Alliance proportion of the vote since the last parliamentary election. However, apart from any increase or decrease in the Alliance vote, there was never really any doubt that the Alliance would win; it would almost certainly have won, although not as easily, even without confrontation. Its position as a non-authoritarian, dominant party has not so far been seriously challenged.[50] It is only a slight exaggeration to say that, at least on the parliamentary scene, the opposition consists of 'relatively small left-wing or traditionalist and particularist movements'.[51] In 1964 only the SF and the PMIP put up candidates in more than half the parliamentary seats, sixty-three and fifty-three respectively. But many of these candidates were fighting hopeless seats. Only the Front has any serious claim to approximate to a 'nation-wide' rival to the Alliance, and even it has no footing on the north-east coast. Under such circumstances the only possibility of victory for the opposition parties is through a coalition, and attempts to form one were as unsuccessful in 1964 as they were in 1959.

[50] Comparison with the Congress Party in India is relevant. As far back as 1952 Asoka Mehta wrote that some members of the Congress Party thought that the party was a transitory party and doomed to disappear: *The Political Mind of India.* Bombay, 1952, pp. 61-2. But in 1962 a commentator wrote, '...barring a national schism in the Congress, it is hard to see how the opposition could reduce Congress to a minority at the central level for another ten or fifteen years'. Myron Weiner, 'India's Third General Elections', *Asian Survey*, Vol. II, No. 3, 1962, p. 6.

[51] See footnote 20 of this Chapter.

It does not follow, however, that the elections were not keenly fought, or that in any sense they constituted only a sham battle. Several of the opposition parties had reason to hope that they might capture control of the legislature of at least one of the states,[52] and the UDP and PAP would have been well satisfied if they had won, say, half-a-dozen seats each at their first venture into a federal election.

It is a familiar theme of political commentators that eventually politics in Malaya (and presumably Malaysia) will become 'polarised'. Usually the two 'poles' are identified as 'class' poles. This type of prediction probably includes an element of wishful thinking. British observers foresee a comforting approach to the British two-party system. Extreme left-wingers visualize a line-up in which the class-struggle can most suitably be staged. Opponents of racial politics see class cleavages as less harmful to the health of the body politic than ethnic cleavages, because they are less deep and less permanent. Certainly the decline in the PMIP vote, by about 7 per cent., from 1959 to 1964, provides evidence that such a trend exists. As the north-east coast of Malaya, the PMIP stronghold, is opened up to outside influences through improved roads and bridges and better education,[53] this trend may well continue. It is also true that the dispute inside the MCA in 1959 over Chinese education, which led to Chinese Independents splitting the vote at the 1959 election, has now subsided. Apparently

[52] For example, the PMIP in Trengganu, Perlis and Kedah (while retaining control of Kelantan); the SF in Penang, and possibly also Malacca and Selangor; the PPP (in alliance with the UDP) in Perak.

[53] Alliance officials in Kelantan claim (partly on the basis of a post-election survey by the Information Department) that PMIP support is highest among women and old people, groups which are easily influenced by religious leaders. If this is correct, the spread of education, both formal and informal, and changes in the composition of the electorate, through deaths and through young persons reaching voting age, should benefit the Alliance in the long run.

many of the votes lost by the Alliance then were regained in 1964.[54]

However, without going too deeply into the course of Malaysian politics since the elections were held in April 1964, this is not quite the whole story. The dispute between the PAP and the MCA before the federal election, later on became largely a dispute between the PAP and UMNO. It became entangled with quarrels between the Federal Government and the Singapore State Government, and was exacerbated by racial riots in Singapore in the second half of 1964. The PAP proceeded to set up branches in the larger towns in Malaya. Press statements and counter statements by Federation and Singapore State Ministers and their political secretaries were supplemented by pro-Alliance propaganda in *Utusan Melayu* and by pro-PAP propaganda on Singapore radio and television. Eventually the PAP took the line that it wanted a 'Malaysian Malaysia',[55] in which the rights of all ethnic groups were safeguarded, while some of the right-wing UMNO 'ultras' wanted a Malay Malaysia. The UMNO countered with denunciations of Mr. Lee Kuan Yew for having raised such sensitive communal questions in public statements and discussions.

In 1965 there was a new development; the PAP and four other parties, the UDP, PPP,[56] SUPP and Party MACHINDA[57] formed a Solidarity Convention. Two significant points stand out about the formation of the

[54] See Chapter XII.

[55] The concept of a Malaysian Malaysia is defined in the Declaration by the Convenors of the Malaysian Solidarity Convention, para. 6, signed 9 July 1965. For further explanations of the concept, see *Towards a Malaysian Malaysia*. Singapore, 1965; *Are there Enough Malaysians to save Malaysia?* Singapore, 1965; and *The Battle for a Malaysian Malaysia*. Singapore, 1965, all by Lee Kuan Yew.

[56] For about a year previously there had been persistent rumours that PPP branches would disband and would be replaced by the PAP, which would 'move into' Perak.

[57] SUPP and MACHINDA, two Sarawak parties, are referred to in Chapter X, above. Extremists in the SUPP objected to the moderate leadership joining the Convention, so SUPP membership was originally provisional.

Convention. All the member parties (with the exception of MACHINDA which is a new party), were in effect 'non-Malay communal' parties, whose supporters were largely Chinese. Also, the most important 'non-Malay communal' party in Malaya, the SF, was not a member of the Convention.

The resulting situation was paradoxical. The PAP claimed to be in spirit a non-communal party. But its political base is in Singapore where three-quarters of the population is Chinese. UMNO's rejection of PAP over-tures, the racial riots in Singapore and the disputes between the Singapore Government and Federal Government had helped to make UMNO the PAP's deadly enemy.[58] Consequently, when the PAP organized the Opposition Convention, the slogan, 'a Malaysian Malaysia' could be directed only against the UMNO leadership in Malaya. And in banding together to support a Malaysian Malaysia, four of the five parties concerned, the exception being MACHINDA, in effect identified themselves as non-Malay communal parties. The future of the Convention was placed in doubt when Singapore separated from Malaysia in August 1965. But, in the event,

[58] Some of these disputes related to the PAP's sources of strength in its Singapore base. When Malaysia was formed in 1963 Singapore was given much more extensive powers than the other state governments, and it used these to set up, even inside the Federation of Malaysia, something approaching an *imperium in imperio*. After April 1964 some of the main sources of the Singapore Government's (and the PAP's) power were under attack. The Federal Government proposed a reduction in the percentage of the tax revenues collected in Singapore which the Singapore State Government was allowed to retain, thus threatening Singapore's considerable degree of financial autonomy. Also, by the *Malaysia Agreement* (Annex K), while the Federal Government was given general control over policy as regards radio and television in Singapore, the Singapore Government retained control over day-to-day operation and used the media extensively to publicize its (and the PAP's) point of view. On the other hand, the Federal Government put forward the idea that there should only be 'one voice' for these media (Inche Senu, *Straits Times*, 28 May 1965). The tension aroused by these, and other, controversies might have seriously impaired Malaysia's viability. However, in August 1965 the solution was adopted that Singapore should be separated from Malaysia.

it was decided that it would continue its activities, the
original PAP being replaced by a 'PAP Malaya' which
would have no organizational links with the party in
Singapore.[59] However, without the PAP leaders from
Singapore, it is possible that the Convention will lose
much of its original drive.

It appears that the next federal election in Malaya
might be fought by the following major parties or groups
of parties: the Alliance; the Malay-communal PMIP;
those components of the new Convention which will
operate in Malaya; and the SF. The last two of the
four will be competing for non-Malay votes with the
MCA and the MIC.

What will be the racial composition of the electorate
in Malaya, to which these, and possibly other, parties
will appeal at future parliamentary elections? Between
1959 and 1964 the proportion of Malays fell by about
2 per cent. and the proportion of Chinese rose by about
2 per cent., while the proportion of 'Indians' was roughly
constant. In the long run, say a generation or so, when,
to put the matter broadly, nearly all residents will have
become citizens and will be entitled to vote, the racial
composition of the electorate in Malaya will approximate
closely to the racial composition of the population *which
is of voting age*.[60] The proportion of Malays in the
electorate would then be about 50 per cent. However,

59 After Singapore's separation, PAP Malaya declared itself a separate
party in order to continue having a legal existence in Malaya. But this
move failed to satisfy the Registrar of Societies, who argued that
such action was not possible under the original registration. (*Straits
Times*, 10 September 1965.) An application was then made for registration as a new party, to be called the Democratic Action Party, (DAP),
and this succeeded in 1966.

60 This proviso is necessary, because the age-distribution of the
various ethnic groups may be different. The racial composition of the
whole population of Malaya at the last (1957) census was approximately
49.8 per cent. Malay, 37.2 per cent. Chinese and 13.1 per cent. Indians
and others. In Chapter XII, it was said that the Chinese constituted about 38 per cent. of the electorate in 1964. Also, we know
that there are some Chinese who are not qualified to vote. So, if in
1964 all Chinese *had* been qualified to vote the age-distribution of

any threat to Malay political dominance from such a change will probably be more than counterbalanced by alterations to constituency boundaries in Malaya. Before the next general elections the Election Commission must propose boundary changes on which Parliament (in effect, the Government) will have the final say. In drawing up the new boundaries, the 'weightage' in favour of rural areas, which already existed in 1964, is likely to be greater than before. Almost certainly any 'loss' in the proportion of Malay votes will be more than compensated for by the extra weightage given to rural, predominantly Malay, areas.

Consequently, as far as Malaya is concerned, the non-Malay communal parties will not have a bigger share of the electoral 'cake' to compete for. The number of seats with a majority of non-Malay electors may actually fall. In striving to win these, the UDP, PPP and the DAP will be in competition, not only with the Socialist Front, but also with the MCA. The MCA lacks an ideology, but it is well-financed and in many areas well-organized. In recent years it has won extra support in local council elections in the former 'new villages'. And in some states, such as Johore, the MCA has built up a following, and also votes, by providing 'services', for example, by helping electors with personal problems or in dealings with the Government.

The preceding discussion has dealt with trends in Malaya at some length, because the Malayan 1964 elections form the principal subject of this book. But estimates of the outcome of future elections for the Federal Parliament must take into account not only the seats for Malaya (at present 104) but also those for Sabah (16) and Sarawak (24). If the new Convention continues to exist, SUPP and MACHINDA in combination could win most of the Chinese votes and a proportion of the

_____

Chinese in Malaya must have been such that a higher proportion of them than of the population as a whole was aged twenty-one years or over.

indigenous non-Malay votes, respectively, in Sarawak. The Convention did not include any Sabah party. However, the younger Chinese electors there are a potential source of support and so, potentially, are some members of UPKO if they feel that they are being pushed too hard by the Federal Government (and the USNO) on the issue of states' rights.[61]

Yet the Alliance position continues to be strong. In Malaya the MCA is still intact, perhaps even strengthened by having braced itself to meet the PAP challenge. If put on the defensive by heavy anti-Malay communal attacks, in the last resort UMNO could count on PMIP support, although perhaps at a price. Regardless of party realignments in Sarawak and Sabah, the Malaysian Alliance can count on the loyalty of some of the Native parties, particularly Malay- or Muslim-dominated parties, to UMNO. It is sad, but probably true, that there is little immediate prospect that Malaysia will have an effective two-party system, organized on non-racial lines. If the Alliance retains its multi-racial appeal, it will constitute a dominant non-authoritarian party. If it loses that appeal, a two-party system may result, but it would most likely have a markedly racial basis.

[61] Some of Mr. Lee Kuan Yew's calculation on possible 'racial' and 'non-racial' majorities in the Malaysian Federal Parliament are reproduced in *Are There Enough Malaysians to save Malaysia?*, op. cit. pp. 7-8 and 12-13. Since then, of course, the situation has been altered by the removal of Singapore from Malaysia.

APPENDIX I

1964 STATE AND PARLIAMENTARY GENERAL ELECTIONS
SEATS WON BY POLITICAL PARTIES AND INDEPENDENT CANDIDATES

SEATS WON

State	Alliance S.	Alliance P.	PMIP S.	PMIP P.	SF S.	SF P.	PPP S.	PPP P.	UDP S.	UDP P.	PAP S.	PAP P.	PN S.	PN P.	(MP) S.	(MP) P.	IND S.	IND P.
Perlis	11 (12)	2 (2)	1 (–)	– (–)	– (–)	– (–)	– (–)	– (–)	–	–	–	–	(–)	(–)	(–)	(–)	(–)	(–)
Kedah	24 (24)	12 (12)	– (–)	– (–)	– (–)	– (–)	– (–)	– (–)	–	–	–	–	(–)	(–)	(–)	(–)	(–)	(–)
Kelantan	9 (2)	2 (1)	21 (28)	8 (9)	– (–)	– (–)	– (–)	– (–)	–	–	–	–	(–)	(–)	(–)	(–)	(–)	(–)
Trengganu	21 (7)	5 (1*)	3 (13)	1 (4)	– (–)	– (–)	– (–)	– (–)	–	–	–	–	(4)	(1)	(–)	(–)	(–)	(–)
Penang	18 (17*)	6 (5)	– (–)	– (–)	1 (7)	1 (3)	– (–)	– (–)	4	1	–	–	(–)	(–)	(–)	(–)	(1)	(1)
Perak	35 (31)	18 (15)	– (1)	– (–)	– (–)	– (–)	5 (8)	2 (4)	–	–	–	–	(–)	(–)	(–)	(–)	(1)	(–)
Pahang	24* (23*)	6 (6)	– (–)	– (–)	– (–)	– (–)	– (–)	– (–)	–	–	–	–	(–)	(–)	(–)	(–)	(1)	(–)
Selangor	24 (23*)	12 (9)	– (–)	– (–)	4 (3)	1 (5)	– (–)	– (–)	–	–	–	1	(–)	(–)	(–)	(–)	(–)	(–)
N. Sembilan	24 (20)	6 (4*)	– (–)	– (–)	1 (3)	– (–)	– (–)	– (–)	–	–	–	–	(–)	(–)	(–)	(–)	(1)	(–)
Malacca	18 (20)	4 (3)	– (–)	– (–)	2 (–)	– (–)	– (–)	– (–)	–	–	–	–	(–)	(–)	(–)	(1)	(1)	(2)
Johore	32* (28*)	16* (16*)	– (–)	– (–)	– (3)	– (–)	– (–)	– (–)	–	–	–	–	(–)	(–)	(–)	(–)	(–)	(–)
Total	**240 (207)**	**89 (74)**	**25 (42)**	**9 (13)**	**8 (16)**	**2 (8)**	**5 (8)**	**2 (4)**	**4**	**1**	**–**	**1**	**(4)**	**(1)**	**(–)**	**(1)**	**(5)**	**(3)**

S = State Elections. P = Parliamentary Elections. * Includes uncontested constituencies.

For purposes of comparison, 1959 General Election figures are given in brackets. 1959 figures are not given in respect of the UDP and the PAP as they did not contest the 1959 General Elections. Conversely, 1959 and not 1964 figures are given in respect of the Malayan Party as this party did not contest the 1964 General Elections.

Malaysia, The Election Commission. *Report on the Parliamentary (Dewan Ra'ayat) and State Legislative Assembly General Elections, 1964 of the States of Malaya.* Kuala Lumpur, 1965, p. 27.

1964 STATE AND PARLIAMENTARY GENERAL ELECTIONS
VOTES CAST FOR POLITICAL PARTIES AND INDEPENDENT CANDIDATES. TOTAL VALID VOTES, NUMBERS OF REJECTED VOTES AND PERCENTAGE OF POLLS

State		Alliance	PMIP	SF	PPP	UDP	PAP	PN	(MP)	IND.	TOTAL VALID VOTES	REJECTED VOTES	TOTAL VOTED	TOTAL ELECTORATE IN CONTESTED CONSTITUENCIES	PERCENTAGE POLLED
Perlis	S	21,905 (19,521)	13,354 (9,697)	547 (393)	—— (——)	——	——	—— (——)	(——)	164 (978)	35,970 (30,589)	2,044 (642)	38,014 (31,231)	46,491 (38,355)	81.8 (81.4)
	P	23,007 (17,653)	13,369 (11,950)	—— (——)	—— (——)	——	——	—— (——)	(——)	—— (——)	36,376 (29,603)	1,564 (223)	37,940 (29,826)	46,491 (38,355)	81.6 (77.8)
Kedah	S	164,817 (138,560)	61,294 (45,979)	12,088 (6,046)	—— (——)	4,256	——	—— (3,666)	(——)	1,386 (512)	243,841 (194,763)	14,255 (8,062)	258,096 (202,825)	336,858 (268,025)	76.6 (75.7)
	P	168,995 (127,965)	61,861 (52,235)	11,794 (14,142)	—— (——)	3,849	——	—— (——)	(——)	—— (1,605)	246,499 (195,947)	10,973 (2,481)	257,472 (198,428)	336,858 (268,115)	76.4 (74.0)
Kelantan	S	89,379 (48,509)	118,498 (114,858)	—— (4,071)	—— (——)	——	——	—— (9,371)	(——)	—— (3,256)	207,877 (180,065)	9,852 (3,547)	217,729 (183,612)	271,731 (240,552)	80.1 (76.3)
	P	89,710 (53,382)	118,770 (116,087)	414 (——)	—— (——)	——	——	—— (292)	(——)	—— (——)	208,894 (169,761)	8,875 (1,446)	217,769 (171,207)	271,731 (240,552)	80.1 (71.2)
Trengganu	S	58,951 (27,806)	34,922 (29,125)	3,965 (6,404)	—— (——)	——	——	8,040 (12,846)	(——)	828 (2,793)	106,706 (78,974)	5,717 (2,984)	112,423 (81,958)	145,217 (114,904)	77.4 (71.3)
	P	60,792 (25,237)	34,522 (32,124)	4,919 (595)	—— (——)	——	——	7,319 (7,986)	(——)	—— (1,497)	107,552 (67,439)	4,786 (898)	112,338 (68,337)	145,217 (97,164)	77.4 (70.3)
Penang	S	96,814 (67,918)	4,305 (10,772)	65,911 (39,069)	670 (7,612)	35,971	1,059	—— (1,124)	(——)	453 (6,518)	105,183 (133,013)	6,437 (2,596)	211,620 (135,609)	253,455 (182,515)	83.5 (74.3)
	P	97,204 (60,249)	5,527 (14,829)	64,986 (52,237)	—— (3,899)	37,151	778	—— (——)	(——)	—— (5,569)	205,646 (136,783)	5,902 (1,358)	211,548 (138,141)	253,455 (188,668)	83.5 (73.2)
Perak	S	216,688 (165,792)	45,107 (46,280)	29,045 (11,731)	82,273 (73,792)	18,321	——	—— (——)	(——)	5,218 (5,753)	396,652 (303,348)	20,299 (6,918)	416,951 (310,266)	524,487 (450,094)	79.5 (68.9)
	P	222,141 (154,056)	41,941 (47,757)	32,339 (8,862)	66,330 (83,509)	26,094	——	—— (——)	(——)	10,931 (16,296)	399,776 (310,480)	17,344 (3,881)	417,120 (314,361)	524,487 (449,969)	79.5 (69.9)
Pahang	S	68,252 (51,366)	8,525 (18,165)	18,528 (6,172)	—— (——)	593	——	—— (——)	(——)	3,864 (5,049)	99,762 (80,752)	6,539 (1,956)	106,301 (82,708)	136,322 (105,940)	78.0 (78.1)
	P	74,323 (52,786)	11,237 (9,169)	18,996 (16,936)	—— (——)	——	——	—— (——)	(——)	—— (——)	104,556 (78,891)	5,358 (790)	109,914 (79,681)	141,592 (109,535)	77.6 (72.7)
Selangor	S	148,253 (105,134)	9,344 (21,273)	90,241 (32,296)	7,239 (7,177)	——	13,743	—— (3,742)	(2,567)	195 (10,476)	269,015 (182,665)	15,502 (4,711)	284,517 (187,376)	388,211 (263,510)	73.3 (71.1)
	P	146,002 (87,577)	6,528 (15,691)	86,210 (59,987)	2,219 (7,821)	——	30,025	—— (——)	(4,008)	—— (22,477)	270,984 (197,561)	13,581 (2,259)	284,565 (199,820)	388,211 (271,360)	73.3 (73.6)
Negri Sembilan	S	68,461 (48,492)	3,837 (9,941)	24,154 (15,513)	2,318 (——)	13,434	——	—— (3,438)	(——)	4,368 (9,499)	116,572 (86,883)	5,238 (2,033)	121,810 (88,916)	152,114 (111,336)	80.1 (79.9)
	P	68,855 (37,634)	—— (12,103)	26,484 (7,934)	1,349 (——)	11,487	5,410	—— (4,369)	(——)	2,578 (10,607)	116,163 (72,647)	5,548 (756)	121,711 (73,403)	152,114 (95,573)	80.0 (76.8)
Malacca	S	66,593 (48,390)	5,416 (10,464)	27,421 (8,215)	—— (——)	——	2,666	—— (——)	(4,993)	90 (238)	102,186 (72,300)	3,640 (1,308)	105,826 (73,608)	125,585 (93,740)	84.3 (78.5)
	P	67,898 (44,186)	3,759 (12,133)	27,478 (8,684)	—— (——)	——	3,461	—— (——)	(9,396)	—— (265)	102,596 (74,660)	3,192 (680)	105,788 (75,344)	125,585 (93,737)	84.2 (80.4)
Johore	S	178,929 (140,217)	6,334 (5,471)	62,762 (20,411)	—— (——)	8,785	1,098	—— (32,288)	(——)	6,727 (10,755)	264,635 (209,142)	13,343 (5,354)	277,978 (214,496)	344,922 (282,161)	80.6 (76.0)
	P	185,413 (140,219)	3,673 (4,992)	57,278 (30,311)	—— (2,162)	9,642	2,456	—— (19,931)	(——)	—— (15,878)	258,462 (213,493)	11,981 (2,534)	270,443 (216,027)	334,359 (280,244)	80.9 (77.1)
TOTAL	S	1,179,042 (861,705)	310,936 (322,025)	334,662 (150,321)	92,500 (88,581)	81,360	18,566	8,040 (66,475)	(7,560)	23,293 (55,827)	2,048,399 (1,552,494)	102,866 (40,111)	2,151,265 (1,592,605)	2,725,393 (2,151,132)	78.9 (74.0)
	P	1,204,340 (800,944)	301,187 (329,070)	330,898 (199,688)	69,898 (97,391)	88,223	42,130	7,319 (32,578)	(13,404)	13,509 (74,194)	2,057,504 (1,547,269)	89,104 (17,306)	2,146,608 (1,564,575)	2,720,100 (2,133,272)	78.9 (73.3)

S = State Elections.   P = Parliamentary Elections.

For purposes of comparison, 1959 General Election figures are given in brackets. 1959 figures are not given in respect of the UDP and the PAP as they did not contest the 1959 General Elections. Conversely, 1959 and not 1964 figures are given in respect of the Malayan Party as this party did not contest the 1964 General Elections.

Malaysia Election Commission, *1964 Election Report, op. cit.* p. 29.

INDEX

263; in Pasir Puteh, 228-9, 239, 241; reports from, 238, 240; of Labour Party in Batu, 253, 259; of PAP in Batu, 262; of Alliance in Batu, 263; of SUPP, 281; in Singapore, 334-5, 337

Pasir Panjang constituency, Singapore, 353

Pasir Puteh, Kelantan, 80, 183; election campaign in, 225-42; result of election in, 241

Pasir Puteh Tengah, 241

Pasir Puteh Tenggara, 241

Pasir Puteh Utara, 241

Pauker, G.J. (cited), 5

Paya Lebar constituency, Singapore, 353

Payne, R. (cited), 267

Penang: a Straits Settlement, 8; and Federation, 10; result of 1955 and 1959 elections in, 14; SF in, 17, 20, 91, 171, 193, 432; PPP in, 20; Islamic Advisory Council in, 50; UDP in, 53, 193, 363, 371; election petition in, 81; PAP in, 139, 141; status of port of, 152, 155-8; injured by confrontation, 155; malpractices alleged at, 188; Lee Kuan Yew on, 339; chief parties in, 363-5

Penchala, Batu, 242, 245-6, 247, 248, 252, 255, 264, 265

Penggawas, 232-3, 239

Penghulus, in Kelantan, 232-3, 238, 239, 242; in Sarawak, 291

Pensiangan, Sabah, 307

People's Action Party (PAP) in Malaya: its late intervention in 1964 election, 3, 7, 22, 23, 24-6, 39, 138-9, 141, 172, 416; agrees with PPP not to contest some seats, 20; and MCA, 22, 24-5, 39, 139-49, 166, 213, 416, 423, 429, 430; and UMNO, 24, 139-40, 141, 147-8, 150, 166; its importance in Malaysian politics, 53; and Borneo territories, 54; withdraws some candidates,

72-3, 139; candidates of, 83, 84, 96, 98, 99, 100-1, 107, 184, 251, 252, 394; and allocation of seats, 93-4; and non-Malays, 109; and SF, 109, 113-14, 116, 139-40, 151-2, 175, 220, 261; and Indonesia, 110, 118-19, 133, 429; and Alliance Party, 111, 114-15, 132, 220, 429-30, 433; and Malays' privileges, 126; and Chinese education, 129-30; and communism, 130, 144, 148-50; and communalism, 131, 142; PMIP and, 132; and Penang, 157; organization of, 172, 254; its successful rallies, 174, 175; newspapers of, 203; Press coverage for, 204-6, 207, 208-10, 211, 212-13; compared with PPP, 206; wins Bungsar, 210, 385-6, 397, 426, 430; Singapore broadcasts for, 224; in Batu, 249, 253, 254, 261-3, 264; votes and seat obtained by, 361, 366, 373; in Selangor, 364; its area of activity, 369-71; its effect on Alliance prospects, 378, 379, 380-1, 384, 385-9, 417; its effect on SF's prospects, 385-6, 390; in Solidarity Convention, 391, 433-5; leaders of, 424; trade unionists in, 426; election hopes of, 432; in Perak, 433; succeeded by 'PAP Malaya', 435

People's Action Party (PAP) in Singapore: its stronghold in Singapore, 53; and Chinese education, 129-30, 342-4; and 'guided democracy', 146; in Opposition in 1955, 312; in control of Singapore City Council, 313; wins 1959 election, 313; rises in importance, 313; loses its left-wing, 314, 319; changes (1959-63) in, 315, 316-19; its campaign (1963), 324-49; its candidates, 327; Press coverage for, 333-4; and

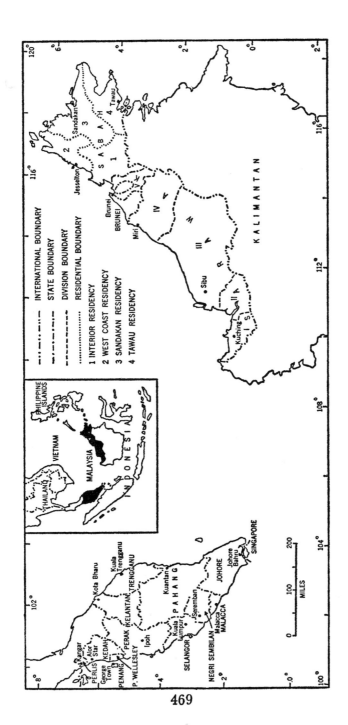

469